Managing Information Risk and the Economics of Security

Managing Information Risk and the Economics of Security

Edited by

M. Eric Johnson
Center for Digital Strategies
Tuck School of Business at Dartmouth
Hanover, NH, USA

Springer

Editor
Dr. M. Eric Johnson
Tuck School of Business Administration
Dartmouth College
Hanover, NH 03755, USA
M.Eric.Johnson@tuck.dartmouth.edu

ISBN: 978-1-4419-3529-8 e-ISBN: 978-0-387-09762-6

Printed on acid-free paper

springer.com

List of Contributors

Managing Information Risk and Economics of Security
M. Eric Johnson, Tuck School of Business at Dartmouth

Nonbanks and Risk in Retail Payments
Terri Bradford, Federal Reserve Bank-Kansas City
Fumiko Hayashi, Federal Reserve Bank-Kansas City
Christian Hung, Federal Reserve Bank-Kansas City
Stuart Weiner, Federal Reserve Bank-Kansas City
Zhu Wang, Federal Reserve Bank-Kansas City
Richard Sullivan, Federal Reserve Bank-Kansas City
Simonetta Rosati, European Central Bank

Security Economics and European Policy
Ross Anderson, University of Cambridge
Rainer Boehme, Dresden University of Technology
Richard Clayton, University of Cambridge
Tyler Moore, University of Cambridge

BORIS – Business-Oriented Management of Information Security
Sebastian Sowa, Ruhr-University of Bochum
Lampros Tsinas, Munich Re
Roland Gabriel, Ruhr-University of Bochum

Productivity Space of Information Security in an Extension of the Gordon-Loeb's Investment Model
Kanta Matsuura, University of Tokyo

Communicating the Economic Value of Security Investments; Value at Security Risk
Rolf Hulthén, TeliaSonera AB

Modelling the Human and Technological Costs and Benefits of USB Memory Stick Security
Adam Beautement, UCL
Robert Coles, Merrill Lynch
Jonathan Griffin, HP Labs
Christos Ioannidis, University of Bath
Brian Monahan, HP Labs
David Pym, HP Labs and University of Bath
Angela Sasse, UCL
Mike Wonham, HP Labs

The Value of Escalation and Incentives in Managing Information Access
Xia Zhao, Tuck School of Business at Dartmouth College
M. Eric Johnson, Tuck School of Business at Dartmouth College

Reinterpreting the Disclosure Debate for Web Infections
Oliver Day, Harvard University
Rachel Greenstadt, Harvard University
Brandon Palmen, Harvard University

The Impact of Incentives on Notice and Take-down
Tyler Moore, University of Cambridge
Richard Clayton, University of Cambridge

Studying Malicious Websites and the Underground Economy on the Chinese Web
Jianwei Zhuge, Peking University
Thorsten Holz, University of Mannheim
Chengyu Song, Peking University
Jinpeng Guo, Peking University
Xinhui Han, Peking University
Wei Zou, Peking University

Botnet Economics: Uncertainty Matters
Zhen Li, Albion College
Qi Liao, University of Notre Dame
Aaron Striegel, University of Notre Dame

Cyber Insurance as an Incentive for IT Security
Jean Bolot, Sprint
Marc Lelarge, INRIA-ENS

Conformity or Diversity: Social Implications of Transparency in Personal Data Processing
Rainer Böhme, Technische Universitat Dresden

Is Distributed Trust More Trustworthy?
Kurt Nielsen, University of Copenhagen

Preface

Security has been a human concern since the dawn of time. With the rise of the digital society, information security has rapidly grown to an area of serious study and ongoing research. While much research has focused on the technical aspects of computer security, far less attention has been given to the management issues of information risk and the economic concerns facing firms and nations. *Managing Information Risk and the Economics of Security* provides leading edge thinking on the security issues facing managers, policy makers, and individuals. Many of the chapters of this volume were presented and debated at the 2008 Workshop on the Economics of Information Security (WEIS), hosted by the Tuck School of Business at Dartmouth College. Sponsored by Tuck's Center for Digital Strategies and the Institute for Information Infrastructure Protection (I3P), the conference brought together over one hundred information security experts, researchers, academics, reporters, corporate executives, government officials, cyber crime investigators and prosecutors. The group represented the global nature of information security with participants from China, Italy, Germany, Canada, Australia, Denmark, Japan, Sweden, Switzerland, the United Kingdom and the US.

This volume would not be possible without the dedicated work Xia Zhao (of Dartmouth College and now the University of North Carolina, Greensboro) who acted as the technical editor. I am also grateful for the service of the WEIS program committee: Alessandro Acquisti (Carnegie Mellon University), Ross Anderson (Cambridge University), Jean Camp (Indiana University), Huseyin Cavusoglu (University of Texas, Dallas), Ramnath Chellappa (Emory University), Neil Gandal (Tel Aviv University), Anindya Ghose (New York University), Eric Goetz (Dartmouth College), Larry Gordon (University of Maryland), Karthik Kannan (Purdue University), Marty Loeb (University of Maryland), Tyler Moore (Cambridge University), Andrew Odlyzko (University of Minnesota), Brent Rowe (RTI), Stuart Schechter (Microsoft), Bruce Schneier (BT Counterpane), Sean Smith (Dartmouth College), Rahul Telang (Carnegie Mellon University), Catherine Tucker (MIT), and Hal Varian (University of California, Berkeley).

Many thanks also go to the individuals and the organizations that helped us organize WEIS: Hans Brechbühl, Jennifer Childs, Scott Dynes, Eric Goetz, David Kotz, Xia Zhao (all of Dartmouth), and Stuart Schechter (Microsoft), as well as the support of Tuck School of Business and Thayer School of Engineering at Dartmouth College; the Institute for Information Infrastructure Protection (I3P); the Institute for Security Technology Studies; and Microsoft. WEIS and the efforts to compile this book were partially supported by the U.S. Department of Homeland Security under Grant Award Number 2006-CS-001-000001, under the auspices of the Institute for Information Infrastructure Protection (I3P) and through the Institute for Security Technology Studies (ISTS). The I3P is managed by Dartmouth College. The views and conclusions contained in this book are those of the authors and should not be interpreted as necessarily representing the official policies, either expressed or implied, of the U.S. Department of Homeland Security, the I3P, ISTS, or Dartmouth College.

September 2008 M. Eric Johnson

Table of Contents

Managing Information Risk and the Economics of Security

M. Eric Johnson[1]

Center for Digital Strategies, Tuck School of Business, Dartmouth College

Abstract Information risk and the economics of managing security is a concern of private-sector executives, public policy makers, and citizens. In this introductory chapter, we examine the nature of information risk and security economics from multiple perspectives including chief information security officers of large firms, representatives from the media that cover information security for both technical and mass media publications, and agencies of the government involved in cyber crime investigation and prosecution. We also briefly introduce the major themes covered in the five primary sections of the book.

1 Introduction

Information is the lifeblood of the global economy. With more and more organizations maintaining information online, that information has also become a source of growing risk. Once viewed as little more than the occasional teenage hacker creating a nuisance, risks today are fueled by more sophisticated, organized, malicious groups. The evolving risks impact the reliability of national infrastructures

[1]Many people contributed to this overview by framing panel discussions at WEIS, recording panelist discussions, and directly contributing to related publications. In particular, I thank Jane Applegate of Tuck's Center for Digital Strategies and Eric Goetz of the I3P for their direct contributions to this manuscript. This material is based upon work partially supported by the U.S. Department of Homeland Security under Grant Award Numbers 2006-CS-001-000001 and 2003-TK-TX-0003, under the auspices of the Institute for Information Infrastructure Protection (I3P) and through the Institute for Security Technology Studies (ISTS). The I3P is managed by Dartmouth College. The views and conclusions contained in this document are those of the authors and should not be interpreted as necessarily representing the official policies, either expressed or implied, of the U.S. Department of Homeland Security, the I3P, ISTS, or Dartmouth College.

M.E. Johnson (ed.), *Managing Information Risk and the Economics of Security*,
DOI: 10.1007/978-0-387-09762-6_1, © Springer Science + Business Media, LLC 2009

(Goetz and Shenoi 2008), the protection of intellectual property of firms and countries (Andrijcic and Horowitz 2006), the financial integrity of investment firms (Jolly 2008), and the control of individuals' identity (Camp 2007). Research has shown that information security requires not only technology (Anderson 2008), but a clear understanding of potential risks, decision-making behaviors, and metrics for evaluating business and policy options. Researchers have made substantial progress analyzing both the internal investment decisions of firms (Gordon and Loeb 2006) and the market-based pressures that impact cyber security (Anderson and Moore 2006, Kannan and Telang 2005).

In this introductory chapter, we present a collage of information risk challenges facing individuals, firms, and governments. In the first section, we examine risk and security from the perspective of the media. Based upon panel discussions conducted at the 2008 Workshop on the Economics of Security (WEIS), hosted by the Tuck School of Business at Dartmouth College, we highlight journalists' perspectives from a range of outlets including the information technology trade media, business publications, and the popular press. In the next section, we examine the risk as seen by cybercrime investigators and prosecutors. Again based on a panel held at WEIS, we present insights from investigators and prosecutors including the FBI and state police along with federal and state prosecutors. Then we turn our attention to firms in the private sector, discussing practices to incorporate information risk into the overall evaluation of business risk. We include the chief information security officer (CISO) perspective of many different global firms from technology providers like Cisco and investment banks like Goldman Sachs to pharmaceutical provider Eli Lilly and retailer CVS Caremark.

Finally, we introduce the chapters contained within the five major sections of the book: Cyber Policy and Regulation, Risk Management and Security Investment, Technology and Policy Adoption, Combating Cybercrime, Privacy and Trust. *Information Risk and the Economics of Security* presents the latest research on the economics driving both the risks and the solutions. These chapters represent some of the best, cutting-edge research within the wide range of research traditions from economics and business to computer science. Following in the strong tradition of WEIS, this collection of papers well represents the peer-reviewed scholarship of the annual workshop. The volume provides managers and policy makers alike with new thinking on how to manage risk.

2 Communicating Security – The Role of Media

The global proliferation of cybercrime has driven wide-spread public recognition of need for better information security. Over the past few years, the steady drumbeat of reported breaches has escalated into a hail storm of media attention. From mainstream mass publications to the trade press, the number of stories and the depth of coverage on security have ballooned as the media seeks to shed light on the shadowy, evolving threat landscape (Acohido and Swartz 2008). While stories about "hackers" and "breaches" have captured the public's imagination, trying to move to a more nuanced discussion has proved challenging. Journalists from every corner of the media, from national mass publications and to security-focused websites and blogs struggle with the challenges of communicating problems that involve both technical and behavioral elements. Many wonder if the media can move beyond the shock factor of large failures, like the Jerome Kerviel story (January 2008 Sociétè Gènérale trading loss (Jolly 2008)), to the underlying drivers of such failures? With so many evolving issues it is exceedingly difficult to research and write credible stories on internal corporate failures or crimes like whaling (where the targets are corporate executives). Journalists struggle to uncover the truth in a world where: 1) organizations rarely see any benefit in coverage and often don't report losses; b) organized crime is thought to be the perpetrator; and c) many of the targets are loathe to discuss their gullibility with the press. Some wonder if cyber journalists can really verify the truth behind international cyber espionage and warfare. In reporting on these stories journalists often struggle with their responsibility of informing the public vs. protecting national security. Likewise, editors must address challenges of tracking and developing journalistic expertise in a rapidly evolving field, where nuances matter, technical jargon rules and the terminology and concepts can be difficult to master. Yet, the growth in cyber crime continues to bring the stories to the forefront of many publications.

At the Workshop of the Economics of Information Security (WEIS), reporters from USA Today, BusinessWeek, CIO Magazine, ZDNet Magazine and Tech Target took part in a provocative panel discussion, providing a fresh perspective on key issues relating to the economics of information security. The group noted that much of the research in security and information risk wasn't front page news five or ten years ago, but that has changed with the increase in the number of breaches and identity thefts. Certainly, this reporting is impacting the public perception about security, public policy making, and funding availability and focus for security research.

Stories detailing identity theft and personal computers being infected by 'bots' and malware are making headlines every day. Cyber criminals based in Eastern Europe, Russia and China are busy stealing and selling sensitive information, according to panelists. Massive data breaches, ranging from the theft of thousands of credit card account numbers from retailer T.J. Maxx (Sidel 2007), to the French trader who misdirected funds at Societe Generale (Jolly 2008), are keeping reporters busy.

"From my perspective, the next great business story is the business of cyber-crime," said Brian Grow, who covers cybercrime for BusinessWeek magazine. "It's the fastest growing crime in America and in the world. The numbers have exploded….so, from a media perspective that makes it relevant because it affects millions of people."

Reporters said their challenge is twofold; selling the cybercrime story to their editors and trying to persuade corporations and law enforcement officials to help them expose the alleged scams. They said many corporations are reluctant to discuss embarrassing data breaches, despite new laws requiring them to report problems to law enforcement agencies and the public.

Of course, selling stories to editors requires public interest that is sometimes lagging. Dennis Fischer, a reporter for Tech Target, said "There probably needs to be more finance coverage crossing with information security coverage. …But, I've constantly been puzzled by the unending levels of apathy on the consumers part. To some extent, when you are following stories, you have to follow what people are concerned about or want to read about, yet a lot of readers just meet those stories, with "eh," it's strange.

On the other hand, researching stories is equally challenging. "It's easier to get sources in the criminal underground (to talk to us) than it is to get the law enforcement, the government and the business sources to talk about it," said Scott Berinato, of CIO/CISO magazines (and now Harvard Business Publications).

The panelist agreed that companies often choose to keep the data breach a secret rather than risking a negative reaction from investors or a public relations nightmare.

"It's only through public awareness that the public will put pressure on the bottom line of corporations to make that change," said Byron Achohido, of USA Today. "Otherwise, they'll just do an accounting trick and assign it as an acceptable loss and spread it out. They (corporations) are assigning a very low premium to the ongoing threat of my Social Security number being out there with 300 million people in a stored database that the bad guys are just doing low level stuff on now and can figure out what else to do in the future."

"The credit bureaus in particular are wide open for reform," continued Achohido. However, the industry is resisting change and the public seems to be apathetic when it comes to demanding more security. He said consumers are also "addicted to convenience" and often release personal information and conduct business online without adequate security precautions in place.

Dennis Fischer, a reporter for Tech Target, said he realized that companies need to focus on security in general, not just protecting information. Fraud is committed in many ways, not just by hacking into computer systems.

"Once I understood the fraud triangle; opportunity, motivation, rationalization, that started to bring to light that all of these cybercrimes were just fraud," said Fischer. "Somebody wants to make money, and so my physical security reporting really helped me write stores which I think the general public understood better because I was just talking about fraud."

However, he said it's tough to get people who have been defrauded to discuss what happened.

"They have a hard time dealing with it and they don't want to talk about it," he said. "But every once in a while, you come across a person whose method of dealing with it is to open up and talk about it. They feel like they are helping to solve the problem by making others aware."

Even when a so-called victim of a computer fraud is willing to be interviewed, Fischer said most corporations are reluctance to publicize a data breach because they don't want bad publicity. "Businesses have this beautiful thing called accepted loss budgets, so they just kind of bury their shame in the acceptable loss budget."

Despite the fact that many computer fraud stories still go unreported, BusinessWeek's Grow said "it's an endless story because it's going to take on new forms and going to shift and we're going to continue to say,' here's how they tricked you."

The group agreed that stronger firewalls and software solutions have eliminated many of the worms and viruses that made stories by from taking down computer systems. Now, the big threat is from malware and bots send out by criminals to infect personal computers.

"They're basically after stealing sensitive data and then marketing the sensitive data to fraudsters who want to use it," said Byron Achiodo, a cybercrime reporter for USA Today.

Apart from fouling up computer systems with Trojans, 'bots' and malware, computer crime is now a national security issue, according to BusinessWeek's Brian Grow. He shared a recent story he covered about an email with a malicious attachment that was made to appear as if it came from the Secretary of the Air Force.

"It was aimed at a military procurement guy at a consulting firm and it contained a request for proposal from the Indian government for 126 fighter jets…the real bid that Boeing and others were bidding on."

Clicking on random email is the quickest way to infect your computer system, according to Ryan Naraine, a reporter for ZDNet Magazine.

"It's fascinating to me that people still just click and install stuff," he said. "They'll install a Trojan for you…you can tell someone, 'here's Britney, she's half naked, click here and people just click."

TechTarget's Fischer said a friend recently sent out two emails to test response rate.

"In one, he said, 'this is a bad email with an attachment,' and the other he said, 'this is a bad email with an attachment, click here.' Naraine said the click rate for the bad email that ordered people to 'click here" had a response rate about 80 percent higher than the other one.

One strategy to protect digital information is to require several types of authentication before allowing access to any sort of sensitive information.

"The Europeans and the Asians to some extent are already several steps ahead of us," said Byron Acohido. "We're still locked at this level, essentially by and large, single factor, username and password. That's really all you need to open all the doors and windows you want on U.S. accounts." Firms are reluctant to move to multi-factor authentication for fear of alienating customers. Hopefully the glare of the media will change user perspective on authentication.

3 Investigating and Prosecuting Cybercrime

Investigating and prosecuting cybercrime has become exceedingly complex. Globalization has fueled virtual, organized crime groups that innovate at dizzying rates. From collecting evidence to convicting cyber criminals, local, state, and federal agencies working with partners around the world must navigate the maze of jurisdictions and constantly evolving technology. Law enforcement must establish who has jurisdiction over investigations; how to coordinate efforts; and how to uncover the link between virtual and physical operations. Often investigators must work with reluctant witnesses as firms often fail to report losses (Pereira et al. 2008).

Law enforcement officials are spending millions of dollars on training and investigations as part of a global effort to thwart the theft and disruption of digital information, according to experts who participated in a WEIS cybercrime panel

"Our primary focus is counter-intelligence and counter-terrorism using computers, so called cyber-terrorism," said Jim Burrell, assistant special agent in charge of the Federal Bureau of Investigation's Boston office. "I put about 80% of my resources there. The other side is everything else…from intellectual property theft to internet fraud and child pornography, things along those lines where the computer is used to facilitate a more traditional crime."

Burrell, an internationally respect expert on cybercrime, said back in the late 1990's, "we treated cybercrime and a lot of these issues as a single violation. Now, we have about 300 different cyber-criminal violations as well as national security issues."

He said the FBI is investing millions of dollars in training top agents to fight cybercrime with assistance from law enforcement agencies in 48 countries. When dealing abroad, Burrell said, the first priority for investigators and agents is to preserve digital data. Without intact data, it's almost impossible to build a strong case again savvy cybercriminals.

"The issue we worry about first is preserving the evidence so it doesn't get deleted or altered," said Burrell, who also teaches digital forensics at Boston University. "That doesn't mean they (local agents) have to turn it over to us, but (we ask them to) make it so it doesn't go away until we can figure out what's going on. Then, we can get the proper diplomatic or legal process in order to obtain physical custody of the information or the data."

Federal prosecutor Arnold Huftalin, agreed that data preservation is critical to successful prosecutions.

"I learned early on in my computer crime experience that data is extraordinarily volatile," said Huftalin, an assistant U.S. attorney based in New Hampshire. He said his biggest challenge was tracking down how criminals are accessing the internet. For example, a few years ago, he had a case where he had to locate hundreds of people around the country through IP addresses that they were using to access servers.

"I was appalled to find out there was no nationwide database of internet service providers," said Huftalin. To remedy that, he assigned a paralegal to set up an extensive database, which is still being used by cybercrime prosecutors around the country.

Once the providers were found, subpoenas for information could be issued, but that's tough because people can change ISP's (internet service providers) on a moment's notice, he said.

"Nobody but the dumbest of the dumbest people in the world is going to go into somebody's (computer) system from their own static IP (address)," he said. "They are going to come in through some innocent person's box in Romania which is going to be access through some other innocent person's box in Turkey."

He said the federal Electronic Communications Privacy Act (ECPA) dictates how federal, state and local law enforcement agencies can compel disclosure in order to collect data for criminal cases.

Because organized crime is now heavily involved in computer crimes, Huftalin said it's actually easier to track them down.

"They tend to be a bit more static and they're not as elusive as the 19 year-old whiz kid who just happens to want to bounce through 18 machines and they for giggles and grins, destroys somebody's network."

Huftalin said cracking computer cases is tough and "there are a lot of prosecutors who, when they see a laptop, will walk away from it," because it takes computer savvy to work in the field.

"When there's a bank robbery and it's in the winter, you follow the footprints in the snow," he said. "But when somebody intrudes into, let's say, Google, there aren't any footprints in the snow."

Despite firewalls and sophisticated software, panelists said corporations continue to be attacked by cybercriminals, the panel said. "Corporations that experience security breaches may be reluctant to provide information to law enforcement because it will affect their bottom line," said Huftalin, the federal prosecutor from New Hampshire. "But, if they don't provide the information, then law enforcement can't share that information with other corporations so they can plug the holes or take security measures in advance, as opposed to after the fact."

He said there is a program called "InfoGuard" which encourages companies to report data breaches to law enforcement agencies so criminals can be prosecuted in a timely manner.

In addition to the FBI's efforts, panelists said state and local officials are working hard to combat cybercrime at all levels.

"Almost every crime that we deal with at the state level has some kind of computer component," said Lucy Carrillo, assistant attorney general for the New Hampshire Criminal Justice Bureau. "Whether it's the drug dealer who has lists, phone numbers addresses on his cell phone or whether it's a homicide scene where the individual has done research on how he was going to commit a homicide."

William "Trip" Cantwell, with the New Hampshire State Police, said public awareness is critical to thwarting all sorts of computer crime. For example, he makes presentations to school children about the dangers of the internet.

"We reach out to them and show them some presentations," he said. "Hopefully it will hit home and prevent one kid from being victimized."

4 CISO Perspective – Evaluating and Communicating Information Risk

While security professionals have long talked about risk, moving an organization from a "security" mindset to one that thoughtfully considers information risk is a challenge. Managing information risk means building risk analysis into every business decision. From a CISO panel held at WEIS and from earlier CISOs workshops hosted by the Center for Digital Strategies, security executives outlined how they are working to move the conversation from security towards information risk. Three key themes of action emerged from these discussions (Johnson, Goetz, Pfleeger (2008); and Johnson and Goetz (2007)):

- **Rank the information risks.** Developing a process to identify and prioritize information risks brings security into the business discussion.
- **Communicate the information risk.** A communication strategy helps the organization quickly recognize and understand economically driven risks. Often this involves embedding information risks into an overall risk communication process. Likewise, managing the risk within a firm's supplier and partner organizations requires ongoing communication and education.
- **Measure progress.** Developing a set of key performance metrics enables the firm to understand if information risk practices are making a difference.

4.1 Ranking the Information Threats

For many firms, information risk management is increasingly being integrated into the broader enterprise risk management conversation. However, this development is uneven—there are still some firms where information risk management is focused more at the project management level. At a recent CISO workshop held at the Tuck School of Business (Goetz and Johnson 2007), security executives from twenty-five Fortune 500 firms gathered to discuss information risk. Neil Hershfield gave a good summary of the real objectives of Dow's risk prioritization activities: "In terms of prioritizing the threats, two things came to mind: Number one, we've got to secure our sites, our chemical sites. So the process of keeping control of our systems and not letting somebody hack in is a big deal for us because if somebody does that, they could cause an incident. The biggest threat is some kind of actual physical incident that's created through cyber. Second, is the risk of insider problems."

From the executive discussion one thing became clear. Risk management is structured in different ways at different companies (i.e., there is no single, unified methodology that is widely used to identify and prioritize risks). In some cases risk management is based around applications, in other cases the focus is on assets or specific projects. In some firms, the emphasis is on aligning information risk management as directly as possible with business strategies.

Workshop participants shared with the group how they prioritize and rank threats. It soon became clear that there are lots of different approaches to risk management and ranking risks along a spectrum from the more quantifiable methods (we measure this) to the softer (we know through experience or through interviews) and intuitive (we just kind of know) methods.

There was a lot of common ground in terms of the elements that firms use to help them categorize and address risk. Common risk elements included data classification; governance; compliance; brand; insider risk; infrastructure; availability; and mission assurance. Different firms use a different combination of these elements to structure their information risk management programs; they also weigh the elements in different ways. Underneath each of these high-level categories, firms have a second-tier of specific factors (often data-driven) that they use for their risk evaluations and prioritizations. The risk elements are then viewed in the context of other company-specific factors, such as the state of current control (i.e., the security baseline); the sophistication of vulnerabilities and threats; the cost of mitigation; the potential consequences of inaction; and, in some cases, the infosec impedence (i.e., the risk to program execution or the risk to innovation if information security controls are put in place). The notion of impedence implies that firms should periodically step back and make sure that protective measures that once made sense are still necessary and are not still in place just by default. Such an approach may help realize additional business opportunities or justify security spending.

For example, United Technologies uses a structured approach for overall risk management calculations. Elements of the model come from all business functions. Some of the elements that help feed the model include data classification, governance, insider risk and infrastructure. As Lee Warren explained it, "We're just starting down this path. There's a lot to do. What we're doing is we pick the risk and we take what we think of as large risk areas and we plot them on an eMap. For instance, governance, how are we doing on governance? Are we red, yellow, or green? Then we try to make a more mathematical model by digging down deeper into why we think governance is in the green. And then we'd weigh all those attributes. And then in future years, we'll add to it as the environment changes. If some of those attributes change, then we'll automatically shift those as opposed to being subjective. But the point is, we're trying to put a structure around the whole thing, starting on a very high level."

Several companies are using some version of a risk matrix that has the X axis dedicated to the potential 'Impact' and the Y axis dedicated to 'Probability' of a negative outcome. Different elements of their risk management approach are plotted on the matrix to see how much attention they require. A potentially high-impact event with a high probability of occurring would require an immediate, focused response. These matrices are updated regularly, perhaps quarterly, to reflect changes in business priorities and the risk environment. BT uses a process called BRAT, which is a step-by-step, ladder process where each hurdle has to be taken in order to move to the next step in the process or project. Some of the steps that would need to be overcome could include: Is this legal? Is it in line with contractual obligations? Does it adhere to established business processes? Is there sufficient protection of sensitive data?

An interesting outcome of the discussion was that it became clear that several companies use back testing (i.e., applying actual incidents or audit and assessment findings) to validate or calibrate their risk management approaches and methods. This focus on continuous improvement seems promising in an area that is still immature.

Other tools to help identify and rank risks include Archer Technologies, RiskWatch, and SecureCompass. John Stewart explained how Cisco is using the RiskWatch tool to help prioritize its risks: "The software itself is an application. The input is by an individual. For example, let's say you would want to take a set of government audit requirements against your environment, and it's a formal set. You put them in, and then are entering them in the known state as you can ascribe it today as any audit would traditionally do. That's subjective data. Then you take the objective data, which is what the audit findings are, of any of your given facilities by the external auditors, and then, over time, it will assert what the categories of risk are with an objective equal to your current areas of effort sorted ostensibly by priority. That's the thinking. Now the question is how people will actually use it. We're going in with the idea that that becomes our risk methodology, so our risk process is subjective/objective data in; this is then sorted and ordered into a priority list of areas to work on. The input doesn't have to be just one project. You could put many projects in, or you could put a business process into it." Other firms are using similar tools to help them with data classification, security awareness and making the risk prioritization process more objective and repeatable.

Ranking and measuring risk is also important across a firm's vendor base. Phil Venables of Goldman Sachs outlined an initiative within the financial industry to rank vendors using an outside rating agency. Working with one of the leading credit rating agencies, Moody's, a group of financial firms are developing an information risk ratings service. Firms could use those ratings to qualify vendors and even negotiate prices and contracts based on the risks posed by that provider. Venables stated, "We intend on primarily using this to rate outsourced service companies. We want to have Moody's go and rate them. And from that we'll be able to adjust the amount of money we're going to pay for a contract in relation to the cost of extra mitigants. When their cyber security risk has been evaluated and rated, we can decide based on clear, consistent evidence whether we need to take on more or less of the risk for that provider and can make contracting decisions accordingly. This in turn can be augmented by similar industry efforts like BITS/FISAP."

There is no single, established process or method that is universally used for ranking risks, but information risk management is maturing and becoming more integrated with overall risk management programs.

4.2 Communicating the Information Risks

Communicating risks within the organization is critical in embedding information risk into the firms overall risk management process. Finding ways to effectively communicate the risk both internally and with suppliers/partners is the challenge.

Many CISOs have emphasized the importance of storytelling in getting the security message across. Telling a compelling story—both in terms of scenarios and using external events to tell a story about how something happened—can be a powerful methodology. Through a good story, people can better visualize a problem or risk and find it easier to understand the implications of a potential security event. However, participants at the Tuck CISO workshop stressed the importance of having the story be accompanied by some analysis that makes the story relevant for a particular company. Sheldon Ort from Eli Lilly emphasized that, "It's the limits of imagination that preclude us from taking seriously some of the real risks out there. It's going to that next step to try and bring it in to a realistic scenario that they can relate to." So, for instance, some threats make great stories, but a firm may already have security measures in place to defend against them, while other stories can really highlight a company's specific vulnerabilities. Security-related stories are most effective if they are told in the context of a firm's risk environment and goals.

The group also discussed the need to have awareness of the audience and how important it is to interface at different levels, to really know at different levels what it is that the audience will respond to. The point was not that a story should be changed for different audiences, but that it should be packaged and emphasized differently—"hitting the right notes for the right level of audience", as one participant put it. Further, the importance of creating a dialogue and engendering real engagement, as opposed to just doing a briefing, was also highlighted by the group. Mauricio Guerra from Dow related how up until recently they had always just gone into the board every six months and told their half hour story, their PowerPoint, and left with a "Thank you very much," and how important it was that they've recently changed to a much more dialogue oriented discussion where the board is actually engaged and suddenly the board cares much more about security risks.

The timing of security communications is also an important factor. Sometimes it is possible to get senior management's attention if a message is communicated on the heels of a high-profile event or new regulations. In the words of Pete Stang from General Dynamics, "But this interest is perishable, whether it's 9/11 or SOX. You have their attention and the board will listen to you for a short time. But after a while, they get bored with it and they'll move on to something else, or they get annoyed with it. We found that out. So you've got to jump when you have the opportunity because you'll lose that window."

Some firms have found great success in informally spreading the security message through the rotation of people. In some firms security people are sent out to spend a day, several days, or even several weeks in the company's operational units - in the factory or a store or a distribution center—in order to get a better sense for the real operational needs of the business. Cisco has taken this approach one step further, sending some of their best security people to work permanently in different jobs elsewhere in the business. That's one way to inculcate security within the company. Several participants spoke about their goal to make more use of informal communications across different levels of their organizations in order to improve their security posture, and increase awareness of security risks.

Another communications strategy used by some firms involves hitching security communications to other successful wagons in a company. For example, if a company pays a lot of attention to their audit group, legal, or regulatory compliance, then it would be a productive approach to partner with those groups to raise awareness about security. This works especially well with groups where there's already a natural affinity that can be echoed. In other cases, piggy-backing security on successful or topical initiatives, such as privacy, within a company can also bear fruit. Terri Curran noted that she successfully worked with R&D at Bose to help communicate IP risk. Working with R&D was naturally helped move the security agenda forward because, at Curran noted, "In our company, R&D is the driver. It's the lifeblood of what we do."

Russ Pierce of CVS/Caremark, also noted that communication must be tailored to roles to maximize its impact. "Awareness, especially role based awareness, is a significant component of our overall strategy. We recognize that in order to achieve, and maintain, good security we need to empower all employees with the appropriate knowledge to work securely with today's, and tomorrow's, technology."

Many of the same innovative internal communications program can work with suppliers and partners across the value chain. However, many of the firms represented at WEIS and our earlier workshops have been struggling to move beyond security audits of their vendors to a point where rapid and ongoing risk communication regularly occurs.

4.3 Measuring Progress

Finally, information risk metrics close the loop on an effective risk management program. Without measurement, how do firms know if their information risk practices are making a difference? Measuring risk, or security metrics, has been a central theme for CISOs for the past few years (Johnson and Goetz 2007). While many firms have developed a set of metrics, questions remain on what should be measured. Most companies now have a variety of security measurements that include empirical or systems data such as the number of hits to the firewall, the number of viruses detected, the percentage of machines patched, the percentage of communications encrypted, etc. Specific programs, such as awareness and communications, are also measured, for instance, by capturing how many people have gone through training. Standards or regulations are also used to measure a company's posture against.

Many companies have dashboards and displays that are fed by the measurements to show the security status of various functions. For example, they could be red, yellow or green on fighting spam, based on some internal metrics. However, a big concern that was repeatedly expressed at our CISO workshop was that measuring security was becoming an exercise in checking boxes, which would not necessarily make the company more secure or better able to handle new risks. The dangers of such a check box mentality include complacency and a loss of personal initiative and innovative thinking. Measuring changes in user behavior over time can help firms see real underlying improvement. At WEIS, Kavitha Venkita of the Corporate Executive Board described how they had developed a single index of secure behavior based on surveys of user security hygiene, such as sharing passwords or avoiding phishing scams. By repeatedly conducting the survey over time, firms could measure the impact of user education.

Companies use a variety of different techniques and methods to measure security, including information from self assessments, audits, objective risk scoring, compliance efforts and interviews. In some cases, context can be added to empirical rankings through the use of scenario stories. There are also many ways to display and structure the results of measurement. The use of rankings and dashboards is very common, but other options, such as heat maps and maturity models, are also being explored to express risk effectively.

Measuring risk still remains problematic for a number of reasons. One of the main difficulties is that a risk equation requires some level of quantification of the threat and the probability of that threat occurring. These two elements are notoriously hard to quantify, thereby making some of the other risk metrics less effective. Another challenge is measuring progress—is my company improving its security posture? The threat landscape and a company's vulnerabilities and technologies change constantly, leaving few options in terms of measuring continuity. Good security measurements have to be able to adapt to internal and external changes. Finally, how are security metrics used, and how much faith is placed in them when it comes to making business decisions, including investment decisions? These are questions that need to be explored further.

5 Overview of Book

Ongoing research is illuminating many open questions presented in the previous sections. The subsequent chapters included in this book examine many such questions and cover a wide variety of important topics. The chapters are broken into five sections: Cyber Policy and Regulation, Risk Management and Security Investment, Technology and Policy Adoption, Combating Cybercrime, Privacy and Trust (see Table 1). We begin with cyber policy and regulation, with a chapter examining the risks of nonbanks in retail payments, both within the United States and Europe. The second chapter in this section broadly examines security economics and public policy, including information asymmetries and breach notification, externalities and the costs of malware, liability and software patching, and the current fragmented state of legislation and law enforcement – focusing on the European Union.

The next section has two chapters examining risk management and security investment. The first chapter outlines an approach (called BORIS) that considers a complete program from strategy to evaluation. The second chapter provides an extension of the popular Gordon-Loeb investment model to consider the productivity of vulnerability and threat reduction. The last chapter in this section addresses communication of the economic value of security investment – a perennial challenge for CISOs.

We then turn to technology and policy adoption with a pair of chapters. The first chapter examines the human and technological costs of USB memory stick security and its related benefits. This is followed by a chapter that examines access governance within an organization and the value of incentives to drive good user behavior.

Combating cybercrime has attracted significant research attention over the past years and we present five cutting-edge chapters on this topic. The first chapter illuminates the debate over disclosure of web infections, discussing the attack trends, methods for identifying infected hosts, and recent analysis of the host infections. The next chapter shows how economic incentives impact site take-down behavior of hosting services. Examining a range of criminal activity from child pornography to phishing, the authors find that economic motivation of harmed organizations speeds response. The next chapter provides a fascinating view into the underground economy of the Chinese web followed by a chapter analyzing Botnet economics. We close this section with a chapter examining the ongoing debate over cyber insurance and its ability to both compensate victims and drive security investment.

Table 1. Chapters within Each Major Section

Cyber Policy and Regulation
Nonbanks and Risk in Retail Payments: EU and U.S.
Security Economics and European Policy
Risk Management and Security Investment
BORIS –Business Oriented management of Information Security
Productivity Space of Information Security in an Extension of the Gordon-Loeb's Investment Model
Communicating the Economic Value of Security Investments; Value at Security Risk
Technology and Policy Adoption
Modelling the Human and Technological Costs and Benefits of USB Memory Stick Security
The Value of Escalation and Incentives in Managing Information Access
Combating Cybercrime
Reinterpreting the Disclosure Debate for Web Infections
The Impact of Incentives on Notice and Take-down
Studying Malicious Websites and the Underground Economy on the Chinese Web
Botnet Economics: Uncertainty Matters
Cyber Insurance as an Incentive for Internet Security
Privacy and Trust
Conformity or Diversity: Social Implications of Transparency in Personal Data Processing
Is Distributed Trust More Trustworthy?

In the final section, we present a pair of chapters focused on privacy and trust. The first chapter examines the social implications of transparency in personal data while the second chapter asks the question "is distributed trust more trustworthy."

We are certain that managers and researchers alike will find many new insights to better manage information security within the pages of *Information Risk and the Economics of Security.*

References

Acohido, B. and Swartz, J. *Zero Day Threat*, Steerling Publishing, New York, NY, 2008.

Andrijcic, E and Horowitz, B. "A Macro-Economic Framework for Evaluation of Cyber Security Risks Related to Protection of Intellectual Property," *Risk Analysis*, Vol. 26(4), 2006, pp. 907–923.

Anderson, R. *Security Engineering*, Second Edition, Wiley Publishing Inc, Indianapolis, IN, 2008.

Anderson, R and Moore, T. "The Economics of Information Security," *Science* 314(5799) 2006, pp. 610–613.

Camp, J.,*Economics of Identity Theft*, Springer Science+Business Media, New York, NY, 2007.

Goetz, E. and Johnson, M.E. "Security through Information Risk Management." I3P Technical Report. Dartmouth College, 2007. http://mba.tuck.dartmouth.edu/ digital/Programs/Corporate Events/CISO2007/Overview.pdf.

Goetz, E. and Shenoi, S. *Critical Infrastructure Protection*, Springer Science+Business Media, New York, NY, 2008.

Gordon, L.A. and Loeb, M.P. "Process For Deciding on Information Security Expenditures: Empirical Evidence," *Communications of the ACM*, (January), 2006, pp. 121–125.

Johnson, M.E., Goetz, E., and Pfleeger, S.L. "Security through Information Risk Management," forthcoming in *IEEE Security and Privacy*, 2008.

Johnson, M.E. and Goetz, E. "Embedding Information Security Risk Management into the Extended Enterprise," *IEEE Security and Privacy*, 5(3), 2007, pp. 16–24.

Jolly, D. "Fraud Costs French Bank $7.1 Billion," *New York Times*, 2008.

Kannan, K. and Telang, R. "Market for Software Vulnerabilities? Think Again," *Management Science* (51:5), 2005, pp. 726–740.

Pereira, J., Levitz, J., and Singer-Vine, J. "Some Stores Quiet Over Card Breach," *Wall Street Journal*, August 11, 2008, B1.

Sidel, R. "Stores Blame Checkout Software for Security Breaches," *Wall Street Journal*, January 18, 2007, D1.

Nonbanks and Risk in Retail Payments: EU and U.S.

Terri Bradford[1], Fumiko Hayashi[1], Christian Hung[1], Simonetta Rosati[2], Richard J. Sullivan[1], Zhu Wang[1] and Stuart E. Weiner[1]

[1]Federal Reserve Bank of Kansas City Payments System Research Function

[2]European Central Bank Oversight Division

Abstract This chapter documents the importance of nonbanks in retail payments in the United States and in 15 European countries and analyses the implications of the importance and multiple roles played by nonbanks on retail payment risks. Nonbanks play multiple roles along the entire payment processing chain. They are prominent in the United States and their presence is high and growing in Europe as well, although there are differences among the various countries and payments classes. The presence of nonbanks has shifted the locus of risks in retail payments towards greater relevance of operational and fraud risk. The chapter reviews the main safeguards in place, and concludes that there may be a need to reconsider some of them in view of the growing role of nonbanks and of the global reach of risks in the electronic era.

1 Introduction

Retail payment systems throughout the world continue to evolve in many ways. Chief among them is the continued migration from paper-based to electronic-based systems. Accompanying this electronification of payments has been an increase in the prevalence of nonbanks in the payment systems.

In an earlier paper (ECB, FRBKC 2007a), we took a first step in documenting and analysing the role of nonbanks in European and U.S. retail payment systems. We found that nonbanks are most prominent in the United States but are prominent—and becoming ever more so—in many European countries as well. We also found that the regulatory framework surrounding nonbank payments participants is uneven both within and across countries.

This second finding is particularly important for central banks because central banks are almost uniformly charged with ensuring that payment systems are safe as well as efficient. At the core of "safety" considerations, of course, is the presence and mitigation of various types of risk. Our earlier paper spent some time exploring

M.E. Johnson (ed.), *Managing Information Risk and the Economics of Security*,
DOI: 10.1007/978-0-387-09762-6_2,

risk issues, but at a fairly general level. The purpose of this chapter is to delve more deeply into risk issues.

Specifically, we explore the various types of risk associated with the many activities along the payments chain, and ask, to what extent does the presence of nonbanks heighten or lessen these risks? As with the first paper, this chapter draws on the results of a joint study undertaken by staff at the European Central Bank (ECB) and the Federal Reserve Bank of Kansas City. The focus is on electronic (non-paper) retail payment services in the European Union (EU) and the United States. We adopt a common set of definitions and a uniform analytical framework.

The following questions are addressed:

1. What payments activities and subactivities are performed along the payments chain?
2. What types of risk are associated with these activities and subactivities?
3. Do the risks associated with various payments activities and subactivities vary by type of payments instrument?
4. Does the increased presence of nonbanks in various payments activities heighten or lessen the degree of risk?
5. Are adequate safeguards—private and/or public—in place to ensure that risk levels are manageable and acceptable?

The chapter is organized as follows. The next section assesses the importance of nonbanks in retail payments. It first summarizes the methodology used in this and the previous paper: the definition of "nonbank," the difference between front-end and back-end payment services, and the various categories of payment types and payment activities. It then documents the role played by nonbanks in the EU and the United States. The third section takes up risk in retail payments. It first describes the various types of risk that may be present in a payments environment, for example, settlement risk, operational risk, reputational risk, and so forth. It then examines which types of risk are most likely to be associated with which types of activities along the payments processing chain. The fourth section "superimposes" this risk analysis on the prior section's documentation of nonbank presence by activity, permitting one to evaluate, at a relatively detailed level, nonbanks' potential impact on payments risk. Finally, the chapter closes with a summary and suggestions for future research.

2 Nonbanks in Retail Payment Systems

2.1 Methodology

Nonbanks can perform functions at all stages of the payments process. For all forms of payment (credit cards, debit cards, electronic-cheques, credit and debit transfers, e-money, and stored-value transactions) and for all points on the payments chain (hardware and software provision, consumer and merchant interaction, backroom processing, clearing and settlement, and post-transaction accounting) nonbanks can play a major role.[2] This subsection provides a framework for documenting and analyzing these roles.

2.2 Definitions

A nonbank payment service provider is defined in this study as any enterprise that is not a bank and which provides, primarily by way of electronic means, payment services to its customers. In the European context, nonbanks include all entities that are not authorized as a credit institution; hence, electronic money institutions (ELMIs) are considered to be nonbanks. In the U.S. context, nonbanks include all entities that do not accept demand deposits. A nonbank payment service provider may be either bank-controlled or nonbank-controlled.[3]

A nonbank payment system provider's customers may be either: (i) end-users of retail payment services, in which case the nonbank is providing front-end services; (ii) banks or other nonbank payment service providers, in which case the nonbank is providing back-end services; or (iii) both types of customers. Examples of front-end services include money transfer services provided to households and acquiring services provided to merchants. Examples of back-end services include back-office data processing, authentication and authorization, and hosting of payments-enabled web sites. An example of a firm with both types of customers is a company that is leasing point-of-sale (POS) devices to merchants and at the same time performing processing and routing services on the data captured on those devices for the banks issuing the associated payment cards. Such a firm would be considered to be providing front-end services to the merchants and back-end services to the issuing banks.

---

[2] In Europe, e-money is defined as "monetary value as represented by a claim on the issuer which is: (i) stored on an electronic device, such as a chip card or computer memory; (ii) issued on receipt of funds of an amount not less in value than the monetary value issued; (iii) accepted as means of payment by undertakings other than the issuer" (EC 2006). Thus, strictly speaking, e-money is not a payment instrument but a means of payment, that is, a substitute for cash and deposits. E-money issuance is usually accompanied by the service or device needed to transfer it, and for simplicity in this survey with the term e-money we refer to the payment devise or instrument used to transfer e-money. E-money can be issued only by banks and by e-money licensed institutions (ELMIs), entities subject to a simplified prudential regime, which is however, modelled on that of banks, and are subject to certain limitations (for instance in terms of activities they can carry out, and investment of the funds).

[3] Examples of bank-controlled nonbank payment service providers include subsidiaries of banks, for example, TSYS, a large U.S. processor owned by Synovus Bank (although about to be spun off), and bank associations, for example, Visa Europe, the large European credit and debit card network. Nonbank-controlled service providers are firms without a governing bank affiliation, for example, First Data Corporation, PayPal, Hypercom, Vodafone, etc.

2.3 Payment Types and Payment Activities

There are two ways to think about the payments process. One is to think about payment types—the means and instruments through which a transaction is undertaken. Examples are credit card transactions, debit card transactions, credit and debit transfers, and person-to-person Internet payments. The second way is to think about payment activities—the various steps and services that are provided as a given transaction takes place. These two concepts—payment types and payment activities—are clearly very closely related.

Five broad payment types are considered in this chapter. Categories include electronic cheques; credit transfers; direct debits; payment (credit and debit) cards; and e-money and other prefunded or stored-value instruments, including Internet person-to-person (P2P) payments.[4] The first category, electronic-cheques, are those payment types that begin with a paper cheque, or information from a paper cheque, but are converted to an electronic payment at some point in the process; end-to-end, traditional paper cheques are excluded. The second and third categories, credit transfers and direct debits, utilize agreements that credit or, with preauthorization, debit accounts. The fourth category, payment (credit and debit) cards, relies on networks to access either a line of credit or a demand deposit account to enable a payment. The fifth category, e-money and other prefunded or stored-value instruments, uses an electronic store of monetary value, which may not necessarily involve a bank account, to make a payment.

A second way of thinking about the payments process is to examine payment activities, that is, the various steps and services that are undertaken as a transaction moves from beginning to end. The payments process can be thought of as a chain of events in which four principal categories of services are performed:

- *pre-transaction activities* encompassing customer acquisition and the provision of front-end infrastructure;
- *during-transaction Stage 1 activities* encompassing connection, communication, authorization, and fraud detection activities;
- *during-transaction Stage 2 activities* encompassing clearing and settlement activities; and
- *post-transaction activities* encompassing statement provision and reconciliation activities.

All in all, one can identify twenty-three primary payment activities that underlie, to varying degrees, all payment transactions. Within these twenty-three primary activities, there are, in turn, a host of subactivities numbering over fifty. The full list of primary activities and subactivities is shown in Table 1.

---

[4] ECB, FRBKC (2007a) includes two additional instrument categories: money remittance and transfer transactions; and other payment instruments. They are not considered here because of insufficient data in some of the surveyed countries.

2.4 *Nonbank Prevalence*

2.4.1 Overview

A payment transaction can be initiated in several ways, and the related payment information and instructions can be captured and transmitted using several methods. Nonbanks can be involved at many points along the processing chain, as well as in the direct provision of payment services to end customers.

Nonbanks have long had a presence in core payments processing, as banks and other financial institutions have sought to outsource such activities as data processing, file transmission, and related tasks. Other during-transaction activities in which nonbanks have been heavily involved include network services such as gateway provision and switching services, authorization services, and fraud and risk management services. All of these activities are important elements of the retail payments process and are of key importance in maintaining public confidence in the safety of payment instruments.

Additionally, nonbanks have been active in the range of activities that take place before and after the execution of a given payment transaction. Examples of such pre-transaction activities include the development and provision of hardware for electronic payments (for example, card production and POS devices) and the establishment of contractual relations with cardholders and merchants. In the case of emerging payments, in many cases these pre-transaction services involve new ways of providing access to traditional payment types, for example, credit transfers initiated via the Internet or via mobile phones or web portals that consolidate billing and facilitate payment initiation. Moreover, nonbanks have also been important in many post-transaction services, including statement provision, reconciliation, and retrieval.

Table 1. Payment Activities

Primary Activity		Subactivity	
Pre-Transaction			
1	Customer acquisition	a	Registration and enrollment of customers as payers (consumers)
		b	Registration and enrollment for merchant accounts or deployments of ATMs
2	Services for issuer's front-end customer (payer) acquisition	a	Provision of credit evaluation/credit risk assessment tools
		b	Application processing services
3	Provision of payment instruments/devices to the front-end customer (payee or payer)	a	Card issuance; card production; card personalization; card delivery; card activation
		b	Hardware and software production (such as a card reader) for usage with a consumer's online device (PC, mobile, handheld)
		c	Provision of e-money wallet/access code to e-money values
		d	Cheque manufacturing

Primary Activity		Subactivity	
4	Provision of hardware to accept payment instruments/devices	a	Provision of ATM terminals (sell/lease; manage)
		b	Provision of POS terminals
		c	Provision of cheque readers/cheque POS terminals
5	Provision of software to accept payment instruments/devices	a	Web hosting services
		b	Provision of shopping cart software
		c	Provision of software to connect payment gateway service providers
		d	Provision of cheque verification software
6	Provision of internet security-related technology/support	a	Certificate-authority services (such as PKI-based secure environments); provision of digital identity services for consumer authentication
		b	Provision of online transaction security systems to front-end customers (payees, merchants), and back-end customers (such as 3D-secured card transactions via Internet)
		c	Provision of e-signatures and other e-authori sations for payment authorisation purposes
7	Payment Card Industry (PCI) compliance services to merchants and/or payers	a	
8	Provision of data center services to back-end customers	a	Outsourcing complete data center functions/ secured, supervised floor space/multi-site backup storage for disaster recovery
9	E-invoicing	a	Creation and delivery of electronic invoices to front-end customers (payer)
During-Transaction Stage 1			
10	Communication connection for merchants	a	Provision of gateway to acquirer/payment processors
		b	Provision of gateway to various networks/ check or ACH authorization vendors
11	Transaction authorization (fund verification)	a	Provision of network switch services; a back-end service
		b	Provision of communication connection between networks and payment instrument issuers
		c	Provision of decision management/fraud screening/neutral network scoring system to card issuers for authorization
		d	Process to verify and confirm if payer has sufficient funds (or credit lines) available to cover the transaction amount
12	Fraud and risk management services to front-end customers (payees)	a	Verification services (address, IP address, card verification number, other data), payment instrument authentication and authorisation services
		b	Identity authentication
		c	Decision management/fraud screening/neutral network scoring system (hosted at third-party service providers)

Primary Activity			Subactivity
13	Fraud and risk management services to card issuers	a	Monitoring transactions and notifying cardholders of potential fraud, enabling them to take immediate action
14	Initiate the debiting of the front-end customer's (payer's) account (during transaction)	a	Debiting the front-end customer's (payer's) account/e-money purse
15	Ex-ante compliance services	a	Anti-money laundering and terrorist financing regulation such as controls to identify suspicious transactions (database, software etc.)
During-Transaction Stage 2			
16	Preparation	a	Sorting merchant's sales information by payment instrument/network for clearing
		b	Submission of sales information to each payment instrument network
		c	Calculation of each network member's net position and transmission of net position information to each member
		d	Provision of transformation services into other payment instrument formats (such as MICR to ACH)
		e	Provision of sorting transactions by destination groups to financial institutions
17	Clearing	a	Transmission of clearing orders to a financial institution
		b	Transmission of clearing orders to ACH operator
		c	Distribution of advices showing the amounts and settlement dates
		d	Clearing (different from an ACH)
18	Settlement	a	Posting credit and debit at each financial institution's central bank account
		b	Posting credit and debit at each financial institution's commercial bank account
		c	Posting debit (credit in case of a return) to front-end payer account
		d	Posting credit (debit in case of a return) to merchant (payee) account
		e	Check settlement
Post-Transaction			
19	Statement	a	Provide statement preparation/delivery services for front-end customers (payers) (such as mobile credit advice; online bank/card account statements)
		b	Provision of statement/payment receipt notification services for merchants (payees)
20	Reconciliation, collection and receivable management services	a	Matching invoices and payments
21	Retrieval	a	Provision of chargeback and dispute processing services

Primary Activity		Subactivity	
22	Reporting and data analysis services	a	to merchants, such as support services for treasury and accounting
		b	to consumers
		c	to financial institutions
23	Ex-post compliance services	a	Compliance with anti-money laundering and terrorist financing regulation, such as reporting to authorities, back-feeding to ex-ante databases

This subsection documents the role played by nonbanks in the EU and U.S. retail payment systems. The analysis is conducted through the use of tables showing, for each of the various payment activities and each of the various payment types, the importance of nonbanks relative to banks.

2.4.2 EU Nonbank Prevalence

The role of nonbanks in payments in Europe was analyzed by carrying out a survey among Payment Experts of the National Central Banks (NCBs). The survey was voluntary, and not all of the ESCB National Central Banks participated. Results were obtained for 15 countries, 10 from the euro area (Austria, Belgium,[5] Germany, Finland, France, Greece, Italy, the Netherlands, Portugal and Slovenia) and five from EU Member States that have not yet adopted the euro (Bulgaria, Cyprus, Czech Republic, Latvia and Lithuania). These countries together process about 67 percent of the number of payment transactions in the European Union.

However, as the NCBs of the largest non-euro area Member States did not participate in the survey (in particular the U. K., which alone counts for more than 20 percent of the number of payments processed in the EU), the focus of the analysis is mainly on the euro area: the above-mentioned 10 euro area countries in the survey together process about 92 percent of the total number of euro area payment transactions, and 66 percent of the total EU payment transactions.[6] All in all, these 10 countries represent 65 percent of the EU GDP (88 percent of the euro area), and 54 percent of the EU population (86 percent of the euro area population).

The survey was carried out using a common methodology. Some respondents stressed that they faced data limitations that did not allow considering the results as a comprehensive and exhaustive description of the role of nonbanks in their respective countries. Thus, the survey does not imply that these are the only activities that nonbanks perform in payment processing or that all payment solutions offered to customers in the surveyed countries are covered. Moreover, the level of detail and the quality of the data varies from country to country, as

[5] For Belgium an assessment of the importance of nonbanks was available only for cards and e-money payments.

[6] The percentages provided are based on 2003 data and include the countries that joined the EU in 2004 (that is, excluding Bulgaria and Romania who joined in 2007).

respondents relied on different data sources and research methodologies, ranging from publicly available information to interviews with major banks and nonbanks. For some countries, the survey's findings provide more of an overview than a fully representative picture. These differences in comprehensiveness and quality of data gathered in the various countries make it difficult to carry out cross-country comparisons, and require care in considering the results. Nevertheless, in the absence of more precise or homogeneous data, we accept these data limitations and believe that the survey provides a useful overview of the role of nonbanks in payments, shedding some light on an aspect of the European payment industry that was not thoroughly investigated previously.

A number of results emerge.

First, and most important, nonbanks play an important role in several European countries, and we expect their role to grow further, particularly at the back-end, in those countries where their role is still somewhat more limited. Drivers will be (i) the growth of cashless payments; (ii) SEPA, and the resulting restructuring and consolidation ongoing within the payments processing outsourcing industry, and; (iii) the maturing of payments markets segments and substitution among payment classes favouring instruments whose growth is largely supported by nonbanks (cards and direct debits).

Second, nonbank presence varies significantly by country. In general, when considering the importance of nonbanks across all payment instruments for each country, countries can be divided into three groups (ECB, FRBKC 2007a). In the first group, including Austria, Germany, the Netherlands and Italy, nonbanks play a larger role compared to other countries in the activities of most payment types. Finland, France, Latvia and Slovenia are in a second group, where nonbanks seem to play a more limited role. The last group includes the remaining countries: Bulgaria, Cyprus, Czech Republic, Greece, Lithuania and Portugal. Nonbank presence in these countries can be considered somewhere in between.

Third, in the majority of the 15 countries, the role of nonbanks for payment cards is high or prevalent in many of the activities considered. This is probably due to the high automation of the pre-transaction and during-transaction Stage 1 activities (such as switch routing, authentication, and real-time authorization of the transaction) and, also, to the international dimension of cards-processing standards. It should be noted that in Europe there are a number of national card schemes that are usually co-branded with the international schemes like Visa and MasterCard to allow customers to use the card abroad. In addition to co-branding, in Europe there are also a few examples of (bilateral) interoperability agreements between national (mainly debit cards) schemes, particularly to allow use in the EU cross-border context. As a result, cards processing is largely organized around a common model.

And, fourth, irrespective of the role played in pre-transaction and other during-transaction activities, the settlement phase largely remains a prerogative of the banking sector in Europe, and this is true for all payment instruments, not only for cards. In the case of traditional payment instruments, this may be explained by the fact that banks are normally those entities that have access to the retail payment systems (and, in many cases, national banking associations actually have set up or own the national clearing and settlement companies) and/or those who are allowed to hold payment settlement accounts. For e-money and other innovative payment solutions, settlement also remains largely dominated by banks, which is consistent with that innovation typically focusing on alternative means (such as Internet and mobile technology) to accessing traditional banking fund transfers services rather than offering fundamentally new payment instrument alternatives.[7]

As an example of the detailed results obtained, the degree of nonbank participation in payment cards is presented in Table 2.[8] In this table, moving from left to right, the degree of nonbank prevalence is shown for the surveyed countries accounting for the largest share of EU27 card payments to the countries accounting for the smallest share of EU27 card payments. Thus, the table is a matrix, in which the rows are payment activities, the columns are countries, and the entry in an individual cell is the authors' assessment of whether nonbank presence is prevalent (P), high (H), medium (M), low (L), or nonexistent (N) for that particular payment activity-payment type-country combination. Cells with parallel lines are not applicable, while cells in white indicate insufficient information to judge. The assessments are based on survey results, industry data, and other sources.

2.4.3 U.S. Nonbank Prevalence

To assess the role of nonbanks in payments in the United States, staff at the Federal Reserve Bank of Kansas City completed the same survey as that distributed to EU survey respondents. Information utilized included industry directories and news articles, interviews with nonbanks and industry observers, and other sources more anecdotal in nature.

Table 3 presents the results for the United States. Rows are the various payments activities and subactivities previously explained. Columns are the principal payment types found in the United States. Payment types are listed in descending order, from those accounting for the highest share of noncash transactions in the United States (in terms of number of transactions) to those accounting for the lowest share of noncash transactions. Shares are based on 2004 data. In 2004, payment cards accounted for 45.9 percent of noncash transactions, direct debits accounted for 6.9 percent, credit transfers accounted for 6.0 percent, e-cheques

[7] See ECB (2005), where reporting the results of a survey on payment innovation (with a scope wider than e-money products only), it is concluded that "two-thirds of the (surveyed) companies are related to the banking sector, either by license or by ownership and, as a consequence, most of the e-products include a link to settlement." This is also consistent with what was reported by Masi (2004), who notes that "the greatest part of the new payment initiatives does not modify the clearing and settlement phases of the payment cycle which are managed and regulated by banks."

[8] Tables for the other four broad payment types are shown in ECB, FRBKC (2007b).

Table 2. Nonbank Importance: EU: Payment Cards

		FR	DE	NL	IT	PT	BE	FI	AT	CZ	SI	GR	CY	LT	LV	BG
% of EU27		22.7	10.5	6.3	5.1	3.5	3.2	2.7	1.0	0.3	0.4	0.3	0.1	0.1	0.1	0.0
Pre-Transaction																
1	a		L	L	M	L	L	H	H	M	L	M			M	L
	b		H	M	M	M	P	L	H	M	L	M	P	L	M	L
2	a	H			P		L	P	H	M	L	M				M
	b	P	H		P		P		H	M	L	H			H	L
3	a	P	H	H		H	P	H	H		M	H	H	H	H	
	b	P	H	H	P		L		H	M	P	H		H		P
	c		H		P		L			M						
	d															
4	a	P	H	H	P	H	P	P	H	M	M	H	P	P	P	H
	b	P	H	H	P	H	P	P	H	M	M	H	P	P	H	H
	c															
5	a	P	H		P		P	M	H		L	P	P		L	M
	b	P	H	H	P		P		H		H	P	M		P	H
	c	H		H	P		P	M	H	M	H	H	P	P	P	H
	d								H							
6	a	M	H	H	M	H	P				H		M		H	
	b	P	H	H	P		P		H		M		P	P	H	
	c	M		H		L			H	M	H					
7	a		H		P		P	H	H	M		H			M	M
8	a	M	H	M	P	H	P	P	H	M	L	P			M	
9	a		H	H	P		P			M		M				

Notes: P=Prevalent; H=High; M=Medium; L=Low; N=Nonexistent

Prevalent; High

Medium; Low, Nonexistent

Not applicable

Not able to judge

Table 2. Nonbank Importance: EU: Payment Cards (Cont.)

		FR	DE	NL	IT	PT	BE	FI	AT	CZ	SI	GR	CY	LT	LV	BG
During-Transaction – Stage 1																
10	a	M	H	H	P	H	P	P	H	M	P	H	P	P	H	H
	b	H	H	H	P	H	P		H	M	H	H	P	P	H	P
11	a	L	H	H	P	H	P	P	H	M	H	P	P	P	H	P
	b	M	H	H	P	H	P		H	M	H	P	P	P	H	P
	c	M	H	L	H		P	P	H	M	M	P	P	P	H	P
	d	M	H	L	M		L	M	H	M	L	H	P	H	M	H
12	a	M	H	H	P	H	P	L		M	M	H	P	H	L	
	b	M	H	H	P	H	P		H	M	L	H		L	L	L
	c	M	H	M	P	H	P	P	H	M	M	H	P	H	L	
13	a	M	H	L	H	H	P	M	H	M	M	H	P	H	M	M
14	a	M		L	H	M	L		H	M	L	P	H	M	M	
15	a	L	H	L				L	L	M		P			L	
During-Transaction – Stage 2																
16	a	L		H	M	H	H	M	H	M	M	H	P	P	M	
	b	L		H	M		P	M	H	M	M	H	P	P	H	M
	c	L		H	M	H	P	M	H	M	H	P	P	P	H	P
	d		H	H					L		L					
	e	M	H	H			P		H	M			P	P		
17	a	L		H			M	M	H	M	M	P	P	H		P
	b	L		H	H		P		H	M	M	H	P			
	c	L	H	H	H		P		H	M	M	H	P	L	M	P
	d	L	H	H								H			H	

Notes: P=Prevalent; H=High; M=Medium; L=Low; N=Nonexistent

Prevalent; High

Medium; Low, Nonexistent

Not applicable

Not able to judge

Table 2. Nonbank Importance: EU: Payment Cards (Cont.)

		FR	DE	NL	IT	PT	BE	FI	AT	CZ	SI	GR	CY	LT	LV	BG
During-Transaction – Stage 2																
18	a	L		H			P		H	M	M					
	b	L		L			P		H	M	M					
	c	L					N	L	H	M	M	L			L	H
	d	L		L			N	L	H	M	M	L	P		L	H
	e			L												
Post-Transaction																
19	a	M		M	H		M		H	M	M	M	P		M	M
	b	M		L	H			L	H	M	M	M		M		L
20	a		H		P			L	H	M	M	M	P			
21	a		H	M	H		M	L	H	M	M	M	P	M	L	
22	a		H	H	P		P		H	M	M	M	P	H		
	b		H		P		N		H	M	M	M	P			
	c		H	H	P	H	P		H	M	M	M	P	H		H
23	a	L			P		M		L	M	M	M			L	

Notes: P=Prevalent; H=High; M=Medium; L=Low; N=Nonexistent

Prevalent; High (dark shading)
Medium; Low; Nonexistent (light shading)
Not applicable (hatched)
Not able to judge (blank)

Table 3. Nonbank Importance: United States

Payment Activity		Type of Payment and Share of Noncash Payments											
		Payment Cards 45.9%			Direct Debits 6.86%			Credit Transfer 6.03%	e-Cheque 4.41%	e-Money 0.00%			
		4-party Credit/ Sig. Debit	PIN-Debit	3-party Credit	Automatic	One-time	Tempo/ PayBy Touch			Prepaid Card Open-Loop	Prepaid Card Closed-Loop	PayCash	PayPal
Pre-Transaction													
1	a	P	P	P	P		P			P	P	P	P
	b	P	P	P			P			P	P	P	P
2	a	H		H			P						
	b	P	P	P	P		P			P	P	P	P
3	a	P	P	P			P			P	P		
	b												
	c											P	P
	d								P				
4	a	H	H	H									
	b	P	P	P			P		P	P	P		
	c								P				
5	a	P	P	P	P	P		H	P	P	P	P	P
	b	P	P	P		P			P	P	P	P	P
	c	P	P	P	P	P	P		P	P	P	P	P
	d												
6	a	P	P	P	P	P	P	P	P	P	P	P	P
	b	P	P	P	P	P	P	P	P	P	P	P	P
	c	P	P	P	P	P	P	P	P	P	P	P	P
7	a	P	P	P						P			
8	a												
9	a	P	P	P	P	P		P	P				

Notes: P=Prevalent; H=High; M=Medium; L=Low; N=Nonexistent
Prevalent; High
Medium; Low, Nonexistent
Not applicable
Not able to judge

Table 3. Nonbank Importance: United States (Cont.)

Payment Activity		Type of Payment and Share of Noncash Payments											
		Payment Cards 45.9%			Direct Debits 6.86%			Credit Transfer 6.03%	e-Cheque 4.41%	e-Money 0.00%			
		4-party Credit/ Sig. Debit	PIN-Debit	3-party Credit	Automatic	One-time	Tempo/ PayBy Touch			Prepaid Card Open-Loop	Prepaid Card Closed-Loop	PayCash	PayPal
During-Transaction – Stage 1													
10	a	P	P	P	P	P	P		P	P	P	P	P
	b	P	P	P	P	P	P		P	P	P	P	P
11	a	P	P	P						P			
	b	P	P	P			P			P			
	c	P	P	P			H			P			
	d	H	H	H		P	P		P	H	P	P	P
12	a	P	P	P		P		P	P	P	P	P	P
	b	P	P	P	P	P	P	P	P	P	P	P	P
	c	P	P	P		P		P	P	P	P	P	P
13	a	H	H	H			P						
14	a		P										
15	a	H	M	P	M	M	M	M	M	H	P	P	P
During-Transaction – Stage 2													
16	a	P	P	P	P	P	P		P	P	P	P	P
	b	P	P	P	P	P	P		P	P	P	P	P
	c	P	P	P						P			
	d								P				
	e												

Notes: P=Prevalent; H=High; M=Medium; L=Low; N=Nonexistent

Prevalent; High — Not applicable

Medium; Low; Nonexistent — Not able to judge

Table 3. Nonbank Importance: United States (Cont.)

Payment Activity		Type of Payment and Share of Noncash Payments											
		Payment Cards 45.9%			Direct Debits 6.86%			Credit Transfer 6.03%	e-Cheque 4.41%	e-Money 0.00%			
		4-party Credit/ Sig. Debit	PIN-Debit	3-party Credit	Automatic	One-time	Tempo/ PayBy Touch			Prepaid Card Open-Loop	Prepaid Card Closed-Loop	PayCash	PayPal
During-Transaction – Stage 2													
17	a	P	P	P	H	H	P		H	P	P		
	b												
	c	P	P	P	P	P	P	P	P	P	P		P
	d												P
18	a	N	N	N	N	N	N	N	N	N	N	N	N
	b	N	N	N	N	N	N	N	N	N	N	N	N
	c	P		P	P	P	P	P	P	P	P	P	P
	d	P	P	P	P	P	P	P	P	P	P	P	P
	e												
Post-Transaction													
19	a	P	P	P	P	P	P	P	P			P	P
	b	P	P	P	P	P	P	P	P	P	P	P	P
20	a	P	P	P	P	P	P		P	P	P	P	P
21	a	P	P	P	P	P	P		P	P	P	P	P
22	a	P	P	P	P	P	P		P	P	P	P	P
	b												
	c	P	P	P						P			
23	a	L	L	P	L	L	L	L	L	L	P	P	P

Notes: P=Prevalent; H=High; M=Medium; L=Low; N=Nonexistent

Prevalent; High
Medium; Low, Nonexistent
Not applicable
Not able to judge

accounted for 4.4 percent, and the e-money share was nearly negligible.[9] Within some of these broader categories, in turn, are shown more specific payments instruments: three types of payment card transactions (four-party credit and signature debit (such as MasterCard and Visa), PIN-debit, and three-party credit (such as American Express, Discover, and private-label); three types of direct debits (automatic, one-time, and those completed under, for example, the Tempo and PayByTouch schemes); and four types of e-money and other prefunded or stored-value instruments (open-loop prepaid card, closed-loop prepaid card, PayCash, and PayPal transactions).

The most striking general observation about Table 3 is the high degree of "P" and "H" cells in the table, indicating that where nonbanks can play a role in the payments process, that role is almost always an integral one. Looking across the payment type columns, almost all payment types show a significant nonbank presence in almost all facets of the payments process, with two exceptions. The first are those activities that are not applicable, either because (i) they are inherently bank functions involving demand deposits, for example, some pre-transaction activities for credit transfers and automatic and one-time direct debits, or (ii) they are activities that are not applicable to that payment type, be it bank or nonbank, for example, transaction authorization activities for automatic debit transactions. The second exception to significant nonbank presence is settlement activities that involve posting credits and debits to financial institutions' commercial and central bank accounts—here banks dominate.[10] Virtually everywhere else, nonbank presence relative to banks is high, and, indeed, prevalent.

The message from Table 3 is clear—nonbanks are a force in the U.S. retail payments system, dominating a large number of payments activities for a large number of payment types.

3 Risks in Retail Payments Processing

3.1 Risks in Retail Payments

During the payments process various types of risks may arise, affecting different parties at different stages, and to varying degrees. This subsection provides a brief review of various risk categories relevant to processing retail payments and to clearing and settlement procedures.[11]

---

[9] An e-cheque is created when a written cheque is either truncated and becomes an ACH payment at some point of cheque processing or is used as a device to capture information to create an ACH payment at the point of transaction.

[10] This also is a principal finding of Bradford, Davies, and Weiner (2003).

[11] The definitions used in this section derive from various sources: for definitions of risks in the context of payments clearing and settlement (credit risk, liquidity risk, operational risk,

- *Liquidity and credit risks*: the risk that a counterparty will not settle an obligation for full value, either when due (liquidity risk) or at any time thereafter (credit risk).
- *Settlement agent risk*: the risk of failure of the entity (settlement agent) whose assets are used to settle payment obligations. This is a specific form of credit risk.
- *Operational risk*: the risk that deficiencies in information systems, internal controls, human errors, or management failures will result in unexpected losses (internal and external events). Recent discussions of operational risk in payments point to subcategories that have grown in importance:
  - *Malfunctions and related problems*: malfunctions that are the result of unintentional circumstances or events (e.g. a computer breakdown or a processing slowdown, or organisational deficiencies) or intentional circumstances or events (such as attack or misuse of information or procedures).
  - *Data security risk*: unauthorized modification, destruction, or disclosure of data used in transactions or used to support transactions. Payment data need to be secured to prevent illicit use and to protect privacy.
  - *Counterfeit and associated fraud*: the risk of financial loss for one of the parties involved in a payment transaction arising from wrongful or criminal deception where either the identity of the payer cannot be easily ascertained or the payee does not have a legitimate claim on the payer. Traditionally, the crime of counterfeiting applies to paper money that is reproduced without authorization. Due to recent technological developments, some payment cards and tokens may store monetary value (e-money stored on a card/ e-wallet). E-money that is reproduced or altered without authorization has characteristics that are comparable to counterfeit paper money. The term counterfeit is now also commonly applied to unauthorized manufacture of cheques, card payment instruments or other physical tokens used in monetary transactions.[12]

Operational risk is, in general, relevant along the entire processing chain in the form of malfunctions. Other types of operational risk may be specific to a certain activity or a certain payment instrument. For example, fraud risk is most relevant for those steps of the processing chain involving authentication or identification. For payment instruments that involve the use of specific hardware (such as card readers), fraud risk is relevant if the hardware can be compromised or altered for illicit purposes (such as skimming or cloning of cards). Data security risk is

---

settlement risk, and systemic risk) see CPSS (2003) and the glossary annexed to ECB (2007b). On various aspects of settlement risk, see also Basel Committee on Banking Supervision (2000). On risks concerning, more specifically, retail payments (e.g. fraud risk, risk of a system-wide impact and reputational risk) see ECB (2007a) and CCBS (1996).

[12] A cheque that bears a false signature or has been altered is properly called forgery. For our purposes, we include forgery with counterfeit risk.

relevant for all activities involving the storage and transit of payment data that may be used for identity theft or for illicit authentication or authorisation of payment transactions. Data security risk may result in fraud risk if exposed records are then used for illicit purposes.

- *Compliance risk*: the risk of loss associated with non-compliance with laws, rules, regulations, prescribed practices, or ethical standards. The risk is borne by the issuing, the distributing, and the transaction archiving institutions and in general by the institutions subject to a compliance duty. The activities where this risk is most relevant are those related to security-related technology where market standards are in place (such as the Payment Card Industry (PCI) data security standard), and those where public regulations and laws aimed at combating the criminal use of the payment system (such as ex-ante anti-money laundering and terrorist financing controls). At times these standards may affect a payment participant indirectly, such as when bank payment acquirers are directly responsible for PCI standards but they hold firms to which they outsource payment processing responsible for the standards.[13] To the extent that payment schemes are subject to oversight by the central banks (as is the case in several European countries), compliance risk may arise if the rules and management of the payment scheme do not comply with the regulatory standards.
- *Risk of illicit use*: the risk of penalties if the failure to comply with required guidelines to curb illicit use of payments is discovered. One of the traditional focuses of law enforcement efforts to curb illicit use of payments is money laundering. Payment participants, such as a bank, are sometimes required to monitor use of bank accounts and to report suspicious activities. More recently, policymakers have been concerned with the use of the payments system to fund terrorist activities. A tool used to combat illicit use of the payments system is to carefully identify and screen new customers before granting access to the payments system. Banks are also obligated to carefully identify and screen merchants before accepting them as clients for payment services, and to monitor their ongoing use of payments.

There are a number of additional risks that are a concern in payments but are excluded from extensive discussion for various reasons. Principal among these is systemic risk (the risk that the failure of one participant in a transfer system, or in financial markets generally, to meet its required obligations will cause other participants or financial institutions to be unable to meet their obligations when due). We say little about systemic because there is a widely held perception that it is well controlled in retail payment systems. We say little about settlement risk (the risk that settlement in a transfer system does not take place as expected), for

[13] Similarly, manufacturers of point-of-sale payment terminals and ATM manufacturers are not directly obligated by contractual relationships with payment networks, but must comply with network security standards if they hope to successfully market their products.

similar reasons.[14] Finally, we limit discussion of some other risk categories, such as reputational, legal, and system-wide risk, because they are of a general nature and are often present whenever a disruption or problem in the payment system arises.

3.2 Risks along the Processing Chain

As briefly described in the previous subsection, various types of risks may arise during the payment process, and parties involved may be exposed to some of them at different stages, and to different degrees. Operational risk is present when payment orders are transmitted over communication networks. Parties that exchange assets to extinguish payment obligations may be exposed to financial risks (for example, liquidity and credit risk). All parties entering into contractual relations in the context of payments processing may be exposed to legal risk. Financial institutions that participate in clearing and settlement systems are vulnerable to operational, liquidity, and credit risk. These risks sometimes compound one another; if operational risk results in a computer outage, one payment participant may not receive funds from other participants, and it may need to refinance at higher prices, or suffer liquidity risk if it is unable to fulfil subsequent payment obligations, or incur legal risk if it is held liable to other parties.

In case of outsourcing of activities to third parties, financial institutions may become subject to legal risks (if the responsibilities of the parties are not sufficiently clear or legally sound), and operational risk (if the outsourcing party becomes dependent on an improperly managed third party). In the case of outsourcing to a third party that concentrates the activities for a whole payment market segment, system-wide risk may arise if the third party becomes suddenly impaired or unable to operate. For payment service providers whose outsourcing activities are subject to regulation (as in the case of banks), compliance risk may arise.

In this section we look at the vulnerability of certain payment activities to specific categories of risk by using a matrix representation (Table 4). Our aim is to identify the types of risk to which specific payment activities are exposed, but we do not attempt to indicate the magnitude of the risk exposure.

In the matrix we show liquidity risk, credit risk, and settlement agent credit risk. The matrix highlights with a shaded background where these risks materialize in the settlement process (settlement risk). Outside of the settlement process, credit and liquidity risk is borne by various parties involved in a payment scheme depending on the timing of the process, what party has custody of funds, and on the design of (and legal and contractual provisions governing) the specific payment instrument involved. For instance, typically a merchant accepting a payment

[14] Settlement agent risk is a variation of settlement risk. We include settlement agent risk because settlement agents are used principally in retail payment systems.

Table 4. Payment Activities and Selected Risks

Payment Activity		Type of Risk: Liquidity and Credit: Liquidity	Liquidity and Credit: Credit	Liquidity and Credit: Settlement agent credit risk	Operational: Malfunctioning and/or other operational problems	Operational: Data security risk associated with fraud or violations of privacy responsibilities	Operational: Counterfeit and associated fraud	Compliance	Illicit use (AML, terrorist financing)
Pre-Transaction									
1	a		x			x	x	x	x
	b	x	x			x	x	x	x
2	a		x		x	x			
	b				x	x			
3	a				x	x	x	x	
	b				x	x		x	
	c					x			
	d				x	x	x		
4	a				x	x		x	
	b				x	x		x	
	c				x	x			
5	a				x	x		x	
	b				x	x	x	x	
	c				x	x		x	
	d				x	x	x		
6	a					x	x	x	
	b				x	x	x	x	
	c				x	x	x	x	
7	a					x		x	
8	a				x	x		x	

Note: Data security risk is associated with the online environment.

Table 4. Payment Activities and Selected Risks (Cont.)

Payment Activity		Type of Risk							
		Liquidity and Credit			Operational				
		Liquidity	Credit	Settlement agent credit risk	Malfunctioning and/or other operational problems	Data security risk associated with fraud or violations of privacy responsibilities	Counterfeit and associated fraud	Compliance	Illicit use (AML, terrorist financing)
Pre-Transaction									
9	a				x	x		x	
During-Transaction – Stage 1									
10	a				x	x		x	
	b				x	x		x	
11	a				x	x		x	
	b				x	x		x	
	c		x		x	x	x		
	d		x		x	x	x	x	
12	a		x			x	x	x	
	b					x	x	x	
	c					x	x		
13	a					x		x	
14	a	x	x		x	x			
15	a							x	x
During-Transaction – Stage 2									
16	a				x	x		x	
	b				x	x		x	
	c				x	x			
	d				x	x			
	e				x	x			

Note: Data security risk is associated with the online environment.

Table 4. Payment Activities and Selected Risks (Cont.)

Payment Activity		Type of Risk: Liquidity and Credit – Liquidity	Liquidity and Credit – Credit	Liquidity and Credit – Settlement agent credit risk	Operational – Malfunctioning and/or other operational problems	Operational – Data security risk associated with fraud or violations of privacy responsibilities	Operational – Counterfeit and associated fraud	Compliance	Illicit use (AML, terrorist financing)
During-Transaction – Stage 2									
17	a				x	x			
	b				x	x			
	c				x	x			
	d				x	x			
18	a	x	x		x				
	b	x	x	x	x				
	c	x	x	x	x				
	d	x	x	x	x				
	e	x	x	x	x				
Post-Transaction									
19	a				x			x	
	b				x			x	
20	a				x	x		x	
21	a				x	x			
22	a					x			
	b					x			
	c					x			
23	a					x		x	x

Notes: Shading of table cells indicate activities and components of settlement risk.
Data security risk is associated with the online environment.

instrument in exchange for goods or services is exposed to credit risk unless the payment is settled with success in real time or at the same time of the delivery of the goods or services, or unless the payment instrument contractual framework provides for its mitigation or transfer to another party (for example, payments by cards may be assisted by a guarantee provided by the card issuer or by the card scheme). In card schemes, the card issuer is typically exposed to credit risk vis-à-vis cardholders of its cards. When a card transaction is properly authorised and accepted for execution by/within a card scheme, the card issuer takes the credit risk by guaranteeing payment to the merchant.

In the case where a retail payment is executed using a debit transfer order (for example, a direct debit) the payee's account may be credited in some cases before the actual debiting of the payer's account in the books of its bank. When this is the case, and if the payee's bank has advanced the funds to its customer before the successful final debiting of the payer's account, it may be exposed to liquidity risk or credit risk if the payee has already withdrawn the credited funds. In general, prepaid payment instruments entail a credit risk for the holder of the instrument vis-à-vis the issuer (such as in case of prepaid cards or e-wallets), while in case of post-paid payment instruments it is the payment service provider of the payee or the payee itself that is exposed to credit or liquidity risk. For example, this happens with post-billing payment services provided by certain mobile and telecommunication companies. This may also happen when a payment service is provided in real time to both payer and payee, but the top-up covering the specific payment is settled at a later stage (for example, a PayPal payment topped-up by direct debit on the payer's bank account).

As far as operational risk is concerned, we represent in Table 4 its general aspect (such as malfunctioning or human error) which is applicable to all activities and operational risk in connection with data security and counterfeiting. Data security has recently attracted attention because numerous data breaches have allowed unauthorized access to sensitive data. Because the primary concern of data security is the potential for payments fraud as well as violation of responsibility to protect privacy of customers, the column notes these consequences in its label. Counterfeiting does not generally get the attention of data security, but statistics for the United States suggest that in terms of its cost, fraud through counterfeiting is far more costly than that from data breaches. Cheque fraud, for example, is estimated to cost 10 to 20 billion dollars per year in the United States, a sum that is larger than estimates of fraud in all other forms of retail payments.

Although operational risk is relevant to the settlement process, it has a particular prominence for retail payments, and we find it useful to highlight those activities where the payments process may be particularly vulnerable to it.

The next-to-last column of Table 4 shows compliance risk. Payment participants can be required to comply with specific laws, regulations, and contractual arrangements. In the United States, payments are subject to legal requirements under the uniform commercial code and regulations such as the Federal Reserve's Regulation E. Members of payment networks (ATM, ACH, PIN-debit, signature debit, and credit card) are contractually bound to comply with operating and security standards set by the network. One of the most significant recent efforts to improve data security in card payments is the PCI data security standard.[15] The standard was revised in January 2005 and the payments industry is in a transition phase to the new standard. Merchants and payment processors that participate in a card network are responsible for complying with the standard. Payment participants subject to compliance risk can face significant penalties if it is found that they do not properly follow guidelines set forth for data security and other operational requirements.

The last column of Table 4 is for risk associated with illicit use of payments. For example, in the United States, payment providers are required to use reliable forms of identifying consumers when they provide payment services and banks must monitor accounts and file reports for suspicious activity.[16] In Europe, not only banks but also other parties are required by the Third Anti Money Laundering Directive to comply with obligations concerning customer due diligence, reporting of suspicious transactions, record keeping and statistical data, and to take other supporting measures, such as ensuring the proper training of personnel and the establishment of appropriate internal preventive policies and procedures.[17]

In Table 4 we associate the various payment activities with liquidity, credit and settlement risks, with operational risk and its main subcategories, and with compliance and illicit use risk. We believe there are three broad messages evident in the table. First, settlement risk is a prominent feature of retail payments. But, though it is present, analysts and policymakers generally believe that settlement risk in retail payments is well controlled.[18] Second, counterfeit risk is limited to a small number of payment activities. However, despite the limited impact on payment activities, counterfeit risk is one of the most significant problems in payments today, accounting for most of the losses due to payments fraud. Third, operational risk is one of the most prominent sources of risk in terms of the number of payment activities it affects. Most of the risk is in problems such as malfunctions and in data security. Associated with the prominence of operational risk is compliance risk, because imposition of rules and regulations on payment participants is a major containment tool used by regulators and payment networks

---

[15] The standards were developed as collaboration between American Express, Discover Financial Services, JCB, MasterCard Worldwide, and Visa International.

[16] As required by the Bank Secrecy Act (1970) and the USA PATRIOT Act (2001).

[17] Directive 2005/60/EC of the European Parliament and of the Council of 26 October 2005 on the prevention of the use of the financial system for the purpose of money laundering and terrorist financing is applicable to the financial sector as well as lawyers, notaries, accountants, real estate agents, casinos, trust, and company service providers. Its scope also encompasses all providers of goods, when payments are made in cash in excess of €15,000.

[18] This serves as a reminder that the purpose of Table 4 is to help identify where risk occurs in the many activities that underlie payments, not their severity.

to compel behaviour that properly manages operational risk.[19] The key to understanding the prominence of operational risk is the shift of payments toward electronic forms. The payment activities and subactivities listed in the table are dominated by processes that facilitate or depend upon electronic forms of messaging. These processes have emerged as we have adopted electronic payments. As a result the locus of retail payments risk has shifted toward operational risk.

In the light of the above results, do nonbanks raise special risk considerations? We address this question in the next section.

4 Impact of Nonbanks on Risk

4.1 Changing Risk Profile

The risk profiles of payment systems (and the risk mitigation techniques employed to minimize exposure to them) may change over time, following the introduction of new business models, the restructuring of business processes, the reorganization of systems, or simply the introduction of new technologies and the adoption of innovative means of communication. In particular, the recent use of open communication networks for the transmission and storage of payment related information (including sensitive personal data) has affected all payment systems. This has added to the prominence of data security risk, fraud risk and counterfeit risk for e-money.

This section addresses the question of how the widespread and rising presence of nonbanks in retail payment processing affects risks that are normally present in payment systems. Included are examples of incidents involving nonbanks that in theory could have affected the safe functioning of payments systems and payment schemes or affected public confidence in payment instruments.

Access to payment systems traditionally has been restricted, at least in part, to banks and other intermediaries that are subject to prudential supervision. One reason is to reduce risk exposures that may emerge among payment systems participants during the clearing and settlement process. Another reason is that the accounts used by banks to settle reciprocal payment obligations are accounts held either one-with-another (as in correspondent banking) or with one central institution that serves a larger banking community. Examples of such central institutions are central banks, which have a long tradition of establishing and operating payment systems for the banking sector. Both self-interest and regulation have led banks to develop strong safeguards against illicit intrusion in their information technology systems and networks.

[19] This method of containing risk in retail payments is common, in part because methods such as pricing for risk or insurance have proven inadequate to bring the level of risk in retail payments to tolerable levels (see Braun et al, forthcoming 2008).

The rising importance of nonbanks and the multiple roles they play both at the front-end and back-end of the payments chain has changed this traditional setting. In some ways, nonbanks contribute to an increase in the relevance of certain risks. In other ways, nonbanks decrease the relevance of other risks or facilitate the containment of risks.

Nonbank presence may increase the vulnerability of payment systems to certain risks. This may happen in at least three ways.

First, on the simplest level, nonbanks pose risk because they may offer alternative points of entry for criminals into the payments system, particularly in the early stage of the introduction of new methods to initiate payments. One example of this kind occurred in 2000, when two individuals used unauthorized access to Internet service providers (ISPs) in the United States to misappropriate credit card, bank account, and other personal financial information from more than 50,000 individuals, hijacked computer networks and then used the compromised processors to commit fraud through PayPal and the online auction company eBay (U.S. Department of Justice 2002). Since this incident, PayPal has been successful at improving its data security and fraud detection systems (Cox 2001; Garver 2005).

Second, and more broadly, banks traditionally act as gatekeepers to the payments system. When banks outsource payment processing services to nonbanks, they provide nonbanks with technical access to the payments systems that may increase vulnerability to various sources of operational risk. Traditionally, banks have managed these relationships to reduce this risk, but incidents do materialize, as shown by several recent examples.

In 2005, the U.S. company CardSystems, Inc. experienced a breach of its computer system that exposed 40 million transaction records with 263,000 records stolen. Credit card associations determined that CardSystems violated their security and record retention standards and, as a result, Visa chose to refuse transactions from CardSystems. At the beginning of 2007, another major data breach occurred at the large retailer group TJX, which operates over 2,000 stores in various countries, including the UK and Ireland. The breach exposed more than 90 million card account numbers. Losses to banks and other issuers have been estimated at between 68 million and 83 million USD for the 65 million Visa accounts exposed alone (Kerber 2007). Another incident involved data breaches related to unloyal staff of outsourcing companies. For instance, a UK journalist reported that he was able to buy details about 1,000 UK customers from a Delhi call centre worker, for GBP 4.25 each, saying that both cards credit numbers and account passwords were for sale (McKenna 2005).

According to a Visa Europe report on account data security in 2005 there were 91 incidents (one every four days), and there were several hacks involving European acquirers and merchants. This resulted in over 1 million cards exposed, and the cost of fraud amounted to USD 30 million (Littas 2006).

In addition to outsourcing, similar risks may arise when banks sell payments services to nonbanks. Banks mitigate this risk with know-your-customer practices that allow banks to detect attempts to exploit payment services and carry out illicit activities. An example of bank liability for improper monitoring of payment services provision to a nonbank customer was reported in the United States in 2003, when the Federal Trade Commission issued press releases explaining how it had closed down several companies (the Assail Telemarketing Network and affiliates) that engaged in fraudulent telemarketing activities. Assail used the ACH services of First Premier Bank; the bank admitted that it had failed to perform due diligence on the activities and legitimacy of its customers (but it did supply information to the investigative agencies); the bank later paid $200,000 in fines as part of a wider settlement and agreed to vigorously engage in know-your-customer actions and ongoing monitoring of customer activity (Iowa Attorney General 2005).

To limit such risks, banks must screen and understand potential nonbank clients and service providers, execute contracts that delineate responsibilities and liabilities, and monitor the business activity and internal control environment of the nonbank. While this risk is not new to banks, the difficulty faced today is that the payment system gatekeeping function may be more of a challenge because established methods of screening and monitoring may be inadequate given the development of new payment types and emergence of new types of business (such as online retailers). Moreover, this gatekeeping function may have become more critical compared to the past because of the complexity of the computer technology involved, which can be exploited in a manner that is fast, can be scaled to large values, and can be difficult to detect or trace.

Third, in some cases nonbanks play a key role for the functioning of an entire retail payment system, either because they run the infrastructure used by it, or because they concentrate processing for an entire retail payments market segment. Under these circumstances, nonbank presence may have implications at the system level. While concentration is often the natural consequence of the huge scale economies present in the payment industry, it also makes these key service providers a potential single point of failure that could trigger a large scale disruption (McPhail 2003). For example, the international credit card system relies on very few cards schemes. A major disruption at a key player may have the potential to impair the ability of millions of customers in several countries to make card payments.

The above discussion points out that nonbank access to payment systems may entail some risks. Furthermore, such risks may be exacerbated by the trend toward electronic payments, as electronic payment networks require a high degree of simultaneous coordination among all participants, with an increased need for cooperation between banks and nonbanks. In principle, this is not directly related to the nonbank status of the new service providers, but rather to the fact that the presence of many different entities in a payment network complicates its design, its functioning, the sequence and execution of transactions, and the regulation and implementation of security standards.

Nonbanks have been very active in introducing new access modalities to traditional bank payment services, and in facilitating the conversion of one payment instrument into an electronic format that allows its processing in the infrastructures that were originally designed for other payment instruments. This innovation has caused some blurring of the lines between payment channels. Various U.S. payment channels, for example, are becoming less distinct. Most visibly, some cheque payments are now being converted into ACH payments. But there are other changes that make the lines between payments systems less obvious. The ACH system is developing its systems to be more and more useful for retail payments. The ACH is also being used for some significant large-scale payments, such as the settlement of payments arising from the credit cards networks. A useful concept for resiliency in the payments system is redundancy: if one channel has problems, users may be able to get by using another channel until the problems are solved. But because of the interdependence of payments channels, the level of redundancy may have decreased, with adverse effects on service continuity. The extension of payments systems to new uses also increases potential for cross-channel risk. For example, criminals typically exploit weaknesses in the payments system. If one payment channel improves its security, criminals will probe other channels as alternatives. This may explain why fraud attacks concentrate on innovative payment communication networks and do not seem to attempt the relatively more isolated and protected established transmission networks such as SWIFT.

Nonbanks also bring new technology and perspectives that can significantly contribute to reducing risk in the payments system. Outsourcing some security-related activities like customer authentication to specialized firms may result, in principle, in better management by the outsourcing banks of certain threats to payments security and, thus, in an improvement of the risk mitigation techniques they employ. In addition, cooperation of payment service providers with Internet providers is key to combating payment fraud via IT systems in terms of promptly shutting down fraudster web sites and phishing sites. In general the payments industry benefits from the adoption of innovative process designs for traditional payment instruments. For example, the overall level of credit risk exposure may decrease by the adoption of online real-time controls of funds or credit limit coverage for submitted payment instructions. Nonbank service providers are proposing significant innovative technological solutions to the industry, such as biometric authentication, which may reduce fraud exposure.

4.2 Risk Management

Management of risk in retail payments depends highly on efforts of bank and nonbank participants in the payment system. But limitations of incentives to control payment risk leads to both industry self-regulation and government regulation. In general, available measures of retail payment risk show that risk in retail payments is well controlled, but there are significant limits to data on payment risk, especially regarding the role of nonbanks in payments.

Self-interest will lead both bank and nonbank providers of payments to limit risks that they can control within their organization. They will also be aware that some risks will affect them from outside of their organizations and may take extra precautions to protect themselves from such contingencies. But the interrelated nature of payment networks, and the exposure to outside threats that are very difficult to anticipate, implies that self-interest may not be sufficient to protect the payment system.

As a result, industry self-regulation is significant in the payments industry. These efforts are typically conducted at the network level where rules and requirements are set regarding standards that participants must meet regarding controls and management of operational, data security, and other risks. The fact that the PCI standards have been strengthened recently shows that these standards evolve in an effort to meet new risks as payment technology advances.

Because successful payment systems depend to a large extent on public confidence, there is also a public policy interest in the safe and smooth functioning of the payment system. In most countries this leads to some regulatory requirements that influence risk management in payments. Banks are at the center of the payment systems and bank supervisors do look at the payments activities of banks (and any payment processing subsidiary affiliated with the bank) to ensure controls over payment risk are in place.

Regulatory treatment of payments services for nonbank payment providers and processors can vary more widely across various countries. In the European Union, for example, front-end payment services provided by nonbanks vary significantly from country to country (EC 2003) and the regulatory provisions for the different types of payment services vary significantly across the Member States, ranging from no license requirement in one country to the restriction of the activity only to banks or other licensed financial institutions in another country.[20] The recently adopted Payment Services Directive changes this differential treatment. The Directive opens the market by allowing actors other than banks and e-money institutions to provide payment services. These new "payment institutions" are entitled to provide the payment services listed in annex to the Directive (Margerit 2007). The payment institutions will be subject to a simplified prudential framework compared to that applied to banks and e-money licensed institutions, with the aim to ensure their safe and prudent management and to protect users from risks arising from payments services provisions.

Similarly, regulatory safeguards regarding outsourcing by other nonbank providers of payment services are not harmonized at the EU level, but they will be once the Payment Services Directive comes into force: the Directive prescribes information

---

[20] Comparative tables of the national regimes in place in the various Member States are available at ec.europa.eu/internal_market/payments/framework/comparison_en.htm.

requirements to the competent authorities and sets conditions and limits for outsourcing of "important operational activities."[21] The Directive also specifies that the authorities supervising the payment institutions would also be entitled to carry out on-site inspections with any entity to which payment services activities are outsourced.

Similarly, bank and nonbank regulations differ for payment participants in the United States. Supervisors will look to see that financial institutions comply with requirements to keep sensitive information secure.[22] There is no similar requirement for nonbanks participants in payments, although the Federal Trade Commission has filled this gap by enforcing data security standards for retailers and other organizations.[23] In general there is no prudential supervision of nonbank payment providers, but a handful of larger nonbank payment providers are examined by federal financial institution supervisors under a technology service provider supervision program.[24] The actual protection this program provides for the payment system is uncertain because its primary purpose is to protect banks, not the payment system. Moreover, many payment providers are not overseen because they are not in an outsourcing relationship with a bank.

The important public policy questions are whether the effort toward risk management by individuals, banks and other payment providers is sufficient and whether the mix of individual effort, industry self-regulation, and regulatory oversight is adequate in the face of a payments industry that is increasingly dependent on nonbank organizations. Unfortunately, comprehensive data that bears on these questions is thin and generally does not parse out the role of nonbanks. Anecdotal examples point to criminal attacks on an increasingly large scale through IT technology (Anderson et al. 2008) or to nonbank responsibility for data breaches, but most analysts would say that the actual level of fraud is low. For example, according to Visa Europe Annual Report 2006, the fraud to sales ratio was only 0.069 percent of total POS spending.

The UK has a more advanced effort to statistically monitor payment fraud. Even though the UK is not included in our survey, their figures may provide a general idea of the size of the potential losses involved. The UK is also an important case study because it is the first country to adopt EVM payment cards, which provide a higher level of security by using computer chips to add

---

[21] An operational function shall be regarded as important if a defect or failure in its performance would materially impair the continuing compliance of a payment institution with the requirements of its authorization or its other obligations under the Directive, or its financial performance, or the soundness or the continuity of its payment services (Article 11).

[22] As required by the Gramm-Leach-Bliley Act of 1999.

[23] Examples include the retailer DSW, the credit agency ChoicePoint, and software vendor Guidance Software.

[24] Sullivan (2007). At year end 2004, 87 payments processors were supervised, while news reports suggest that there are roughly 500 companies that process credit card payments (Dash 2005).

encryption and other features to payment authorization. UK card issuers began the rollout of EMV cards and associated infrastructure in late 2003 and the year 2007 is the first complete year where all card payments had been required to be used in retail and ATM transactions. Total fraud losses in 2007 on cards issued by UK financial institutions are 6 percent higher than in 2004 but the mix of fraud from various sources as well as the distribution of losses in and out of the UK changed substantially over this time period (APACS 2008). Losses due to lost or stolen cards and card ID theft fell by 50.9 percent, reflecting the fact that the card requires a PIN. Fraud at UK retailers and ATMs both declined by large margins. The reduction in fraud on lost or stolen cards is a significant accomplishment and UK issuers achieved a major goal of EMV deployment.

There was, however, an increase of 92.6 percent in fraud losses on card-not-present transactions (phone, internet, and mail order). Surprisingly, losses due to counterfeit cards rose by 11.3 percent, despite the difficulty of counterfeiting a smart card. This happened because the UK EMV cards carry all the information necessary to make them backwards compatible with magnetic stripe cards. If criminals intercept this information, they can create a counterfeit magnetic stripe card for use in locations outside of the UK where they are still accepted. And in fact, fraud outside of the UK rose by 124.5 percent from 2004 to 2007.

The only systematic information on payment risk that allows a comparison of banks and nonbanks concerns data breaches in the United States. Data breaches are widely reported as a problem for payments and may serve as a measure of data security risk that could potentially lead to payments fraud. From January 2005 to April 2007, nearly 154 million records were compromised in 541 publicly reported data breaches.[25] Nonbank payment processors accounted for only 2.5 percent of all data breaches, but 26.5 percent of compromised records. Banks and other financial service companies accounted for 9.4 percent of incidents and 4.1 percent of records compromised over the entire period. A large number of data breaches have occurred in education, retail, health care, and government sectors. These four sectors together account for 77 percent of data breaches and 67.2 percent of records compromised in this particular period.

While conclusions are tentative, it appears that actual payments fraud is well contained. The UK experience shows how difficult it is to upgrade payment security standards because criminals adjust their efforts to exploit security weaknesses. And while analysis of data breaches show that payment security should involve all payment participants, the impact of data breaches on payments fraud appears limited at this time.

Insufficient incentives to manage risk in the payments system may contribute to payment risk. However, it is difficult to know the severity of incentive problems. Self-interest will lead to some risk management efforts by all participants in payments. Moreover, if everyone in the payments system managed risk in a

[25] Sullivan (2007), based on publicly disclosed data breaches listed by the Privacy Rights Clearinghouse (www.privacyrights.org/).

socially optimal manner, we would still observe some amount of security problems and payments fraud. As a result, a balanced public policy toward management of risk in payments seems warranted. Efforts by private industry to manage payment risk should be encouraged and supported. Carefully designed regulations can help coordinate industry efforts and maintain industry standards. Laws and criminal penalties can deter fraud and other misuse of the payments system. Finally, the importance of confidence in the overall payments system—a public good—should not be underestimated.

5 Conclusions and Closing Remarks

In this chapter we have reviewed the role played by nonbanks in the retail payments industry, both as front-end and back-end providers of services. We assess this role as being prominent in the United States and high in several of the surveyed European countries. In the United States, this is true across all payment instruments and along the entire processing chain. In Europe, this is true for cards in most countries and, in some countries, for most payment instruments, although there are differences concerning national preferences in the use of certain payment products, as well as in available data. In Europe, for some payment instruments, little information is available, particularly for payment instruments that are not widely used or whose use is declining.

We conclude that the role of nonbanks has margin for further growth in Europe, driven by the SEPA project, the restructuring and consolidation of the payments processing industry, and the growth of payment instruments whose processing models rely more heavily on third-party processors (for example, cards, which imply real-time authorisation and interplay among the parties involved in the scheme). Card transactions are growing significantly in Europe, particularly in those countries where maturing payment instruments are being replaced with electronic-based payments. Finally, changes in the regulatory environment will soon allow nonbank front-end payment service providers (the payment institutions) to operate within Europe in a harmonised framework, and their role is expected to increase.

Next, we analysed the risk categories that are most relevant for retail payments and showed that, while some of them (legal risk, reputational risk, and systemic risk) are of a general nature, others may be associated directly with specific activities along the payments processing chain. Due to the adoption of advanced technologies and more complex processing and business models (characterised by the interplay of numerous parties, IT systems, and databases), we found that some categories of risk have become more prominent. This is particularly the case with operational risk in its various forms (malfunctioning, data security, and fraud), and associated compliance risk.

Evaluating how these developments impact the nature and balance of risks between banks and nonbanks and the multiple roles they play, we conclude that controlling for risk may have become more challenging in the new environment.

First, nonbanks increasingly have gained access to payment systems (directly, or indirectly in the form of a technical access following outsourcing), and the resulting more complex networks of systems, relations, and interactions require a higher degree of coordination among participants. The regulation and implementation of security standards, for example, may have become more complex, and different incentives and interests may need to be reconciled. In principle, unless safeguards are in place, a heightened nonbank presence could present new points of entry for criminals into the payments system. Looking to the future, as new technologies are introduced and new contact points and players enter the picture, new potential vulnerabilities may need to be addressed. For example, vulnerabilities in WiFi communication networks could present new security challenges, and telephone malware could be used to spread viruses to consumer applications and to gain control of payments data stored in cell phones or data warehouses. These are just examples to show that the more contact points there are between networks and users and the more complex their functioning, the more challenging is risk control.

Second, the trend toward using a given payment infrastructure for different payment instruments (for example, converting one payment type into another for easier processing, or introducing payment instruments that present features of other instruments), increases potential for cross-channel risk. For instance, criminals may tend to focus attacks on more recently adopted open networks instead of bank-controlled proprietary networks. If criminals are able to misappropriate authentication and authorisation data and procedures, they may be able to submit "apparently" correct instructions to banks and into the payment system. The result would be fraud, with the ultimate cost, in terms of both financial cost and reputational damage, borne in many cases by banks.

Third, to the extent nonbank processors concentrate a larger share of payments in a certain market, a system-wide impact of disruption at a key player is possible.

While some of these risk issues do not originate from the bank or nonbank status of payment service providers, their control may be more challenging because the implementation of risk safeguards, particularly those introduced by regulation, may be designed and enforced starting from the assumption that payments' safety depends on banks. These models may in some cases need to be reconsidered or complemented in light of the increased importance of nonbanks. In Europe, for example, the regulatory framework for banks and nonbanks providing payment services has been harmonised both at the front-end and back-end. Furthermore, the Eurosystem has clear statutory competence in oversight of payment systems and may take action in various forms, if deemed appropriate, to safeguard the safety and efficiency of payment systems, as well as public confidence in the payment instruments, irrespective of the bank or bank-nature of the entities involved.

We also note that nonbanks and some of the technologies they have introduced into payments processing have in many instances contributed to a reduced exposure to various sources of risks. Such contributions should not be underestimated, as they support banks' and other nonbanks' efforts toward reducing operational risk and fraud risk, in particular.

Given the global reach and open-access nature of many of the technologies currently being utilised in payments networks, increased cooperation among bank and nonbank supervisory authorities, and among bank and nonbank industry players performing functions at various stages of the payments chain, would be appropriate, not only at the domestic level but, increasingly, at the international level as well.

Finally, we note that many of the observations and conclusions in this chapter are necessarily preliminary. Reflecting the lack of comprehensive and comparable data, we could not assess the severity of the various risks categories, or the net overall effect on payments safety. Although efforts are being made by both the private and public sectors, particularly in regards to the relevance of fraud risk, this is an area where more research is clearly warranted. Regarding the role of nonbanks in Europe, the analysis of this chapter could be complemented once more detailed and comparable data for the surveyed countries were available. This study has focused primarily on the euro area. A more complete assessment of nonbanks' role in Europe would require data for the remaining European markets.

Acknowledgments

The views expressed in this chapter are those of the authors and do not necessarily reflect the views of the ECB, the Eurosystem, the Federal Reserve Bank of Kansas City, or the Federal Reserve System. A longer, more detailed version of this article is available in (ECB, FRBKC 2007b). This research has benefited from comments by participants at the Joint ECB-Bank of England Conference on Payment Systems and Financial Stability, Frankfurt, November 12-13, 2007, from seminar participants at the Banca d'Italia and the Reserve Bank of Australia, and from comments by anonymous referees for the WEIS conference.

References

Anderson, R., Böhme, R., Clayton, R., and Moore, T. "Security Economics and European Policy," paper presented at *the Workshop on the Economics of Information Security*, June 2008.

APACS. "Fraud Abroad Pushes Up Losses on UK Cards Following Two-year Fall," press release, March 12, 2008. Available at www.apacs.org.uk/2007Fraudfiguresrelease.html#.

Basel Committee on Banking Supervision. *Principles for the Management of Credit Risk*, Bank for International Settlement, 2000. Available at www.bis.org/publ/bcbs54.htm.

Bradford, T., Davies, M., and Weiner S.E. *Nonbanks in the Payments System,* Federal Reserve Bank of Kansas City, 2003. Available at www.kansascityfed.org/publicat/psr /BksJournArticles/ NonBankPaper.pdf.

Braun, M., McAndrews, J., Roberds, W., and Sullivan, R.J. "The Economics of Managing Risks in Emerging Retail Payments," Federal Reserve Bank of New York *Economic Policy Review*, forthcoming 2008. Available at www.newyorkfed.org/research/epr/ forthcoming /0711brau. pdf.

Centre for Central Bank Studies. Bank of England, *Payment Systems*, Handbooks in Central Banking no. 8, 1996. Available at www.bankofengland.co.uk/education/ccbs/handbooks/pdf/ ccbshb08.pdf.

Committee on Payment and Settlement Systems. *A Glossary of Terms Used in Payment and Settlement Systems*, Bank for International Settlement, March 2003. Available at www.bis.org/ publ/cpss00b.htm.

Cox, P. "PayPal and FBI Team Up," *Wall Street Journal*, June 22, 2001.

Dash, E. "Take a Number," *The New York Times*, July 30, 2005.

European Central Bank. *Report on Retail Payment Innovations 2005,* Frankfurt am Main, Germany, 2005. Available at epso.intrasoft.lu/papers/Report-Retail-payment-innovations-2005. pdf.

_____. Consultation Announcement: Oversight Framework for Card Payment Schemes, press release, and Draft Oversight Framework for Card Payment Schemes, May 3, 2007a. Available at www.ecb.int/press/pr/date/2007/html/pr070503.en.html.

_____. Blue Book 2007, Payments and Securities Settlement Systems in the European Union, August 2007b.

European Central Bank Oversight Division and Federal Reserve Bank of Kansas City Payments System Research Function. "Nonbanks in the Payments System: European and U.S. Perspectives," paper presented at the Federal Reserve Bank of Kansas City *Conference on Nonbanks in the Payments System*, 2007a. Available at kansascityfed.org/econres/PSR/ PSRConferences/ 2007/pdf/Rosati_Weiner.pdf.

_____. "Nonbanks and Risk in Retail Payments," Working paper 07-02, Federal Reserve Bank of Kansas City, 2007b. Available at www.kc.frb.org/Econres/PSR/RWP/NonbanksRWP07-02.pdf.

European Commission. "Comparative Tables of National Rules," 2003. Available at ec.europa.eu/ internal_market/payments/framework/comparison_en.htm.

_____. "Commission Staff Working Document on the Review of the E-Money Directive (2000/46/EC)," Commission of the European Communities, SEC (2006) 1049,19.07.2006, Brussels: Belgium, 2006.

Garver, R. "eBay and Banking: Is PayPal a Serious Rival?" *American Banker*, November 15, 2005.

Iowa Attorney General. "First Premier Bank Agrees to Deny Automatic Withdrawal Services to Telemarketing Scams," July 6, 2005. Available at www.iowa.gov/government/ag /latest_news/ releases/july_2005/First_Premier.html.

Kerber, R. "Court Filing in TJX Breach Doubles Toll," *Boston Globe*, October 24, 2007. Available at www.boston.com/business/articles/2007/10/24/court_filing_in_tjx_breach _doubles_ toll/.

Littas, R. "Fraud Prevention Challenges After the Chip Card Migration," presentation delivered at Seminar on Payment Fraud in the EU Member States, the EU Accession Countries & Other European Countries, Brussels, March 8–9, 2006. Available at ec.europa.eu/internal_market /payments/docs/fraud/taiex_seminar/littas1st.pdf.

Margerit, V. "The Payment Services Directive," Banque de France Bulletin, August 2007.

Masi, P. "The Evolution of Electronic Payment Systems and Instruments," in Giorgio Pacifici and Pieraugusto Pozzi, eds., *Money-on-line.eu Digital Payment Systems and Smart Cards.* Milan: Franco Angeli, 2004.

McKenna, B. "Credit Card Details in the Clear and Up For Sale in India," *Network Security*, July 2005.

McPhail, K. "Managing Operational Risk in Payment, Clearing, and Settlement Systems," Working Paper 2003-2, Department of Banking Operations, Bank of Canada, February 2003. Available at www.bankofcanada.ca/en/res/wp/2003/wp03-2.pdf.

Sullivan, R.J. "Risk Management and Nonbank Participation in the U.S. Retail Payments System," Federal Reserve Bank of Kansas City *Economic Review* (second quarter), 2007, pp. 5-40. Available at kansascityfed.org/PUBLICAT/ECONREV/PDF/2q07sull.pdf.

U.S. Department of Justice. "Russian Computer Hacker Sentenced to Three Years in Prison," October 4, 2002. Available at www.cybercrime.gov/gorshkovSent.htm.

Visa Europe. Annual Report 2006, released 2007.

Security Economics and European Policy

Ross Anderson[1], Rainer Böhme[2], Richard Clayton[1] and Tyler Moore[1]

[1]Computer Laboratory, University of Cambridge, UK

[2]Technische Universität Dresden, DE

Abstract In September 2007, we were awarded a contract by the European Network and Information Security Agency (ENISA) to investigate failures in the market for secure electronic communications within the European Union, and come up with policy recommendations. In the process, we spoke to a large number of stakeholders, and held a consultative meeting in December 2007 in Brussels to present draft proposals, which established most had wide stakeholder support. The formal outcome of our work was a detailed report, "Security Economics and the Internal Market", published by ENISA in March 2008. This chapter presents a much abridged version: in it, we present the recommendations we made, along with a summary of our reasoning.

1 Introduction

Until the 1970s, network and information security was the concern of national governments. Intelligence agencies used eavesdropping and traffic analysis techniques against rival countries, largely in the context of the Cold War, and attempted to limit the penetration of their own countries' networks by rival agencies. From the 1970s until about 2004, however, the centre of gravity in information security shifted from governments to companies. As firms became ever more dependent on networked computer systems, the prospect of frauds and failures has increasingly driven investment in research and development.

Since about 2004, volume crime has arrived on the Internet. All of a sudden, criminals who were carrying out card fraud and attacks on electronic banking got organised, thanks to a handful of criminal organisations and a number of chatrooms and other electronic fora where criminals can trade stolen card and bank account data, hacking tools and other services. Hacking has turned from a sport into a business, and its tools are becoming increasingly commoditised. There has been an explosion of crimeware – malicious software used to perpetrate a variety of online crimes. Keyloggers, data theft tools and even phishing sites can be constructed using toolkits complete with sophisticated graphical user interfaces.

M.E. Johnson (ed.), *Managing Information Risk and the Economics of Security*,
DOI: 10.1007/978-0-387-09762-6_3, © Springer Science + Business Media, LLC 2009

The 'quality' of these tools is improving rapidly, as their authors invest in proper research, development, quality control and customer service.

Most commonly, crimeware is spread by tricking users into running code that they got in email attachments or downloaded from a malicious web site. However, its distribution is becoming more sophisticated as the criminal economy develops. For example, one so-called affiliate marketing web site offers to pay webmasters a commission ranging from US$0.08 to US$0.50 per infection to install iframes that point to an attacker's site which distributes crimeware (Jakobsson and Ramzan 2008). Meanwhile, network and information security is of growing economic importance in Europe (as elsewhere): sales of anti-virus software, cryptographic products, and services ranging from spam filtering through phishing site 'take-down' to brand protection and copyright enforcement are in the billions of euros per annum. The economic study of information security is thus of rapidly growing relevance to policy makers.

Since about 2000, researchers have realised that many security failures have economic causes (Anderson and Moore 2006). Systems often fail because the organisations that defend them do not bear the full costs of failure. For example, in countries with lax banking regulation, banks can pass more of the cost of fraud to customers and merchants, and this undermines their own incentive to protect payment systems properly. In addition, so long as anti-virus software is left to individuals to purchase and install, there may be a less than optimal level of protection when infected machines cause trouble for other machines rather than their owners.

Our key message is that in order to solve the problems of growing vulnerability and increasing crime, policy and legislation must coherently allocate responsibilities and liabilities so that the parties in a position to fix problems have an incentive to do so. For a variety of reasons, the state will have a role to play, either as policeman, or regulator, or coordinator. In the specific case of the European Union, regulatory options range from direct legislation (previous examples being the Data Protection Directive and the Electronic Commerce Directive), sector-specific regulation (such as the recent Payment Services Directive), coordinating groups (such as the Article 29 Working Party on data protection law), the funding of research, public procurement, down to the collection and publication of information.

In our complete report[26], we provide a more complete regulatory context and weigh the different options in greater detail. In this chapter, we describe just the final recommendations we made, along with our reasoning. By way of disclaimer, we note that these recommendations are our own and do not necessarily reflect the policy of ENISA or any other European institution.

---

[26] "Security Economics and the Internal Market", available at http://www.enisa.europa.eu/doc/pdf/report_sec_econ_&_int_mark_20080131.pdf.

1.1 Economic Barriers to Network and Information Security

We used five general headings to classify and analyse the economic barriers to network and information security, which form the structure of our chapter: information asymmetries, externalities, liability, diversity, and the fragmentation of legislation and law enforcement.

Information Asymmetries Asymmetric information can be a strong impediment to effective security. Akerlof's model of the 'market for lemons' (Akerlof 1970) appears to apply to many security product markets. The tendency of bad security products to drive out good ones from the marketplace has long been known, and at present the main initiative to overcome asymmetric information supported by the Commission and Member State governments is the Common Criteria.

It has also long been known that we simply do not have good statistics on online crime, attacks and vulnerabilities. Companies are hesitant to discuss their weaknesses with competitors even though a coordinated view of attacks could allow faster mitigation to everyone's benefit. In the USA, this problem has been tackled by information-sharing associations, security-breach disclosure laws and vulnerability markets.

Externalities Many important security threats are characterised by negative externalities. For example, home computers are increasingly being compromised and loaded with malware used to harm others. As a result, a user who connects an unpatched computer to the Internet does not face the full economic consequences of her action. A further set of externalities affect Internet service providers (ISPs). Small-to-medium ISPs have an incentive to clean up user machines (as being a source of spam damages their peering relationships (Serjantov and Clayton 2005)) while large ISPs at present enjoy a certain impunity.

Network externalities also affect many protective measures. For example, encryption software needs to be present at both ends of a communication in order to protect it; the first company to buy encryption software can protect communications with its branches, but not with its customers or its suppliers. In other circumstances, investments can be strategic complements: an individual taking protective measures may also protect others, inviting them to free ride.

Liability Dumping Firms seeking to manage risk often dump it on less powerful suppliers or customers. Software and service suppliers impose licenses on customers disclaiming all liability, including for security failures, and may also take 'consent' to the installation of spyware. This may delay the emergence of a market for more secure languages and tools, and lessen demand for the employment of professional software engineering methods.

Another example is the problem of mobile phone security; mobile phones have a long and complex supply chain, starting from the intellectual property owners, the chipmaker, the software supplier, the handset vendor, the network operator and the service provider. Each of these players seeks to have others bear the costs of security as much as possible, while using security mechanisms to maximise its own power in the chain. One side effect has been the failure of the OMA DRM Architecture V2 to come into widespread use, which in turn may have depressed the market for music downloads to mobile phones.

A third example is in payment services. The recent Payment Services Directive (European Union 2007) goes some way towards harmonisation of service rules across the EU but still leaves consumer protection significantly behind the USA. Banks are allowed to set dispute resolution procedures by their terms and conditions, and do so in their favour – as found for example in the recent report of the UK House of Lords Science and Technology Committee into Personal Internet Security (House of Lords 2007), which recommended that the traditional consumer protection enshrined in banking law since the nineteenth century should be extended to electronic transactions too.

Lack of Diversity Lack of diversity is a common complaint against platform vendors, whether Microsoft or Cisco or even Symbian. This is not just a matter for the competition authorities; lack of diversity makes successful attacks more devastating and harder to insure against, as high loss correlation renders some market segments uninsurable. Thus the market structure of the IT industry is a significant factor in society's ability to manage and absorb cyber risks.

Communication service providers are also affected; smaller ISPs find it cheaper to use single peering points, with the result that only large ISPs offer their customers resilience against peering point outage. This not only places these smaller ISPs (which are mainly small-to-medium enterprises (SMEs) and providing services to SMEs) at a disadvantage but shades over into critical national infrastructure concerns.

Fragmentation of Legislation and Law Enforcement The fragmentation of jurisdictions hinders rapid response. For example, the most important factor in deterring and frustrating phishing attacks is the speed of asset recovery. A bank learning of a customer account compromise needs to be able to trace and freeze any stolen assets quickly. The phishermen send hot money through the banks of Member States with a relaxed attitude to asset recovery. This issue spills over to money laundering.

A serious problem is that traditional mechanisms for international police cooperation are too slow and expensive for the Internet age. They evolved when international investigations were infrequent and dealt with matters that were either procedurally simple (such as the extradition of a fugitive) or a large investigation of mutual interest (such as drug smuggling). They do not cope well (or in some cases at all) with volume crime that crosses national boundaries.

2 Information Asymmetries

There has long been a shortage of hard data about information security failures, as many of the available statistics are not only poor but are collected by parties such as security vendors or law enforcement agencies with a vested interest in under- or over-reporting. These problems are now being tackled with some success in many US states with security-breach reporting laws, which we describe in Section 2.1. We also consider other opportunities for collecting relevant data in Section 2.2.

2.1 Security-Breach Notification

The first security-breach notification law to be enacted in the United States was California's A.B.700 in September 2002 (California State Senate 2002). It applies to public and private entities that conduct business in California and requires them to notify affected individuals when personal data under their control has been acquired by an unauthorised person. The law was intended to ensure that individuals are given the opportunity to take appropriate steps to protect their interests following data theft, such as putting a 'lock' on their file at credit agencies. It was also intended to motivate companies holding personal data to take steps to keep it secure. Indeed, (Acquisti et al. 2006) found a statistically significant negative impact on stock prices following a breach. Breach disclosure laws have also had the positive effect of contributing valuable data on security incidents to the public domain.

The California law has been followed by further laws in at least 34 other states[27], although they differ somewhat in their details. The variations have led to calls for a federal statute, but although bills have been introduced in Congress, none have had much success so far. In Europe, a security breach notification law has been proposed that would require notification to be made where a network security breach was responsible for the disclosure of personal data (European Commission 2007). This is a very narrow definition and will only deal with a small fraction of the cases that a California-style law would cover. Many incidents, such as criminals fitting an automatic teller machine (ATM) with a skimmer that steals card details (BBC 2007), would only be covered by a California-style law.

The US experience demonstrates the disadvantages of a patchwork of local laws, and the obvious recommendation is that a security breach notification law should be brought forward at the EU level, covering all sectors of economic activity rather than just telecomms companies. Indeed, the point of security breach notification is to avoid all the complexity of setting out in detail how data should be protected; instead it provides incentives for protection. It does not impose the

---

27 http://www.ncsl.org/programs/lis/cip/priv/breach.htm.

burden of a strict liability regime across the whole economy, but relies on 'naming and shaming'. Competent firms should welcome a situation where incompetent firms who cut corners to save money will be exposed, incur costs, and lose customers. This levels up the playing field and prevents the competent from being penalised for taking protection seriously.

Recommendation 1: We recommend that the EU introduce a comprehensive security-breach notification law.

As well as informing the data subjects of a data breach, a central clearing house should be informed as well. This ensures that even the smallest of breaches can be located by the press, investors, researchers, and sector-specific regulators. The law should set out minimum standards of clarity for notifications – in the US some companies have hidden notices within screeds of irrelevant marketing information. Finally, notifications should include clear advice on what individuals should do to mitigate the risks they run as a result of the disclosure; in the US many notifications have just puzzled their recipients rather than giving them helpful advice.

2.2 Further Data Sources

While breach-disclosure notification laws also serve as a useful data source on information security, a wider selection of data needs to be collected in an unbiased manner. A number of sources already collect relevant data, which comes in many forms. For the past twelve years, the US-based Computer Security Institute has annually surveyed enterprises, asking respondents whether they have been attacked and, if so, what the resulting losses were (Computer Security Institute 2007). In 2003, Eurostat started collecting data on Internet security issues from both individuals and enterprises in its "Community Surveys on ICT Usage" (European Commission 2006). Many security vendors also regularly publish reports on attack trends (e.g., (Symantec 2007)). Industry groups also sometimes disclose useful statistics, including the Anti-Phishing Working Group and APACS, the UK payments association. Finally, some academics conduct useful data collection and analysis (e.g., analysing phishing website lifetimes (Moore and Clayton 2007) and tracking botnets (Zhuge et al. 2007).

While governments can specify requirements for data collection, it is up to the stakeholders to actually provide the data. Security vendors will feel it in their interest to provide inflated statistics; phishing statistics often seem particularly fishy. For example, the anti-phishing group PhishTank has boasted about the large number of sites it identifies (OpenDNS 2007), when in reality the number of duplicates reduces the overall number several fold. APACS provides another example by asserting a 726% increase in phishing attacks between 2005 and 2006 (with merely a 44% rise in losses) (APACS 2007).

ISPs, by contrast, have an incentive to undercount the amount of wickedness emanating from their customers, particularly if they are held to account for it. But there is an even more pernicious problem with ISP reporting: ISPs hold important private information about the configuration of their own network that influences measurements. In particular, policies regarding dynamic IP address assignment can greatly skew an outside party's estimate of the number of compromised machines located at an ISP. ISPs also regard the size of their customer base as a company secret, which makes cross-ISP performance comparisons difficult.

In more mature sectors of the economy, we can see useful examples of statistical institutions collecting business data jointly with industry bodies. For example, safety and accident statistics for cars are collected by police and insurers, while media circulation figures are typically collected by private firms, some of them jointly owned and controlled by publishers and advertisers.

At the behest of the European Commission, ENISA recently investigated whether to establish a framework for sharing collected data on information security indicators between interested parties (Casper 2008). They identified around 100 potential data sources, then surveyed a core of potential partners (CERTs, MSSPs, security vendors, etc.) who were invited to a workshop to further gauge interest. Unfortunately, there was very little desire for sharing raw data, aggregated data, or indeed any information that doesn't already appear in the publicly-issued reports. Hence mandatory reporting of particular indicators may be required for sharing to happen.

We recommend that ENISA's information sharing efforts focus on industries with a clear benefit but where sharing is not already taking place in every Member State – and the two industries where more information should be made available are the financial industry and ISPs.

Individual banks are usually keen to keep data on fraud losses private. But one notable exception is the UK, where APACS has published aggregated figures for the annual amount lost to phishing attacks, as well as ATM crime and other financial fraud (APACS 2007). While the incentives are against individual financial institutions revealing losses publicly, a country-wide aggregation may still aid policymakers without inhibiting honest reporting very much. As far as we can tell, no other Member State publishes statistics of this kind. As banks collect such statistics for operational, internal control and audit purposes, and aggregating them nationally is straightforward, we believe this practice should become standard practice in the EU. The statistics are particularly critical to the formulation of policy on network and information security since the majority of the actual harm that accrues is financial. Without a good measure of this, other figures – whether of vulnerabilities, patches, botnets, or bad traffic – lack a properly grounded connection to the real economy.

Recommendation 2: We recommend that the Commission (or the European Central Bank) regulate to ensure the publication of robust loss statistics for electronic crime.

In many cases, fraud statistics are already collected by the police or banking associations, so regulatory action should aim at harmonisation of definitions, metrics and release cycles across Member States. A good first step would be to require figures broken down broadly as the APACS statistics are and show losses due to debit and credit card fraud (subdivided into the useful categories such as card cloning versus cardholder-not-present, national versus international, and so on).

As for the information that should be published by and about ISPs, it is well known at present within the industry that some ISPs are very much better than others at detecting abuse and responding to complaints of abuse by others. This is particularly noticeable in the case of spam. A small-to-medium sized ISP may find its peering arrangements under threat if it becomes a high-volume source of spam, so such ISPs have an incentive to detect when their customers' machines are infected and recruited into botnets. Large ISPs don't face the same peering-arrangement pressures, so as a result some send significantly larger quantities of spam and other bad traffic than others. We feel it would strongly be in the public interest for quantitative data on ISPs' security performance to be made available to the public.

Recommendation 3: We recommend that ENISA collect and publish data about the quantity of spam and other bad traffic emitted by European ISPs.

As Europe has some 40,000 ISPs, a staged approach may be advisable – with initial reports collected using sampling, followed if need be by action through telecomms regulators to collect more detailed statistics. However, even rough sample data will be useful, as it is the actions of the largest ISPs that have the greatest effect on the level of pollution in the digital environment.

Anyway, we feel that ENISA should take the lead in establishing these security metrics by setting clear guidelines, collating data from ISPs and other third parties, and disseminating the reported information. To begin with, ENISA could make a positive contribution by collecting and disseminating data on the rate at which ISPs are emitting bad packets. Such data could serve as a useful input to existing interconnection markets between ISPs since high levels of bad traffic can be costly for a receiving ISP to deal with.

The types of digital pollution to be measured must be defined carefully. To track spam, useful metrics might include: the number of spam messages sent from an ISP's customers; the number of outgoing spam messages blocked by an ISP; the number and source of incoming spam messages received by an ISP; and the number of customer machines observed to be transmitting spam for a particular duration. To track other types of malware, the number of infected customer machines would be relevant, along with the duration of infection.

Once data are available on which ISPs are the largest polluters, the next question is what should be done about them. This moves us from the heading of 'information asymmetries' to our next heading, 'externalities'.

3 Externalities

Externalities are the side effects that economic transactions have on third parties. Just as a factory belching smoke into the environment creates a negative externality for people downwind, people who connect infected PCs to the Internet create negative externalities in that their machines may emit spam, host phishing sites and distribute illegal content such as crimeware. The options available are broadly similar to those with which governments fight environmental pollution (a tax on pollution, a cap-and-trade system, or private action). Rather than a heavy-weight central scheme, we think that civil liability might be tried first. We first discuss the different stakeholders to whom pressure might usefully be applied before detailing our recommendation.

3.1 Who Should Internalise the Costs of Malware?

At present, malware used to harm others is the backbone of the underground economy in electronic crime. Such malware is installed using social engineering, by exploiting weaknesses in core platforms (operating systems, communications systems and server software) or via applications. Responsibility for correcting the externality might plausibly fall on several stakeholders.

One option is to assign responsibility to the software vendors for making software vulnerable in the first place. We consider what can be achieved using the stick of software liability in Section 4. However, we note here that the incentives are not as misaligned for core platforms – Microsoft has been improving its security for some time and suffers negative publicity when vulnerabilities are publicised. However, exploits at the application level require a different approach. Users readily install add-on features to web browsers, load web applications from untrustworthy firms, and run unpatched or out-of-date software. Users might also not install or update anti-virus software.

The machine owner is another important stakeholder. But there is a big difference between large and small owners. Large companies manage their machines by having a network perimeter where devices such as firewalls minimise exposure to compromise and restrict outbound communications from compromised machines; they also employ technicians to repair infected devices.

Individual end users and SMEs can do much less. They can and should maintain updated software, from the OS to applications and anti-virus tools; but they cannot protect themselves at the network perimeter as effectively as large businesses can, and can have tremendous difficulty repairing compromised devices.

The next influential stakeholder is the ISP. Compared to the others, ISPs are in a good position to improve the security of end-user and SME machines. ISPs control a machine's Internet connection, and therefore its ability to harm others.

There are many steps an ISP can take to limit the impact of malware-infected customer devices onto others, from disconnection to traffic filtering. ISPs can also communicate with customers by telephone or post, not just by Internet channels.

ISPs are divided on whether they should actively isolate infected customer machines, let alone whether they should try to prevent infections. One survey found that 41% of ISP respondents believed that they should clean up infected hosts, with 30% disagreeing and 29% uncertain (McPherson et al. 2007). Taking costly steps to repair customer machines, potentially including the unpopular move of temporarily cutting off service, is undesirable for ISPs when most of the negative effects are not borne by others.

3.2 Policy Options for Coping with Externalities

If ISPs should take action to raise the level of end-user security, then how can we best encourage them? A laissez-faire approach of encouraging best practice through self-regulation is tempting but likely to be insufficient. This is because the incentives on taking costly remedial action are weak at best (van Eeten and Bauer 2008), and since the poor performance of even a minority of ISPs can overshadow the operations of the best. Assigning liability for infected customers to ISPs is undesirable in practice due to the potentially high transaction cost of lawsuits, and the difficulty of valuing the monetary loss associated with individual events.

An alternative is to introduce fixed penalty charges if ISPs do not take remedial action within a short time period of notification. Upon notice of malicious activity, ISPs should place the machine into quarantine, clean up the offending content and reconnect the user as soon as possible. At present, there is great variation in the response times for ISPs when notified that a customer's machine is infected – the best ISPs remove phishing sites in less than one hour, while others take many days or even weeks to respond. Introducing a fixed penalty for machines that continue to misbehave after a reasonable duration, say 3 hours, would drastically speed up remedial action.

Fixed penalties are useful because they avoid the problem of quantifying losses following every infringement. They have been used effectively in the airline industry, where the EU has introduced penalties for airlines that deny passengers boarding due to overbooking, cancellations or excessive delays. The goal of this regulation is to provide an effective deterrent to the airlines. Fixed penalties are also routinely used for traffic violations. Again, the penalties deter violations while simplifying liability when violations occur. The threat of penalties should alter behaviour so that, in practice, fixed penalties are rarely issued.

For fixed penalties to work, a consistent reporting mechanism is important. Fortunately, existing channels can be leveraged. At present, several specialist security companies already track bad machines and notify ISPs to request cleanup.

This process could be formalised into a quarantine notice. End users could also send notifications to `abuse@isp.com`, as is already possible for reporting spam.

One issue to consider is to whom the fixed penalty should be paid. To encourage reporting, the penalty could be paid to whoever sent the notice. What about duplicate payments? One compromised machine might send millions of spam emails. If a fixed penalty had to be paid for each received report, then the fine may grow unreasonably large. Instead, the penalty should be paid to the first person to report an infected machine, or perhaps to the first ten who file reports.

Given the threat of stiff penalties for slow responses, ISPs might become overzealous in removing reported sites without first confirming the accuracy of reports. This might lead to a denial-of-service-attack where a malicious user falsely accuses other customers of misdeeds. There is also the established problem that firms who want a machine taken down for other reasons – because they claim that it hosts copyright-infringing material, or material defamatory of their products – are often very aggressive and indiscriminate about issuing take-down notices. These notices may be generated by poorly-written automatic scripts, and result in risk-averse ISPs taking down innocuous content.

In theory, a user can tell her ISP to put back disputed content and assume liability for it, but often the ISP will then simply terminate her service, rather than risk getting embroiled in a legal dispute. In many countries, ISPs have got into the habit of writing their contracts so that they can terminate service on no notice and for no reason. So there has to be a 'put-back' mechanism that users can invoke to get their ISPs to reconnect an incorrectly classified machine quickly by assuming liability for any wicked emanations. Consumers only need assume liability if they skip the quarantine process. In practice, we anticipate most consumers will elect to participate in the ISP's cleanup service.

It is not the purpose of our report to provide a detailed design of a fixed-penalty system, as this would have to evolve over time in any case. We nonetheless feel that it is the single measure most likely to be effective in motivating the less well-managed ISPs to adopt the practices of the best.

Recommendation 4: We recommend that the European Union introduce a statutory scale of damages against ISPs that do not respond promptly to requests for the removal of compromised machines, coupled with a right for users to have disconnected machines reconnected by assuming full liability.

We learned from the stakeholders' meeting that this is the most controversial of our recommendations. We therefore say to the ISP industry: do you accept it is a problem that infected machines remain connected to the Internet, conducting attacks for extended periods of time? And if so, what alternative means do you propose for dealing with it? Do we need policemen in each ISP dealing with infected machines, or could the ISPs' own staff deal with them more efficiently and cheaply?

4 Liability Assignment

A contentious political issue is liability for defective software. The software industry has historically disclaimed liability for defects, as did the motor industry for the first sixty years of its existence. There have been many calls for governments to make software vendors liable for the harm done by shoddy products. As society depends more on software, we will have to tackle the 'culture of impunity' among its developers.

To illustrate the many complexities surrounding software liability, we now describe an example using a navigation system. Suppose that a citizen purchases a navigation system to use with a mobile home and, relying on it, is directed by a software error down a small country lane where his mobile home gets stuck, as a result of which he incurs significant towing and repair costs. This case is interesting because navigation can be supplied in a number of ways as a product, as a service, or as a combination of both, for example:

1. one could buy a self-contained GPS unit in a shop;
2. a driver can also get a navigation system in the form of software to run on his PDA or laptop computer;
3. navigation is also available as a service, for example from Google Maps;
4. many high-end mobile phones have built-in GPS, and can also provide route advice either through embedded software or an online service;
5. a GPS receiver in a driver's mobile phone might connect to route-finding software in his laptop;
6. a driver's proprietary system might run on an open platform such as Linux;
7. as well as proprietary route-finding systems, there is a project[28] to build a public-domain map of the whole world from GPS traces submitted by volunteers.

So which of the above suppliers could the mobile home owner sue? Certainly it is common for GPS equipment vendors to put up disclaimers that the driver has to click away on power-up, but the Product Liability Directive (European Economic Community 1985) should aid consumers. This suggests that, at least at the consumer level, we should be able to deal with the liability issues relating to embedded systems – that is, the software inside cars, consumer electronics and other stand-alone devices – as a product-liability matter.

However, the Product Liability Directive does not apply to business property. Thus although our mobile-home driver can sue, a truck driver whose load of seafood got stuck and spoiled in exactly the same narrow lane has no recourse under the Product Liability Directive. The Unfair Contract Terms Directive, or other legal doctrines, might come to the rescue. To be fair, this complexity is a general problem for Community law and is not IT-specific. There is a further

[28] http://www.openstreetmap.org.

problem of jurisdiction: a business might rely on software downloaded from a website in California, which makes it clear that the contract is governed by the laws of California, and subject to the exclusive jurisdiction of that state. If the contract contains an exclusion that is valid under California law, then there may be little that the business can do if it is damaged by a software failure. Again, this is a general problem: there may be little the Community can do, as even if EU courts took jurisdiction their judgments would not be enforceable in California.

4.1 Software and Systems Liability Assignment

The above example should illustrate that software liability is both widely misunderstood and complex. But something may still need to be done. Our civilisation is becoming ever more dependent on software, and yet the liability for failure is largely disclaimed and certainly misallocated. We take the pragmatic view that software liability is too large an issue to be dealt with in a single Directive, because of the large and growing variety of goods and services in which software plays a critical role. We suggest that the Commission take a patient and staged approach. There are already some laws that impose liability regardless of contract terms (e.g., for personal injury), and it seems prudent for the time being to leave stand-alone embedded products to be dealt with by regulations on safety, product liability and consumer rights. Networked systems, however, can cause harm to others, and the Commission should begin to tackle this.

A good starting point would be to require vendors of PCs and other network-connected programmable devices to certify that their products are secure by default. It is illegal to sell a car without a seatbelt, so why should shops be allowed to sell a PC without an up-to-date operating system and a patching service that is switched on? This gives a more direct approach to the problem than assigning more specific rights to sue for damages. However, vendors who sell insecure systems should then be exposed to lawsuits from ISPs and other affected parties.

Recommendation 5: We recommend that the EU develop and enforce standards for network-connected equipment to be secure by default.

The precise nature of 'secure by default' will evolve over time. At present, the most important issue is whether the operating system is patched when the customer first gets it, and subsequently. The most likely solution would be to redesign the software so that the machine would not connect to any other online service until it had visited the patching service and successfully applied an update. Regulation should seek to enforce the principle of security by default rather than engineer the details, which should be left to market players and forces. Note that we are careful to specify 'all network-connected equipment', not just PCs; if we see more consumer electronic devices online, but lacking mechanisms to patch vulnerabilities, then in due course they will be exploited.

One of the stakeholders expressed concern at the likely costs if all consumer electronics required Common Criteria certification to EAL4; our view is that it would be quite sufficient for vendors to self-certify. However, the vendor should be liable if the certification later turns out to have been erroneous. Thus if a brand of TV set is widely compromised and used to host phishing sites, the ISPs who paid penalty charges for providing network connectivity to these TV sets should be able to sue the TV vendor. It would then be a matter for the court to decide fault on the facts. (We expect that once one or two landmark cases have been decided, the industry will rapidly adapt.)

In this way the Commission can start to move to a more incentive-compatible regime, by relentlessly reallocating slices of liability in response to specific market failures. The next question is what other liability transfers should be made initially. The most important matters at the present time have to do with patching – at which we now look in greater detail.

4.2 Patching

Patching is an unfortunate but essential tool in managing the security of information systems. Patching suffers from two types of externality. First, it is up to the software developer to create patches, but the adverse effects of a slow release are felt by consumers and the online community generally, rather than the companies directly involved. Second, the deployment of patches is costly, especially for large organisations. The publication of a patch often reveals the vulnerability to attackers, and then the unpatched, compromised machines are used to harm others; so the local benefits of patching may be less than the local costs, even when the global benefits greatly exceed the costs.

The first key challenge is to speed up patch development. The lag between vulnerability discovery and patch deployment is critical. During this period, consumers are vulnerable to exploits and have no recourse to protect themselves. Software vendors are often slow in deploying patches, and there is great variation in the patch-development times exhibited by different vendors. Among 5 leading OSs, Microsoft and Red Hat are fastest, Sun and HP are slowest by far, and Apple is in the middle (Symantec 2007). Consumer-oriented OSs tend to patch faster, perhaps because there is greater consumer demand and awareness.

For a sample of vulnerabilities exploited by Chinese websites in 2007 (Zhuge et al. 2008), nearly half were actively exploited in the wild before a patch was disclosed. Furthermore, the time lag between a vulnerability being disclosed and appearing in the wild is just two days, while patches took nearly two weeks to be published (if they were released at all). This suggests that there is scope for speeding up patch dissemination.

Vulnerability disclosure is often what triggers the development and deployment of patches. Yet the process by which the vulnerability is disclosed can affect the time vendors take to release patches. Some security researchers advocate full and immediate disclosure: publishing details (sometimes including exploit code) on the Bugtraq mailing list[29]. While undoubtedly prompting the vendors to publish a patch, full and immediate disclosure has the unfortunate side effect of leaving consumers immediately vulnerable. Vendors, for their part, typically prefer that vulnerabilities never be disclosed. However, some vulnerabilities might go undiscovered by the vendor even when they're being exploited by miscreants, and non-disclosure creates a culture in which vendors turn a blind eye.

A more balanced alternative is responsible disclosure as pioneered by CERT/CC in the US. CERT/CC notifies vendors to give them time to develop a patch before disclosing the vulnerability to the public. When the vulnerability is finally disclosed, no exploit code is provided. Empirical analysis comparing the patch-development times for vulnerabilities reported to Bugtraq and to CERT/CC revealed that CERT/CC's policy of responsible disclosure led to *faster* patch-development times than Bugtraq's full disclosure policy (Arora et al. 2005). The researchers also found that early disclosure, via CERT/CC or Bugtraq, does speed up patch-development time.

Another option is to assign liability for vulnerabilities to the software vendor until a patch is made available and consumers have had a reasonable chance to update. (Cavusoğlu et al. 2006) compare liability and cost-sharing as mechanisms for incentivising vendors to work harder at patching their software. It turns out that liability helps where vendors release less often than they should.

Recommendation 6: We recommend that the EU adopt a combination of early responsible vulnerability disclosure and vendor liability for unpatched software to speed the patch-development cycle.

While quantitative measurements are difficult to obtain, the view among security professionals is that patches are already available for the majority of exploits used by attackers. Over half of the exploits in the study by (Zhuge et al. 2008) first appeared on Chinese websites only after a patch had already been made available. Hence, a second key challenge is to increase the uptake of patches among users.

So why do some users remain unpatched? While most operating systems offer automatic patching, many third-party applications like web browser add-ons do not. Vendors who do not provide automated patches could be held liable as part of the 'secure default' approach discussed in Recommendation 5. Meanwhile, some perfectly rational users (especially at the enterprise level) choose not to patch immediately because of reliability and system stability concerns.

Vendors must make patching easier and less of a nuisance for consumers. One simple way of doing this is to decouple security patches from feature updates.

---

[29] http://www.securityfocus.com/archive/1.

Users may not want to add the latest features to a program for a variety of reasons. Feature updates could disrupt customisation, slow down performance, or add undesirable restrictions (e.g., DRM). Even though most feature updates are beneficial, the few exceptions can turn users off patching, even when it is in their interest to do so.

Recommendation 7: We recommend security patches be offered for free, and that patches be kept separate from feature updates.

4.3 Consumer Policy

Where consumers are involved one may need more protection. A particularly important context is the resolution of payment disputes. Many online frauds result in debits from bank accounts, whether via transactions for nonexistent goods or services, via fraudulent use of credit card data, or via direct attacks on online banking systems. The impact of fraud on the citizen thus depends critically on the ease of obtaining restitution. However, this varies rather widely across Member States. Where banks can dump liability for fraud on merchants, or where banks and merchants can dump it on the customer, there arises a further moral hazard; when the parties most able to reduce fraud are shielded from its effects, they may make less effort than they should to prevent it.

The question of varying fraud liability and dispute resolution procedures has been raised from time to time, and so far has been avoided by legislators – most recently when the Payment Services Directive was being negotiated from 2002 to 2005 (European Union 2007). It is time for the Commission to tackle this issue.

Recommendation 8: The European Union should harmonise procedures for the resolution of disputes between customers and payment service providers over electronic transactions.

Competition is relevant here too. Consumers are in a weak position vis-à-vis competing vendors of products where there is an 'industry position' of disclaiming liability for defects (as with cars two generations ago, or software and online services today), yet they are in an even weaker position facing a monopoly supplier. In both cases, they are faced with shrink-wrap or click-wrap licenses that impose contract terms on them on a take-it-or-leave-it basis.

Shrink-wrap licenses are thought by legal scholars to be defective. The main applicable law in the EU is the Unfair Contract Terms Directive (European Union 1993), which makes a consumer contract term unfair "if, contrary to the requirement of good faith, it causes a significant imbalance in the parties' rights and obligations arising under the contract, to the detriment of the consumer". This is widely flouted by the software industry. For example, Article 5 requires that "terms must always be drafted in plain, intelligible language"; yet in practice, end-user license agreements (EULAs) are written in dense legalese and made difficult to access; for example, a large amount of text may appear via a small window, so that the user has to scroll down dozens or even hundreds of times to read it. Some companies use deceptive marketing techniques that break various EU laws. Spyware programs "monitor user activities, and transmit user information to remote servers and/or show targeted advertisements" (Edelman 2008). Spyware's installation strategies violate the Unfair Contract Terms Directive. In almost all cases, the installation will be done without valid, free consent, so spyware also violates the Data Protection Directive and the E-Privacy Directive (European Union 2002). As if that were not enough, spyware programs are often made deliberately hard to uninstall.

Dealing with spyware through regulation is difficult, since most spyware companies are based outside the EU (typically in the US). While directly regulating the practices of spyware vendors is difficult, effective sanctions are still possible by punishing the companies that advertise using spyware. In the 1960s, a number of unlicensed 'pirate' radio stations aimed at UK consumers were launched from ships just outside the UK's jurisdiction. The Marine Broadcasting Offences Act of 1967 made it illegal for anyone subject to UK law to operate or assist the stations. This immediately dried up advertising revenues, and the unlicensed stations were forced to fold. A similar strategy could undermine spyware, since many of the advertisers are large international companies that do business in the EU (Edelman 2004). While advertisers might object that they could be framed by competitors, an examination of the resulting evidence should vindicate any false accusations.

Another abusive practice already the target of regulation is spam. The EU Directive on Privacy and Electronic Communications (European Union 2002) attempts to protect consumers from spam. For the most part, it prohibits sending any unsolicited messages to individuals, requiring their prior consent. However, Article 13 Paragraph 5, states that protections only apply to 'natural persons', and leaves it up to Member States to decide whether to allow unsolicited communications to business. Direct marketing lobbies argued that spamming businesses was essential to their trade. In practice, the business exemption has undermined the protections for consumers. It gives spammers a defence against all messages sent to 'work' domains. It also drives up costs for businesses, who must contend with spam sent from potentially millions of other businesses. Finally, it is difficult (in practice perhaps impossible) to draw clear lines between 'natural' and 'legal' persons in this context: some businesses (one-man firms, barristers, partners in some organisations) are legally 'natural' persons, while email addresses of identifiable individuals in companies relate to 'natural' persons. So there is a strong case to abandon the distinction. Therefore, we recommend repealing Article 13 Paragraph 5, the business exemption for spam.

Putting all these together:

Recommendation 9: We recommend that the European Commission prepare a proposal for a Directive establishing a coherent regime of proportionate and effective sanctions against abusive online marketers.

The issues raised in this section on consumer policy are not limited to abusive marketing and unfair banking contracts. Perhaps the most important example concerns the foundation of the Single Market itself. It is a long-established principle that EU citizens can buy goods anywhere in the Union. The challenge now is that physical goods are increasingly bundled with online services, which may be priced differently in different Member States, or even unavailable in some of them. The bundling of goods and services is an area of significant complexity in EU law. Moreover, the segmentation of online service markets can affect information security. Sometimes market segmentation in B2B transactions impacts consumers; for example, citizens in one country can find it hard to open a bank account in another because of how credit-reference services are bundled and sold to banks. This in turn reduces consumers' ability to exert pressure on banks in countries where online banking service is less competitive by switching their business elsewhere.

The 2006 Services Directive takes some welcome first steps towards harmonising the market for services (European Union 2006). This Directive tries to remove many protectionist measures erected over the centuries by Member States to cosset domestic service providers. In our view another aspect warrants attention: the deliberate use of differential service provision as a tool by marketers, both as a means of discriminatory pricing and in order to undermine consumer rights.

Single-market service provision is much broader than the scope of our report. Like the liability for defects in software – and in services – it is such a large topic that it will have to be tackled a slice at a time, and by many stakeholders in the Commission. We encourage ENISA to get involved in this policy process so that security aspects are properly considered in consumer-protection questions.

Finally, universal access to the Internet may also benefit from action under the heading of consumer rights. If all the ISPs in a country align their terms and conditions so that they can disconnect any customer for no reason, this should be contrary to public policy on a number of grounds, including free speech and the avoidance of discrimination. Even those citizens who are unpopular with some vocal lobby group must have the right to Internet connectivity.

Recommendation 10: ENISA should conduct research, coordinated with other affected stakeholders and the European Commission, to study what changes are needed to consumer-protection law as commerce moves online.

5 Dealing with the Lack of Diversity

Diversity can help security. Physical diversity deals with geographical distribution of redundant infrastructure components and network routes, whereas logical diversity means that distributed systems do not share common design or implementation flaws. A lack of diversity implies risk concentration which negatively affects insurability and thus an economy's ability to deal with cyber risks.

5.1 Promoting Logical Diversity

For logical diversity to happen, alternatives must be widely available and adoption well-balanced. In information industries, this has rarely occurred: technical lock-in, positive network externalities and high switching costs tend to yield dominant-firm markets (Shapiro and Varian 1999). Nonetheless, there are steps governments can take to improve, or at least not hinder, the prospects for diversity.

A policy to foster diversity must first ensure the availability of viable alternatives. One option is to promote open standards to facilitate market entry. But even successful open standards do not always deliver diversity. Another option is to promote diversity in public procurement. Consumers and firms are shortsighted when selecting software; positive network externalities lead them to discount increases in correlated risk. Governments need not be so myopic, but there are limits to the impact governments can have through public procurement policies alone.

Regulatory responses may occasionally be required. However, regulation tends to work more slowly than the industry. Cisco used to have a very dominant market position in the routers deployed in the Internet backbone. A vulnerability in Cisco routers (Zetter 2005) was disclosed that could have removed a significant portion of the Internet backbone if a flash worm had been disseminated. So the lack of diversity among routers used to be a critical concern. But the market for backbone routers has balanced recently, given competition from Juniper and others. The market for mobile phone software similarly used to be dominated by Symbian, but that has also corrected itself somewhat thanks to challenges by Apple, Google, Microsoft and others. Finally, the market for web browsers is now more competitive following years of dominance by Internet Explorer. In general, we feel the authorities should maintain a watching brief for competition issues that persist and have security implications.

Recommendation 11: We recommend that ENISA should advise the competition authorities whenever diversity has security implications.

5.2 *Promoting Physical Diversity in CNI*

Pitcom, a UK parliamentary group, has published a useful overview of critical national infrastructure (CNI) vulnerability aimed at legislators (Pitcom 2006). They show how an Internet failure could damage other parts of the CNI such as finance, food and health. Telecomms and power are known to be closely coupled: if a high voltage power line fails, the engineers who go to fix it will keep in touch by mobile phone. But the mobile phones depend on the power supply to keep base stations operating. This particular problem can be fixed using satellite phones; but what other problems should we anticipate?

In principle, network designers avoid single points of failure using redundant components. However, as systems scale, they may be introduced beyond an individual network's control. For example, a major concern about single points of failure for the Internet is the growth of Internet Exchange Points (IXPs) such as LINX in London, AMSIX in Amsterdam, DECIX in Frankfurt, etc., and how one IXP per country tends to grow much larger than its rivals. ISPs use IXPs to reduce the costs of providing their customers with connectivity to the rest of the Internet.

The value of joining an IXP can increase as more ISPs join, leading to winner-take-all dynamics where one IXP is much larger than its local rivals. 11 EU countries have just one IXP; in almost all the others the largest IXP is 4 or more times the size of the next largest – the exceptions being Estonia, Spain, Belgium, and Poland (in each of which there are 2 roughly equal sized IXPs, not a stable equilibrium), and France which, for complex historical reasons, is much more fragmented with 5 similar sized exchanges. These pressures towards a dominant IXP lead to possible single points of failure at the IXP itself. Some leading IXPs have invested heavily in redundancy; others haven't, mainly because of the expense.

CNI is now understood to be a multi-national issue. One of the key difficulties in this area is that CNI companies do not wish to discuss how they might be vulnerable, while governments have limited understanding of the real world: for example the COCOMBINE project in Framework 6 examined IXPs but failed to understand why peering does or does not take place between particular ISPs, and merely attempted to find spatial patterns, with limited success (D'Ignazio and Giovanetti 2006a; D'Ignazio and Giovannetti 2006b). Hence the most obvious policy option to adopt is that of encouraging information sharing – and more, better informed, research into the actual issues.

Recommendation 12: We recommend that ENISA sponsor research to better understand the effects of IXP failures. We also recommend they work with telecomms regulators to insist on best practice in IXP peering resilience.

6 Fragmentation of Legislation and Law Enforcement

As well as providing the right incentives for vendors and service providers, and protection for consumers, it is important to catch cyber criminals, who at present act with near impunity thanks to the fragmentation of law enforcement efforts. In order for the police to prosecute the criminals they catch, cyber crimes must be offences in all Member States. Furthermore, as nearly all cyber crimes cross national borders, cooperation across jurisdictions must be improved.

To a first approximation, existing legal frameworks have had no difficulty in dealing with the Internet. However, the cross-jurisdictional nature of cyberspace has meant that many criminals commit their offences in another country (often many other countries) and this leads to difficulties in ensuring that they have committed an offence in the country in which they reside.

The practical approach that has been taken is to try and harmonise national laws within a consistent international framework. The relevant treaty for the specific harms that cannot be dealt with by existing 'offline' legislation is the 2001 Convention on Cybercrime (Council of Europe 2001) which sets out the required offences, provides the requisite definitions and sets out a uniform level of punishments. All of the EU states have signed the convention, but some six years later only 12 have ratified, while 15 have failed to do so. If the harmonisation approach is to bear fruit, this process needs to be speeded up.

Recommendation 13: We recommend that the European Commission put immediate pressure on the 15 Member States that have yet to ratify the Cybercrime Convention.

Cooperation across law enforcement jurisdictions is essential for online crime, yet there are very serious impediments against police forces working together. Police forces must make tough choices in deciding which crimes to investigate. In the case of electronic crime, one of the first questions is how many local citizens are affected, and how many local computers are being used to launch attacks. Using this criterion, most attackers are not worth pursuing, even if in aggregate they are having a devastating effect. Even those cases that are deemed worth pursuing invariably lead to computers located in other countries. The current structures for international cooperation were designed for physical crimes, where cross-border activity is rare. They slow down investigations and drive up costs.

When a crime involves another country, law enforcement agencies may first attempt to establish a joint operation between police forces. In a typical joint operation, the country where the investigation began does most of the work while the cooperating country serves warrants and obtains evidence as requested by the originating force. Joint operations are largely unfunded and carried out on a quid pro quo basis, so they cannot be relied upon as the baseline response to all cybercrimes. Cooperation may also be possible via a mutual legal assistance treaty

(MLAT). MLATs require a political decision taken by the requested country's foreign ministry to determine whether cooperation can commence, and are very slow to process. So many investigators prefer to avoid using them where possible.

The problem of countries working together for a common cause while preserving national sovereignty has already been tackled by the military – whether it was SHAPE in World War II or NATO today. The model is that each country takes its own political decision as to what budget to set aside for fighting cybercrime. Part of this budget funds liaison officers at a central command centre. That command centre decides which tasks to undertake, and the liaison officers relay requests to their own countries' forces. This is in effect a permanent 'joint operation' that avoids the glacial speed of MLATs. The key is that countries trust their liaison officers to assess which requests carry no political baggage and can be expedited.

Recommendation 14: We recommend the establishment of an EU-wide body charged with facilitating international cooperation on cyber crime, using NATO as a model.

7 Security Research and Legislation

Security research is important, and occurs at a number of places in the value chain. First, blue-sky (typically academic) researchers think up new algorithms, protocols, operating-system access-control schemes and the like. Second, applied researchers investigate how particular types of systems fail, and devise specific proposals for submission to standards bodies. These researchers can be academic, industrial, or a mix. Third, research and development engineers produce prototypes and write code for specific products and services. Fourth, users of these products or services discover vulnerabilities. These are often design or implementation errors rather than flaws in the underlying security technology.

Public policy has gotten in the way of security research on a number of occasions. The debate on cryptography policy during the 1990s led to EC Regulation 1334/2000 on Dual Use Goods under which the export of cryptographic software in intangible form (e.g. researchers swapping source code) became subject to export control. Many small software developers are unaware of this control regime and may be technically in breach of its implementation provisions in some Member States. More recently, in some Member States, well-meant but poorly drafted legislation has impeded security research. In Germany, the criminal law code (Strafgesetzbuch) has been amended with a new section 202c that makes it an offence to produce, supply, sell, transmit, publish or otherwise make accessible any password, access code or software designed to perpetrate a computer crime, or in preparation for such a crime. This has been opposed as excessive by many researchers who see it as threatening those who possess system engineering tools for innocuous purposes (Anderson 2007). In the UK, the government amended the Computer Misuse Act to make it an offence to "supply or offer to supply, believing that it is likely to be used to commit, or to assist in the commission of [a computer offence]" so that it is the meaning of 'likely' which will determine whether an offence has been committed. The government's response to concern about the circumstances in which an offence would be committed has been to promise to publish guidance for prosecutors as to when the law should be invoked.

In both cases the concern is that IT and security professionals who make network monitoring tools publicly available or disclose details of unpatched vulnerabilities could be prosecuted. Indeed, most of the tools on a professional's laptop, from nmap to perl, could be used for both good and bad purposes. The resulting legal uncertainty has a chilling effect on security research (Clayton 2007).

The industry needs an advocate in Brussels to ensure that its interests are taken into account when directives and regulations are being formulated – and as they evolve over time. In the case of export control, we recommend that ENISA push for cryptography to be removed from the dual-use list. In the case of dual-use tools that can be used for hacking as well as for bona-fide research and administrative tasks, we recommend ENISA take the position that sanctions should only apply in the case of evil intent.

Recommendation 15: We recommend that ENISA champion the interests of the information security sector within the Commission to ensure that regulations introduced for other purposes do not inadvertently harm security researchers and firms.

8 Conclusions

As Europe moves online, information security is becoming increasingly important: first, because the direct and indirect losses are now economically significant; and second, because growing public concerns about information security hinder the development of both markets and public services. While information security touches on many subjects from mathematics through law to psychology, some of the most useful tools for both the policy analyst and the systems engineer come from economics.

In our report, of which this is an abridged version, we provided an analysis based on security economics of the practical problems in network and information security that the European Union faces at this time. We have come up with fifteen policy proposals that should make a good next step in tackling the problems. We therefore hope that they will provide the basis for constructive action by ENISA and the European Commission in the future.

Acknowledgments

The authors are grateful to acknowledge input from the attendees at the ENISA stakeholders' meeting on December 10th, 2007; from people in the security industry who talked to us, mostly off the record; from colleagues in the security groups at Cambridge and Dresden; from members of the Advisory Council of the Foundation for Information Policy Research, particularly Nick Bohm, Alan Cox, Douwe Korff, Jim Norton and Martyn Thomas; and from Alexander Korff of Clifford Chance. Responsibility for any errors and omissions of course remains with the authors alone.

References

Acquisti, A., Friedman, A., and Telang, R. "Is There a Cost to Privacy Breaches? An Event Study", in *5th Workshop on the Economics of Information Security (WEIS)*, Cambridge, United Kingdom, June 2006.

Akerlof, G. "The Market for 'Lemons': Quality Uncertainty and the Market Mechanism". *Quart. J. Economics (84)*, 1970, pp. 488—500.

Anderson, N. "German 'Anti-Hacker' Law Forces Hacker Sites to Relocate". *Ars Technica*, 14 August 2007. http://arstechnica.com/news.ars/post/20070814-german-anti-hacker-law-forcing-hacker-sites-to-relocate.html

Anderson, R., and Moore, T. "The Economics of Information Security", *Science* (314:5799), October 2006, pp. 610—613.

APACS. "Card Fraud Losses Continue to Fall", Press Release, APACS, 14 March 2007. http://www.apacs.org.uk/media_centre/press/07_14_03.html

Arora, A., Krishnan, R., Telang, R., and Yang, Y. "An Empirical Analysis of Vendor Response to Disclosure Policy", in *4th WEIS*, Cambridge, Massachusetts, June 2005.

BBC. "Devices Attached to Cash Machines", *BBC News*, 15 October 2007.http://news.bbc.co.uk/1/hi/england/cambridgeshire/7044894.stm

California State Senate. *Assembly Bill 700*, 2002. http://info.sen.ca.gov/pub/01-02/bill/asm/ab_0651-0700/ab_700_bill_20020929_chaptered.pdf

Casper, C. "Examining the Feasibility of a Data Collection Framework", *ENISA*, February 2008.

Cavusoğlu, H., Cavusoğlu, H., and Zhang, J. "Economics of Patch Management", in *5th WEIS*, Cambridge, United Kingdom, June 2006.

Clayton, R. "Hacking Tools are Legal for a Little Longer", *Light Blue Touchpaper*, 19 June 2007. http://www.lightbluetouchpaper.org/2007/06/19/hacking-tools-are-legal-for-a-little-longer/

Computer Security Institute. "The 12th Annual Computer Crime and Security Survey", October 2007. http://www.gocsi.com/

Council of Europe. *Convention on Cybercrime*, CETS 185, November 2001. http://conventions.coe.int/Treaty/Commun/QueVoulezVous.asp?NT=185&CL=ENG

Edelman, B. "Advertisers Using WhenU", July 2004. http://www.benedelman.org/spyware/whenu-advertisers/

Edelman, B. "Spyware: Research, Testing, Legislation, and Suits", June 2008.http:/www.benedelman.org/spyware/

van Eeten, M., and Bauer, J. "The Economics of Malware: Security Decisions, Incentives and Externalities", *OECD*, May 2008. http://www.oecd.org/dataoecd/25/2/40679279.pdf

European Commission. "i2010 Benchmarking Framework", November 2006.http://ec.europa.eu/information_society/eeurope/i2010/docs/benchmarking/060220_i2010_Benchmarking_Framework_final_nov_2006.doc

European Commission. "Report on the Outcome of the Review of the EU Regulatory Framework for Electronic Communications Networks and Services in Accordance with Directive 2002/21/EC and Summary of the 2007 Reform Proposals", November 2007. http://ec.europa.eu/information_society/policy/ecomm/doc/library/proposals/com_review_en.pdf

European Economic Community. "Council Directive of 25 July 1985 on the Approximation of the Laws, Regulations and Administrative Provisions of the Member States Concerning Liability for Defective Products (85/374/EEC)", July 1985.

European Union. "Directive 93/13/EEC of 5 April 1993 on Unfair Terms in Consumer Contracts", April 1993. http://eur-lex.europa.eu/smartapi/cgi/sga_doc?smartapi!celexapi!prod!CELEXnumdoc&lg=EN&numdoc=31993L0013&model=guichett

European Union. "Directive 2002/58/EC of the European Parliament and of the Council of 12 July 2002 Concerning the Processing of Personal Data and the Protection of Privacy in the Electronic Communications Sector (Directive on Privacy and Electronic Communications)", July 2002. http://eur-lex.europa.eu/LexUriServ/LexUriServ.do?uri=CELEX:32002L0058:EN:HTML

European Union. "Directive 2006/123/EC of the European Parliament and of the Council of of 12 December 2006 on Services in the Internal Market", December 2006. http://eur-lex.europa.eu/LexUriServ/LexUriServ.do?uri=OJ:L:2006:376:0036:0068:EN:PDF

European Union. "Directive 2007/64/EC of the European Parliament and of the Council of 13 November 2007 on Payment Services in the Internal Market Amending Directives 97/7/EC, 2002/65/EC, 2005/60/EC and 2006/48/EC and Repealing Directive 97/5/EC Text with EEA Relevance", November 2007. http://eurlex.europa.eu/LexUriServ/LexUriServ.do?uri=OJ:L:2007:319:0001:01:EN:HTML

House of Lords Science and Technology Committee. *Personal Internet Security, 5th Report of 2006—07*, The Stationery Office, London, August 2007.

D'Ignazio, A., and Giovannetti, E. "Spatial Dispersion of Peering Clusters in the European Internet", *Cambridge Working Papers in Economics 0601*, January 2006.http://econpapers.repec.org/paper/camcamdae/0601.htm

D'Ignazio, A., and Giovannetti, E. "'Unfair' Discrimination in Two-sided Peering? Evidence from LINX", *Cambridge Working Papers in Economics 0621*, February 2006. http://econpapers.repec.org/paper/camcamdae/0621.htm

Jakobsson, M., and Ramzan Z. *Crimeware: Understanding New Attacks and Defenses*, Addison Wesley, Upper Saddle River, New Jersey, 2008.

McPherson, D., Labovitz, C., and Hollyman, M. "Worldwide Infrastructure Security Report Volume III", *Arbor Networks*, 2007. http://www.arbornetworks.com/report

Moore, T., and Clayton, R. "Examining the Impact of Website Take-down on Phishing" in *2nd Anti-Phishing Working Group eCrime Researcher's Summit (APWG eCrime)*, Pittsburgh, Pennsylvania, October 2007, pp. 1—13.

OpenDNS. "OpenDNS Shares April 2007 PhishTank Statistics", Press Release, 1 May 2007. http://www.opendns.com/about/press_release.php?id=14

Pitcom. "Critical National Infrastructure, Briefings for Parliamentarians on the Politics of Information Technology", November 2006. http://www.pitcom.org.uk/briefings/PitComms1-CNI.doc

Serjantov, A., and Clayton, R. "Modelling Incentives for E-mail Blocking Strategies", in *4th WEIS*, Cambridge, Massachusetts, June 2005.

Shapiro, C., and Varian, H. *Information Rules. A Strategic Guide to the Network Economy*, Harvard Business School Press, Boston, Massachusetts, 1999.

Symantec. "Internet Security Threat Report Volume XII", September 2007. http://www.symantec. com/business/theme.jsp?themeid=threatreport

Zetter, K. "Router Flaw is a Ticking Bomb", *Wired*, 1 August 2005. http://www.wired.com/politics/security/news/2005/08/68365

Zhuge, J., Holz, T., Han, X., Guo, J., and Zou, W. "Characterizing the IRC-based Botnet Phenomenon", *Reihe Informatik Technical Report TR-2007-010*, December 2007. http://honeyblog.org/junkyard/reports/botnet-china-TR.pdf

Zhuge, J., Holz, T., Song, C., Guo, J., Han, X., and Zou, W. "Studying Malicious Websites and the Underground Economy on the Chinese Web", in *7th WEIS*, Hanover, New Hampshire, June 2008.

BORIS –Business ORiented management of Information Security

Sebastian Sowa[1], Lampros Tsinas[2] and Roland Gabriel[3]

[1] Institute for E-Business Security (ISEB), Ruhr-University of Bochum, GC 3/29, 44780 Bochum, Germany

[2] Munich Re, Koeniginstr. 107, 80802 Munich, Germany

[3] Chair of Business Informatics, Ruhr-University of Bochum, GC 3/132, 44780 Bochum, Germany

Abstract The present chapter aims to successfully deal with the needs of information security functions by providing a management tool which links business and information security objectives. In the past terms, information security has fortunately become a top management topic due to the recognition of the continuously increasing dependencies of the overall business success on secure information and information processing technologies and means. While the focus of information security management primarily lay on the implementation of solutions to assure the achievement of the enterprises' security objectives and their management, the business oriented management objectives were typically not regarded as major concern. Today, information security management executives are severely confronted with a different situation. An increasing pressure forces them to manage the security measures not only using their security, but also business glasses. To handle this challenge, a framework is presented in this chapter. It supports any information security functions with a strong economic focus, whereby it specifically links business and information security objectives. The core of the presented methodology has proven to be reliable, user friendly, consistent and precise under real conditions over several years.

1 Introduction

1.1 Background

Because of the community's increasing dependency on secure and private information, the establishment and continuous management of information security today is one of the most challenging tasks (Lange 2005; Laprie 1995). Several

M.E. Johnson (ed.), *Managing Information Risk and the Economics of Security*,
DOI: 10.1007/978-0-387-09762-6_4, © Springer Science + Business Media, LLC 2009

models, methods and measures were introduced in the past, each covering particular aspects of the subject of matter. Most of the approaches focus primarily on technical issues but business-oriented approaches for managing information security also raised an interest in the recent past.

A wide range of economic approaches have then been presented which indicate the increasing interest in security management methods with an economic focus (i.e. Anderson and Moore 2006; Camp and Wolfram 2004; Gordon and Loeb 2002; Gordon and Loeb 2004; Soo 2002). But many of these approaches mainly focus on narrow and specialized fields without meeting the challenges of a holistically integrated concept. They especially lack in integrating the high number of different actors and their interests that the enterprise's information security system contains. And even more important, they lack in establishing a systematic method that directly and transparently links business with information security objectives and measures as well as the information security objectives and measures with a method for defining optimal investment policies. To handle these challenges, a framework for managing information security with a strong economic focus is presented in the following paragraphs. To set the record straight from the beginning, this task starts with the clarification of the appreciation of used terms and intended goals.

1.2 Terms

Information as the first relevant term used in the discussion of information security management topics can linguistically be derived from the Latin informatio. Informatio in this turn stands for explanation or interpretation of ideas. It can also be used in the meaning of education, training or instruction which gives a first consideration about an accurate and precise definition. Information in this chapter is defined as an explanatory, significant assertion that is part of the overall knowledge, and it is also seen as specific, from human beings interpreted technical or non-technical processed data (Biethahn et al. 2000; Gabriel et al. 2003). This definition is precisely in line with the ISO/IEC standards which explain that information "can exist in many forms. It can be printed or written on paper, stored electronically, transmitted by post or by using electronic means, shown on films, or spoken in conversation" (ISO 2005a; ISO 2005b). This – mostly trivial – way to use the term information unfortunately does not reflect the common sense in the information security community. There, it is quite often assumed to only affect electronic data, and thereby information security management mostly has to deal with IT. In this chapter, we clearly focus on a broad and comprehensive denotation, which the described methodology has to deal with.

As consequence of the appreciation of information, information security also has to cover technical as well as non-technical challenges. In this context, the ISO explains that whatever "form the information takes, or means by which it is shared or stored, it should always be appropriately protected. Information security is the protection of information from a wide range of threats in order to ensure business continuity, minimize business risk, and maximize return on investments and business opportunities" (ISO 2005a; ISO 2005b). As seen in the citation, the standard explicitly accentuates the importance of the link of information security to business management which leads to the first of the requirements that are defined for the business-oriented information security management framework presented in this contribution. This requirement and others are described in the following.

1.3 Goals

As information security is seen as both a business and strategic management topic, the information security management framework then has to enable executives to transparently link business to information security objectives (R1). Therefore, the framework should support answers to top management's questions about information security performance as well as support information security management to address areas suitable or necessary to improve the performance influencing indicators (R2).

Shifting the view to the information security management itself, more detailed information is typically needed. From this background, the framework should support the process of defining concrete and measurable indicators for the security target as well as for the current state in different levels of detail (R3).

To close identified gaps by planning, introducing and managing adequate measures and programs, investment decisions have to be addressed in the context of the regarded business-oriented management framework. The framework should support the executives in the processes of finding and defining cost benefit balanced investment strategies (R4).

Wherever and whenever investments are done and measures are already running, the framework should include a method for evaluation that can be used for the task of optimizing the economic and strategic performance of the overall information security infrastructure (R5).

As last requirement at this point, the evaluation and optimization process as well as the other named aspects of the management framework have to be integrated into a management process that enables the continuous and especially sustainable business-oriented information security management (R6).

The defined requirements are based on individual interviews with information security management executives and are additionally in line with findings in several near-topic publications like (Cavusoglu 2004; Cavusoglu et al. 2004) for instance.

2 BORIS design

2.1 Overview

The framework meeting the described requirements and presented in this contribution is the result of the evolutionary advancement of the management approach presented in (Klempt et al. 2007). It consists of four layers, whereby each layer covers particular aspects of strategic, tactical and operational (STO) challenges.

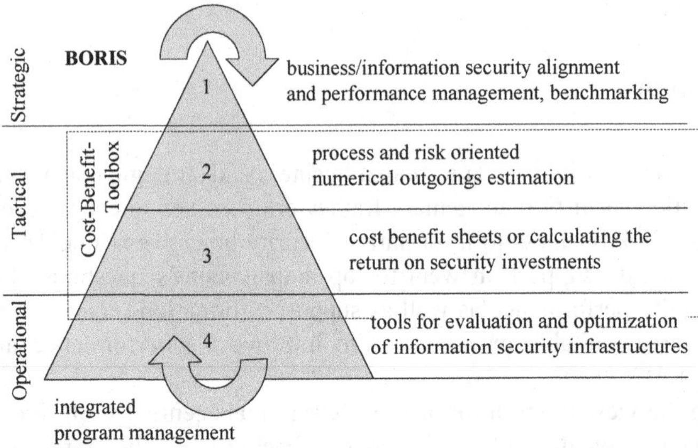

Figure 1. BORIS General Topology

As seen in Figure 1, the top level focuses on the business and information security management interaction, the second layer deals with linking the results of the strategic methods to specific information security objectives as well as supports addressing the current state. The third layer replenishes the tactical methods as it deals with defining a balanced investment policy for implementing and managing measures targeted to close identified gaps. Because of the strong interdependencies of the second and third layers in regard to the financial alignment, they are combined in the so-called Cost-Benefit-Toolbox (CB-Toolbox) which also contains elements of the fourth layer. The fourth layer holds tools for the evaluation and optimization of an information security infrastructure which closes the STO view. A program management cycle rounds the framework off.

2.2 Business Strategic Methods

As visualized, the top layer of the framework deals with business/information security alignment and performance management. It consists of a transferring system for linking strategic as well as compliance drivers to information security objectives and a central scorecard system with which the performance can be measured (see Figure 2).

The theoretical basis of the scorecard system is laid out by the Balanced Scorecard which *Norton* and *Kaplan* have developed (Kaplan and Norton 1996; Kaplan and Norton 2005). It provides a framework with which performance influencers are anchored classically in four dependent dimensions, each containing objectives, metrics, targets and measures. Historically, the multidimensional system of the Balanced Scorecard was established to overcome one of the main problems arising in measuring the original aimed overall enterprise performance on financial indicators: Because the traditionally solely used financial indicators could only reflect a small range of the entire performance influencers, they have been linked to customer and process indicators which again have been linked to indicators which visualize the dependency of the customer and process efficiency on the enterprise ability for learning and developing.

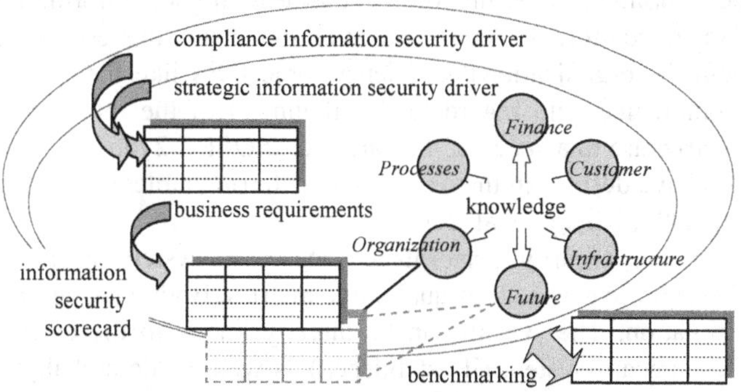

Figure 2. Conceptualization of Business Strategic Methods

Besides the implementation of Balanced Scorecard systems in several branches and industries, the general idea was also recognized quite early in the field of information management (i.e. Gabriel and Beier 2002; Gabriel and Beier 2003), where information security sometimes was even implemented as its own, additional dimension (Baschin 2007). Other, proprietary systems (ISF; Information Security Forum) have adopted the original four axes and embedded information security objective therein.

Because of the aim of connecting the BORIS system with an enterprise Balanced Scorecard, the business strategic method defined in the BORIS framework integrates information security performance objectives and metrics in the traditional dimensions of finance, customer, processes and future (similar to learning and development). An organization dimension is defined, in addition, aiming to match the requirements of several standards which accentuate the importance of organizational information security performance. The sixth dimensions then cover the importance of the technological information security infrastructure and address relevant performance indicators for the objectives. All sixth dimensions are connected through a knowledge-based steering methodology.

The compliance and strategic requirements are transferred to security objectives by the use of a systematic and formally defined process, whereby relevant players such as the chief information officer, business process owners, and compliance officers have to cooperatively agree. Transferring tables, containing columns for the business objectives and related security dimension and objectives, are offered to support the executives in the defining and agreement process. The table – based on the underlying process – propagates business requirements (formulated in "business language") to information security requirements without losing the vital connection between them. It is only this explicitly applied connector philosophy between business and ISMS that validates the right to exist to any security control.

When the business objectives are linked to security dimensions and transferred to concrete security objectives, metrics for the measurement of the level of objectives' fulfillment have to be defined as well as processes have to be established for ensuring the continuous measure of the business aligned information security indicators. As an example for the organization dimension that aims to answer the question about the organizational efficiency, objectives like the improvement of regulatory compliance with regard to the alignment of the information security organization structure to a specific standard like ISO/IEC 27001, or any other one the executives have defined in the objective transferring tables, could be addressed (Gabriel et al. 2008; Klempt et al. 2007).

The information security performance scorecard system itself enables the handling of quantitative as well as qualitative metrics. Both types are brought into a balanced situation. The system can be directly linked to the entire enterprise performance scorecard system (if established) as well as hierarchally be brought down as far as to the operational level of the enterprises' information security organization. Furthermore, the cascading character offers the use of a flexible and expandable instrument that directly links business to information security objectives, as well as helps to link the resulting strategies with human individual objectives' systems. Thereby, the prerequisite agreement process regarding the definition of the security objectives ensures to overcome the limited view of an autonomous set of ever reachable objectives as well as brings together the quantum of information security relevant players in a cooperative manner (Fitzgerald 2005).

Benchmarking at this point replenishes the set of strategic methods. It supports the identification of the own level of maturity while the individual records of performance are set in relation to a peer group of interest for the enterprise. Benchmarking is widely used and accepted (Powell 2007; Xerox Corporation 1987). The method offers to benefit from the results if the data is correctly interpreted and the peers are of adequate competitive importance (Lapide 2006; Supply Chain Consortium 2007). The key factor for success regarding the BORIS framework is to have a comprehensive database, a sophisticated model, and a clear focus to the subject of matter, namely information security which reduces the quantum of suitable as well as available benchmark platforms to only a few

(Klempt et al. 2007). For the BORIS framework, the Information Security Status Survey provided for the members of and by the Information Security Forum (ISF) is currently used in this context.

To transfer benchmarking results to concrete improvement results, the strategies, objectives and identified gaps between the objectives and the current states in each of the six dimensions of the business/information security alignment and performance management method have to be linked to process tactical methods. These methods are anchored in the next layer of the BORIS framework and explained in the following.

2.3 *Process Tactical Methods*

While the first layer of the BORIS framework aims to answer the question about the alignment grade of the information security infrastructure with business, and thereby including compliance requirements as well as relevant performance indicators addressed for monitoring, the results are used for the information security concerned process tactical methods described in the following paragraphs.

The process and risk oriented numerical outgoings estimation (PRONOE) method is the first one of the process tactical methods and is introduced in detail in (Tsinas 2007). It is directly linked to the introduced security strategic performance scorecard and fulfills a top-down as well as a bottom-up function: The performance objectives are used as operational guidelines while the data processed in PRONOE again is delivered up to the six dimensions of the strategic performance scorecard in an aggregated form. Figure 3 shows that PRONOE contains three main components (Klempt et al. 2007): A risk assessment layer for determining qualitative actual and debit states, the (100- X)% rule for determining the quantitative debit state and a process for the cost-benefit balancing comparison of the qualitative and quantitative actual and debit state values which especially supports addressing financial investment policy goals that are then used by the financial tactical methods described in section 2.4.

As shown in the top layer configuration of the BORIS framework, a management forum should determine the security performance objectives which concretely mean to agree on a specific level of acceptable risk exposure and on the areas which require additional risk controls. It is naturally not responsible for making explicit proposals for risk minimization/mitigation, as this is the domain of the security specialists who select appropriate controls (including security awareness programs (Lardschneider 2007; Peltier 2005) in the context of establishing and maintaining suitable security architectures (Sherwood et al. 2005).

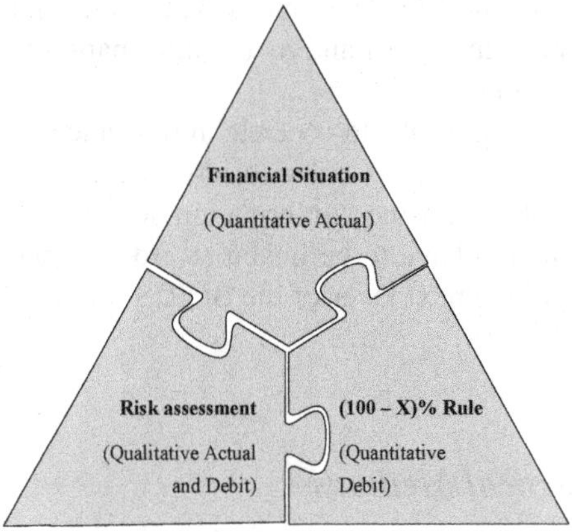

Figure 3. PRONOE Core Components

The current security situation is then assessed using risk assessments or scorecard analyses instruments. The scorecard analysis practice in this context has been outlined by *Loomans* (Loomans 2004) and is also part of the work of the Information Security Forum pertaining FIRM (Fundamental Information Risk Management) (Information Security Forum 2008). It ultimately reflects a structured component for ascertaining current and target values in various risk areas (i.e. so-called R_i risk areas) and thereby follows the construct of the scorecard system established for the business strategic methods in layer one.

For practicality reasons, the scorecard system used for the risk assessment process should hold the dimensions up to a value of about ten. A desirable distribution of the dimensions thereby could use the structure of acknowledge standards like ISO/IEC 17799 (ISO 2005a), the CObIT framework (ITGI 2007) or any other theoretical affirmed or best practice bases. Currently, the five dimensions defined in the implemented version of the risk scorecard were derived from FIRM (Information Security Forum 2008). They address:

- Criticality
- Level of threat
- Business impact
- Vulnerability – status of arrangements
- Vulnerability – special circumstances

As the second component of PRONOE, the (100- X)% rule transfers the level of the acceptable risk exposure agreed on by the members of the management forum to protection areas which are defined as 100 percent minus the accepted level of risk in percentage. It is based on the following rules:

- Each assertion about the acceptable risk level directly implicates that any further level of risk is not accepted.

- As a consequence, each assertion also defines the areas for investment in order to reduce the overlapping risk levels to acceptable ones.

What directly follows out of the named rules is that the protection areas constitute the areas of investment. Therefore, they are used for investment decision-making processes as well as are linked to the next component of PRONOE – the cost-benefit balancing comparison of the qualitative and quantitative actual and debit state. For cost-benefit balancing comparisons, the quantitative actual situation has of course to be assessed first by what is done for each risk area R_i. Completed, the result of the (then following) comparison enables information security management executives to visualize and analyze the total amount of information security relevant investments as well as those per risk area R_i. This, in turn, supports the determination whether the established security level could have been realized using the defined resources or whether an objective has been left unmet because sufficient resources were not available, which as a consequence supports the identification of the so-called "money drains" as well as chronically under-funded areas (Klempt et al. 2007).

To sum up to this point, the first and second layer support the strategic alignment and performance measurement as well as answering process tactical questions of information security interests. They hold up methods to transfer business to security objectives, to define information security protection areas and to evaluate the reached level of maturity. But for a holistic approach, two more questions have to be addressed, namely how to handle financial questions arising from process tactical results and how to handle optimization challenges at the operational dimension.

2.4 *Financial Tactical Methods*

Whenever the process tactical methods result in the identification of protection areas where measures have to be implemented in order to reduce risks, questions about optimal investments on a more detailed level arise. Here, BORIS offers two general methods to support executives in decision making:

- Return on Security Investment (RoSI)
- Cost Benefit Sheets (CoBS)

Approaches for the definition of RoSI were highly recognized in the past due to the aspiration for having a method that could handle the problematic financial investment decision question. Its structure and goals are similar to the concept of the Return on Investment (ROI) used to justify traditional financial investment decisions. The calculation of a RoSI is based on four steps (Wei 2001):

1. Defining the Annualized Rate of Occurrence (ARO) for a specific risk.
2. Identifying the Single Loss Expectancy (SLE) for the given risk.

3. Determining the Annual Loss Expectancy (ALE) as product of ARO times SLE.
4. Comparing the ALE without risk concerned security investment with the ALE if the investment is done, plus the costs for this investment.

The problem about RoSI is that it is only meaningful where the calculation is based on existent and statistically significant data (Klempt et al. 2007; Tiller 2003). In all other situations, when these data are missing, an equivalent methodology must be applied. In this case, Cost Benefit Sheets (CoBS) as shown in Figure 4 can be used.

Investment No. X	
What are the adressed risks (vulnerabilities x threat) ?	
+ What is the aim of the investment ?	
+ What is the degree of effectiveness of the investment ?	
+ What is the financial loss and likelihood of occurrence ?	
+ What could happen, if we would reject the investment ?	

Figure 4. Cost Benefit Sheet (CoBS) for Information Security Investment

This approach is very much similar to the approach introduced by *Schneier* in (Schneier 2006). In antithesis with this proposal, the CoBS model is characterized by a coherent schema, a well-sorted order which is reflecting the psychological aspects during the assessment, and is layered in a way, that a negative response of any layer leads directly to a rejection of an investment proposal.

Using CoBS, all existing data should theoretically be considered while completing the sheets. Here, a systematic documentation can enhance the CoBS quality as well as enable it to appropriately justify but also revise an investment decision. So what CoBS or the RoSI method can do is to justify and especially document investment decisions on the basis of BORIS process tactical results. On the other side, these methods link the risk areas R_i defined in PRONOE to the operational evaluation methods anchored in the next layer of the BORIS framework.

2.5 Operational Evaluation and Optimization Methods

So far, strategic, process and financial tactical methods are introduced and linked to each other which demonstrates a closed chain from enterprise business to security business management. For rounding of the quantum of methods for the BORIS approach, the operational level of the presented framework holds methods for:

- Evaluating the current controls infrastructure (ECI)
- Optimizing the necessary controls infrastructure (OCI)

Whereas the aforementioned methods support comparison of an actual and debit state regarding strategic performance, respectively the risk-investment-ratio, the operational methods in the following support the comparison of the actual and debit states on the level of implemented and operationally running measures, like physical or technical ones for instance. The methods are based on the process for evaluation and control of IT risks which is introduced in detail by (Klempt 2007; Werners and Klempt 2005) and which is also part of the first version of the approach presented in this contribution (Klempt et al. 2007). Here, the German "IT-Grundschutz Catalogues" (BSI 2005) linked approach is structurally separated from the German standard and used as for FIRM aiming to better harmonize the different layers of the BORIS framework. Thereby, the methods make use of the Fuzzy-Sets-Theory introduced in detail by (Zimmermann 1993; Zimmermann 2001) for algorithmic.

As described before, the FIRM scorecard offers five dimensions, each containing a questionnaire regarding different aspects of risk assessment. Thereby, the addressed controls are directly linked to the control areas of the ISF Standard of Good Practice for Information Security which in turn is aligned to ISO 17799 (ISO 2005a) as well as CObIT 4.1 (ITGI 2007). Each of the currently six control areas contains sections. Each section again contains control objectives which can be used on an operational level of information security management. The set of control areas in the following is defined as *C*, the set of sections as *S*, and the considered enterprise *e* is the element of the set of overall enterprises *E*.

For ECI, the first step is to proof whether S_{ij} for $i = 1 \text{ to } N_j$ (N_j is the number of sections for control area *j*) and $j = 1 \text{ to } 6$ is relevant or expendable for the considered *e*. The identified individual relevant sections define the fuzzy set *R* as visualized through the following function:

$$\mu_R\,(S_{ij},\, e) = \begin{cases} 1 \textit{ if } S_{ij} \textit{ is relevant for } e \\ 0 \textit{ if } S_{ij} \textit{ otherwise} \end{cases} \tag{1}$$

For each $r \in R$, it is cross-checked with the FIRM questionnaires, whether the required control is in place, in progress, planned or if nothing is done yet. With the aim of evaluating the actual set of controls, planned and not-started actions lead to the same result, namely that controls are not implemented. For this reason and with the background of the assumption that the identified not-started actions are followed by immediate planning activities, planned and not-started actions are regarded as one characteristic in the used algorithmic of the evaluation method. The result of this step shapes the fuzzy set of the implementation grade *G* with the function:

$$\mu_G\,(S_{ij},\, e) = \begin{cases} 1 & \textit{if } S_{ij} \textit{ is completed} \\ 0{,}5 & \textit{if } S_{ij} \textit{ is in progress} \\ 0 & \textit{otherwise} \end{cases} \tag{2}$$

As only relevant sections are regarded, the average out of R and S defined using the minimum operator then gives the fuzzy set for the section status SG (Werners and Klempt 2005):

$$\mu_{SG}(S_{ij}, e) = \{ min \quad \mu_R(S_{ij}, e); \mu_S(S_{ij}, e) \} \vee \neg e \in E, S_{ij} \in S \qquad (3)$$

In the next step of the evaluation process, the importance of the individual sections for the specifically considered e are addressed by matching the security performance objectives set in the upper layers of the BORIS framework ,with the risk assessment results specially focusing on the criticality, level of threat and the business impact of the regarded information resource. According to the FIRM process, a classification of five characteristics is chosen: Very high (A), high (B), medium (C), low (D), and very low (E). On the basis of this classification, the degree of importance of each section is determined resulting in the functions for the fuzzy sets $\mu_A(S_{ij})$, $\mu_B(S_{ij})$, $\mu_C(S_{ij})$, $\mu_D(S_{ij})$, and $\mu_E(S_{ij})$, each containing the value of 1 if S_{ij} is classified or O if S_{ij} is not classified as A respectively B, C, D, or E sections.

For each control area C, μ_{SG} with regard to A- to E-sections is set in relation to μ_A to μ_E which then results in five quantitative values, one for each importance oriented section implementation grade. Following the evaluation process, these values are used for the determination of the quantitative values of the security level of each control area C. It follows the steps: fuzzification, inference, and defuzzification.

During the fuzzification, the quantitative values of the importance oriented section implementation grades are linked to relating fuzzy set functions for implementation grades due to algorithmic reasons. Analogue, fuzzy set functions for output data are defined. During the inference, a set of rules which explicitly considers the individual importance of a section transfers differently combined input data (for grades A to E) to one output each. On the basis of firing rules, the inference leads to the containment of the relevance area of the fuzzy output functions. In the next step, defuzzification supports extraction of a quantitative value out of the relevance area. In this context, the barycentric method is used to harmonize the domain between the function of the lowest up to the function of the highest possible output, as well as used to address the final quantitative security level value on the basis of the harmonized domain in combination with the contained area of relevance. Thereby, the γ-operator is used in the aggregation process for the weighting of sections (Zimmermann 2001) in order to recognize the weakest links adequately.

For OCI, a technical implementation of ECI supports to automatically apply an otherwise time-consuming calculation, and the technological support enables to transparently visualize evaluation results (Klempt et al. 2007). As a result, a realized optimization process can rank the measures necessary and leading to a strong enhancement of security, down to rounding off ones so that limited resources can be invested targeted.

2.6 *Integrated Program Management*

Four layers have been presented so far, each containing methods to handle the specific STO challenges of information security management, and each with a strong economic focus. As a linking element, an integrated program management that supports annual planning including Resource Management and the definition of the key performance indicators is defined. It stretches over the whole BORIS pyramid and summarizes all initiatives, projects and services under one umbrella, aiming to guarantee a transparent overview over the security infrastructure landscape, to minimize project redundancies, to install a proper prioritization process and to directly derive thorough resource management duties (Klempt et al. 2007).

So, program management in this case is more than only about managing programs. It is also about providing services for managing the continuing and ongoing activities and about the alignment of these activities to the overall enterprise goals. Thereby, it follows a systematic called PDCA (Plan-Do-Check-Act) that achieved attention especially with the work of *Deming* (Deming 2000) and is also part of security management standards (ISO 2005; ISO 2005b; Nyanchama 2005). For the BORIS needs, this process was slightly modified in order to better handle the specific challenges of the introduced methods in a holistic and integrated manner, which by no means represents a departure from the fundament of the PDCA principle. The adopted process is defined as:

1. Transferring strategic and compliance driver top-down to information security objectives and defining the business security performance measurement system.
2. Deriving and defining acceptable risk levels and comparing actual and debit state in order to extract information about the adequacy of objectives and measures.
3. Optimizing the information security infrastructure and linking planning activities to financial tactical methods in order to strongly follow economic principles.
4. Analyzing the operational level of the information security infrastructure in order to extract detailed information about optimization potentials.
5. Executing new measures and linking the measures' characteristics bottom-up to the tactical, and the tactical again to the strategic performance measurement level.

Whereas the four layers address methods for the vertical supply chain of a business-oriented information security management, the program management cycle rounds the framework off by establishing the necessary systematic and closed control loop.

3 Evaluation

Regarding the defined goals at the beginning of this chapter, BORIS can fulfill all of them. As layer one holds a system for aligning business to security objectives, R1 is fulfilled. Additionally, a performance scorecard system is outlined that enables visualization of information security performance on a high level of aggregation in different but linked dimensions. The system strongly focuses on business management interests and fulfills R2 in consequence. Thereby, a balanced set of quantitative as well as qualitative metrics support in visualizing financial, customer, process, organizational, infrastructural and future aspects which ensures a holistic view on the performance influencers and their causes and effects, even if they are not quantitative measurable.

On the tactical layer, PRONOE is introduced to handle risk-investment oriented challenges. It holds a scorecard for assessing enterprises' risk areas and supports in visualizing actual and debit state comparisons which collectively fulfills R3. Because the process tactical methods are directly linked to the financial tactical ones, R4 can be fulfilled. Thereby, PRONOE has several degrees of freedom which make it highly adjustable to individual circumstances which concern, for instance:

- The weighting of each risk aspect
- The interdependent weighting of risk aspects
- The aggregation criteria for the management summary

As described before, PRONOE is currently implemented on the basis of the FIRM dimensions. It is running in a real-time environment of an enterprise with worldwide presence, leading their industry (Klempt et al. 2007). Figure 5 shows an example of this implementation for the qualitative comparison of actual and debit states in regard to the FIRM dimensions. Thereby, the dimensions are even weighted. The green line indicates the management objectives, the red one the assessment results. If the green one is closer to the centre, the objectives are fulfilled and no action is required, otherwise, initiatives have to be initiated to close the gaps between both lines.

The quantitative results, where the actual investments per dimension are compared with the targeted volumes, are visualized in the same structure as the qualitative ones as shown in Figure 5.

It is stressed that the structure of the implementation can of course influence the numerical results. However, this is neither the case for the defined process nor for the interpretation of results for what reason it is implemented and ongoing, running in a real and active information security management system.

If gaps are identified, the CB-Toolbox of the BORIS framework offers CoBS or ROSI calculations for dealing with investment decisions on the project level. To support this process, BORIS contains the ECI and OCI methods for explicitly addressing the areas of action from the bottom-up perspective.

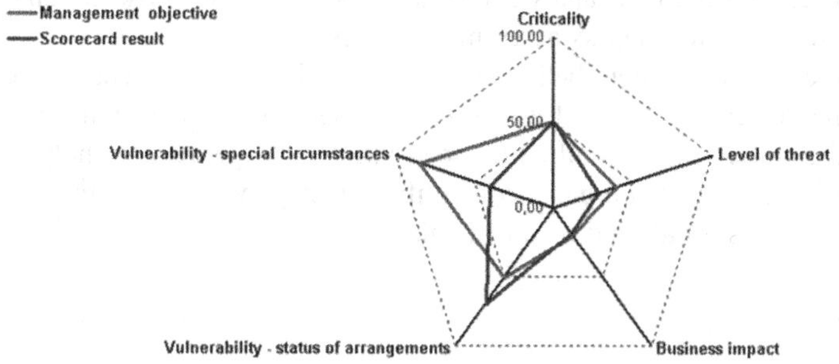

Figure 5. PRONOE: Example of Qualitative Results

While ECI uses the Fuzzy-Sets-Theory in order to extract hard data out of fuzzy input, specific quantitative results can be calculated. Additionally, the ECI method can be used as the conceptual basis for a technology supported optimization process (OCI), which together fulfills R5. The program management cycle is added in order to link the layers in a planned and systematic matter, which fulfills R6.

The structure of the framework is evaluated by interviewing several information security professionals, and most parts are already implemented and tested in real industrial environments.

4 Conclusion and Outlook

The chapter introduced BORIS, a framework for information security management which consists of four layers connected with a program management cycle in order to ensure a closed control loop. Each layer holds methods to deal with strategic, tactical or operational challenges of the topic of interest.

In comparison to currently existing information security management frameworks, the main and innovative advantage of the BORIS framework is that it strictly ensures business orientation in the entire process of information security management. The defined methods systematically follow the chain from business goals, including compliance requirements, to information security measures. Qualitative and quantitative metrics as well as instruments to deal with financial concerns are offered, which stresses the character of the framework of being a concept for business-oriented management.

Although the contribution presents a systematic and holistic concept, the authors point out that ongoing work has to be done. For example, the system for transferring business goals to security goals has to be enhanced. In this context, the authors currently examine the opportunity to directly link the strategic information security scorecard dimensions and objectives to an enterprise balanced scorecard.

Furthermore, it should be analyzed which system is the most suitable one to constitute the basis for the risk assessment process.

Nevertheless, the authors believe that the already presented, current version of BORIS enables enterprises and its information security management to overcome several difficulties in the daily life of security management. It helps to get a transparent insight into the gaps to identify not only what to do, but what to do aligned to business goals and financial balance.

References

Anderson, R., and Moore, T. "The Economics of Information Security," *Science* (314:5799), 2006, pp. 610-613.

Baschin, A. *Die Balanced Scorecard für Ihren Informationstechnologie-Bereich. Ein Leitfaden für Aufbau und Einführung*, Frankfurt/Main, 2001,

Biethahn, J., Mucksch, H., and Ruf, W. *Ganzheitliches Informationsmanagement. Band I: Grundlagen*, 5., unwes. veränd. Auflage, M. et al., 2000.

BSI *IT Basic Protection Catalogues*, German Federal Office for Information Security (BSI), http://www.bsi.de/english/publications/bsi_standards/index.htm, 2005.

Camp, J.L., and Wolfram, C. "Pricing Security", in *Economics of Information Security*, Camp, J.L., Lewis, S. (Eds.), Boston et al., 2004, pp. 17-34.

Cavusoglu, H., Cavusoglu, H., and Raghunathan, S. "Economics of IT Security Management: Four Improvements to Current Security Practices," *Communications of AIS* (2004:14), 2004, pp. 65-75.

Cavusoglu, H. "Economics of IT-Security Management," in *Economics of Information Security*, Camp, J.L., Lewis, S. (Eds.), Boston et al., 2004, pp. 71-83.

Deming, W.E. *Out of the Crisis*, Cambridge, MA, 2000.

Fitzgerald, T. "Building Management Commitment through Security Councils," *Information Systems Security* (14:2), 2005, pp. 27-36.

Gabriel, R., Beier, D. *Informationsmanagement in Organisationen*, Stuttgart, 2003.

Gabriel, R., and Beier, D. *Informationsmanagement, Band 3: Spezialthemen des Informationsmanagements*, Lehrmaterialien im Studienfach Wirtschaftsinformatik 36/02, Lehrstuhl für Wirtschaftsinformatik, Ruhr-Universität Bochum, Bochum, 2002.

Gabriel, R., Sowa, S., and Wiedemann, J. "Improving information security compliance – A process-oriented approach for managing organizational change," in *Multikonferenz Wirtschaftsinformatik 2008 (MKWI 2008)*, Bichler, M., Hess, T., Krcmar, H., Lechner, U., Matthes, F., Picot, A., Speitkamp, B., and Wolf, P. (Eds.), Berlin, 2008, pp. 247-248.

Gordon, L.A., and Loeb, M.P. "The Economics of Information Security Investment," in *Economics of Information Security*, Camp, J.L., Lewis, S. (Eds.), Boston et al., 2004, pp. 105-127.

Gordon, L.A., and Loeb, M.P. "Return On Information Security Investments: Myths vs Realities," *Strategic Finance* (84:5), 2002, pp. 26-31.

Information Security Forum *Fundamental Information Risk Management (FIRM)*, http://www.securityforum.org/ (member access only), 2008.

ISO (International Organization for Standardization) *ISO/IEC 17799:2005 "Information technology - Code of practice for information security management"*, Geneva, 2005.

ISO (International Organization for Standardization) *ISO/IEC 27001:2005 "Information technology - Security techniques - Information security management systems – Requirements"*, Geneva, 2005.

ITGI *CObIT 4.1, Framework, Control Objectives, Management Guidelines, Maturity Model*, IT Governance Institute, Rolling Meadows, 2007.

Kaplan, R.S., and Norton, D.P. "The Balanced Scorecard: Measures That Drive Performance," *Harvard Business Review* (83:7/8), 2005, pp. 172-180.

Kaplan, R.S., and Norton, D.P. "Using the Balanced Scorecard as a Strategic Management System," *Harvard Business Review* (74:1), 1996, pp. 75-85.

Klempt, P. *Effiziente Reduktion von IT-Risiken im Rahmen des Risikomanagementprozesses*, Bochum, Univ., Diss., 2007.

Klempt, P., Schmidpeter, H., Sowa, S., and Tsinas, L. "Business Oriented Information Security Management – A Layered Approach," in *On the Move to Meaningful Internet Systems 2007: CoopIS, DOA, ODBASE, GADA, and IS, OTM Confederated International Conferences, CoopIS, DOA, ODBASE, GADA, and IS 2007*, Meersman, Robert; Tari, Zahir (Eds.), Berlin et al., 2007, pp. 1835-1852.

Lange, J.A. *Sicherheit und Datenschutz als notwendige Eigenschaften von computergestützten Informationssystemen. Ein integrierender Gestaltungsansatz für vertrauenswürdige computergestützte Informationssysteme*, 1. Auflage, Wiesbaden, 2005.

Lapide, L. "Questions to Ask when Reviewing the Benchmarking Data," *Journal of Business Forecasting* (25:4), 2007, pp. 4-7.

Laprie, J.C. "Dependability of Computer Systems: from Concepts to Limits," in *Proceedings of the Sixth International Symposium on Software Reliability Engineering*, 1995, pp. 2-11.

Lardschneider, M. "Security Awareness – Grundlage aller Sicherheitsinvestitionen," *DuD, Datenschutz und Datensicherheit*, (31:7) 2007, pp. 492-497.

Loomans, D.C. "Information Risk Scorecard macht Sicherheitskosten transparent," in *HMD 236 "Praxis der Wirschaftsinformatik - IT-Sicherheit*," Mörike, M. (Ed.), 2004, pp. 43-51.

Nyanchama, M. "Enterprise Vulnerability Management and Its Role in Information Security Management," *Information Systems Security* (14:3), 2005, pp. 29-56.

Peltier, T.R. "Implementing an Information Security Awareness Program," *Information Systems Security* (14:2), 2005, pp. 37-48.

Powell, R. "The Boom in Benchmarking Studies," *Journal of Financial Planning* (20:7), 2007, pp. 5-23.

Schneier, B. *Beyond Fear, Thinking Sensibly About Security in an Uncertain World*, New York, 2006.

Sherwood, J., Clark, A., and Lynas, D. *Enterprise Security Architecture, A Business Driven Approach*, 2005.

Soo H., and Kevin J. "How Much Is Enough? A Risk Management Approach to Computer Security," *Workshop on Economics and Information Security*, University of California. Berkeley, CA, 2002.

Supply Chain Consortium "Benchmarking Do's and Don'ts," *Industry Week/IW* (256:12), 2007, p. 50.

Tiller, J. "The Business of Security," *Information Systems Security* (12:5), 2003, pp. 2-4.

Tsinas, L. "PRONOE, Process and Risk Oriented Numerical Outgoings Estimation – Vorschlag für eine Methodik zur risikoorientierten Kosten-Nutzen-Balance im Informations-Sicherheits-Management," *KES, Zeitschrift für Informations-Sicherheit* (23:4), 2007, pp. 44-49.

Wei, H., Frinke, D., Carter, O., and Ritter, C. "Cost-Benefit Analysis for Network Intrusion Detection Systems," *CSI 28th Annual Computer Security Conference*, October 29-31, 2001, Washington, DC, http://www.csds.uidaho.edu/deb/costbenefit.pdf, 2001.

Werners, B., Klempt, P. *Verfahren zur Evaluation der IT-Sicherheit eines Unternehmens*, Arbeitsbericht Nr. 12, Institut für Sicherheit im E-Business (ISEB), Bochum, 2005.

Xerox Corporation *Leadership through quality: Implementing competitive benchmarking*, 1987.

Zimmermann, H.J. *Fuzzy set theorie – and its applications*, 4th ed., Boston et al., 2001.

Zimmermann, H.J *Fuzzy Technologien: Prinzipien, Werkzeuge, Potentiale*, Düsseldorf, 1993.

[illegible]
[illegible]
[illegible]
[illegible] "[illegible] to [illegible] Return on Security Investment" [illegible]
[illegible]
[illegible]
[illegible]
[illegible] Information Security [illegible]
[illegible]
[illegible]
[illegible]
[illegible]
[illegible]
[illegible]
[illegible]
[illegible]
[illegible]
[illegible]
[illegible]
[illegible]
[illegible]

Productivity Space of Information Security in an Extension of the Gordon-Loeb's Investment Model

Kanta Matsuura

Institute of Industrial Science, the University of Tokyo

Abstract Information security engineers provide some countermeasures so that attacks will fail. This is vulnerability reduction. In addition, they provide other countermeasures so that attacks will not occur. This is threat reduction. In order to study how the optimal investment for information security is influenced by these reductions, this chapter introduces a *productivity space* of information security. In the same manner as in the Gordon-Loeb model, where vulnerability reduction is only considered, I suppose a productivity of information security characterizes economic effects of information security investment. In particular, I consider a productivity regarding threat reduction as well as a productivity regarding vulnerability reduction, and investigate a two-dimensional space formed by the two productivities. The investigation shows that the productivity space is divided into three areas: the no-investment area where both the productivities are low, the mid-vulnerability intensive area where the vulnerability reduction productivity is high but the threat reduction productivity is low, and the high-vulnerability intensive area where the threat reduction productivity is high.

1 Introduction

Management and evaluation of information security is a bridge between security engineering and society. On the engineering's side, engineers provide some technologies so that attacks will fail. This is vulnerability reduction. In addition, they provide other technologies so that attacks will not occur. This is threat reduction. We can see the same two reductions also when we consider countermeasures that are not purely technological. On the society's side, users wish to know how significant these reductions are. This chapter constructs a simple analytical bridge between the two sides by introducing a *productivity space* of information security.

The first thing to do is to review how the vulnerability reduction and the threat reduction have been studied in the research community so far. This review is done in Section 2. We then go on to Section 3 where a productivity space of information

M.E. Johnson (ed.), *Managing Information Risk and the Economics of Security*,
DOI: 10.1007/978-0-387-09762-6_5, © Springer Science + Business Media, LLC 2009

security is introduced in the context of extending an existing optimal investment model for information security. After implications and limitations of the extended model are mentioned in Section 4, concluding remarks are given in Section 5.

2 The Two Reductions

2.1 Vulnerability Reduction

To inspire managers to information security risk management, some studies documented the status of information security and potential losses due to security breaches (Gordon et al. 2005; Kuper 2005), and others showed the return on security investment to convince managers of the benefits of security efforts (Geer 2001; Hoo et al. 2001; Purser 2004). More importantly, managers should know how to appropriately invest in countermeasures to defend against security incidents effectively and efficiently. Some researches use figures and rankings to identify the actual threats and currently available countermeasures (Gordon et al. 2005; Whitman 2003). Others provide security management methods and generally evaluate the efficiency of their methods by conducting a case study in a company or other organizations (Dynes et al. 2005; Karabacak and Sogukpinar 2005; Kim and Lee 2005; Lovea et al. 2005). In these qualitative models and heuristic approaches, it is difficult to find a vulnerability reduction model that is rich in implications.

On the other hand, quantitative models and analytical approaches are relatively fewer, but a seminal model proposed in (Gordon and Loeb 2002) has some empirical supports (Liu et al. 2007; Tanaka et al. 2005). The essence of the Gordon-Loeb model (GL model, hereafter) is in its formalization regarding the effect of vulnerability reduction. This formalization is extensively helpful in discussing information-sharing and the free-rider problem of information security (Gordon et al. 2003).

Let us consider a one-period economic model of a firm contemplating the additional security efforts to protect a given information set. The information set is characterized by the following three parameters:

- λ: the monetary loss conditioned on a breach occurring. It is assumed that λ is a fixed amount as estimated by the firm (for simplicity) and that λ is finite and less than some very large number so that we can assume risk-neutrality.
- t: the threat probability, defined as the probability of a threat occurring. For notational simplicity, they define the potential loss L as $L=t\lambda$. Since t is a probability, $0 \le t \le 1$.
- v: the vulnerability, defined as the conditional probability that a threat once realized would be successful. Since v is a probability, $0 \le v \le 1$.

Let $z>0$ denote the monetary investment in information security to protect the given information set, measured in the same units (e.g., yen) used to measure the potential loss L. In the GL model, they let $S(z,v)$ denote the probability that the information set will be breached, conditional on the realization of a threat and given that the firm has made an investment of z. $S(z,v)$ is called the *security breach probability function* (SBP function for short, hereafter). Some classes of functions have been discussed as candidates for the SBP function, and the class of the highest interest among researchers so far is:

$$S(z,v) = v^{\alpha z+1} \tag{1}$$

where the parameter $\alpha>0$ is a measure of the productivity of information security regarding vulnerability reduction. The aforementioned interest comes from the fact that this class of SBP function, called the class-II SBP function, has empirical supports (Liu et al. 2007; Tanaka et al. 2005) and from its implication of an intuitively easy-to-accept strategy: managers allocating an information security budget should normally focus on information which falls into the midrange of vulnerability.

This strategy was derived by solving the maximization problem of the ENBIS (Expected Net Benefits from an investment in Information Security):

$$ENBIS(z) = \{v - S(z,v)\}L - z \to \max. \tag{2}$$

In summary, the GL model tells that the economic benefit from the information security investment originates from the reduction of the vulnerability from v to $S(z,v)$.

2.2 *Threat Reduction*

There are some security technologies that do not reduce vulnerabilities and yet are expected to have practical effects. A good example is deterrents to Denial-of-Service (DoS) attacks against handshake protocols. One well-known deterrent is a Proof-of-Work (POW) mechanism in which protocol initiators must demonstrate that they have expended processing cost in solving a cryptographic puzzle (Juels and Brainard 1999; Matsuura and Imai 1998; Matsuura and Imai 2000). This cost for one execution of the protocol must avoid being prohibitively high because not only DoS attackers but also legitimate users must expend it.

A more traditional POW mechanism is a tool to combat against junk e-mails (Dwork and Naor 1992). In the context of this POW, there have been some economic debates. The point is whether a system with the POW is accepted by users (non-spammers) or not. The answer is not trivial because the extra cost by the POW depends on the statistics of actual traffic and so on.

In 2004, Laurie and Clayton showed that it is not possible to discourage spammers by means of a POW system with keeping an acceptable impact on legitimate users (Laurie and Clayton 2004). Their study is based on an economic estimation of the cost of each POW processing, and on a real-world data from a large ISP (Internet Service Provider). Two years later, Liu and Camp showed that POW can work when combined with proper reputation systems (Liu and Camp 2006). In this series of debate, their interests have been not in the formalization of the effect of the threat reduction but in the numerical estimation of the users' incentive reduction accompanied with how to interpret the estimation results.

3 Productivity Space of Information Security

3.1 Threat Reduction Productivity

As included in the concluding comments of (Gordon and Loeb 2002), extension of the GL model is recommendable to study dynamic issues. So let us consider an extension toward the formalization of the effect of the threat reduction.

In particular, let us assume that the information security investment z can reduce the threat probability and that the reduction depends only on the investment z and the current level of threat probability t. So let $T(z,t)$ denote the probability that a threat occurring, given that the firm has made an investment of z. Let us call $T(z,t)$ the *security threat probability function* (STP function for short, hereafter). In this extended model, our investment strategy should be discussed by solving the following ENBIS maximization problem:

$$ENBIS(z) = vt\lambda - S(z,v)T(z,t)\lambda - z \rightarrow \max. \tag{3}$$

By analogy with the empirically-supported class of the SBP function, the remainder of this article considers

$$T(z,t) = t^{\beta z+1} \tag{4}$$

where the parameter $\beta(\geq 0)$ is a measure of the productivity of information security regarding threat reduction. We call α the *vulnerability reduction productivity* and β the *threat reduction productivity*. The case of β=0 corresponds to the original GL model.

The features of the above class of the STP function include the following:

- $T(z,0)$=0 for all z. That is, if the information set is completely free from a threat, then it will remain perfectly safe for any amount of information security investment, including a zero investment.

- For all t, $T(0,t)=t$. That is, if there is no investment in information security, the threat probability is that inherent to the given information set's environment.
- For all $t \in (0,1)$, and for all z, we have $\frac{\partial T(z,t)}{\partial z} < 0$ and $\frac{\partial^2 T(z,t)}{\partial z^2} > 0$. That is, as the information security investment increases, the environment gets safer due to the discouragement to attackers, but at a decreasing rate.
- For all $t \in [0,1)$, $T(z,t) \to 0 \; (z \to \infty)$. That is, by investing sufficiently in information security, the threat probability can be made to be arbitrarily close to zero unless the threat is inevitable (i.e., t=1).

3.2 *Optimal Investment*

Let z^* denote the optimal investment as the solution to the ENBIS maximization problem (3). When we use Eq. (1) and Eq. (4) in the problem (3), the optimum is characterized by the first-order condition

$$-\alpha(\ln v)v^{\alpha z+1}t^{\beta z+1}\lambda - \beta(\ln t)v^{\alpha z+1}t^{\beta z+1}\lambda = 1 \tag{5}$$

where the left-hand side of Eq. (5) represents the marginal benefit from the investment and the right-hand side of Eq. (5) represents the marginal cost of the investment. However, we must note that the optimal level of investment z^* equals zero if the marginal benefit at z=0 is less than or equal to the marginal cost of such investment. So paying attention to $L=t\lambda$, we can rewrite the condition for having a zero value of the optimal investment as follows:

$$F(v) \equiv v \ln v + \frac{\beta \ln t}{\alpha} \cdot v + \frac{1}{\alpha L} \geq 0 . \tag{6}$$

That is, when $F(v)$ is larger than or equal to zero, we have z^*=0. On the other hand, when $F(v)$<0, we obtain

$$z^* = \frac{\ln\left\{-1/\left(vt\lambda \ln(v^\alpha t^\beta)\right)\right\}}{\ln(v^\alpha t^\beta)} = \frac{\ln\left\{\dfrac{1}{-vL(\alpha \ln v + \beta \ln t)}\right\}}{\alpha \ln v + \beta \ln t} \tag{7}$$

by solving Eq. (5) with respect to z.

3.3 Productivity Space

Let us investigate how the optimal level of investment z^* behaves for different values of the productivities α and β of information security. To see this, knowing the characteristics of the function $F(v)$ is helpful.

First, from Eq. (6), we can see $F(v) \to 1/(\alpha L)\ (v \to +0)$. Since $1/(\alpha L) > 0$, we have $z^* \to 0\ (v \to +0)$.

Second, we have the derivative of $F(v)$ as

$$\frac{dF(v)}{dv} = \frac{\beta \ln t}{\alpha} + \ln v + 1. \tag{8}$$

So by letting $v_0 = e^{-1-(\beta \ln t)/\alpha}$, we have $\frac{dF(v)}{dv} = 0 \Leftrightarrow v = v_0$. The derivative given by Eq. (8) is monotonically increasing with respect to v, and v ranges from 0 to 1. Therefore, paying attention to the fact that $F(v)$ approaches to a positive constant when v approaches to +0, we evaluate the sign of $F(v_0)$ and/or $F(1)$ in order to see whether the condition (6) is satisfied or not (i.e., whether the optimal investment z^* is zero or not). The equivalence

$$F(v_0) = \frac{1}{\alpha L} - e^{-1-(\beta \ln t)/\alpha} \geq 0 \Leftrightarrow \beta \leq \frac{\alpha\{\ln(\alpha L) - 1\}}{\ln t} \tag{9}$$

is helpful when we use the following breakdown in order to investigate the behavior of z^* in the α-β plane.

- **[Case I]** When $F(v_0) \geq 0$;
  - Since $F(v) \geq F(v_0) \geq 0$, the condition (6) is satisfied and hence $z^*=0$.
- **[Case II]** When $F(v_0)<0$;
  - This condition can be rewritten as $\beta > \frac{\alpha\{\ln(\alpha L) - 1\}}{\ln t}$.
  - From $F(v_0) = \frac{1}{\alpha L} - v_0 < 0$, we have $v_0 > \frac{1}{\alpha L}$.
  - **[Case II-A]** When $\frac{1}{\alpha L} \geq 1$ in addition to the condition of Case II; This additional condition can be rewritten as $\alpha \leq \frac{1}{L}$. From $\alpha \leq \frac{1}{L}$ and $v_0 > \frac{1}{\alpha L}$, we have $v_0>1$. Therefore, the minimum of $F(v)$ is $F(1) = \frac{\beta \ln t}{\alpha} + \frac{1}{\alpha L}$. Since we are interested in the sign of this $F(1)$, we divide Case II-A into the following two subcases.

[Case II-A-1] When $\beta \le -1/(L \ln t)$ in addition to the condition of Case II-A; Since $F(v) \ge F(1) \ge 0$, the condition (6) is satisfied and hence z^*=0.

[Case II-A-2] When $\beta > -1/(L \ln t)$ in addition to the condition of Case II-A; Since $F(1)<0$, there exists $V_1 \in (0,1)$ such that the condition (6) is satisfied for the region $0 < v \le V_1$ (and hence z^*=0) and that the condition (6) is not satisfied for the region $V_1 < v \le 1$ (and hence z^* is given by Eq. (7)).

– **[Case II-B]** When $\alpha > 1/L$ in addition to the condition of Case II; Paying attention to $v_0 \ge 1 \Leftrightarrow \beta \ge -\alpha/\ln t$, we divide Case II-B into the following subcases.

[Case II-B-1] When $\beta \ge -\alpha/\ln t$ in addition to the condition of Case II-B; We have $v_0 \ge 1$ and therefore the minimum of $F(v)$ is $F(1) = \dfrac{\beta \ln t}{\alpha} + \dfrac{1}{\alpha L}$. Since $\alpha > 1/L$ and $\ln t < 0$, we have $\beta + \dfrac{1}{L \ln t} > \beta + \dfrac{\alpha}{\ln t} \ge 0$, and hence

$$F(1) < -\frac{1}{L \ln t} \cdot \frac{\ln t}{\alpha} + \frac{1}{\alpha L} = 0. \tag{10}$$

Therefore, there exists $V_1 \in (0,1)$ such that the condition (6) is satisfied for the region $0 < v \le V_1$ (and hence z^*=0) and that the condition (6) is not satisfied for the region $V_1 < v \le 1$ (and hence z^* is given by Eq. (7)).

[Case II-B-2] When $\beta < -\alpha/\ln t$ in addition to the condition of Case II-B; Since $v_0<1$, the minimum of $F(v)$ is $F(v_0)<0$. So paying attention to $F(1) = \dfrac{\beta \ln t}{\alpha} + \dfrac{1}{\alpha L}$, we find the following.

[Case II-B-2-a] When $F(1)>0$ in addition to the condition of Case II-B-2; We have $\beta < -1/(L \ln t)$ since $F(1)>0$. There exist V_1 and V_2 ($0<V_1<V_2<1$) such that the condition (6) is satisfied (and hence z^*=0) for the regions $0 < v \le V_1$ and $V_2 \le v \le 1$, and that the condition (6) is not satisfied (and hence z^* is given by Eq. (7)) for the region $V_1<v<V_2$.

[Case II-B-2-b] When $F(1) \le 0$ in addition to the condition of Case II-B-2; We have $\beta \ge -1/(L \ln t)$ since $F(1) \le 0$. There exists V_1 ($0<V_1<v_0<1$) such that the condition (6) is satisfied (and hence z^*=0) for the region $0 < v \le V_1$ and that the condition (6) is not satisfied (and hence z^* is given by Eq. (7)) for the region $V_1 < v \le 1$.

The cases investigated above can be recognized as illustrated in Figure 1.

The lower left area composed of Case I and Case II-A-1 is a no-investment area; the optimal investment z^* equals zero regardless of the vulnerability v. A numerical example in this area is given in Figure 2. The curve $-\alpha v \ln v - \beta v \ln t$ is shown in Figure 2 so that one can see whether the condition (6) is satisfied or not at a glance; Eq. (6) is equivalent to

$$-\alpha v \ln v - \beta v \ln t \leq \frac{1}{L}. \tag{11}$$

Therefore, from the observation that the curve $-\alpha v \ln v - \beta v \ln t$ does not exceed the dashed horizontal line of $1/L$, we see the condition (6) is satisfied for all v (and hence $z^*=0$).

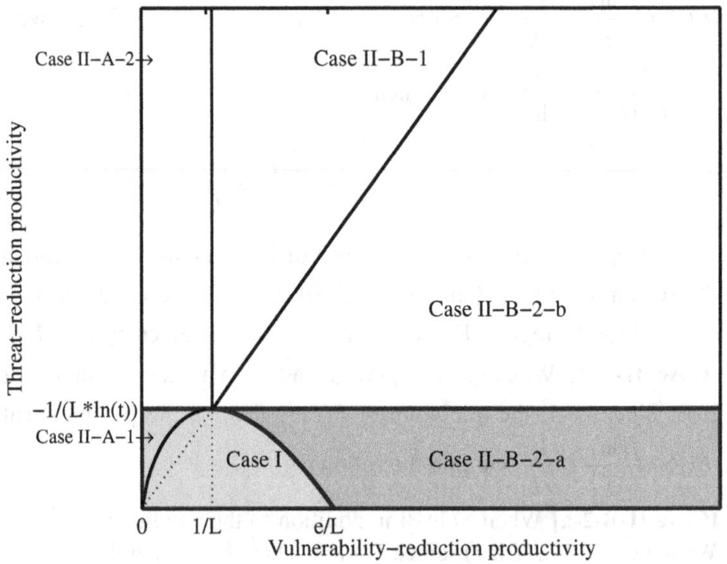

Figure 1. Productivity space of information security, divided into three areas: the lower left area composed of Case I and Case II-A-1 is a no-investment area, the lower right area composed of Case II-B-2-a is a mid-vulnerability intensive area, and the upper large area composed of Case II-A-2, Case II-B-1, and Case II-B-2-b is a high-vulnerability intensive area. The situation studied by the class-II SBP function in the original GL model is included in the mid-vulnerability intensive area, on the horizontal axis.

The lower right area composed of Case II-B-2-a is a mid-vulnerability intensive area; the optimal investment z^* is zero for low $(v \leq V_1)$ and high $(v \geq V_2)$ vulnerabilities whereas the investment occurs ($z^*>0$) for the midrange ($V_1<v<V_2$)

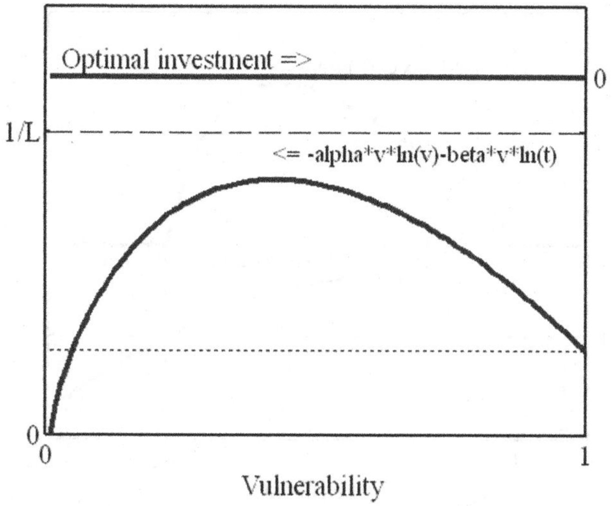

Figure 2. A numerical example of the no-investment area (α=0.000005, β=0.000001, t=0.5, λ=800000). The curve $-\alpha v \ln v - \beta v \ln t$ (its values are labeled on the left vertical axis) as well as the optimal investment (labeled on the right vertical axis) is shown so that one can see whether the condition (6) holds or not. In this example, the curve never exceeds $1/L$ regardless of the vulnerability. This means the condition (6) holds for any $v \in (0,1]$, and the optimal investment is z^*=0. Intuitively, both the productivities are too low and there is no incentive for information security. It should be noted that this happens for the same potential loss L as in page 449 of (Gordon and Loeb 2002) and the vulnerability reduction productivity α is about half of that used by Gordon and Loeb.

vulnerabilities. For these midrange vulnerabilities, the curve exceeds $1/L$ (that is, the condition (6) is not satisfied), and hence the optimal investment is given by Eq. (7). The α-axis in this region corresponds to the situation well-discussed in (Gordon and Loeb 2002). A numerical example in this area is given in Figure 3.

The upper large area composed of Case II-A-2, Case II-B-1, and Case II-B-2-b is a high-vulnerability intensive area; the optimal investment z^* is zero for low $(v \le V_1)$ vulnerabilities whereas the investment occurs (z^*>0) for higher $(v > V_1)$ vulnerabilities. A numerical example in this area is given in Figure 4. The feature shown here is similar to that of the SBP function of class I in (Gordon and Loeb 2002); a firm can be better off concentrating its security resources on high-vulnerability information sets. It is remarkable that this happens in spite of the same values of the potential loss L and the vulnerability reduction productivity α as in (Gordon and Loeb 2002). The very high information security productivity β regarding threat reduction causes this intensity shift from midrange vulnerabilities to high vulnerabilities.

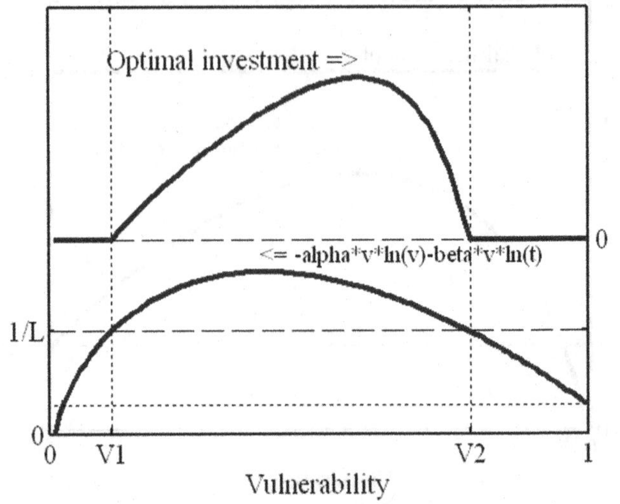

Figure 3. A numerical example of the mid-vulnerability intensive area (α=0.00001, β=0.000001, t=0.5, λ=800000). In the same way as in (Gordon and Loeb 2002), this shows an intuitively easy-to-accept strategy: managers allocating an information security budget should normally focus on information which falls into the midrange of vulnerability.

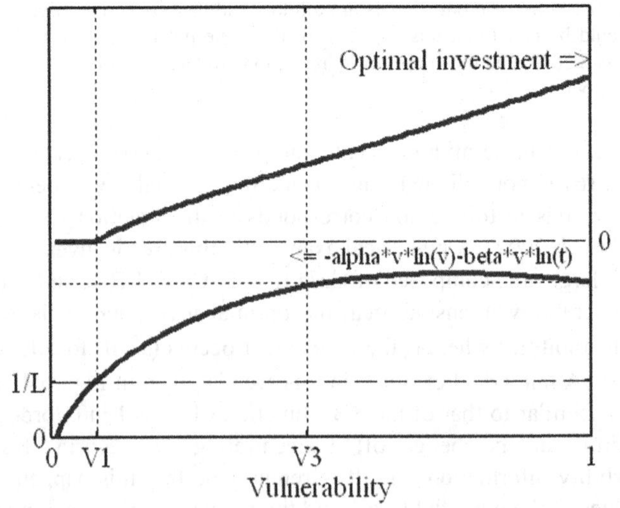

Figure 4. A numerical example of the high-vulnerability intensive area (α=0.00001, β=0.00001, t=0.5, λ=800000). The feature shown here is similar to that of the SBP function of class I in (Gordon and Loeb 2002). The meaning of the vulnerability value V_3 will appear in Theorem 3.

Our next interest is in the effects of productivity improvements on the optimal investment z^* when $z^*>0$. To investigate this, by elementary calculus, we have

$$\frac{\partial z^*}{\partial \alpha} \geq 0 \Leftrightarrow \frac{\partial z^*}{\partial \beta} \geq 0 \Leftrightarrow -v \ln v \leq \frac{\beta \ln t}{\alpha} \cdot v + \frac{e}{\alpha L} \tag{12}$$

from Eq. (7). One can observe that replacing L with L/e in the condition (6) yields the inequality of the right-hand side of Eq. (12). Therefore, based on a similar investigation to that from Case I to Case II-B-2-b, we achieve the following three theorems.

- **Theorem 1**: Suppose the information security productivities satisfy the condition

$$\left(\frac{e}{L} < \alpha\right) \wedge \left(\frac{\alpha\{\ln(\alpha L/e) - 1\}}{\ln t} < \beta < -e/(L \ln t)\right).$$

Then, there exist V_3 and V_4 ($0<V_3<V_4<1$) such that $\frac{\partial z^*}{\partial \alpha} \geq 0$ and $\frac{\partial z^*}{\partial \beta} \geq 0$ for any $v \in (0, V_3]$ and $v \in [V_4, 1)$ as long as $z^*>0$, and such that $\frac{\partial z^*}{\partial \alpha} < 0$ and $\frac{\partial z^*}{\partial \beta} < 0$ for any $v \in (V_3, V_4)$ as long as $z^*>0$.

- **Theorem 2**: Suppose the information security productivities satisfy the condition

$$\left(\beta \leq \frac{\alpha\{\ln(\alpha L/e) - 1\}}{\ln t}\right) \vee \left(\left(\alpha \leq \frac{e}{L}\right) \wedge \left(\frac{\alpha\{\ln(\alpha L/e) - 1\}}{\ln t} < \beta < \frac{-e}{L \ln t}\right)\right).$$

Then, $\frac{\partial z^*}{\partial \alpha} \geq 0$ and $\frac{\partial z^*}{\partial \beta} \geq 0$ for any v as long as $z^*>0$.

The numerical example used for Figure 3 satisfies the condition in Theorem 2.

- **Theorem 3**: Suppose the threat reduction productivity satisfies the condition $\beta > \frac{-e}{L \ln t}$. Then, there exists $V_3 \in (0,1)$ such that $\frac{\partial z^*}{\partial \alpha} \geq 0$ and $\frac{\partial z^*}{\partial \beta} \geq 0$ for any $v \in (0, V_3]$ as long as $z^*>0$, and such that $\frac{\partial z^*}{\partial \alpha} < 0$ and $\frac{\partial z^*}{\partial \beta} < 0$ for any $v \in (V_3, 1)$ as long as $z^*>0$.

The numerical example used for Figure 4 satisfies the condition in Theorem 3, and the parameter V_3 is indicated on the horizontal axis of Figure 4 for reference.

4 Implications and Limitations

4.1 Different Investment Strategies

We must remember that (Gordon and Loeb 2002) showed that different classes of SBP functions may bring different investment strategies such as mid-vulnerability intensive one and high-vulnerability intensive one. By contrast, the formalization of threat reduction in this chapter tells us that not only different classes of functions but also different values of productivities may bring different investment strategies.

4.2 Influence of Productivity-Assessment Failures

Let us regard the no-investment strategy as a special case of the mid-vulnerability intensive strategy as well as of the high-vulnerability intensive strategy. Suppose that we are trying to choose one of the two strategies, mid- and high-vulnerability intensive strategies, by assessing the productivities of information security. In the original GL model, we do not have to be afraid of a wrong choice being made by assessment failure. However, in our extended model, a failure in assessing the threat reduction productivity, β, can lead us to a wrong choice. If the actual vulnerability reduction productivity α is larger than e/L and the actual threat reduction productivity β is larger than $-1/(L\ln t)$, then an underestimate of the latter such that $\beta < -1/(L\ln t)$ brings a wrong strategy of recommending the focus on midrange vulnerabilities. Likewise, if the actual vulnerability reduction productivity α is larger than e/L and the actual threat reduction productivity β is smaller than $-1/(L\ln t)$, then an overestimate of the latter such that $\beta > -1/(L\ln t)$ brings a wrong strategy of recommending the focus on high vulnerabilities. To our annoyance, the threshold value $-1/(L\ln t)$ depends on parameters that are also to be assessed. In light of this, our future work of empirical studies must be carefully designed.

4.3 Upper Limit of the Optimal Investment

An important implication of the original GL model is the relationship between the optimal investment z^* and $vt\lambda$, the loss that would be expected in the absence of any security investment when the SBP functions belong to two particular classes, including the one used in this chapter. In the case of the two classes, called class I and class II, the optimal investment is always less than or equal to 36.79% (i.e., $1/e$) of $vt\lambda$. Our extended model has the same upper limit of the optimal investment; from Eq. (7), it is elementary to observe that we can use the same proof technique as the one used for the class II SBP function in the GL model. That is, we divide Eq. (7) by vL and then let $x = -vL(\alpha \ln v + \beta \ln t)$.

4.4 *Influence of Countermeasure Innovation*

When an innovation of countermeasures happens, we expect that productivities of information security are increased. However, when we discuss the influence of the innovation on information security investment, we must be careful about our current location in the productivity space of information security. This is because the location determines which of the three investment strategies is recommendable (i.e., no investment, mid-vulnerability intensive, or high-vulnerability intensive) and which condition in Theorems 1, 2, and 3 is satisfied (i.e., whether the optimal investment z^* increases or decreases as the productivities increase).

Let us look at Figure 5 that revisits the productivity space with auxiliary dashed lines intended for easier understanding of Theorems 1, 2, and 3. The productivity space is divided into three areas of different investment strategies. The partitioning lines and curves are similar to, but do not overlap, those for describing the conditions regarding the signs of $\frac{\partial z^*}{\partial \alpha}$ and $\frac{\partial z^*}{\partial \beta}$. As a result, we can see the following implications.

Firstly, when $e/L<\alpha$ and $\max\left\{\frac{\alpha\{\ln(\alpha L/e)-1\}}{\ln t}, \frac{-1}{L\ln t}\right\} < \beta < \frac{-e}{L\ln t}$, the point (α, β) is in the high-vulnerability intensive area. In addition, this situation satisfies the condition in Theorem 1. Suppose that information security investment is focused on high vulnerabilities, say, $v>V_4$. Then, from Theorem 1, we have $\frac{\partial z^*}{\partial \alpha} \geq 0$ and $\frac{\partial z^*}{\partial \beta} \geq 0$. Therefore, when an innovation increases information security productivities, the optimal amount of investment could be increased. A numerical example for this situation is shown in Figure 6.

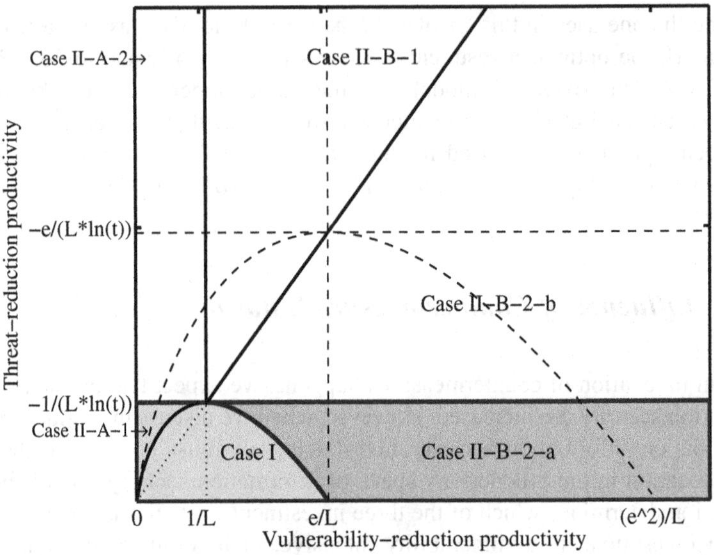

Figure 5. Productivity space of information security, divided into three areas: the lower left area composed of Case I and Case II-A-1 is a no-investment area, the lower right area composed of Case II-B-2-a is a mid-vulnerability intensive area, and the upper large area composed of Case II-A-2, Case II-B-1, and Case II-B-2-b is a high-vulnerability intensive area. Auxiliary dashed lines are appended to help easier reading of Theorems 1, 2, and 3.

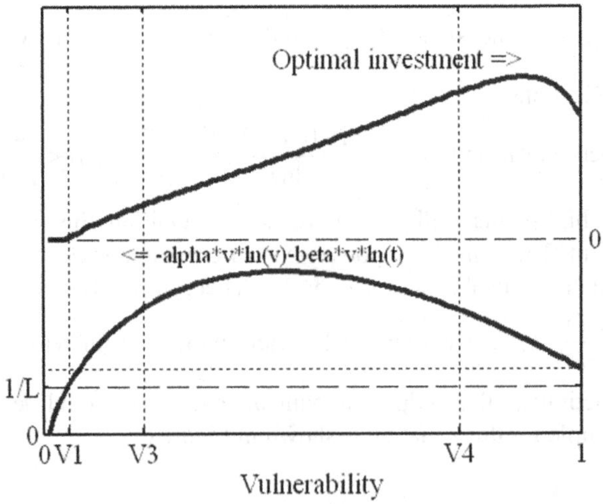

Figure 6. Another numerical example of the high-vulnerability intensive area (α=0.00002, β=0.000005, t=0.5, λ=800000). Whereas the former example in Figure 4 satisfies the condition in Theorem 3, this example satisfies the condition in Theorem 1; for high vulnerabilities such that $v > V_4$, the partial derivative of z^* with respect to a productivity, α or β, is non-negative.

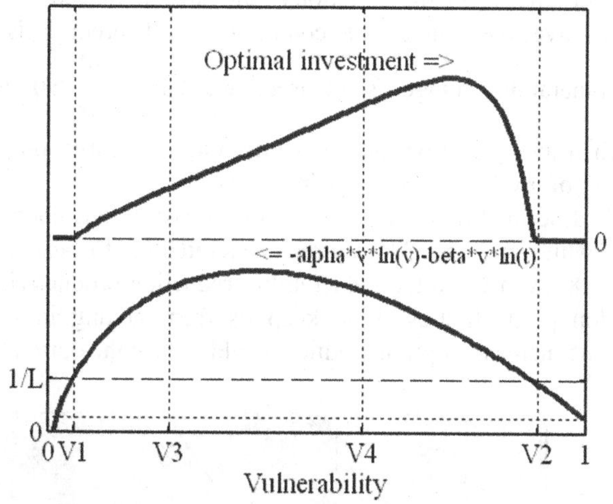

Figure 7. Another numerical example of the mid-vulnerability intensive area (α=0.00002, β=0.000001, t=0.5, λ=800000). Whereas the former example in Figure 3 satisfies the condition in Theorem 2, this example satisfies that in Theorem 1; for relatively high vulnerabilities such that $V_4<v<V_2$, the partial derivative of z^* with respect to a productivity, α or β, is non-negative.

Secondly, when $e/L<\alpha$ and $\frac{\alpha\{\ln(\alpha L/e)-1\}}{\ln t}<\beta<\frac{-1}{L\ln t}$, the point ($\alpha$, β) is in the mid-vulnerability intensive area. In addition, this situation satisfies the condition of Theorem 1. Suppose a strategy of information-security investment focused on midrange vulnerabilities, say, $V_3<v<V_4$. Then, from Theorem 1, we have $\frac{\partial z^*}{\partial \alpha}<0$ and $\frac{\partial z^*}{\partial \beta}<0$ as long as $z^*>0$. Therefore, when an innovation increases information security productivities, the optimal investment is decreased.

However, we must be careful whether the strategy above is realistic or not. In fact, as proved in Appendix A, we have the following claim:

- **Claim 1**: If one rather chooses a strategy of focusing sharply around the maximum of the optimal-investment curve, the focus is outside the vulnerability range $V_3<v<V_4$ (see an example shown in Figure 7).

Thirdly, when $\beta>-e/(L\ln t)$, the point (α, β) is in the high-vulnerability intensive area. In addition, this situation satisfies the condition in Theorem 3. Suppose that information-security investment is focused on high vulnerabilities, say, $v>V_3$. Then, from Theorem 3, we have $\frac{\partial z^*}{\partial \alpha}<0$ and $\frac{\partial z^*}{\partial \beta}<0$ as long as $z^*>0$. Therefore, when an innovation increases information security productivities, the optimal investment is decreased. This situation was visited in Figure 4.

Fourthly and finally, in the situations that have not been described above, except the no-investment area, the condition in Theorem 2 is satisfied. So whichever vulnerability range is focused, we have $\frac{\partial z^*}{\partial \alpha} \geq 0$ and $\frac{\partial z^*}{\partial \beta} \geq 0$. Therefore, when an innovation increases information security productivities, the optimal amount of investment could be increased.

Figure 8 is described to summarize the four observations above. It should be noted that the white and the light-gray regions stretch out toward infinitely further right in Figure 8; even when the vulnerability reduction productivity is high, low threat reduction productivities could keep us from getting into the dark-gray region where the increase of productivities would reduce the optimal investment.

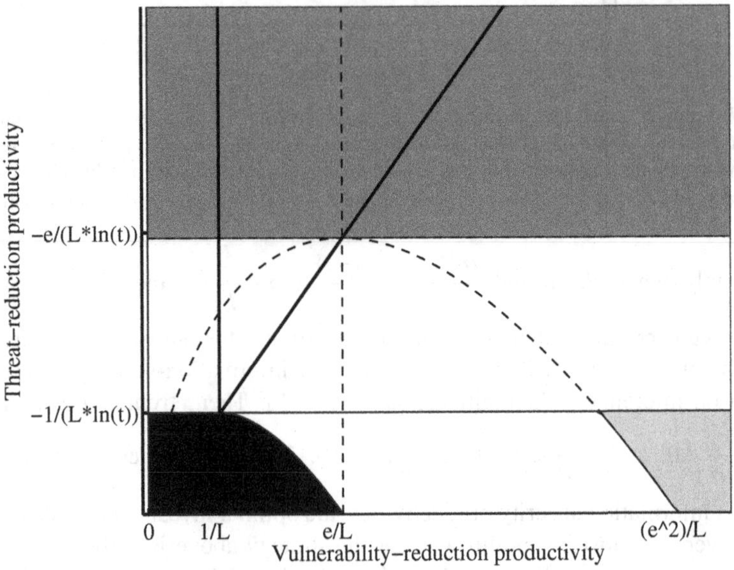

Figure 8. Productivity space of information security, divided into four regions according to the observations regarding the influence of countermeasure innovation. In the first region (painted dark gray in the upper part of this figure), the increase of information security productivities would reduce the amount of the optimal investment determined by the suggested investment strategy of the proposed model. In the second region (painted light gray in the right-lower corner of this figure), the change of the optimal investment in response to productivity increase would strongly depend on how we interpret the midrange vulnerabilities. In the third region (white in this figure), the increase of information security productivities would increase the optimal investment. The final one (black region) is simply the no-investment region where the optimal investment is zero anyway.

4.5 *Trade-off between Vulnerability Reduction and Threat Reduction*

When one makes a threat reduction effort, it could have three different influences on others. Suppose that a family is going to buy a watchdog. First, if their house is a little house on the prairie, then the resultant threat reduction would be discouragement of burgling into the little house only (i.e., no influence on the others). Let us call this a *no-influence* model. Second, if the house is a small one in a densely-populated urban area, then the threat reduction effect (i.e., burglar discouragement) would reach its neighborhood as well; burglars would hesitate to attack not only the house where the watchdog is introduced but also other houses nearby because the watchdog might find and bark at those who make an attempt to enter neighborhood houses. Let us call this a *positive-influence* model. Third, as discussed in (Kunreuther and Heal 2003), there is a possibility of having an opposite effect; a burglar who finds a watchdog may change his target from the house with the dog to another house to which he believes the dog pays no attention. That is, one's investment to reduce one's threat may not reduce but enhance another party's threat. Let us call this a *negative-influence* model. Clearly, the three models above are in close relation to interdependent security.

In the area of the economics of information security, the interdependency and externality problems have been attracting wide attention (Boehme and Kataria 2006; Kesan et al. 2005; Kunreuther and Heal 2003; Ogut et al. 2005; Varian 2002). In fact, after the framework of the original model (Gordon and Loeb 2002), the GL model's formulation method was extensively used to analyze the free-riding problem in the context of information sharing (Gordon et al. 2003).

Likewise, our future works should explicitly include the interdependency and externality problems. In doing that, a care should be made to consider all three models above: no-influence, positive-influence, and negative-influence models regarding threat reduction. For example, it is easy to expect a trade-off between vulnerability reduction and threat reduction in the positive-influence model. If one expects a strong threat reduction on him by other parties' investment, and if he likewise expects a strong threat reduction on other parties by his investment, then he may reduce his incentive for his security investment. Thus, even though the vulnerability reduction is a positive incentive factor for security investment, we will face a trade-off if we consider the threat reduction as well.

Finally, it should be noted that this chapter shows another trade-off between vulnerability reduction and threat reduction although the no-influence model is used. Let us suppose not users but developers of security technologies. While users' efforts would reduce vulnerability and/or threat, developers' efforts could increase the productivities. As observed in Section 4.4, the productivity increase may increase/decrease the (users') optimal amount of security investment. There are two possibilities: some developers may prefer the increase of the optimal investment, and others may prefer the decrease. Let us suppose the former developers and a location in the white region in Figure 8. Then, they may hesitate to make their efforts; while they are probably happy with the contribution of their efforts to the improvement of vulnerability reduction productivity, they may be unhappy with the improvement of threat reduction productivity that could move the location in the productivity space from the white region to the dark-gray region (see Figure 8 again). Although this trade-off is different from the well-known trade-off pointed out in the previous paragraph, we should pay attention to it in a public-policy perspective.

5 Concluding Remarks

In the context of extending the Gordon-Loeb model, this chapter introduced the concept of productivity space of information security, and investigated the behavior of the optimal information security investment there. Security efforts can reduce vulnerabilities. Security efforts can reduce threats. The productivities regarding these two reductions can be enhanced by research, innovation, well-designed public policies, and so on. The optimal investment strategies for different vulnerabilities are characterized by a space formed by these productivities. Although restricted to risk-neutral users and a particular class of functions in the model, the productivity space has three areas of different investment strategies. First, zero investment is optimal in the lower-left area (i.e., where both of the productivities are low). Second, investment focused on mid-range vulnerabilities is recommendable in the lower-right area (i.e., where the vulnerability reduction productivity is high and the threat reduction productivity is low). Third, investment focused on high vulnerabilities is recommendable in the upper area (i.e., where the threat reduction productivity is high).

By using the lines and curves similar to those used for partitioning the productivity space into the three areas above, the effects of productivity improvements on the optimal investment are characterized. Some implications were shown by comprehensive observations based on this characterization and the three investment strategies. In particular, trade-offs between the two productivities will be of further interest in the research community. Although the proposed model does not explicitly deal with the trade-off from the viewpoint of users, one of the implications suggests the trade-off from the viewpoint of developers.

Acknowledgments

This work was partly supported by grant no. 08D49001a from New Energy and Industrial Technology Development Organization. The author gratefully acknowledges the productive comments from the anonymous reviewers.

References

Boehme, R., and Kataria, G. "Models and Measures for Correlation in Cyber-Insurance," *The Fifth Workshop on the Economics of Information Security*, Cambridge, UK, June 2006.

Dwork, C., and Naor, M. "Pricing via Processing or Combatting Junk Mail," *Lecture Notes in Computer Science* (740), Springer, Berlin/Heidelberg, August 1992, pp. 139-147.

Dynes, S., Brechbuhl, H., and Johnson, M. E. "Information Security in the Extended Enterprise: Some Initial Results from a Field Study of an Industrial Firm," *The Fourth Workshop on the Economics of Information Security*, Cambridge, MA, June 2005.

Geer, D. E. "Making Choices to Show ROI," *Secure Business Quarterly* (1:2), 2001, Q4.

Gordon, L.A., and Loeb, M.P. "The Economics of Information Security Investment," *ACM Transactions on Information and System Security* (5:4), November 2002, pp. 438-457.

Gordon, L.A., Loeb, M.P., and Lucyshyn, W. "Sharing Information on Computer Systems Security: An Economic Analysis," *Journal of Accounting & Public Policy* (22:6), November/December 2003, pp. 461-485.

Gordon, L. A., Loeb, M. P., Lucyshyn, W., and Richardson, R. "2005 CSI/FBI Computer Crime and Security Survey," Computer Security Institute, July 2005, Available from: http://gocsi.com.

Hoo, K.S., Sudbury, A.W., and Jaquith, A.R. "Tangible ROI through Secure Software Engineering," *Secure Business Quarterly* (1:2), 2001, Q4.

Juels, A., and Brainard, J. "Client Puzzles: A Cryptographic Countermeasure against Connection Depletion Attacks," in *Proceedings of the Network and Distributed System Security Symposium 1999*, San Diego, CA, February 1999, pp. 151-165.

Karabacak, B., and Sogukpinar, L. "ISRAM: Information Security Risk Analysis Method," *Computers & Security* (24:2), March 2005, pp. 147-159.

Kesan, J. P., Majuca, R. P., and Yurcik, W. J. "Cyberinsurance as a Market-Based Solution to the Problem of Cybersecurity: A Case Study," *The Fourth Workshop on the Economics of Information Security*, Cambridge, MA, June 2005.

Kim, S., and Lee, H.J. "Cost-Benefit Analysis of Security Investments: Methodology and Case Study," *Lecture Notes in Computer Science* (3482), Berlin/Heidelberg, Springer, May 2005, pp. 1239-1248.

Kunreuther, H., and Heal, G. "Interdependent Security," *The Journal of Risk and Uncertainty* (26:2/3), March 2003, pp. 231-249.

Kuper, P. "The Status of Security," *IEEE Security & Privacy* (3:5), September/October 2005, pp. 51-53.

Laurie, B., and Clayton, R. "Proof-of-Work Proves Not to Work," *The Third Annual Workshop on Economics of Information Security*, Minneapolis, MN, May 2004.

Liu, D., and Camp, L.J. "Proof of Work Can Work," *The Fifth Workshop on the Economics of Information Security*, Cambridge, UK, June 2006.

Liu, W., Tanaka, H., and Matsuura, K. "Empirical-Analysis Methodology for Information-Security Investment and Its Application to a Reliable Survey of Japanese Firms," *IPSJ Journal* (48:9), September 2007, pp. 3204-3218.

Lovea, P. E.D., Iranib, Z., Standinga, C., Lina, C., and Burna, J. M. "The Enigma of Evaluation: Benefits, Costs and Risks of IT in Australian Small-Medium-Sized Enterprises," *Information & Management* (42:7), October 2005, pp. 947-964.

Matsuura, K., and Imai, H. "Protection of Authenticated Key-Agreement Protocol against a Denial-of-Service Attack," in *Proceedings of the 1998 International Symposium on Information Theory and Its Applications*, Mexico City, October 1998, pp. 466-470.

Matsuura, K., and Imai, H. "Modified Aggressive Modes of Internet Key Exchange Resistant against Denial-of-Service Attacks," *IEICE Transactions on Information and Systems* (E83-D:5), May 2000, pp. 972-979.

Ogut, H., Menon, N., and Raghunathan, S. "Cyber Insurance and IT Security Investment: Impact of Interdependent Risk," *The Fourth Workshop on the Economics of Information Security*, Cambridge, MA, June 2005.
Purser, S. A. "Improving the ROI of the Security Management Process," *Computers & Security* (23:7), October 2004, pp. 542-546.
Tanaka, H., Matsuura, K., and Sudoh, O. "Vulnerability and Information Security Investment: an Empirical Analysis of e-Local Government in Japan," *Journal of Accounting and Public Policy* (24:1), January/February 2005, pp. 37-59.
Varian, H. R. "System Reliability and Free Riding," Workshop on Economics and Information Security, Berkeley, CA, May 2002.
Whitman, M. E. "Enemy at the Gate: Threats to Information Security," *Communications of the ACM* (46:8), August 2003, pp. 91-95.

Appendix

A. Proof of Claim 1

The proof of Claim 1 goes as follows. From Eq. (7), we have

$$\frac{\partial z^*}{\partial v} = \frac{-\left(\frac{1}{v} - \frac{\alpha/v}{\alpha \ln v + \beta \ln t}\right)(\alpha \ln v + \beta \ln t) + \{\ln(vL) + \ln(-\alpha \ln v - \beta \ln t)\}\frac{\alpha}{v}}{(\alpha \ln v + \beta \ln t)^2}. \quad (13)$$

For $v \in (0,1)$, due to the fact that $\alpha/v>0$ and $(\alpha \ln v + \beta \ln t)^2 > 0$, the sign of Eq. (13) is given by the sign of

$$G(v) \equiv \frac{-(\alpha \ln v + \beta \ln t)}{\alpha} + 1 + \ln(vL) + \ln\left(-\alpha \ln v - \beta \ln t\right) \quad (14)$$

$$= \frac{-\beta \ln t}{\alpha} + 1 + \ln L + \ln\left(-\alpha \ln v - \beta \ln t\right). \quad (15)$$

$G(v)$ is monotonically decreasing for $v \in (0,1)$. And we can see $G(v) \to \infty$ when $v \to +0$. Therefore, with the help of the equivalence (12), we can see that

$$\left(G(V_5) = 0\right) \wedge \left(-V_5 \ln V_5 > \frac{\beta \ln t}{\alpha} \cdot V_5 + \frac{e}{\alpha L}\right) \quad (16)$$

is a necessary condition for z^* to take a maximum at $v=V_5$ such that $V_3<V_5<V_4$ and the point (α, β) is in the mid-vulnerability intensive area. However, if we assume the condition (16) is satisfied, then it brings a contradiction. In fact, from the first part of the condition (16) (i.e., $G(V_5)=0$), we have

$$-\alpha \ln V_5 - \beta \ln t = \frac{t^{\beta/\alpha}}{eL}. \tag{17}$$

Regarding the second part of the condition (16), since $\alpha/V_5>0$, we have

$$-V_5 \ln V_5 > \frac{\beta \ln t}{\alpha} \cdot V_5 + \frac{e}{\alpha L} \Leftrightarrow -\alpha \ln V_5 - \beta \ln t > \frac{e}{LV_5}. \tag{18}$$

Using Eq. (17) and Eq. (18), we have $\frac{t^{\beta/\alpha}}{eL} > \frac{e}{LV_5}$. That is,

$$t^{\beta/\alpha} > \frac{e^2}{V_5}. \tag{19}$$

Since $0 \le t \le 1$ tells $t^{\beta/\alpha} \le 1$ and $0<V_5<1$ tells $\frac{e^2}{V_5} > 1$, the inequality (19) is a contradiction. Thus Claim 1 is proved.

B. List of Abbreviations

For the readers' convenience, this appendix shows the following list of abbreviations used in this article:

- DoS: Denial-of-Service.
- ENBIS: Expected net benefits from an investment in information security.
- GL model: Gordon-Loeb model.
- ISP: Internet service provider.
- POW: Proof-of-Work.
- SBP function: Security breach probability function.
- STP function: Security threat probability function.

Communicating the Economic Value of Security Investments: Value at Security Risk

Rolf Hulthén

TeliaSonera AB

Abstract The information and data security communities and their individual practitioners have long experienced the pedagogical difficulties in communicating to management or funding bodies the importance and relevance of sufficient investments in information and data security.

One reason for this pedagogical failure is that the highly specialized security domain is difficult to penetrate for the average manager with a background in business administration or economics. Consequently, the entities and metrics used by the security community to evaluate security risks and their consequences usually tell very little to people involved in security investment decisions.

Historically, Return on Investment (RoI) has been used for this purpose. However, RoI is not an ideal entity to use, since it generates misunderstanding and misinterpretation. Companies and enterprises already have tools, methods and metrics to express risk levels and their economic consequences: we refer to Value-at-Risk and Value-at-Risk-type metrics.

This contribution transforms or transfers entities and metrics used by the information and data security communities into Value-at-Risk-type entities and metrics. This will allow management to understand, compare and evaluate security risks and their economic consequences with risks generated by other sources, strategies or investment decisions and give management a firmer and more rational basis for security investment decisions.

1 Introduction and Problem Situation

There are several models aiming at answering the questions on how much to spend on security investments, and on the incentives to do so (Geocites 2008; Gordon and Loeb 2002; Hulthén 2007). Usually the models aim at establishing a quantitative relation between investment level and the resulting vulnerability level.

The information and data security communities and their individual practitioners have long experienced the pedagogical difficulties in communicating to management or funding bodies the importance and relevance of sufficient investments in

M.E. Johnson (ed.), *Managing Information Risk and the Economics of Security*,
DOI: 10.1007/978-0-387-09762-6_6, © Springer Science + Business Media, LLC 2009

information and data security, and inside these communities there is almost universal agreement that companies underinvest in security. However, some rational economical support for such a strategy can be raised (Hulthén 2007).

One reason for this pedagogical failure is that the highly specialized security domain is difficult to penetrate for the average manager with a background in business administration or economics. Consequently, the entities and metrics used by the information and data security communities to evaluate security risks and their consequences usually tell very little to people involved in security investment decisions.

Historically, Return on Investment (RoI), sometimes named Return on Security Investment (RoSI) in our applications, (Geocites 2008) has been used for this purpose. However, RoI is not an ideal entity to use, since it generates misunderstanding and misinterpretation: financial officers and managers generally book such spending as *costs* or *expenses*. Thus, RoI as applied is not a financial return on an investment that we can collect and register in accounting books (Pindyck and Rubinfeld 2001; Ittelson 1998) but a *probabilistic expected net prevented loss* due to security breaches per monetary unit spent.

Companies and enterprises already have tools, methods and metrics to express risk levels and their economic consequences to support management in investment decision situations: we refer to Value-at-Risk (VaR) (Jorion 2007; RiskMetrics 2008) and Value-at-Risk-type metrics. We have already seen several such VaR-type metrics, e.g. Credit-, Cash Flow-, Revenue-, Profit-, and Market Value at Risk.

The purpose of this contribution is to add 'Value-at-Security Risk' (VaSR) to this collection by transforming or transferring the entities and metrics (such as Threat, Vulnerability, Security Risk, Breach Loss) already used by the information and data security communities into Value-at-Risk-type entities and metrics. This will allow management to understand, compare and evaluate security risks and their economic consequences with risks generated by other sources, strategies or investment decisions: companies may have corporate guidelines on allowed financial risk levels as a function of investment levels. Credit rating agencies, such as Moody's (Moody's 2008) and Standard & Poor's (Standard & Poor's 2008), have very well-defined demands on financial risk level, investment level, time span and equity capital for a company to qualify for a particular rating level. Thus, our aim is to give to management a metric that will constitute a firmer and more rational basis for security investment decisions.

This contribution establishes a connection between the length of an investment period, risk level and value-at-risk. An earlier contribution (Hulthén 2007) established the connection between length of investment period, investment level, risk level and value to be security protected.

We reach the purpose in the following steps.

Section 2 introduces and lists entities to be used, and Section 3 formulates our problem and defines the concept of Value-at-Risk. Section 4 gives a high-level analytic introduction to our model, whereas Section 5 goes into analytic details and derives the key entity that solves our problem. Section 6 uses this entity to define and calculate the most important Value-at-Risk entities. Section 7 reports conclusions of analysis of authentic security incident data; the analysis tests the validity of model assumptions made in Section 5. Section 8, finally, gives some comments and conclusions.

2 Background and Preliminaries

We import from (Gordon and Loeb 2002) and (Hulthén 2007) the following mean value (or Expected Value in the sense of statistical theory) entities, namely

- *Threat* $T(t)$ is the number of (security) attacks per unit time at time t,
- *Vulnerability* $V(t)$ is the probability that an attack at time t will be successful,
- *Breach Loss* $\lambda(t)$ is the economic loss from a successful attack at time t,
- *Potential Loss per Unit Time* at time t is $T(t)\lambda(t)$; taken over an investment period $(t_j; t_{j+1})$ the *Potential Loss* is $PL(t_j;t_{j+1}) = \int_{t_j}^{t_{j+1}} T(\tau)\lambda(\tau)d\tau$.
- *Security Risk per Unit Time* at time t is $T(t)V(t)$; this is equal to the number of successful attacks per unit time at time t.

  Taken over an investment period $(t_j; t_{j+1})$ the *Security Risk* is

  $SR(t_j;t_{j+1}) = \int_{t_j}^{t_{j+1}} V(z_j;\tau)T(\tau)d\tau$.

  z_j is the investment in monetary units that we make at investment time t_j for the period $(t_j; t_{j+1})$. The resulting vulnerability is $V(z_j;t)$; it will increase during the course of time (Hulthén 2007).

To reach our present purpose, we introduce the following stochastic variables:

- A is the number of (security) attacks per unit time at time t; discrete (and integer) A has power density function (pdf) $p_A(n;t) = \Pr\{A = n; t\}$, i.e. the probability that A equals n at time t. We want the expected value of A to be $E\{A\} = T(t)$ since we want to transform or transfer *Threat* $T(t)$ used by the security community into entities used by the financial risk community.
- S is the number of successful (security) attacks per unit time at time t; discrete (and integer) S has pdf $p_S(m;t) = \Pr\{S = m; t\}$, i.e. the probability that S equals m at time t. We will later present a candidate model for authentic data for $p_S(m;t)$. With the expected value of S as $E\{S\}$, we observe that *Vulnerability* $V(t) = E\{S\}/E\{A\}$ and that $E\{S\} = T(t)V(t)$, i.e. *Security Risk per Unit Time* at time t.
- L is the economic loss we make from a successful attack at time t. Continuous L has pdf $f_L(\ell;t)$, i.e. the probability that L falls in an interval $(\ell;\ell+d\ell)$ at time t is equal to $f_L(\ell;t)d\ell$. We will later present a candidate model for authentic data

for $f_L(\ell;t)$. We want the expected value of L to be $E\{L\} = \lambda(t)$, i.e. *Breach Loss* at time t in the terminology of the security community.

3 Problem Formulations: Value-at-Risk

The core question answered by stating the Value-at-Risk is the following: *In a situation beyond our own immediate control and where value is at risk, what is the maximum loss value that, with a preset level of confidence, will not be surpassed within a defined time span?*

This value is the Value-at-Risk. Within Credit Risk Management, typical values can be 5 M$, 95 %, or 24 hours. Depending on the application, these numbers can be quite different. We refer to (Jorion 2007) for an introduction to the subject.

Thus, Value-at-Risk connects a time period (e.g. a fiscal year or an investment period), a (security) risk level, and the value of the resource at (security) risk.

In principle, there are two methods to arrive at the Value-at-Risk: a non-parametric and a parametric method. The non-parametric method relies on historic data in the sense that we, from such data for the application under consideration, generate a histogram for loss within the defined time span. From this histogram we estimate VaR (and other entities of interest) at the preset confidence level. Provided we have sufficient historic data, this method is simple and quite straightforward. However, it does not generate as much insight into the underlying mechanisms to our risk situation as does the parametric method, which, on the other hand, critically depends on an accurate risk situation model and historic data to normalize our model parameters. The method also relies on the possibility to estimate the value of the resource that we want to protect, which can be very different, e.g. corporate IT infrastructure, competitive information and knowledge such as customer or product data, and brand value. We return to this issue in Section 8.

The parametric method derives a pdf for the loss within a defined time span. From this pdf we calculate VaR and other entities of interest. We will follow the parametric method line and state our own problem situation as follows: *Find the pdf for the total loss $\mathcal{L}$, i.e. the value that, due to security breach attacks, is at risk during an investment period.*

This pdf will use entities already in use by the security community to calculate *Value-at-Security Risk, Expected Breach Loss, Unexpected Breach Loss*, and *Expected Tail Breach Loss;* this is done in Section 6.

4 Value-at-Security Risk Model: Assumptions

Using the stochastic variables S and L introduced above and initially following, but generalizing and adapting to our present application, the approach in (Jorion

2007), Chapter 19.3, we experience the individual losses L_1, L_2, L_3,... during a time unit at time t, so that the total loss per time unit at time t is

$$L_m = \sum_{i=1}^{m} L_i \,.$$

The generalization we make is to introduce time dependent $\lambda(t)$ and $\nu(t)$; this is relevant since we know that Threat, Vulnerability and Breach Loss all vary with time (Richardson 2007).

Further, the probability that the total loss L(t) per time unit at time t is smaller than or equal to some value x is

$$\Pr\{\mathcal{L}(t) \le x\} = \sum_{m=0}^{\infty} \Pr\{L_m \le x \mid m\}\, p_S(m;t) =$$

$$= \sum_{m=0}^{\infty} \Pr\{(\sum_{i=1}^{m} L_i) \le x \mid m\}\, p_S(m;t) \tag{1}$$

Here we have made the assumptions that the individual attacks, as well as their consequent breach losses, are independent. We are aware that this is not always the case and will comment on these assumptions in Section 8.

From this expression we may in principle obtain the pdf $g(x)$ for the total loss L over the investment period $(t_j; t_{j+1})$ as

$$g(x) = \int_{t_j}^{t_{j+1}} (d \Pr\{\mathcal{L}(t) \le x\} / dx)\, dt \tag{2}$$

From $g(x)$ we may determine *VaSR* on the confidence level at our specification, and any additional statistical entity that we prefer under the conditions at hand, i.e. L known, assumed or estimated behaviors of *Threat* $T(t)$, *Vulnerability* $V(t)$, and *Breach Loss* $\lambda(t)$. We will next introduce and make concrete assumptions on these entities and develop $g(x)$ into an operationally useful form.

5 Our Parametric Model

We make the assumption that the number of successful attacks per time unit at time t (i.e. the stochastic variable S) is Poisson-distributed; this is a well-tested model of the number of arrival events (Law and Kelton 1982). Thus, we have

$$p_S(m;t) = (\nu(t)^m/m!)\exp(-\nu(t))\,;\ m \text{ integer} \ge 0 \text{ and } \nu > 0. \tag{3A}$$

$$p_S(m;t) = 0;\ m \text{ integer} \ge 0 \text{ and } \nu = 0. \tag{3B}$$

Here the event intensity $\nu(t) = E\{S\} = T(t)V(t)$, i.e. *Security Risk per Unit Time* at time t. (Jorion 2007) uses a time-independent geometric distribution for the number of events per time unit, which we think is less in agreement with the actual behavior in our application.

We next make the assumption that the economic loss L that we make from a successful attack at time t is exponential distributed with the expected value $E\{L\} = \lambda(t)$, i.e. *Breach Loss* at time t. Thus,

$$f_L(\ell;t) = (1/\lambda(t))\exp(-\ell/\lambda(t));\ \ell \geq 0 \text{ and } \lambda(t) > 0,$$

$$f_L(\ell;t) = 0 \text{ elsewhere.} \tag{4}$$

(Jorion 2007) uses the same distribution but with time-independent parameter λ.

To proceed we need the pdf of $L_m = \sum_{i=1}^{m} L_i$, where all L_i have pdf Equation (4). It is well known (Law and Kelton 1982) that the pdf for a sum of m independent expo ($\lambda(t)$)-distributed stochastic variables is gamma-distributed $\Gamma(m;\lambda(t))$, i.e. L_m has pdf

$$f_{Lm}(\ell;t) = \{\ell^{m-1}/[\lambda(t)^m\,\Gamma(m)]\}\exp[-\ell/\lambda(t)]\,. \tag{5}$$

$\Gamma(m)$ is the Gamma function; $\Gamma(m) = (m-1)!$, m integer ≥ 1. We now have

$$\Pr\{(\sum_0^{\infty} L_i) \leq x \mid m\} = \int_0^x \{\ell^{m-1}/[\lambda(t)^m\Gamma(m)]\}\exp[-\ell/\lambda(t)]d\ell +$$

$$+ \Pr\{(\sum_0^{\infty} L_i) \leq x \mid m = 0\}$$

and, using Equation (3), rewrite Equation (1) to read

$$\Pr\{\mathcal{L}(t) \leq x\} = \sum_{m=1}^{\infty}\{\int_0^x\{\ell^{m-1}/[\lambda(t)^m\Gamma(m)]\}\exp[-\ell/\lambda(t)]d\ell(\nu(t)^m/m!)\exp[-\nu(t)]\} +$$

$$+\exp[-\nu(t)] =$$

$$= \{\int_0^x \exp[-\nu(t)]\exp[-\ell/\lambda(t)]d\ell\}\{\sum_{m=1}^{\infty}\{\ell^{m-1}/[\lambda(t)^m\Gamma(m)]\}[\nu(t)^m/m!]\} +$$

$$+\exp[-\nu(t)],\ x \geq 0 \text{ and } \nu \geq 0. \tag{6A}$$

$$\Pr\{L(t) \leq x\} = 0 \text{ for } x < 0 \text{ and for all } x \text{ when } \nu = 0. \tag{6B}$$

The last term in Equation (6A) is important; it absorbs the case $m = 0$ which is not covered by the pdf of L_m, $\Gamma(m;\lambda(t))$, but contributes to $L(t) \leq x$. We will comment on it in Section 5.2.

Using the *modified Bessel function of the first kind* (Abromowitz and Stegun 1964, Chapter 11), and the fact that $\Gamma(\nu + k + 1) = (\nu + k)!$ for integer ν,

$$I_\nu(z) = \sum_{k=0}^{\infty}(z/2)^{\nu+2k}/[k!(\nu+k)!]$$

we obtain

$$\Pr\{\mathcal{L}(t) \le x\} = \sqrt{\nu(t)/\lambda(t)}\exp[-\nu(t)]\int_0^x I_1(2\sqrt{\ell\nu(t)/\lambda(t)})\exp[-\ell/\lambda(t)]/\sqrt{\ell}d\ell +$$
$$+ H(\nu)\exp[-\nu(t)],$$

i.e. the pdf of $\mathcal{L}(t)$ is

$$f_{\mathcal{L}}(x;t) = d\Pr\{\mathcal{L}(t) \le x\}/dx =$$
$$= C\sqrt{\nu(t)/\lambda(t)}\exp[-\nu(t)]\,I_1(2\sqrt{x\nu(t)/\lambda(t)})\exp[-x/\lambda(t)]/\sqrt{x} +$$
$$+ C\delta_{x,0}\,H(\nu)\exp(-\nu(t)). \tag{7}$$

$\delta_{x,0}$ is the Kronecker delta and $H(\nu)$ is the Heaviside step function. Expressed as in Equation (7), this $f_{\mathcal{L}}(x;t)$ is valid for all $x \ge 0$ and for all values of $\nu \ge 0$. C is a probability normalization constant; using entry 11.4.31 of (Abromowitz and Stegun 1964),

$$\int_0^\infty \exp\left(-a^2t^2\right)I_\mu\left(bt\right)dt = \left(\sqrt{\pi}/2a\right)\exp\left(b^2/8a^2\right)I_{\mu/2}\left(b^2/8a^2\right)$$

when $\Re(\mu) > -1$ and $\Re(a^2) > 0$, which is true in our case, and $I_{1/2}(z) =$ $= \sqrt{2/z\pi}\sinh(z)$, we confirm that $C = 1$ and arrive at the pdf for the total loss $\mathcal{L}(t)$ per time unit at time t

$$f_{\mathcal{L}}(x;t) = \sqrt{\nu(t)/\lambda(t)}\exp[-\nu(t)]\,I_1(2\sqrt{x\nu(t)/\lambda(t)})\exp[-x/\lambda(t)]/\sqrt{x} +$$
$$+ \delta_{x,0}\,H(\nu)\exp(-\nu(t)). \tag{8}$$

With no loss of generality, taking the investment period to be $(0;T)$, we now find the pdf $g_{\mathcal{L}}(x)$ for the total loss $\mathcal{L}$ over the investment period to be

$$g_{\mathcal{L}}(x) = \int_0^T f_{\mathcal{L}}(x;t)dt\,. \tag{9}$$

This is as far as we reach with analytic techniques without making functional assumptions about $\lambda(t)$ and $\nu(t)$.

5.1 Some Observations on $f_{\mathcal{L}}(x;t)$ and $g_{\mathcal{L}}(x)$

Using the approximation $I_\mu(z) \approx (z/2)^\mu/\Gamma(\mu+1)$, valid for $0 < z < \sqrt{\mu+1}$, we have for $x < \lambda/2\nu$

$$f_{\mathcal{L}}(x;t) = [\,\nu(t)/\lambda(t)\exp[-x/\lambda(t)] + \delta_{x,0}\,H(\nu)]\exp[-\nu(t)]$$

so that

$$f_{\mathcal{L}}(0;t) = [\,\nu(t)/\lambda(t) + H(\nu)]\exp[-\nu(t)]\,.$$

Moreover, $f_{\mathcal{L}}(x;t) \to 0$ when $x \to \infty$. Further, for $x > 0$ and using $I_{\mu-1}(z) = dI_\mu(z)/dz + [\nu(t)/z(t)]\, I_\mu(z)$, we learn that $f_{\mathcal{L}}(x;t)$ exhibits a maximum at $x = x_{\max}$ satisfying

$$I_2(z) \,/\, I_1(z) = z/2\,\nu(t), \tag{10}$$

where $z = 2\sqrt{x\nu(t)/\lambda(t)}$; since $I_2(z)/I_1(z) < 1$ for all z, it is always true that $x_{\max} < \nu(t)\lambda(t)$. This is expected. As a consequence, $g_{\mathcal{L}}(x)$ is everywhere finite for finite investment interval $(0;T)$.

5.2 A Special Case: Constant λ and ν

When λ and ν are both constant (i.e. independent of time) and at least when $[2\nu(t)/z]\, I_2(z) - I_1(z) > 0$ over the entire investment period, $g_{\mathcal{L}}(x)$ also has a maximum at $x = x_{\max}$ above. Figure 1 shows such a case for $\lambda = 0.5$ and $\nu = 3.0$. In this case Equation (10) gives $x_{\max} = 0.634$. This may give us some guidance in investment decisions: $0 < x_{\max} < \nu(t)\lambda(t)$ tells us that medium sized breach losses are more frequent than low- and high-cost breaches.

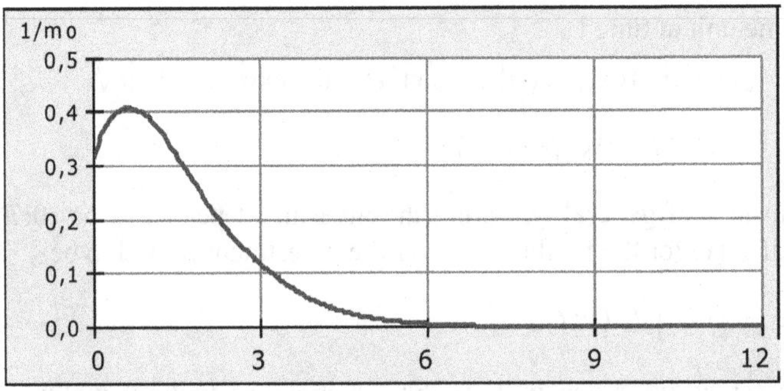

Figure 1. Power Density Function $g_{\mathcal{L}}(x)$ for Total Breach Loss $\mathcal{L}$ over an Investment Period T= 1 Year with Constant λ and ν

We further study the special case when λ and ν are both constant since this gives us an opportunity to check the model in a few details. Using Entry 11.4.29 of (Abromowitz and Stegun 1964) and Equations (8) and (9) and the fact that $\int_{-\infty}^{\infty} f(x)\,\delta_{x,0}\,dx = f(0)$, we obtain the *Expected Breach Loss* over the investment period $(0;T)$

$$E\{\mathcal{L}\} = \int_0^\infty x g_{\mathcal{L}}(x)\,dx = T\int_0^\infty x\, f_{\mathcal{L}}(x)\,dx =$$

$$= T\sqrt{\nu/\lambda}\,\exp(-\nu)\int_0^\infty \sqrt{x}\, I_1(2\sqrt{x\nu/\lambda})\exp(-x/\lambda)\,dx = T\lambda\nu\,.$$

This is exactly what we expect: on an average ν successful attacks per time unit, each causing the average breach loss λ, will give this loss over the investment period. We also calculate the *Breach Loss Variance* over the investment period (Abromowitz and Stegun 1964, Entry 11.4.28)

$$V\{\mathcal{L}\} = E\{(\mathcal{L} - E\{\mathcal{L}\})^2\} = \int_0^\infty (x - T\lambda\nu)^2 g_{\mathcal{L}}(x)\,dx = T\,\lambda^2\nu\left[2 + \nu(1-T)^2\right].$$

This result is of the quality that we expect: on an average ν exponentially distributed stochastic variables per time unit generate a gamma distributed stochastic variable with expected mean $\lambda\nu$ (as above) and variance $\lambda^2\nu$ (Law and Kelton 1982). A multiplicative factor is plausible from the fact that the number of exponentially distributed variables added to form the gamma distributed stochastic variable is also a stochastic variable, thus generating an additional variance beyond $\lambda^2\nu$; the $V\{\mathcal{L}\}$ expression above is confirmed by simulation.

Had we not included the isolated $\exp(-\nu(t))$ –term in Equation (6), and thereby not the $\delta_{x,0}\exp(-\nu(t))$–term in Equation (8), we would instead obtain $E\{\mathcal{L}\} = T\lambda\nu/(1-\exp(-\nu))$, i.e. $E\{\mathcal{L}\} = T\lambda\nu$ only asymptotically when $\nu\to\infty$ and $E\{\mathcal{L}\} = T\lambda$ asymptotically when $\nu\to 0$, which is impossible for an obvious reason: also without successful attacks we would suffer a breach loss $T\lambda$. Similarly, $V\{\mathcal{L}\} \to T\lambda^2\nu^2 \to\infty$ when $\nu\to\infty$ and $V\{\mathcal{L}\} = T^2\lambda^2$ asymptotically when $\nu\to 0$, which again is impossible for the same reason.

6 Value-at-Security Risk Entities

Using Equations (8) and (9), we may derive all quantitative entities of economic and risk evaluation interest, using the entities used by the security community. We list the most important and most frequently used VaR-type entities here and give examples.

Value-at-Security Risk. Writing the Value-at-Security Risk = X_{vasr} for short, this value is defined by the relation

$$\int_0^{X_{vasr}} g_{\mathcal{L}}(x)\,dx = 1 - RL\ ,$$

where RL is our preset risk level; and $1 - RL = CL$, i.e. our confidence level. The explicit interpretation is a standard one: our total loss over the investment period, due to security breaches, will not exceed the value X_{vasr} with probability CL. Figure 2 shows an example with synthetic curves $\lambda(t)$ and $\nu(t)$ and the resulting $g_{\mathcal{L}}(x)$.

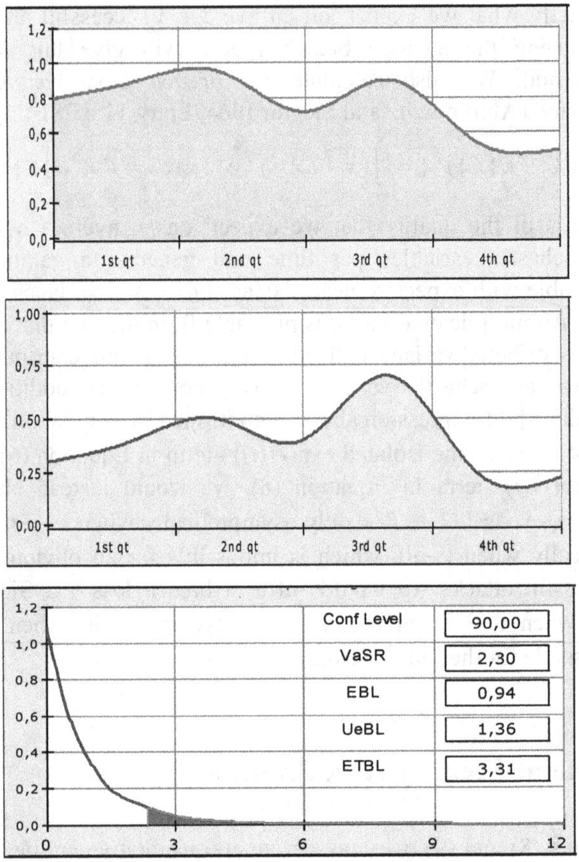

Figure 2. Breach Loss Time Development (upper diagram), Number of Successful Attacks Time Development (middle diagram) and Power Density Function $g_{\mathcal{L}}(x)$ for Total Breach Loss $\mathcal{L}$ (lower diagram) over One Year Investment Period: *Synthetic Data*

Expected Breach Loss (*EBL*) is

$$EBL = E\{\mathcal{L}\} = \int_0^\infty x g_{\mathcal{L}}(x)\, dx \,,$$

and *Unexpected Breach Loss* (*UeBL*) is *VaSR* – *EBL* (Jorion 2007).
Expected Tail Breach Loss (*ETBL*) is the expected loss in case the loss exceeds *VaSR*, i.e.

$$ETBL = E\{\mathcal{L} \mid \mathcal{L} > X_{vasr}\} = \int_{X_{vasr}}^\infty x\, g_{\mathcal{L}}(x)\, dx \Big/ \int_{X_{vasr}}^\infty g_{\mathcal{L}}(x)\, dx \,.$$

Security Risk over the investment period (0;*T*) is

$$SR(0;T) = \int_0^T v(t)\{\sum_{m=0}^\infty p_S(m;t)\}\, dt = \{\text{Equation (3)}\} = \int_0^T v(t)\, dt \,.$$

This expression agrees with the equivalent expression in use by the security community. To calculate the values of these entities, we have to resort to computer simulations.

7 Analysis of Authentic Data: Model Evaluation

To examine the validity of the models in Section 5, we have analyzed portions of data contained in a database collected and maintained by our company. The database contains data on safety and security incidents with connection or association to our company. The database has collected data since 1998. However, only since the end of 2004 has the reporting been fairly complete with respect to incidents that are known to have occurred. This analysis therefore uses data from the period 2005 to (and including) 2007; although available, data from 2008 is not included in our analysis.

We show preliminary results from data on a typical and common telecom fraud of a kind where incidents on good grounds are assumed to be fairly independent. In total, the period contains 2961 incidents. At the onset of this analysis, the material was judged to be rather homogeneous with respect to categorization, also if some incidents could have been listed under other categories without too much objections. To some extent our experience deviated from this, as will be described.

7.1 Number of Incidents per Time Unit

Our model Equation (3) assumes that the number of incidents per time unit is Poisson-distributed with event (incident) intensity $\nu(t)$. Figure 3 shows incident intensity for 2005, calculated as a moving average over 14 days.

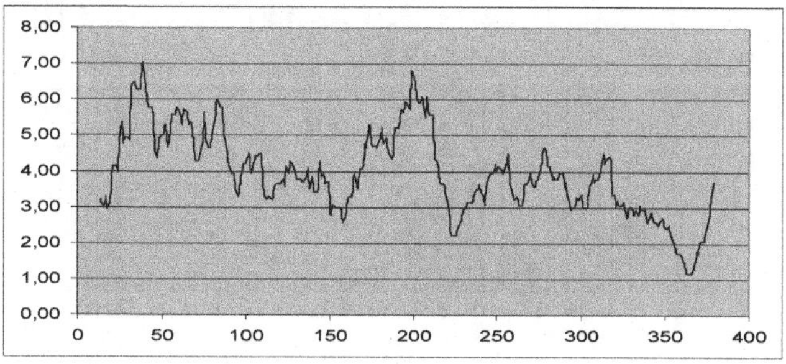

Figure 3. Incident Intensity 2005

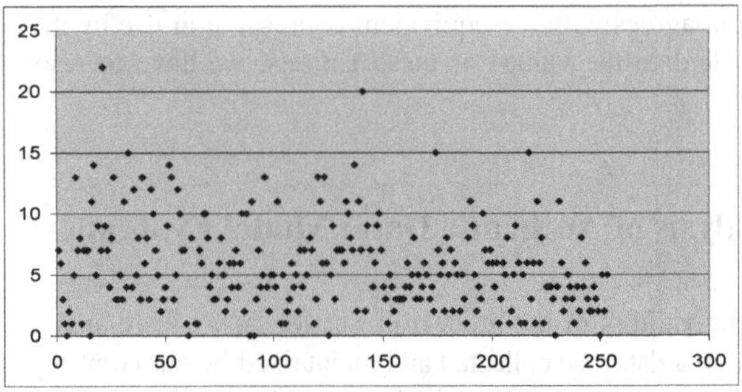

Figure 4. Number of Incidents per Weekday 2005

Figure 4 shows the number of incidents *per weekday* during 2005. The reason for *per weekday* is that individuals almost always register incidents that occur during weekends and holidays during weekdays, but use the same date for incident and reporting despite instructions to distinguish these dates. As a consequence, we expect to find high values of parameter m in Equation (3) overly represented in the authentic material. The few incidents that are reported to have occurred during weekends and holidays have, for the sake of consistency, been randomly distributed

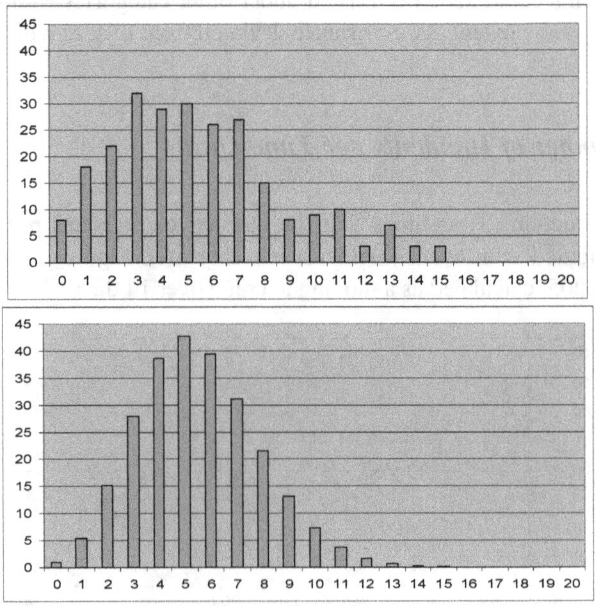

Figure 5. Frequency of Observed (upper diagram) and Expected (lower diagram; ν= 5.51; N= 250) Number of Incidents per Weekday 2005.

to a weekday during the following week. The reporting pattern is the same for 2006 and 2007; therefore, data from these years have been handled as data from 2005.

Figures 5 to 7 show the results for the number of incidents for the years 2005 to 2007. In all cases have the averages over a year of the observed number of incidents per weekday been used to calculate the corresponding expected number of incidents per weekday (N is the number of days with incidents, *not* the number of incidents).

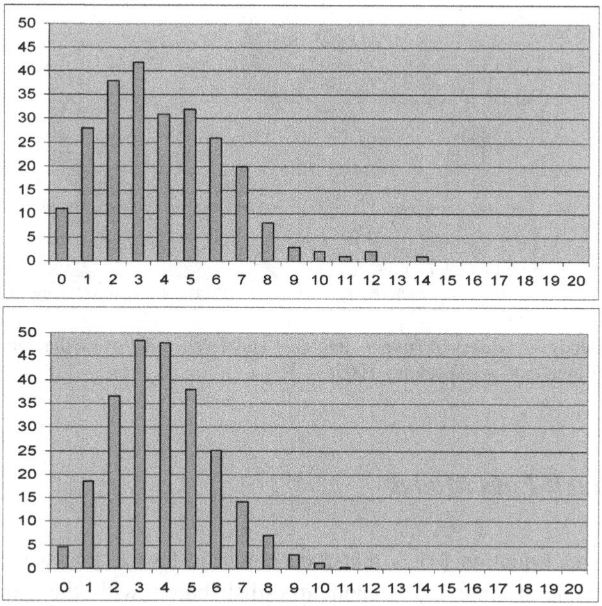

Figure 6. Frequency of Observed (upper diagram) and Expected (lower diagram; ν= 3.96; N= 245) Number of Incidents per Weekday 2006

As expected, higher values of parameter m are overrepresented. The agreement between model and reality is quite satisfying for 2007. For future analyses we therefore accept a Poisson distribution as a valid model for the number of incidents per time unit.

We moreover make the observation that incident intensity $\nu(t)$ decreases from 5,51 (2005) to 3,96 (2006) to 2,06 (2007), due either to deteriorating incident reporting discipline or to the fact that our ability to counteract this type of telecom fraud has increased.

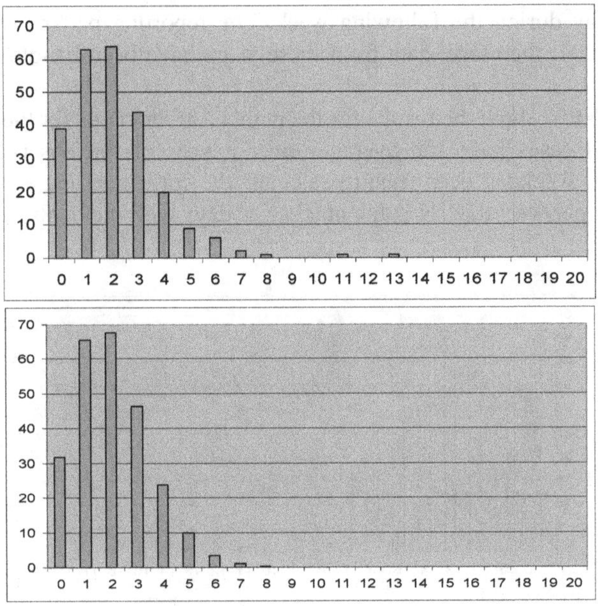

Figure 7. Frequency of Observed (upper diagram) and Expected (lower diagram; ν= 2.06; N= 250) Number of Incidents per Weekday 2007

7.2 Breach Loss Model

Our assumption Equation (4) is that the economic loss L that we make from a successful attack at time t is exponential-distributed with the expected value $E\{L\}= \lambda(t)$, i.e. L is Expo($\lambda(t)$).

In our authentic incident data the economic loss is a direct cost that each incident can be loaded with. It includes manpower costs for troubleshooting, problem solving, cleanup operations, further license costs, stand-still time and lost revenue, and sometimes costs for lawsuit and compensation to customers as well as other direct costs that may have been generated by an incident. We realize that economic losses may be generated by changes of brand value due to security incidents. We give some comments on this issue in Section 8.

Figure 8 shows the frequency of direct costs in 10 k€ intervals for 2005. The corresponding diagrams for 2006 and 2007 are quite similar. Figure 9 shows the 'high direct costs' side for 2005 and with an exponential model inserted. The diagrams for 2006 and 2007 are again quite similar. Figure 10 shows the values for all years under analysis; for costs above 60 k€, they can all be approximated with one and the same exponential.

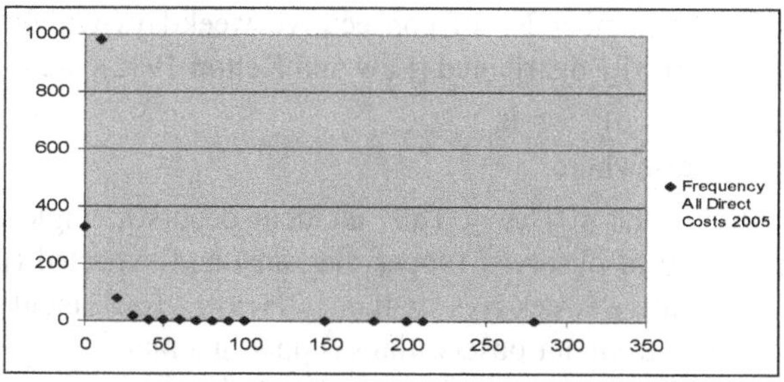

Figure 8. Frequency of All Direct Costs for 2005

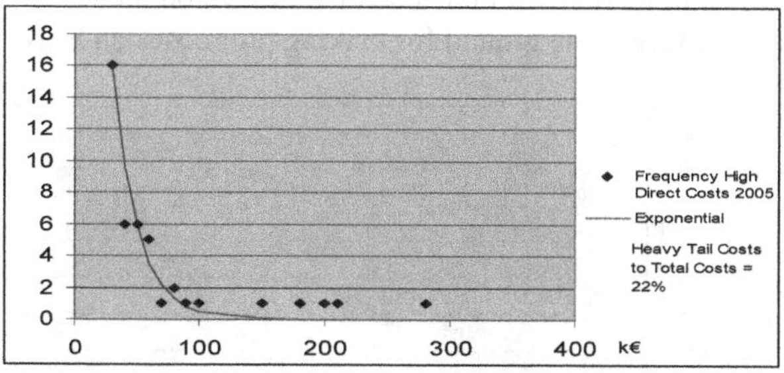

Figure 9. Frequency of 'High Direct Costs' Side for 2005

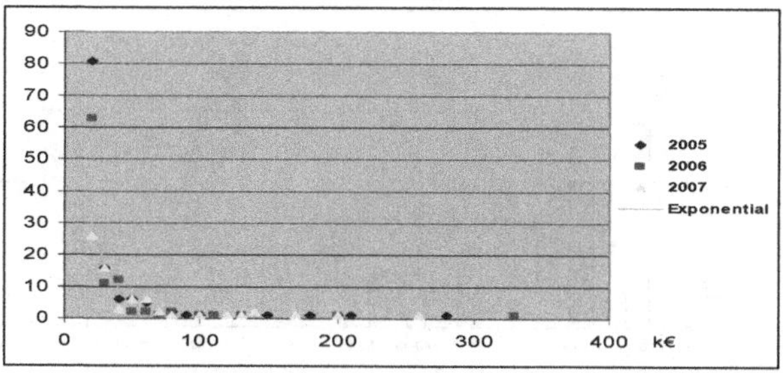

Figure 10. Frequency of 'High Direct Costs' Side for 2005, 2006, and 2007

Figure 9 clearly shows the presence of 'heavy tails', a phenomenon well-known from risk analysis within finance and insurance (Embrechts et al. 2004). In our data material, the heavy tails are costs above 60 k€. Their fraction of total costs increases considerably for 2007, which however is a consequence of the fact that total costs have decreased. Their absolute values have stayed rather constant: 1.40 M€ (2005), 1.07 M€ (2006), and 1.42 M€ (2007), and their average values per incident quite constant: 140 k€ (2005), 134 k€ (2006), and 129 k€ (2007).

Heavy tails usually evade reliable statistical modeling since they are often generated by rare events. This experience is confirmed here, i.e. our 'Heavy Tail' incidents are not covered by our exponential models. We therefore refocus our modeling goals since a more favorable possibility is offered: we make the assumption that the number N_C of consecutive weekdays without 'Heavy Tail' incidents is geometrically distributed (Law and Kelton 1982), i.e.

$$\Pr\{ N_C = x\} = p(1-p)^x, x = 0, 1, 2, \ldots,$$
$$\Pr\{ N_C = x\} = 0 \text{ elsewhere.}$$

p is the probability that a 'Heavy Tail' incident occurs a single day. Figure 11 shows the frequency of observed (upper diagram) and expected (lower diagram) number of consecutive weekdays without 'Heavy Tail' incidents; p (lower diagram) is obtained from our observations (upper diagram).

Considering the relatively sparse data at hand, the agreement between the two is acceptable, so we tentatively (i.e. until falsified by future data) adopt the assumption. In combination with the statement above on the costs of 'Heavy Tail' incidents we now have some ground for making prognoses on heavy tails.

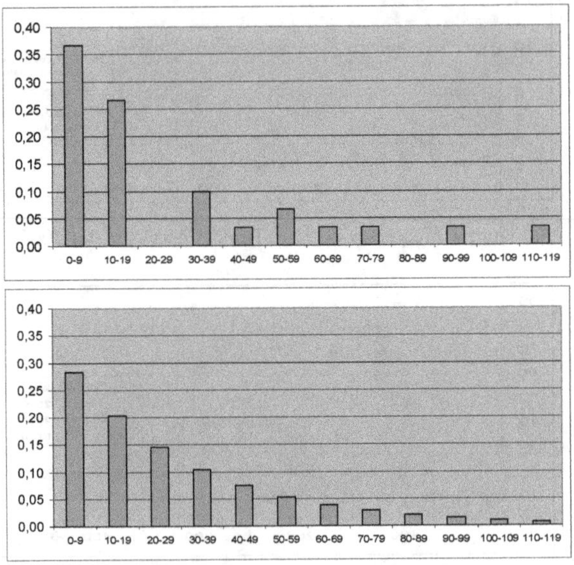

Figure 11. Frequency of Observed (upper diagram) and Expected (lower diagram) Number of Consecutive Weekdays without 'Heavy Tail' Incidents

The 'low direct costs' side is more complex. Figure 12 shows data for 2005 with two alternative candidate exponentials inserted. Neither pleases us since both fail to capture significant data points.

The value at 0.2 k€ is a special case. It is the cost of manpower for reporting and registering the incident into the database system, usually the cost of one or two man-hours. As such it is not included in the model as originally formulated in Section 5. We will therefore disregard this cost in the present analysis but keep it in mind for the future.

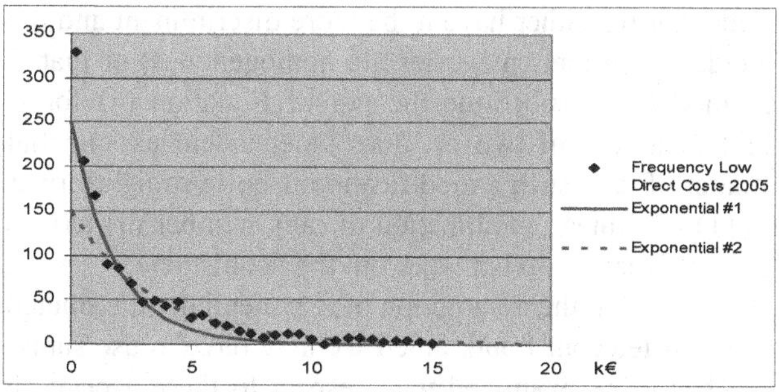

Figure 12. Frequency of 'Low Direct Costs' Side for 2005

Our displease over the poor fits of the candidate exponentials in Figure 12 forces us to reconsider our model Equation (4), and to question the homogeneity of our incident data. Thus, we hypothesize that the cost data is the sum of two independent exponentially distributed costs, i.e. our observed L is $L = L_1 + L_2$, where L_i is Expo(λ_i). Applying elementary statistical theory we derive the pdf of $L = L_1 + L_2$ and arrive at

$$f_L(\ell;t) = [\exp(-\ell/\lambda_1) - \exp(-\ell/\lambda_2)]/(\lambda_1 - \lambda_2);\ \ell \geq 0 \text{ and } \lambda_1(t) > 0,\ \lambda_2(t) > 0$$
$$f_L(\ell;t) = 0 \text{ elsewhere.} \qquad (11)$$

$f_L(\ell;t)$ has a maximum at $\ell = \ell_M = (\lambda_1\lambda_2)/(\lambda_1 - \lambda_2)\ \ln(\lambda_1/\lambda_2)$, which is also where $f_{L1}(\ell;t)$ and $f_{L2}(\ell;t)$ cross, and

$$f_L(\ell_M;t) = (\lambda_2^{\lambda_2/\Delta\lambda})/(\lambda_1^{\lambda_1/\Delta\lambda});\ \Delta = \lambda_1 - \lambda_2.$$

The modified model is inserted in Figure 13. The agreement between model and reality is now better than for any of the candidate exponentials for 2005 in Figure 12. The same is true for data from 2006 and 2007.

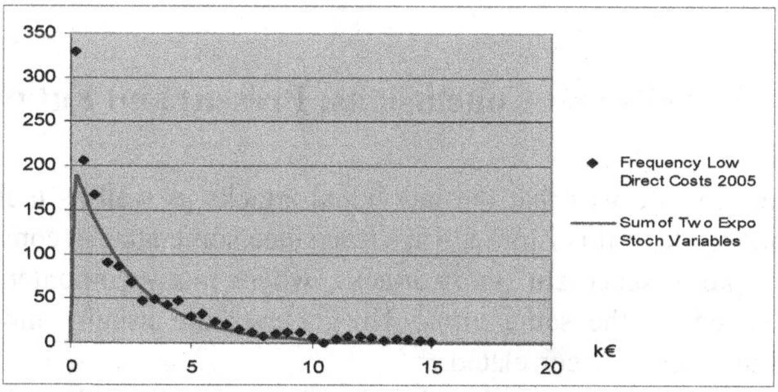

Figure 13. Frequency of 'Low Direct Costs' Side with Modified pdf Model for 2005

We conclude that we either have to be more discriminant and precise when we categorize incidents (so that categories are homogeneous) or that we have to use the modified model and substitute the pdf of Equation (4) for a pdf (such as Equation (11)) of a sum of two or more independent exponentially distributed costs. As a matter of fact, such a modification is quite straightforward since $f_L(\ell;t)$ of Equation (11) is a linear combination of (any number of) terms of the kind in Equation (4). However, we do not work out the details here.

Our conclusion is that the assumption of exponentially distributed costs is valid for this category of telecom fraud, albeit we may have to use sums of such costs. Each category has to be examined with respect to these aspects, in particular if incidents are statistically dependent.

Figure 14 contains all 'low direct costs' data for the years considered. We observe that these costs reduce over time.

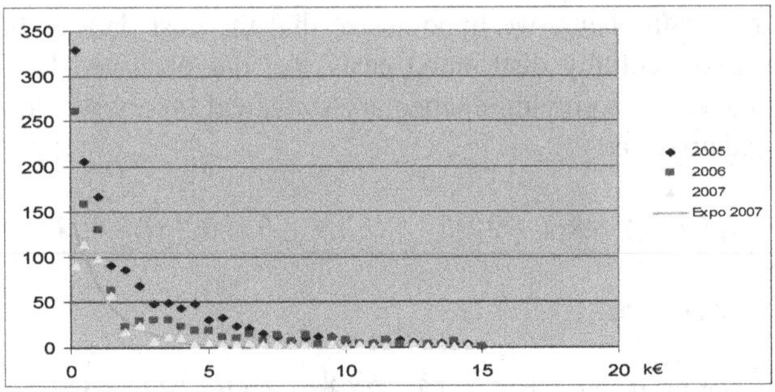

Figure 14. Frequency of All 'Low Direct Costs' Data for 2005 – 2007

At this point we may wonder whether symptoms of a sum of stochastic variables should also appear in the analysis of the number of incidents per time unit. The answer is *no:* the sum of say q independent Poisson-distributed variables with event intensities $\nu_1, \nu_2, \ldots, \nu_q$ is again Poisson-distributed with event intensity $\nu_1+\nu_2+\ldots+\nu_q$.

8 Comments and Conclusions: Present and Future Work

An assumption made was that the individual attacks as well as their consequent costs are independent; this is not always true since some attacks come in bursts. A typical example is successful virus attacks, where many computers and servers become infected by the same virus. Thus, bursts are usually independent but attacks within a burst are correlated.

The present approach can harbor this situation by modeling breach loss $\lambda(t)$ and attack intensity $\nu(t)$ to have coinciding periods with varying combinations of breach loss level and attack intensity level, e.g. frequent low breach loss attacks or rare high breach loss attacks. We are presently modifying the model and the simulation implementation to include a situation with varying and stochastic burst time lengths.

Another critical assumption is that we can estimate the values of the resources to be protected so that we have a fair estimate of breach loss $\lambda(t)$. Admittedly, this is a hard and uncertain activity (Varian 2008; Martin 2006)) and several practitioners within the information and data security communities have strong reservation against the principal possibility of doing so. (Jaquith 2007) is one of them. Despite his explicit rejecting position, the author repeatedly gives good examples of metrics that can be useful for such endeavors. Moreover, individual managers or resource responsible people do make such estimates for specific applications or situations, e.g. by estimating costs caused by virus attacks. These costs include direct costs as listed in Section 7.2 and sometimes loss due to reduced brand value. The estimates may not cover all costs or losses, but they can serve as a floor in security investment decisions.

We make the observation that the model presented does not use the individual entities Threat $T(t)$ and Vulnerability $V(t)$, but their product. As long as Threat and Vulnerability are known individually we may gain additional insight into our security situation, but the present model does not need them such, at least if we do not want to calculate the equivalent of Potential Loss; then we will need the pdf of a stochastic variable Threat $T(t)$ that measures the number of attack attempts per time unit at time t.

Potential Loss is substituted by *VaSR*, *EBL*, *UeBL* and *ETBL* (and others) as defined here, which are much more informative than Potential Loss. With them, we can address management in a terminology that management is familiar with.

References

Abramowitz, M., and Stegun, I. A. (Eds.) "Handbook of mathematical functions," National Bureau of Standard, Washington, DC, 1964, Downloadable from http://www.math.sfu.ca/~cbm/ aands/.

Embrechts, P., Kluppelberg, C., and Mikosch, T. "Modelling Extremal Events," Berlin Heidelberg, Germany, Springer, 2004, Chs. 2-4.

Geocites, "ROI and Economics of Information Security," 2008, Downloadable from http://www.geocities.com/amz/links.html#ROI_ALE .

Gordon, L.A., and M P Loeb, M.P. "The Economics of Information Security Investments," *ACM Transactions on Information and System Security*, **5**^{No4}, November 2002, pp 438-457.

Hulthén, R. "The Gordon-Loeb Investment Model Generalized: Time Dependent Multiple Threats and Breach Losses over an Investment Period," *Workshop on the Economics of Information Security*, 2007-06-07—08. Rump Session presentation. Available from the author rolf.hulthen@telia.com.

Ittelson, T. "Financial Statements. A Step-by-Step Guide to Understanding and Creating Financial Reports," Career Press, Franklin Lakes, NJ, 1998, Chs. 12-13.

Jaquith, A. "Security Metrics. Replacing Fear, Uncertainty, and Doubt," Upper Saddle River, NJ, Addison-Wesley, 2007, Chs. 4 and 7.

Jorion, P. "Value at Risk. The New Benchmark for Managing Financial Risk," 3rd Edition, McGraw-Hill, International Edition, Boston, MA, 2007.

Law, A. M., and Kelton, W. D. "Simulation Modeling and Analysis," McGraw-Hill, New York, NY, 1982.

Martin, L. "The Statistical Value of Information," *The Workshop on the Economics of Securing the Information Infrastructure*, 2006-10-23- -24, Downloadable from http://wesii.econinfosec.org/workshop/.

Moody's http://www.Moody's/cust/default.asp, 2008.

Pindyck, R. S., and Rubinfeld, D.L. "Microeconomics," Prentice Hall International, Inc., Upper Saddle River, NJ, 2001, Chs. 5 and 15.

Richardson, R. "The CSI Survey 2007. The 12th Annual Computer Crime and Security Survey," Downloadable from http://www.GoCSI.com.

RiskMetrics "Risk Management Publications," Downloadable from http://www.riskmetrics.com/, 2008.

Standard & Poor's http://www2.standardandpoors.com/portal/site/sp/en/us/page.my_homepage?lid=us_topnav_mypage, 2008.

Varian, H. R. (Ed.), "The Economics of the Internet, Information Goods, Intellectual Property and Related Issues," Downloadable from http://www2.sims.berkeley.edu/resources/infoecon/, 2008.

Modelling the Human and Technological Costs and Benefits of USB Memory Stick Security

Adam Beautement[1], Robert Coles[2], Jonathan Griffin[3], Christos Ioannidis[4], Brian Monahan[3], David Pym[34*], Angela Sasse[1] and Mike Wonham[3]

[1]UCL, [2]Merrill Lynch, [3]HP Labs, [4]University of Bath

Abstract Organizations deploy systems technologies in order to support their operations and achieve their business objectives. In so doing, they encounter tensions between the confidentiality, integrity, and availability of information, and must make investments in information security measures to address these concerns. We discuss how a macroeconomics-inspired model, analogous to models of interest rate policy used by central banks, can be used to understand trade-offs between investments against threats to confidentiality and availability. We investigate how such a model might be formulated by constructing a process model, based on empirically obtained data, of the use of USB memory sticks by employees of a financial services company.

1 Introduction

Organizations deploy systems technologies in order to support their operations and achieve their business objectives. In so doing, they encounter tensions between the confidentiality, integrity, and availability of information.

In formulating security policies that are intended to resolve such tensions to the organizations' satisfaction, people (e.g., CEOs, CIOs, CISOs, security managers) with responsibility for information and systems security face the following two problems:

1. Poor economic understanding of how to formulate, resource, measure, and value security policies; and
2. Poor organizational understanding of the attitudes of users to both information and systems security and of their responses to imposed security policies (see, for example, the UK Foresight 'Cyber Trust and Crime Prevention' report (Office of Science and Technology 2004)).

---

* Corresponding author.

M.E. Johnson (ed.), *Managing Information Risk and the Economics of Security*,
DOI: 10.1007/978-0-387-09762-6_7,

Consequently, the effectiveness and value of the policies with which users are expected to comply are very difficult to assess, as are the corresponding investment decisions (Anderson 2001; Anderson and Moore 2006). We believe that, in order to assess the effectiveness and value of security investments in a system, be they in people, process, or technology, it is necessary to have a conceptualization (i.e., a model) of the system, including its users, and its economic environment.

In this work, we present an entirely novel approach to the problem of modelling the economic effectiveness of implementing security policies within an organization. The following are the key components of our approach:

- We test the hypothesis that there is a trade-off between the components of investments in information security that address confidentiality and availability (for our present purposes, we suppress integrity);
- For now, we capture primarily conceptually rather than mathematically, the trade-off between availability and confidentiality using a model inspired by a macroeconomic model of the Central Bank Problem (Ruge-Murcia 2001; 2003). Our approach, which considers aggregate values of confidentiality and availability under variation in investment, stands in contrast to the microeconomic approaches described by Gordon and Loeb (Gordon and Loeb 2002; 2006);
- Rather than provide a detailed mathematical formulation, which at this stage in our investigation we are not ready to formulate, we conduct an empirical study together with a (rigorously structured) simulation based on the empirical data and the processes executed by the system. Our simulations embody the dynamics of the conceptual model;
- Our empirical data is obtained from semi-structured interviews with staff at two organizations, a financial services company and a research organization, with a focus here on the financial services organization;
- We demonstrate the use of the model to explore the utility of trade-offs between availability and confidentiality.

The results of our study, and variations upon it, will inform our efforts to design and calibrate economic models of the kind we discuss.

The remainder of the chapter is structured as follows: In Section 2, we explain the form of the economic model of the response of confidentiality and availability to security investments that is of interest to us; in Section 3, we explain how we have obtained our initial empirical data; in Section 4, we explain the key features of our process model of the use of USB memory sticks and, in Section 5, we explain how this model is realized in our systems modelling language, Demos2k (Demos2k); in Section 6, we explain our experimental study, including its relationship to the economic model we sketch in Section 2; and finally, in Section 7, we explain how we intend to pursue this work, explaining the directions of empirical study, process modelling, and economic modelling. We also include two appendices, one containing a summary of the empirical data and one containing the code for our (executable) model; both are available at http://weis2008.econinfosec.org.

2 The Central Bank Problem and Information Security

A well-known problem in macroeconomics concerns the setting of interest rates by a central bank in order to manage, say, inflation and (un)employment. The basic model derives from a line of work including Barro and Gordon (1983), Taylor (1993), and Nobay and Peel (2003).

In very brief summary, for readers who may be unfamiliar with the background, the basic setup of the model is as follows (Ruge-Murcia 2001; 2003):

- Inflation and unemployment are related as

$$u_t = u_t^n - \lambda\left(\pi_t - \pi_t^e\right) + \eta_t,$$

for $\lambda > 0$, where u_t, u_t^n and π_t are, respectively, the rates of unemployment, natural (or target) unemployment, and inflation; π_t^e is the (public) forecast of inflation at time t, constructed at time $t-1$, determined rationally as

$$\pi_t^e = E_{t-1}\pi_t,$$

where E_{t-1} is the expectation conditional on the set of all relevant information available at time $t-1$, denoted I_{t-1}; η_t is an aggregate supply disturbance;

- The natural (or target) rate of unemployment evolves over time, with Δu_t^n depending on the $\Delta u_{t-k}^n s$;
- The central bank affects the rate of inflation via a policy instrument, such as a base interest rate. Such an instrument is imperfect, with imperfections represented by the error term ε_t in the following equation, in which $i_t \in I_{t-1}$:

$$\pi_t = i_t + \varepsilon_t;$$

- The central bank's preferences for inflation and unemployment are captured by a utility, or loss, function of the following form:

$$U\left(\pi_t, u_t\right) = \frac{\phi}{2}\left(\pi_t - \pi_t^*\right)^2 + \frac{\phi}{\gamma^2}\left(\exp\left(\gamma\left(u_t - u_t^*\right)\right) - \gamma\left(u_t - u_t^*\right) - 1\right),$$

where π_t^* and u_t^*, respectively, are the target rates of inflation and unemployment, and ϕ is a parameter; γ is a non-zero real. Here the target unemployment rate is the expected (natural) rate of unemployment:

$$u_t^* = E_{t-1}\left(u_t^n\right).$$

It is assumed that the target inflation, π_t^*, can be approximated by a constant term (Ruge-Murcia 2001; 2003).

Note that the utility function taken in this setup employs the linex function (Varian 1974; Zellner 1986; Clatworthy et al. 2006), of the form

$$g(x) = \left(\exp(\alpha x) - \alpha x - 1\right) / \alpha^2$$

where α is a parameter. In comparison with the use of a quadratic utility function, the linex function admits asymmetry whilst retaining the quadratic as the special (limit) case when α tends to zero.

We argue that a form of the central bank problem (model) can be deployed to explain trade-offs in investments in information security. In our present case, we are concerned with the trade-off between availability and confidentiality, in the particular setting of the overall availability of information derived from the use of USB memory sticks set against the overall increased exposure of confidential information that is a consequence of their use. The analogy goes as follows:

- Availability and confidentiality, respectively, correspond to inflation and unemployment. The policy instrument is the level of investment in information security countermeasures;
- Availability and confidentiality are related as follows:
  - As availability increases, the potential for exposures increases, and confidentiality decreases. Confidentiality is also reduced by increased levels of threat to confidentiality
    $$C = -\lambda A + \varepsilon_C,$$
    where λ is a parameter and ε_C is a non-decreasing stochastic process (so expectation is non-zero) for the threat to confidentiality;
  - Availability depends both on the level of investment in information security, negatively in the case of the study discussed in this chapter, and on the level of threat to availability
    $$A = -\Psi I + \varepsilon_A,$$
    where the instrument I is security investment or, perhaps, system complexity, Ψ is a (possibly negative) parameter and ε_A is a non-decreasing stochastic process for the threat to availability. More generally, we might also require a term in changes ΔI in the instrument I, with various dependencies;
- For utility, in terms of expectations, we might take, for example,
  $$E\left(U(C,A)\right) = E\left(\left(\exp[\alpha A] - \alpha A - 1\right)/\alpha^2 + \frac{\phi}{2}C^2\right),$$
  where ϕ is a parameter, as before;
- Such a formulation does have analytic solutions for I, in terms of expectation, of the form
  $$I = E\left(\frac{1}{\Psi}\left[\varepsilon_A - \frac{\varepsilon C}{\lambda} - \frac{1}{\alpha\lambda^2\phi} + \text{ProductLog}\left[\frac{\exp\left(\frac{\alpha\varepsilon_C}{\lambda} + \frac{1}{\lambda^2\phi}\right)}{\lambda^2\phi}\right]\right]\right),$$
  where, as in Mathematica (2008), ProductLog[z] is a solution for w in $z = w\exp(w)$. A discussion of this solution and its significance is beyond our present scope, as is a discussion of a multi-period model.

As we have remarked, in the context of information systems, the instrument I might be a measure of investment in information security, or a measure of the complexity of the system. For an example of the latter, we might take a 'complexity parameter', $x \in [0,1)$, and then take $I=1/(1-x)$. Then if $x=0$, we have a maximally simple system (a single unit) and, as x approaches 1, and so I approaches infinity, we can obtain an arbitrarily complex system.

In business contexts, systems users who have access to confidential and business-critical information make widespread use of USB memory sticks. They do so for good reasons: these devices efficiently enable data transfer between all manner of business colleagues and partners. The use of these devices also exposes organizations to risks of losses of confidential data, owing to their capability to transfer all kinds of data conveniently and cheaply to anyone capable of receiving it. Thus there is a trade-off between availability and confidentiality (we suppress consideration of integrity issues in this context, where it can be argued that they are minor), and there is an incentive incompatibility between the users of the systems and owners of the policies.

In this chapter, we study the use of USB memory sticks by the staff of a financial services firm, in the context of a model of the form discussed above. We do not attempt to reify such a model analytically, even at this level of detail. Rather, we demonstrate the dynamics of a simple instance using an executable model of the system of USB users using a process model.

The model, built on the basis of empirically obtained data, executes processes that track availability and breaches of confidentiality under specified levels of security investment. In assessing our experimental results within the executable model, we employ, for illustrative purposes, perhaps the simplest form of utility function that might possibly be useful:

$$U(C,A) = \alpha(A - \beta C),$$

where α and β are parameters; the details of the choices here are explained in Section 6.

3 An Empirical Study

To obtain an empirical basis for our model, we conducted a study to elicit factors that contribute to corporate and individual security cost. One of the academic researchers conducted 17 in-depth interviews with security staff, employees, and managers in the two companies that are partners in this research project. The interviews remained anonymous.

The interviews were semi-structured, exploring

- the tasks and responsibilities of interviewees,
- their perception of the risks facing the company,

- their attitudes to the company's security polices and security measures, and
- the perceived impact of security measures on individuals' tasks and responsibilities, as well as company productivity.

Whilst the interviews covered a range of security policies and measures, all interviewees were asked about one specific security problem: USB sticks. They were asked

- if they used USB sticks (all did),
- how they used them as part of their tasks and responsibilities,
- about the relationship between the risks facing their company, and their USB stick usage,
- if whether any of their USB stick usage contravened the company's security policies, and if so,
- why they thought contravening the security policy was justified.

We suggested the company was considering making the use of encrypted USB sticks mandatory (for the financial services company, this was actually the case), and asked interviewees to

- explore the cost and benefits of such a policy for the company, and
- explain the cost and benefit for them and their tasks and responsibilities.

The interviews were transcribed and analyzed using techniques from Grounded Theory. Grounded Theory (Strauss and Corbine 1990) is a qualitative data analysis method widely used in social sciences, which allows identification of salient concepts and relationships between them. Over the past 10 years, the method has been successfully applied to model user perceptions and attitudes in Human-Computer Interaction in general. Adams and Sasse (1999) used this approach to identify factors that affect employees' perceptions of corporate security policies, and Weirich and Sasse (2001) modelled employee decision-making on compliance with password security policies.

For the study reported in this chapter, only the sections on USB stick policies and tasks and situations surrounding their usage were analyzed. We coded the interviews using axial coding (the first stage of Grounded Theory) to produce an inventory of the individual employee's cost and benefit associated with USB stick usage, and the cost and benefit for the organization. The data were coded by two researchers independently.

The range of roles performed by the interview subjects was relatively diverse, from security managers to part-time researchers, as was the range and frequency of security related comments they produced. There were also noticeable differences in USB usage between the various interview subjects. From the interviews, we were able to identify two main USB stick usage scenarios. These scenarios broadly corresponded to the type of organization for which the subject worked. We have focused on the first of these scenarios in which the USB stick is used as a transport medium for data. This scenario is described in detail below. The second scenario, corresponding to the research organization, in which the USB stick is also used as a primary data storage device, will not be covered here.

The following scenario is more representative of the financial services organization. In this scenario, the USB stick is primarily used for temporary storage for transit between locations such as an employee visiting a client company to deliver a presentation. The data required to deliver the presentation would be copied from the company's computer system onto the USB stick and taken to the client's location. Any data which must be brought back to the home company can be copied from the client's system onto the USB stick and brought back by the employee.

The data in this case is always backed up, either on the home company's system or the client company. The data is never unique and so a loss of a security stick cannot constitute a long-term availability issue. While a short-term loss of availability can be detrimental — the cost is to the individual, with possible small collateral reputation loss for the parent company if the clients need to resend data, etc. — it is unlikely to have a significant impact on the company.

A far bigger concern for the security manager in this scenario are the potential confidentiality issues resulting from company data being transported through unsecure locations while in transit to and from the client. If the USB stick were to be lost or stolen at this time, while containing unencrypted data, then the cost in terms of reputation and lost business would be to the company itself rather than the individual. While the company can punish the individual internally, it cannot recoup its losses by doing so. This scenario encourages the security manager to take a 'confidentiality first' approach when designing the USB control policy. We opted to focus on this scenario when describing our individual and organizational costs as it provided a relatively simple set of actions that encompassed the key points.

At this point we created a list of the actions required to complete the task in the scenario. This then was converted into a set of tables detailing the task at each stage, the cost to the individual, the cost to the organization, a possible failure mode at that juncture, and the cost to each of that failure. Appendix A (available at http://weis2008.econinfosec.org) contains the results of the empirical study, in tabulated form.

The data obtained in our empirical study, which has not been explored in this chapter, will be considered in future work.

4 The Conceptual Model

The empirical study discussed in Section 3 has presented ways in which USB sticks are used in two large organizations. In particular, this study shows that certain classes of events and risks arise during the course of the life-histories of USB sticks and their owners. This information provides a rich corpus that we can use to make modelling decisions. Accordingly, we have embodied these classes of events and risks within the process model we now present. More specifically, we take, as the primary input to our model, the data obtained from the financial services organization.

For simplicity, we consider the organization of interest to consist in the collection of its individuals. Thus we can capture the behaviour of the organization, at this rather crude level of abstraction, by capturing the behaviour of a typical individual.

The purpose of our model is to embody the behaviour of our intended macroeconomics-inspired model of the relationship between the confidentiality and availability of information owned by an organization that uses USB memory sticks to support its operations. In this model, the instrument that is available to the organization is investment in information security. For the purposes of this study, we identify the following three types of investment:

- *Training* — individuals are trained to understand and work within the organization's information security policies;
- *IT Support* — the organization provides specialist IT personnel to help individuals resolve problems;
- *Monitoring* — the organization monitors the behaviour of the individuals with respect to its information security policies.

Our focus of attention for this model concerns the use of encryption of data held on USB memory sticks.

For each type of investment, we consider the idea of a *transfer function,* which associates to a given level of investment a certain parameter that is used to calculate the effect of a given level of investment. In the cases of *Training* and *IT Support*, the transfer function returns a value in the real interval [0,1]; in the case of *Monitoring*, the transfer function returns a (real) time interval. There are many reasonable choices for these functions, and we take simple exemplars, chosen primarily for their shape, on the presumption that more investment will generally increase the business proficiency and efficacy of the matter of interest, and they are guided by the following considerations:

- Whether they are monotonic increasing/decreasing;
- What limits they tend to;
- The presence of threshold effects for investment; and
- Algebraic simplicity.

We do not claim anything else for these particular functions — we do not know a priori what these functions ought to be, and so we leave that as an open question for further investigation. We consider them in turn.

First, the Training transfer function: The idea is that this transfer function takes the portion of the overall security investment budget allocated for training and specifies the probability of the individual making support calls. As the budget for training increases, the individual becomes more proficient and needs to make fewer and fewer support calls. We assume, however, that there is always a background need to make some support calls, for example, having to do with aligning the USB encryption with organizational systems configurations. Thus the transfer function has output in [0,1] and is monotonically decreasing with increasing training budget. We further assume that a minimal amount of training is needed before there is any reduction in the probability of an individual making a support call. The form we have chosen for this function, where *inv* is the investment variable, is:

$$trainingTF(inv) = (b - c)(\min(1, a / inv)) + c,$$

illustrated in Figure 1; the parameters *a*, *b*, and *c* are defined as follows:

- *a* = minimum training investment threshold: The amount of investment needed before there is any effect on training and reduction on the probability of needing support;
- *b* = maximum probability of needing support: This value is attained when no training is given at all;
- *c* = minimum probability of needing support: We assume that there is a baseline, underlying need for IT support, no matter how trained the employees are. Clearly, we require $b \geq c$.

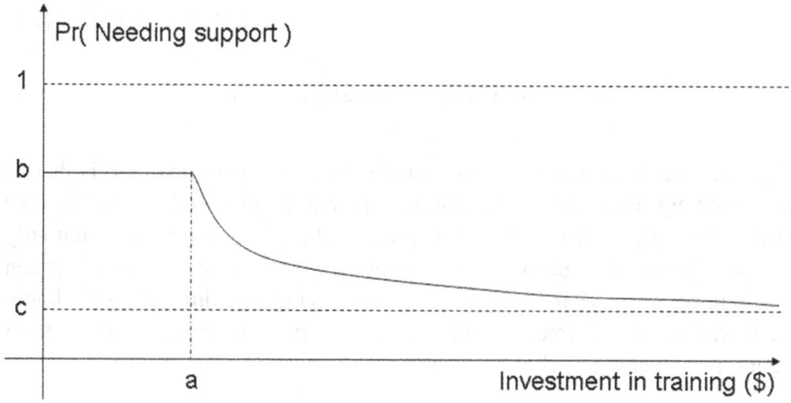

Figure 1. The 'Training' Transfer Function

Second, the IT Support transfer function: The idea here is that as security investment in IT support increases, the probability of a successful interaction with support also increases. The transfer function shows how this investment affects this probability, and is this time monotonically increasing. Just as for training, there is a minimum amount of investment required before any benefit is realised. The form we have chosen for this function is:

$$ITsupportTF(inv) = \max(0, b(1 - a / inv)),$$

illustrated in Figure 2; the parameters *a* and *b* are defined as follows:

- a = minimum IT support threshold: The minimum amount of investment required before there is any effect on the probability of the success of IT support;
- b = maximum probability of successful support: This is naturally a limiting value, which we assume can be achieved arbitrarily closely.

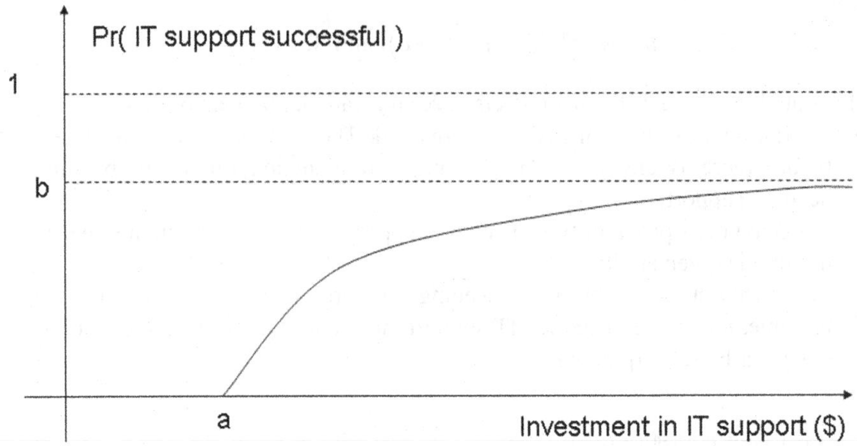

Figure 2. The 'IT Support' Transfer Function

Finally, the Compliance Monitoring transfer function: The idea here is that as security investment in compliance monitoring increases, this leads to an effective increase in the frequency with which compliance checks are made, so potentially improving the effectiveness of monitoring. Consequently, the time interval between checks will decrease. The transfer function specifying the time interval should therefore monotonically decrease as budgeted investment increases — the form of this function is conveniently chosen to be:

$$monitoringTF(inv) = (b - c)(\min(1, a / inv)) + c,$$

illustrated in Figure 3. The parameters a, b, and c are defined as follows:

- a = minimum monitoring investment threshold: The minimum amount of investment required before there is any reduction on the time interval between monitoring checks;
- b = maximum time interval between monitoring checks: A notional maximum amount of time between checks — in practice, this can simply be a very large number;
- c = minimum time interval between checks: It is assumed that each check must take some amount of time to complete — thus the time interval *between* these checks cannot be less than this. Clearly, we require $b \geq c$.

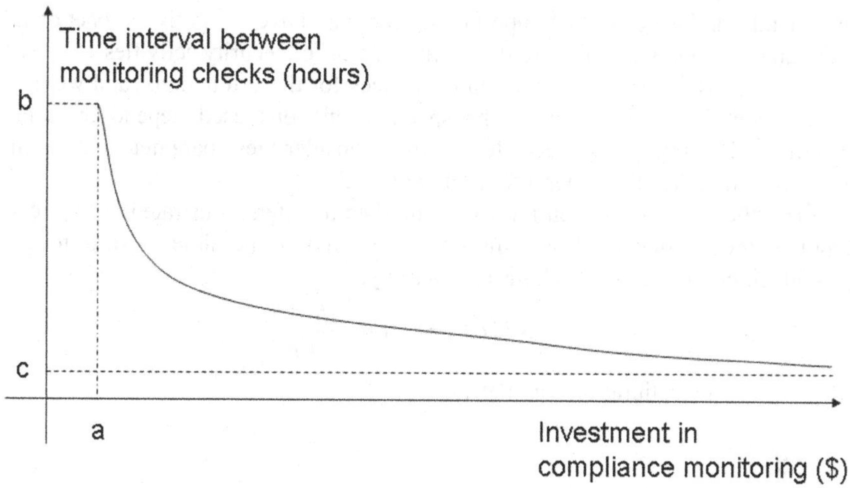

Figure 3. The 'Compliance Monitoring' Transfer Function

The transfer functions are used to determine the probability that a typical individual will employ encryption, in the manner intended by the security policy, when using a USB memory stick. Note that we are not in a position to give an analytic definition of this probability. Rather, this is the point at which we appeal to our empirical data and the simulations provided by our model (the code is given in Appendix B, available at http://weis2008.econinfosec.org). A key component of the model is the *individual's scoring function,*

EQ *indScore*:*R*\s\up5(4)→*R*\,

where *R* denotes the reals, expressing an individual's cost–benefit over the following four indicators:

- Successful data transfers (*trf*) — successful transfer of data is treated as a proxy for an individual's productivity;
- Embarrassments (*emb*) — events which damage the reputation of the individual, such as inability to recall a password in the presence of a customer;
- Reprimands (*ding*) — management may reprimand individuals for failing to comply with policy, and repeated reprimands may lead to serious sanctions;
- Negative experiences with IT Support (*nsup*) — interactions with IT Support may be unsatisfactory, and may fail to solve an individual's problem.

For the present study, we take the scoring function to be given by

$$indScore(trf, emb, ding, nsup) = dtSF(trf) + eSF(emb) + dSF(ding) + nsSF(nsup),$$

where *dtSF*, *eSF*, *dSF*, and *nsSF* are chosen functions that capture the dependency of the overall score on the evident components. Note that the scoring functions *eSF*, *dSF*, and *nsSF* are all negative-valued and decreasing because embarrassments, reprimands, and negative IT Support experiences all have a negative impact on an individual's assessment of the cost-benefit trade-off of security activities.

As usual, there are many reasonable choices for these functions, and we take simple exemplars. In all cases, the specific functions used depend on some specific 'calibration parameters'. Rather than consider these parameters in detail, we explain here just the general form of the functions.

First, the scoring function for successful data transfers, illustrated in Figure 4, captures the existence of a limit on the maximum possible reward to the individual, no matter how high his productivity:

$$dtSF(trf) = a\left(1 - \frac{b}{trf + b}\right),$$

where $a,b>0$ are calibration parameters.

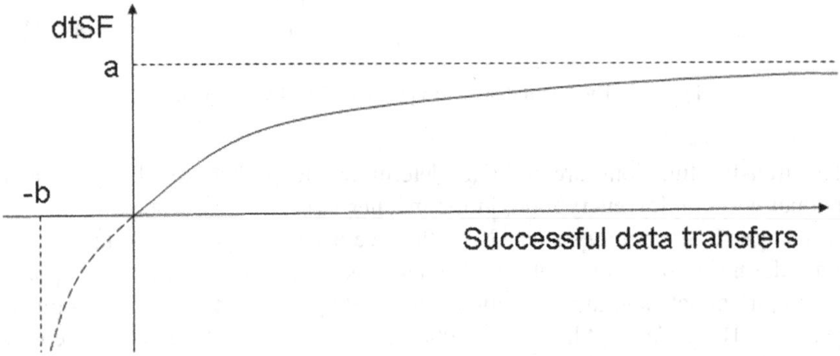

Figure 4. Individual Scoring Function for Successful Data Transfers

Personal embarrassments reduce the individual's score, so the scoring function *eSF*, illustrated in Figure 5, is negative decreasing; we assume that costs of embarrassments accumulate unboundedly:

$$eSF(emb) = -\, a(emb),$$

where $a>0$ is a calibration parameter.

Reprimands from management also reduce an individual's score, and the greater the number of reprimands, the smaller the effect of subsequent reprimands. The function *dSF*, illustrated in Section 6, has the following form:

$$dSF(ding) = a\left(\frac{b}{ding + b} - 1\right),$$

where $a,b>0$ are calibration parameters.

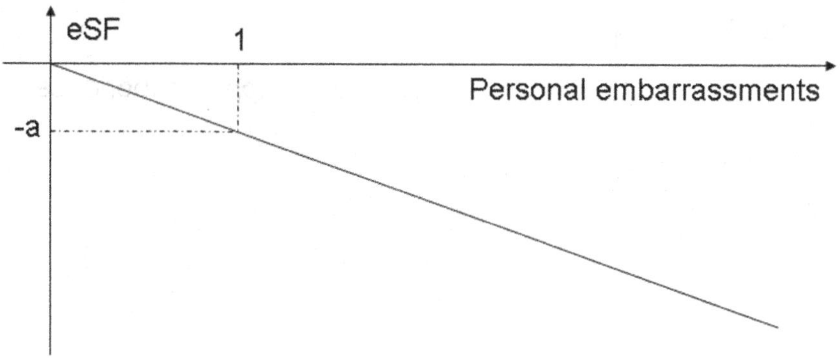

Figure 5. Individual Scoring Function for Personal Embarrassments

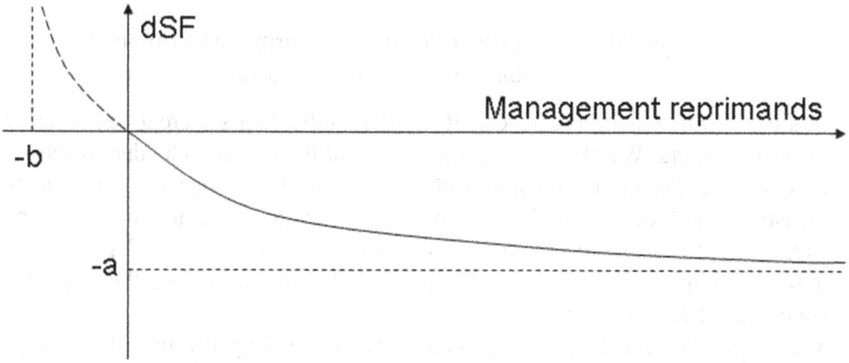

Figure 6. Individual Scoring Function for Management Reprimands

Finally, we consider the function *nsSF*, illustrated in Figure 7. Here we assume that the user's response to his failing to receive adequate support deteriorates as he experiences more such failures. We expect that it eventually overrides other factors, representing the encryption technology's becoming unusable and being given up. We take

$$nsSF\left(n\,\mathrm{s}\,up\right) = -a\left(n\,\mathrm{s}\,up^{2}\right),$$

with a calibration parameter $a > 0$.

The typical individual's probability of using encryption is now obtained as follows:

- By using the above transfer and scoring functions, the model essentially becomes a function with a number of input parameters that maps over security investment, then security budget proportions, then probability of encryption, resulting in an overall numerical score as output. Informally,

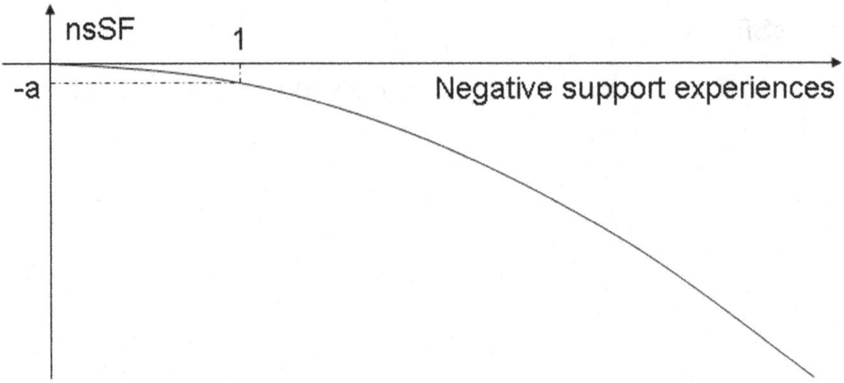

Figure 7. Individual Scoring Function for Support Failures

model : security-investment → security-budget-proportions → probability-of-encryption → score.

Intuitively, this function represents the typical individual's score given all these input parameters. We also assume, however, that the typical individual responds rationally to the organizational environment (as determined by the security investment and the security budget proportions) by choosing how frequently he uses encryption, so as to maximize his perceived overall score. This rational maximization of benefit by the typical individual is therefore the basis for choosing the encryption probability;

- Mathematically speaking, our procedure for computing the probability p of encryption is to take $p \in [0,1]$ such that p is the (unique) value that maximizes the overall score as a function of security investment and security budget proportions:

$$\sup \{ model(sec)(sec\text{–}budget)(p) \in R \mid p \in [0,1] \}$$

where $sec \in sec\text{–}range$ and *sec–range* is a subset of R, representing the range of security investments to be investigated and where *sec–budget* ranges over the budgetary splits we could make (e.g., IT support, etc.). Technically, this function might have several optima as p ranges over [0,1]; that is unlikely since the transfer and scoring functions are clearly monotonic (and also concave/convex) and we assume that they are sufficiently smooth for there to be a unique choice maximizing the score;
- This function is expressed in terms of an executable discrete event model involving stochastically generated events (see Section 5). Therefore, the numerical answers that we obtain are generally approximate. In effect, the computation we are making involves fixing discrete values for the security investment, the security budget proportions and then performing a range of experiments ranging over discrete values for the probability of encryption. Each of these

experimental variations are then performed a large number of times in order to obtain statistically valid outcomes from which we choose the probability value that maximizes the score. Intuitively, the multiple runs performed for each of the choices taken represents finding the average score over our typical population (we assume, for now, a homogeneous population).

The probability of using encryption has direct consequences for the utility function that derives from the model. The calculation of this function is explained in Section 6.

5 An Executable Model

The conceptual model described in the previous section is reified using our modelling tool, Demos2k (Demos2k; Birtwistle 1979], which executes discrete event models of systems of resources and processes. Demos2k has rigorous mathematical semantics (Birtwistle and Tofts 1993; 1994; 1998; 2001a; 2001b) based on process algebra (Milner 1983; 1989; Pym and Tofts 2006; 2007), which can be understood in both asynchronous and synchronous terms. Our modelling technique is to deploy the discrete mathematical tools of resource semantics (Pym 2002; Pym and Tofts 2006; 2007), process algebra (Milner 1989; Pym and Tofts 2006; 2007), and probability theory/stochastic processes (Demos2k; Tofts 1994] in the style of classical applied mathematics (see Yearworth et al. (2006) for another example of the approach); that is, we identify levels of abstraction that are appropriate to the questions of interest, and avoid representing irrelevant detail.

We model the life-history of the composite entity 'a typical individual together with his current USB stick' to illustrate how various forms of risk are encountered within a given amount of time. By modelling these risk encounters explicitly, we can obtain a better quantitative picture of how the risks identified are naturally distributed. Modelling this composite entity (i.e., the 'user') allows us to ignore aspects of an individual's own life that do not involve any dealings with the USB stick.

For there to be any risk to confidentiality or availability, we need to introduce some particular sources of hazard. For this investigation, there are two principal components contributing to the hazards that arise: the user's physical location and the categories of people with whom the user intentionally or unintentionally shares data. For the purposes of this model, we broadly categorize the people we share data with as follows: whether they are a colleague or business partner who might legitimately share the information (i.e., a 'Friend'), or someone who will actively misuse the information gained to somehow harm the organization or the user (i.e. a 'Foe'), or, finally, someone who appears to the user as a Friend but *in actual fact* acts like a Foe (i.e., a 'Traitor'). Both of these aspects — location and categories of people we share data with — are explicitly represented in the model.

The outcome of running the model will be values of various performance indicators gathered as a part of simulating the life-histories:

- Number of successful data transfers to/from the USB device: This is used as a straightforward proxy for productivity — we assume that using a USB stick to transfer data has business benefit;
- Total number of exposures: Occasions on which information was transferred to either a Foe or a Traitor;
- Total number of 'reveals': A 'reveal' is less significant than an exposure and arises when a colleague or business partner (i.e., a Friend) is given information that they did not have a right to see. Because they are Friends, they are not expected to use that information to cause harm to the organization or the user. One way in which this can arise is via 'accidental archiving' — information that was unintentionally made available alongside other information that was intended to be shared.

Various other indicators are also gathered as output from each run; these have already been discussed in Section 4.

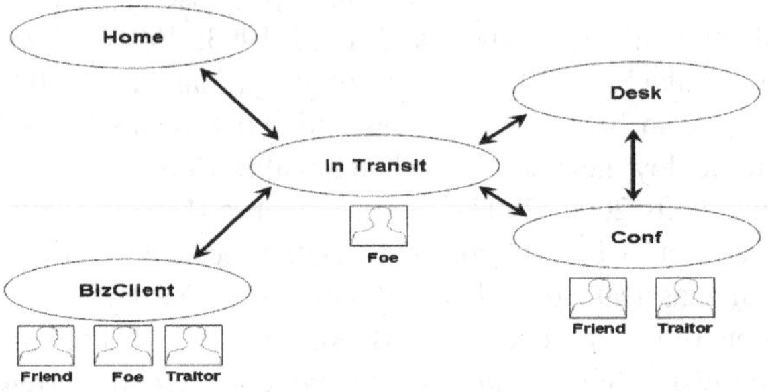

Figure 8. Locations and Roles

The model comprises three main concurrent processes: *lifeUSB*, *movement*, and *measure*:

- *lifeUSB*: This process captures the activities of the 'individual plus his USB stick'. The user essentially interacts with different kinds of people in different locations, and indicators are accumulated as a result. Particular events involving the USB stick, such as *add/modify*, *write*, *delete*, etc., are randomly selected according to (discrete) probability distributions, conditional upon current location. As a result of these actions and interactions, we use a combination of time penalties and indicators to capture and account for the risks encountered.
- *movement*: This process concurrently and independently moves the user from location to location, spending some time in each place. The different locations we use are:
- *Home*: The user's personal home;
  - *Desk*: The main place of (solitary) work for the user;
  - *Conf*: This is where business meetings with Friends (and, potentially, Traitors) occur;

  - *BizClient*: Business meetings/workshops/conferences with business partners or other actors (i.e., principally Friends, but with some potential for talking to Traitors and Foes);
  - *InTransit*: This represents intermediate locations (e.g., on a plane, in a hotel, in a car) between main locations.

  Each location naturally has its own associated risks and opportunities for interaction. The transitions between locations follow the graph presented in Figure 8. Note that we assume that the user can move directly between the workplace locations Desk and Conf without going via the riskier InTransit location. Future locations for the user are chosen according to a location-dependent probability distribution, as well as the period of time they spend there;
- *measure*: A bookkeeping process that samples the various indicators gathered on a regular basis throughout each run.

The Demos2k code for the model we described is given in Appendix B, available at http://weis2008.econinfosec.org.

6 The Experimental Space

Now that we have our executable model, we can use it to explore how the level of security investment by an organization is connected to particular levels of availability and confidentiality, as modulated and affected by changes in typical employee behaviour, vis-à-vis his use of USB memory sticks. The organization's choices of amount and balance of security investment affect the usage of encryption on USB sticks by typical employees. This usage results in levels of information availability and confidentiality loss, which translate into business value for the organization.

Our experiments, performed using Demos2k (Demos2k) and its DXM experiment manager (Monahan 2008), varied the following numerical instruments:

- Security Investment: This indicates the level of yearly investment per individual in security related cost. The range we have explored is: 20, 50, 100, 200, 500;
- Budgetary Proportions: Although we have three areas in which to invest — *training, IT support* and *monitoring* — we have specified a fixed value of training, since it is a one-off cost. So we have investigated the trade-off between investment in IT support on the one hand, and monitoring on the other. In practice, we have chosen to investigate 3 values of support proportion: 0.25, 0.5 and 0.75[30].

[30] A support proportion of 0.25 means that 1/4 of the total security investment goes towards IT support and the remainder goes towards monitoring.

Each of these 15 (3×5) sample points represents a particular experimental variation. Following the approach to obtaining the individual's probability of using encryption, explained in § 4, within each of these variations we then need to range over *Pr*(*Enc*), the probability of encryption, (from 0.1 to 0.9 in steps of 0.2) and finally run each of these 300 times to obtain results of some statistical value.

For simplicity of presentation in this chapter, we have had to restrict the number of experimental simulations, and so we have adopted a coarse-grain 'sampling' strategy to choose parameters. We plan to conduct a more thorough and systematic experimental investigation based on empirical evidence to support the form of the transfer and scoring functions; where that is not possible, we hope to perform a systematic investigation of the space of parameters. The objective of such an investigation is to provide detailed guidance for conditioning economic models of the kind we have discussed.

6.1 Exploratory Fit of Additional Calibration Parameters

The transfer and scoring functions given are each dependent upon a number of numerical parameters. At this stage, it has not been possible to find obvious choices for these parameters — there are no easy and obvious sources of data, and there are no 'natural scales' that we could obviously exploit in order to make considered and easily justified choices. Further empirical study and experimental work will be necessary to address this issue.

Instead, we have taken the pragmatic decision to make choices of these parameters that illustrate a range of behaviour. To do this, we have conducted a series of exploratory (ad hoc) searches through the space of additional calibration parameters, helping to locate values of these parameters that yield useful observable output. We cannot claim therefore that this study has given definitive or canonical results. We instead claim that there is evidence here for examining the connections between these concerns in greater depth.

6.2 Some Confirmation of Expected Behaviour

As investment in monitoring and IT Support increased, we expected to see greater use of encryption; that was observed.

We expected to see a variation in the effectiveness of that investment as the proportion spent on IT Support vs. Monitoring was varied. As illustrated by the results below, we did not observe any such effect: the influence of a given level of investment is roughly the same for different proportions. We expected to be able to see a gradual increase in the use of encryption as investment increased, but the results show a fairly sharp transition from probability of encryption of 0.1 to 0.9 between investment values of 100 and 200. (Examining the data in more detail than shown here emphasizes this effect. The individual's optimal choice of probability (as computed from the experimental results) is always at one of the extremes, and never at a middle value.) We also expected that, above and below certain limits, there would be little extra effect from further increasing or reducing the investment level: this is not contradicted by the model (it is mildly confirmed).

6.3 Results

In Section 4, we described how to extract information about our estimate for *Pr(Enc)* for a given level of security investment and budgetary proportions, based upon the individual's scoring function. Intuitively, this value is the one that produces the maximum value of this scoring function at that investment level.

The table below gives the value of *Pr(Enc)*, for the budgetary proportion dedicated to IT support versus security investment:

Table 1. Value of *Pr(Enc)*

	20	**50**	**100**	**200**	**500**
0.25	0.1	0.1	0.1	0.9	0.9
0.5	0.1	0.1	0.1	0.9	0.9
0.75	0.1	0.1	0.1	0.9	0.9

This table shows that, for security investment of 100 and below, the user's best choice is *Pr(Enc)* = 0.1; that is, rarely to use encryption. For security investment of 200 and above, the user's best choice is *Pr(Enc)* = 0.9; that is, nearly always to use encryption. (We did not consider *Pr(Enc)* of 0 or 1 because such utterly consistent user behaviour is rare.)

Next we tabulate the observed values of the availability measure and of the confidentiality measure over the 15 sample points, with the user's *Pr(Enc)* fixed at the corresponding value shown in the table above.

The availability measure is chosen to be the average number of successful data transfers per year carried out by the user. This is under the assumption that the purpose of the USB stick is to enable the user to transfer data on behalf of the organization.

Table 2. Availability Measure

	20	**50**	**100**	**200**	**500**
0.25	165.093316	164.0433177	165.106651	161.2066513	161.1899847
0.5	163.453318	163.5266511	165.5766509	162.6299845	161.453318
0.75	164.729983	165.6333176	164.2733177	161.2266513	161.6966513

The confidentiality measure we use is a linear combination of the average number of events when confidential data is exposed and the average amount of confidential data exposed, both per year.

Table 3. Confidentiality Measure

	20	50	100	200	500
0.25	10.02999905	8.26666588	9.326665779	5.85666611	6.626666036
0.5	8.176665889	7.876665917	9.123332465	6.106666086	6.886666012
0.75	9.519999094	7.966665909	8.569999185	6.449999386	5.486666145

We can observe that there is a substantial change in both the organization's availability and confidentiality measures as the user's probability of using encryption, *Pr(Enc)*, changes from 0.1 to 0.9.

The results are all obtained as averages over 300 independent runs. These values conservatively have a standard error of less than 10% of the values in the table. Given the number of runs required, it seems that the standard error might be halved by performing 1200 runs.

All of these results are preliminary. Further, and quite extensive, experimental work will be required to obtain adequate confidence interval estimates for the numbers quoted above.

6.4 A Utility Function

We have discussed, in Section 2, a utility function approach to understanding the trade-offs between availability and confidentiality. We suggest that the simplest utility function it seems reasonable to postulate is one of the form

$$U(C, A) = \alpha(A - \beta C),$$

where α and β are parameters, which captures a simple ratio between confidentiality and availability.

Below are some tabulations of values for this function for different values of α,β, based upon the tables of availability and confidentiality numbers presented above. Exploring parameters of the utility function, illustrated in the tables below, we see that for values of β=10 or 3, as spending on support and monitoring increases, the gain from increased confidentiality clearly outweighs the consequent loss of availability. β=0.1 results in the loss in availability as spending increases outweighing the gain in confidentiality. Values of β in the region of 1 didn't give us useful results for utility, because statistical variation in experimental results swamps the difference between availability and confidentiality components of utility.

Table 4. Utility Function for α=1.164, β=10.000

	20	**50**	**100**	**200**	**500**
0.25	75.44987339	94.76066264	83.65550334	119.52117	110.5353456
0.5	95.12164829	98.70045181	86.57055909	118.2674243	107.814368
0.75	80.96557825	100.1055786	91.49626593	112.6352725	124.4002981

Table 5. Utility Function for α=0.714, β=3.000

	20	**50**	**100**	**200**	**500**
0.25	96.33782579	99.36347244	97.85302782	102.4985371	100.8382374
0.5	99.13512178	99.82968844	98.62371136	102.979025	100.4695461
0.75	97.17035435	101.1403263	98.87822724	101.2426083	103.6496

Table 6. Utility Function for α=0.615, β=0.100

	20	**50**	**100**	**200**	**500**
0.25	100.9077518	100.3704883	100.9592029	98.77427677	98.71667626
0.5	100.013201	100.0767461	101.2607345	99.63418527	98.86262497
0.75	100.7156816	101.3667113	100.4932739	98.75008864	99.09835674

7 Conclusions and Directions

We have reported a preliminary study. We have postulated an economic model that is suitable for capturing the utility of trade-offs between investments against confidentiality and availability in the context of the use of USB memory sticks in a financial services company. Building on empirically obtained data and on informed observations concerning policy and technology, we have used a process model to demonstrate that the hypothesized trade-off between confidentiality and availability does indeed exist, so providing evidence for the validity of the model, and to investigate the behaviour of a simple version of this model, giving good evidence to support the approach and motivate further study. We have established that individuals make cost–benefit decisions from their own (economic) perspective; we suggest organizations must understand that when making investment decisions.

The following is a brief list of possible research directions:

- Further exploration of our experimental space, with substantial statistical analyses to inform the detailed formulation of economics models of the kind we have discussed;
- Mathematical and computational studies of the properties of these models;

- An investigation of game-theoretic approaches to the utility of the allocation security investment resources against competing priorities such as confidentiality and availability;
- More basic empirical studies of the kind we have described; for example, more studies of portable data storage media, or studies of network access control policies;
- Developments of our process modelling tool better to handle the structure of distributed systems.

The work reported here is the result of a highly interdisciplinary study. Such an approach seems to us to be necessary to make progress in this area.

Acknowledgments

We are grateful to the many members of staff of HP Labs and Merrill Lynch who generously gave their time to take part in our empirical studies. We also thank Jean Paul Degabriele for his advice on the early stages of this work.

References

Anderson. R., and Moore, T. "The Economics of Information Security," *Science* (314), 2006, pp. 610–613. Extended version available at http://www.cl.cam.ac.uk/~rja14/Papers/toulouse-summary.pdf.

Anderson, R. "Why Information Security Is Hard: An Economic Perspective," in *Proceedings 17th Annual Computer Security Applications Conference*, 2001.

Adams, A.L., and Sasse, M.A. "Users Are Not the Enemy: Why Users Compromise Security Mechanisms and How to Take Remedial Measures," *Communications of the ACM* (42:12), 1999, pp. 40–46.

Barro, R., and Gordon, D. "A Positive Theory of Monetary Policy in a Natural Rate Model," *Journal of Political Economy* (91), 1983, pp. 589–610.

Birtwistle, G. *Demos — discrete event modelling on Simula*. Macmillan, 1979.

Birtwistle, G., and Tofts, C. "An Operational Semantics of Process-Orientated Simulation Languages: Part I,", Demos. *Transactions of the Society for Computer Simulation* (10:4), 1993, pp. 299–333.

Birtwistle, G., and Tofts, C. "An Operational Semantics of Process-Orientated Simulation Languages: Part II," Demos. *Transactions of the Society for Computer Simulation* (11:4), 1994 pp. 303–336.

Birtwistle, G., and Tofts, C. "A Denotational Semantics for a Process-Based Simulation Language," *ACM ToMaCS* (8:3), 1998, pp. 281–305.

Birtwistle, G., and Tofts, C. "Getting Demos Models Right — Part I Practice," *Simulation Practice and Theory* (8:6-7), 2001, pp. 377–393.

Birtwistle, G., and Tofts, C. "Getting Demos Models Right — Part II ... and Theory," *Simulation Practice and Theory* (8:6-7), 2001, pp. 395–414.

Mathematica Documentation Center. http://reference.wolfram.com/mathematica/guide/Mathematica.html. 2008.

Clatworthy, M., Peel, D., and Pope, P. "Are Analysts' Loss Functions Asymmetric?" *Technical Report 005*, Lancaster University Management School, 2006.

Demos2k. http://www.demos2k.org.

Gordon, L.A., and Loeb, M.P. "The Economics of Information Security Investment," *ACM Transactions on Information and Systems Security* (5:4), 2002, pp. 438–457.

Gordon, L.A., and Loeb, M.P. *Managing Cybersecurity Resources: A Cost-Benefit Analysis*. McGraw Hill, 2006.

Milner, R. "Calculi for Synchrony and Asynchrony," *Theoretical Computer Science* (25:3), 1983, pp. 267–310.

Milner, R. *Communication and Concurrency*. Prentice-Hall, 1989.

Monahan, B. "DXM: Demos Experiments Manager," Forthcoming *HP Labs Technical Report*, 2008.

Nobay, R.A., and Peel, D.A. "Optimal Discretionary Monetary Policy in a Model of Asymmetric Bank Preferences," *The Economic Journal* (113:489), 2003. pp. 657–665.

Pym, D., and Tofts, C. "A Calculus and Logic of Resources and Processes," *Formal Aspects of Computing* (18:4), 2006, pp. 495–517, Erratum (with Collinson, M.) *Formal Aspects of Computing* (19) 2007, pp. 551–554.

Pym, D., and Tofts, C. "Systems Modelling via Resources and Processes: Philosophy, Calculus, Semantics, and Logic," in Cardelli, L., Fiore, M., and Winskel, G. (Eds), *Electronic Notes in Theoretical Computer Science (Computation, Meaning, and Logic: Articles dedicated to Gordon Plotkin)*, (107) 2007, pp. 545–587, Erratum (with Collinson, M.) *Formal Aspects of Computing* (19) 2007, pp. 551–554.

Pym, D.J. *The Semantics and Proof Theory of the Logic of Bunched Implications*, *Applied Logic Series* 26 Kluwer Academic Publishers, 2002. Errata and Remarks maintained at: http://www.cs.bath.ac.uk/~pym/BI-monograph-errata.pdf.

Ruge-Murcia, F.J. "The Inflation Bias When the Central Bank Targets the Natural Rate of Unemployment," *Technical Report 2001-22*, Département de Sciences Économique, Université de Montréal, 2001.

Ruge-Murcia, R.J. "Inflation Targeting under Asymmetric Preferences," *Journal of Money, Credit, and Banking* (35:5), 2003, pp. 763–785.

Strauss, A.L., and Corbine, J.M. *Basics of Qualitative Research: Grounded Theory Procedures and Techniques*. Newbury Park, CA: Sage, 1990.

Office Of Science and Technology. Foresight: Cyber Trust and Crime Prevention Project: Executive Summary. 2004.

Taylor, J.B. "Discretion versus Policy Rules in Practice," *Carnegie-Rochester Conference Series on Public Policy* (39), 1993, pp. 195–214.

Tofts, C. "Processes with Probability, Priority and Time," *Formal Aspects of Computing*, (6:5), 1994, pp. 536–564.

Varian, H. "A Bayesian Approach to Real Estate Management," in Feinberg, S.E. and Zellner, A. (Eds) *Studies in Bayesian Economics in Honour of L.J. Savage*, North Holland, 1974, pp. 195–208.

Weirich, D., and Sasse, M.A. "Pretty Good Persuasion: A first Step towards Effective Password Security for the Real World," in *Proceedings of the New Security Paradigms Workshop*, Cloudcroft, NM, ACM Press. September 2001, pp. 137–143.

Yearworth, M., Monahan, B., and Pym, D. "Predictive Modelling for Security Operations Economics," (extended abstract) in *Proc. I3P Workshop on the Economics of Securing the Information Infrastructure*, 2006. Proceedings at http://wesii.econinfosec.org/workshop/.

Zellner, A. "Bayesian Prediction and Estimation Using Asymmetric Loss Functions. *Journal of the American Statistical Association* (81), 1986, pp. 446–451.

[illegible] June 2005.
[illegible] and Pepper [illegible] 2004.
[illegible]
[illegible] pp. 363–418.
[illegible] Prentice-Hall.
[illegible] 2004.
[illegible] Bank Economics [illegible]
[illegible] Computing (1995) [illegible]
[illegible] Computing (1995) [illegible] 570.
[illegible]
[illegible] University of [illegible]
[illegible] Executive Summary, 2004.
Taylor [illegible] (1992) pp. [illegible]
[illegible] pp. 5[illegible]
Varian [illegible] pp. 175–[illegible]
Watson [illegible] the Real World [illegible]
[illegible]
[illegible] the American Statistical Association 81 (1986) pp. 446–451.

The Value of Escalation and Incentives in Managing Information Access

Xia Zhao and M. Eric Johnson

Center for Digital Strategies[31], *Tuck School of Business, Dartmouth College*

Abstract Managing information access within large enterprises is increasingly challenging. With thousands of employees accessing thousands of applications and data sources, managers strive to ensure the employees can access the information they need to create value while protecting information from misuse. We examine an information governance approach based on controls and incentives, where employees' self-interested behavior can result in firm-optimal use of information. Using insights gained from a game-theoretic model, we illustrate how an incentives-based policy with escalation can control both over and under-entitlement while maintaining the flexibility.

1 Introduction

As the global economy evolves from the industrial age to the digital age, its focus has shifted away from the production of the physical goods towards the manipulation of information. Today, rapid access to information has become a critical asset for business success. For example, the literature on supply chain management has emphasized the importance of information sharing on supply chain coordination (e.g., Lee et al. 2000). In the Collaborative Forecast and Replenishment (CFAR) model, manufacturers and retailers share forecast information and jointly develop forecasts and replenishment plans (e.g. Walmart and Warner-Lambert). In the Vendor Managed Inventory (VMI) model, larger manufacturers can obtain inventory and sales data from retailers and better plan production and distribution (e.g. Campbell Soup and VF Corporation). Likewise, the literature on innovation

[31] The Center for Digital Strategies at the Tuck School of Business examines the role of digital strategies in corporations and the use of technology-enabled processes to harness an organization's unique competencies, support its business strategy, and drive competitive advantage. This research was supported through the Institute for Security Technology Studies at Dartmouth College, under award Number 2006-CS-001-000001 from the U.S. Department of Homeland Security (NCSD). The statements, findings, conclusions, and recommendations are those of the authors and do not necessarily reflect the views of the Department of Homeland Security.

M.E. Johnson (ed.), *Managing Information Risk and the Economics of Security*,
DOI: 10.1007/978-0-387-09762-6_8, © Springer Science + Business Media, LLC 2009

has discussed the benefits of free-flowing information, linking it to innovation productivity (e.g., Bakerand and Freeland 1972; von Hippel 1994; Tsai 2001).

However, fears of information misuse force organizations to restrict information availability. Identity and access control systems have been widely deployed to manage access to information and mitigate security risks and privacy concerns. In addition, regulatory compliance, such as Sarbanes-Oxley (SOX), Payment Card Industry Data Security Standard (PCI DSS), Health Insurance Portability and Accountability Act (HIPAA), Gramm-Leach-Bliley Act (GLBA), Personal Information Protection and Electronic Documents Act (PIPEDA), and the European Union Directive on Data Privacy (EU Directive), also leads firms to reduce information access through better controls and governance (Goetz and Johnson 2007).

Thus information governance is needed to help firms balance two goals. On one hand, access governance should enable users to interact with data for value creation; On the other hand, controls are needed to eliminate data misuse. In today's increasingly dynamic environment, firms frequently face unanticipated situations and users' information needs keep changing. Users' access profiles must be synchronized with the users' information needs so that they can seize business opportunities and create value for firms. Flexibility comes to be a prerequisite of information governance for business success.

To achieve flexibility, we consider an access governance system where employees are allowed to escalate into controlled data and applications when needed. Employees are given a baseline level of access for their regular tasks. When they observe opportunities for value creation, they can obtain one-time access without any time-delaying approval process. This system with escalation endows employees with substantial power but potentially breeds significant security risks. Users may abuse their rights and access information not for business reasons but rather for personal benefit. Thus to mitigate misuse, the escalation activities are later audited, and employees found to be abusing their accesses are penalized. In addition to penalties, we also consider the possibility of using rewards for appropriate escalation to motivate employees.

We present insights derived from a game-theoretic model to inform the policy design problem of the information governance system. We argue that combined with the proper incentives, our governance approach can provide the desired access flexibility with a significant level of control.

While we believe that escalation can be a powerful access tool, it must be confined to cases where the risk of failure or the cost of recovery is relatively low compared to the cost of not granting access (e.g., the potential value created through escalation). For example, escalation is very effective in situations where emergency access may save someone's life, or in a time-critical system where the person with the necessary privileges may be unavailable (Povey 2000).

The chapter is organized as follows. In Section 2, we present important background information and illustrate our solution framework. In Section 3, we review the related literature. In Section 4 and Section 5, we outline the model and illustrate the important characteristics of the optimal access governance policy with escalation and incentives. Finally, we conclude with implementation guidance in Section 6.

2 Background and Solution Framework

2.1 Access Control Policies

Access is a specific type of interaction between a subject and an object that results in the flow of information from one to the other (US Department of Defense 1985); For example, the ability to open a file, execute an application, share data with other users, and so on. In the enterprise environment, the subjects are generally users of information systems such as employees, business partners and customers. The objects are various data sources; users who are authorized to fulfill a type of access are said to have the access right (a.k.a. entitlement, privilege, or permission, all of which are used interchangeably in practice.) Access control is the process of dictating access to the resources of a system only to authorized users, programs, or other systems (US Department of Defense 1988). Three different access control policies are commonly used in computer systems:

- Discretionary access control (DAC)
- Mandatory access control (MAC)
- Role-based access control (RBAC)

The first two policies are considered as "classical" for having been used by practitioners for a long time. DAC policies are enforced on the basis of users' identities and authorization. The access is explicitly specified in terms of "who, what, and how—a user or a group of users can access a data source in a specific mode." MAC policies are enforced on the basis of classification of subjects and objects in the system. Each user or data source is assigned a security level (e.g., TopSecret (TS), Secret(S), Confidential(C), Unclassified(U), ordered as descending security levels in the military and civilian government environments.) Access is granted based on a specific principle (e.g., Read Down[32] or Write Up[33].) Role-based access control policies have emerged more recently. A role is a job function with a set of requisite access needs for fulfilling it (e.g., a cashier, a nurse, or a salesperson). A user may be assigned one or multiple roles.

---

[32] The reading right is granted if the security level of the subject dominates that of the object.

[33] The writing right is granted if the security level of the subject is dominated by that of the object.

2.2 Security and Flexibility of Access Control Policies

Access control is enforced with the guideline of preventing misuse of data—either intentionally (such as using the data to make illegal stock trades) or unintentional (such as storing the data on a device that is vulnerable to a security breach). A common approach to access control is known as "the rule of least privilege", i.e., each user is provided with the minimum access rights needed to perform her/his task (Ferraiolo et al. 2007). Therefore, access rights have to be customized and dynamically managed.

Figure 1 shows a typical access control system used to enforce the rule of lease privilege. It includes five components—request, approve, administer, enforce and monitor. Specifically, a user requests an entitlement; the owner examines the request and then approves or rejects it; the administrator modifies the user's entitlements; the user accesses the resource and the system logs the user's activities; and the auditor examines the logs and evaluates the users' activities. With access control, users can interact with data only if they have the corresponding access rights. For example, DAC requires that the access rights of each user (or groups of users) are specified. MAC requires that a security level is assigned to users and data sources and information can only flow along the defined direction (e.g. from low security levels to high security levels.)

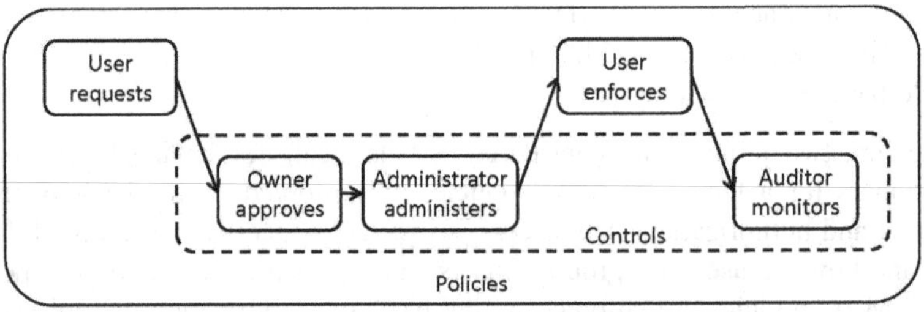

Figure 1. Access Control System

In a dynamic environment, organizations frequently face unanticipated situations and have to adjust their organizational structures and personnel to adapt customers' needs. For example, Sinclair et al. (2007) found in their field study of an investment bank, that a business group of 3,000 people witnessed 1,000 changes to organizational structure within just a few months. The rule of least privilege entails that employees' accesses must be continually updated and audited to remain in synchronization with the changing organization. In large organizations with thousands of users interacting with thousands of different applications and data sources, each having many access rights, the assignment and maintenance of access are daunting.

Rather than customizing the assignment of access rights for every employee, some organizations use a role-based approach and assign users with one or multiple roles. This approach works well for organizations with a few dominant roles that do not change. However, in some cases it is difficult to establish such clear roles and the information needs of those roles quickly change over time. In such cases, the RBAC approach is too rigid to adapt to these dynamic environments.

In practice, the flexibility of access governance is sometimes achieved by "overentitlement"[34]. Sinclair et al. (2007) found in field study that an investment bank had 50-90% of employees overentitled. This practice is rationalized by the argument that long-term employees are valuable and need quick access to information to create value for the firm. But, as the employees are permanently overentitled, they become larger security risks to the organization because their access could be used maliciously or accidentally.

2.3 *Access Governance System with Escalation*

In an increasingly dynamic world, access governance must be flexible, yet secure. In this chapter, we define access governance as an integrated system that includes policies, controls, incentives, and processes that manage user accesses to information resources. The goal of such access governance is to ensure that information systems deliver the right information to the right people at the right time, but also protect the information from misuse, including security and privacy violations. Figure 2 shows the information governance system with escalation. Besides all components in the typical access control system (Figure 1), it includes an escalation component to adapt the dynamic environment. Incentives are enforced through coupling reward and penalty with access and escalation activities.

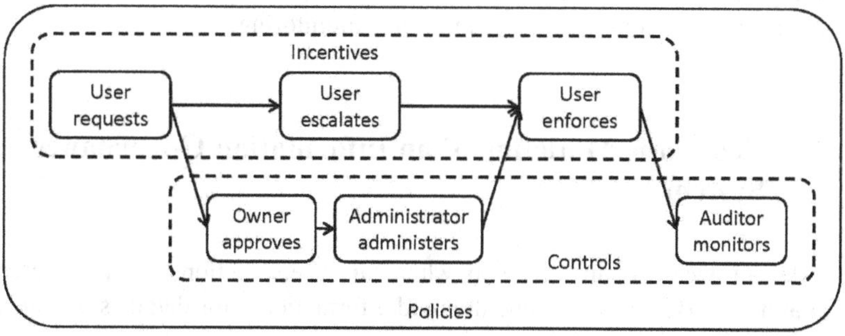

Figure 2. Access Governance System with Escalation and Incentives

[34] "Overentitlement" refers to the situation that an employee has more privileges than s/he needs. "Underentitlement" refers to the situation that an employee has less privileges than s/he needs.

Our solution framework of access management is different from previous approaches in that it expands the scope of access management beyond policies and controls, including incentives and escalation. It empowers users to quickly respond to unanticipated situations and seize business opportunities with controls of data security. This access governance system can be adapted to different types of access control policies including DAC, MAC and RBAC.

3 Literature Review

Many technical issues of implementing escalation into an access control system have been discussed in the computer science literature (e.g., Povey 2000; Rissanen 2004; Ferreira et al. 2006). Chen et al. (2007) focused on the economic aspect of the access governance and evaluated the exceptional access using a risk and benefit analysis. However, the user's escalation behavior is not explicitly studied. Our chapter considers users' incentives and uses a principal and agent setting to explore the policy design problem.

Principle-agent models have been employed in many settings (e.g. Antle and Eppen 1985; Arrow 1985; Baiman 1990; Harris and Raviv 1979; Harris et al. 1982; Holmstrom 1979; or Shavell 1979, etc.). Our chapter closely relates to a large stream of literature that studies financial audit policy in a principal-agent framework (Baron and Besanko 1984; Dye 1986; Harris and Raviv 1996; Kim and Suh 1992; Townsend 1979). In compliance with security regulations, we assume all escalation activities are monitored and audited. We focus on the firm's optimal strategy in response to the audit results, i.e. the penalty for misuse. Since a perfect audit is impossible or extremely costly to achieve, penalty by itself is incapable of eliminating misuse. We consider incorporating a reward scheme, i.e. a bonus, to alleviate the adverse consequence of imperfect monitoring.

4 Economic Modeling of an Information Governance System

We model an access control system where the users' actions are monitored to support auditing. Below we outline the model formation – for details see Zhao and Johnson (2008).

Our game-theoretic model captures the economic parameters of both the employees and the firm. Based on value generated by an employee and the associated information risk, the firm assigns the employee a regular access level to perform regular tasks. Over time employees randomly face opportunities to create more value by seizing an emergent task. We represent the level of information required by the emergent task as a random variable. If the employee's access level is lower than the information requirement, the firm's value from the emergent task cannot be fully monetarized. Therefore, the firm allows employees to escalate access levels temporarily in the emergent situations. To mitigate risk of unnecessary escalation, the firm audits each instance of escalation.

The firm also earns profits from regular tasks at the expense of bearing security risks and providing routine technical support to the regular access level. We assume that the firm's revenue from regular tasks is an increasing and concave function of the regular access level and the associated expense is an increasing and convex function. The firm's revenue from emergent tasks is an increasing and concave function of the employee's total access level including the escalated access.

Employees receive bonuses from the firm based on the value they create from performing emergent tasks. In addition, employees also derive some private benefit from the information. For example, in healthcare, a provider may examine the records of a patient for their private benefit like curiosity. The employee's private benefit from escalation is an increasing concave function of both the regular access level and the escalated access level. The employees bear costs from both regular and escalated access in terms of personal risk (the personal pain of being audited or having a security breach) and in terms of the documentation required when escalating past their regular access. Higher levels of information include more risk and more complex documentation in the audit process. An employee's cost is an increasing and convex function of the regular access level and the escalated access level.

Since employees are self-interested, an employee may escalate to a level that is higher or lower than the information requirement. If the employee's total access level is higher than the information requirement, we say the employee is overentitled. In some cases, risk-averse employees may choose not to escalate to the level needed to achieve the full emergent benefit, which we refer to as underentitled. We assume that all escalation requests receive an audit and that this initial audit cost is fixed, and thus not relevant to our model. However, if overentitlement is suspected, it creates significant security risk that requires more investigation. For example, the firm needs to document and evaluate the overentitlement in compliance with government regulations. The firm incurs additional auditing cost related to overentitlement. On the other hand, underentitlement degrades business performance as represented in the firm's revenue function. To minimize the overentitlement or underentitlement, the firm audits the escalation activities and penalizes employees who abuse their rights or fail to escalate when opportunities arise. Note that the firm can figure out the information requirement ex post through communicating with managers and coworkers of the employee. However, the audit process is imperfect. So the firm does not take action unless the over- or underentitlement exceeds a threshold.

The timing of events is shown in Figure 3. At stage 1, the firm announces the access governance policy including the regular access level, the bonus scheme and the penalty scheme; At stage 2, an employee observes her/his information requirement; At stage 3, the employee escalates her/his access level; At stage 4, the firm's revenue and cost, and the employee's personal benefit and cost are realized; at stage 5, the firm investigates the escalation; Finally the firm rewards and penalizes the employee according to the announced access governance policy. The events above the time line represent the information flow and those below the time line represent the financial flow.

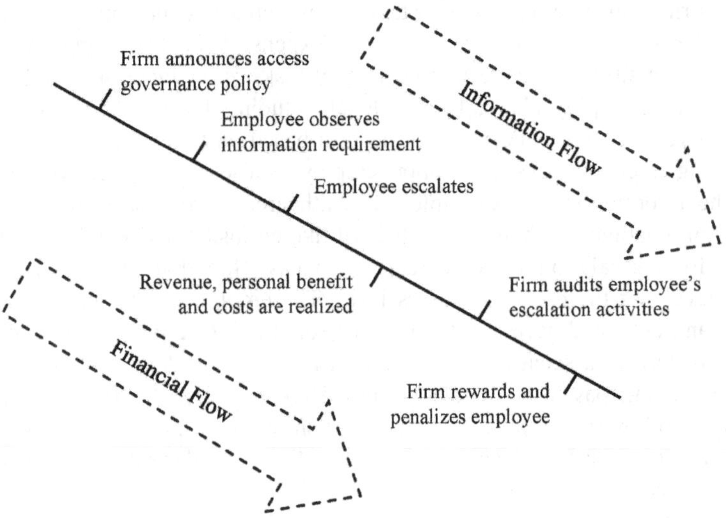

Figure 3. The Timing of Events, Information Flow and Financial Flow

5 Overview of Insights and Results

In this section, we highlight some of the results and intuition we have developed from a mathematical analysis of the model outlined in Section 4 (Zhao and Johnson 2008). Based on the game-theoretic analysis, the firm's access governance policy influences the employee's escalation strategies, and, by backward induction, anticipation of the latter will influence the firm's policy design. Given the policy parameters of the firm, the employee chooses an escalation level to maximize her/his payoff for each business task. Considering the employee's response, the firm chooses the access governance policy to maximize its profit. For ease of communication and implementation, we assume that the firm adopts a linear reward and penalty scheme.

5.1 Employee

Result 1. *Due to the audit error, the employee will be overentitled (or underentitled) if the information requirement is low (or high).*

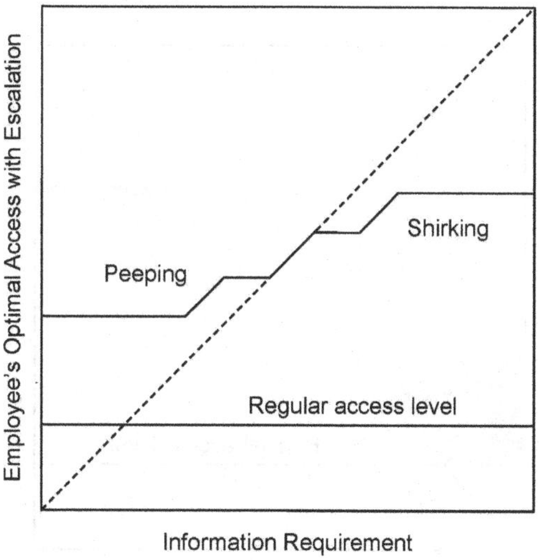

Figure 4. Employee's Strategy

Figure 4 shows an employee's escalation strategy. The horizontal axis represents the level of information requirement and the vertical axis represents the employee's total access level. The graph represents an employee's total access level after escalation given different information requirements of the emergent task. When the information requirement of the emergent task is low, an employee always gains access beyond the information requirement. This "peeping" behavior is driven by the employee's private benefit from accessing extra information. The firm can mitigate the overentitlement by auditing the escalation activities and penalizing employees who are overentitled. This penalty reduces the benefit of the incremental access and the level of escalated access drops. However, due to the audit error, the employee still escalates to a level higher than the information requirement. The dark area in Figure 5 represents all the contingencies where the employee is overentitled.

When the information requirement of the emergent task is high, the cost of escalating to the information requirement dominates the marginal private benefit from the escalated access. In this case, an employee tends towards underentitled, i.e. shirking. The firm motivates the desired behavior using revenue bonuses and penalties. The bonus connects the employee's payoff with the firm's revenue from emergent tasks, and hence increases the marginal benefit of the escalated access. The bonus by itself, however, is not enough to provide employees with incentive to overcome underentitlement. The penalty for underentitlement supplements the bonus, and further increases the marginal benefit of the escalated access. Underentitlement still exists because of the audit error. The light shaded area in Figure 5 represents all contingencies where the employee is underentitled.

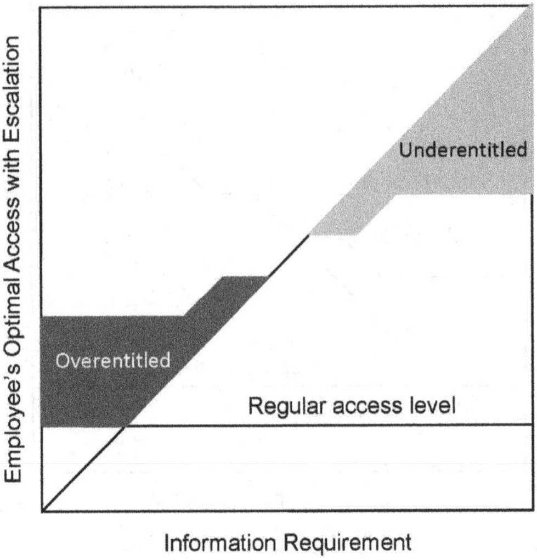

Figure 5. Overentitlement and Underentitlement

5.2 *Firm*

Both over and underentitlement generate organizational inefficiency, which is costly to the firm. The firm sets the penalty rates to minimize such inefficiency. Figure 6 shows the employee's escalation strategy with optimal penalty schemes. Because of the audit error, over and underentitlement still exist.

Implementation of the penalty scheme is based on the assumption that the firm can detect misuse through auditing. If there is no audit error, the penalty scheme can completely eliminate over and underentitlement.

Result 2. *If the audit instrument is perfect (i.e. there is no audit error), the firm will not adopt the reward scheme.*

With an imperfect audit instrument, the penalty scheme by itself cannot completely eliminate the opportunistic behavior. For example, drivers often know that the police will not issue a ticket if they exceed the speed limit within 5 mph,

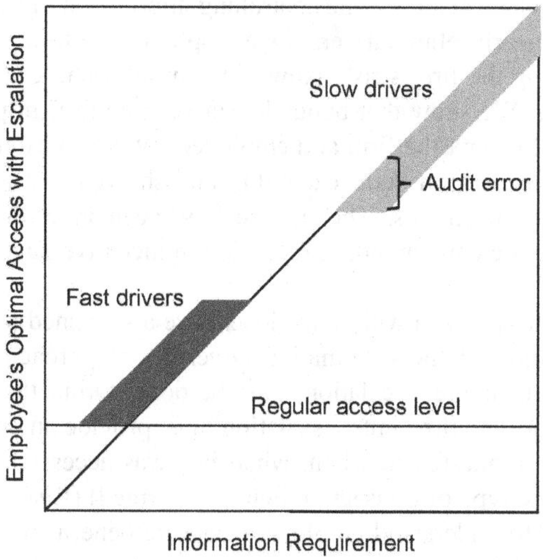

Figure 6. Over-and Underentitlement with Optimal Penalty Scheme

so some fast drivers always drive a bit higher than the speed limit. In contrast, drivers who are concerned about safety may drive slower than the speed limit.

Rewards can be used to overcome underentitlement since the bonus increases the employee's benefit from the incremental access, and this effect is valid only when the total access level is less than the information requirement. However, this incentive is costly to the firm because the firm has to share revenue with employees. The firm needs to balance the above trade-off while determining the optimal bonus rate.

In addition to the penalty and bonus scheme, the level of regular access is also an important decision for the firm. Result 3 gives the relationship between the bonus and the regular access.

***Result** 3. Bonus and the regular access are substitutes in presence of audit error. In particular, the bonus rate is decreasing in the regular access.*

The regular access and the bonus potentially substitute for each other. In particular, if the regular access increases, the bonus rate decreases.

6 Conclusion

In this chapter, we examined a framework of information access governance that includes incentive schemes and an escalation component. Reviewing results from a game-theoretic analysis, we have illustrated how both penalty and reward can be used to encourage value creation while controlling information misuse. Set properly, user penalties can nearly eliminate employees' propensity to access unnecessary information, reducing the firm's risk. However, simple penalties are not sufficient to eliminate misuse. We show that bonus incentives tied to firm performance can improve outcomes for both the firm and employees. We also examined how these results are linked to the firm audit capability and showed that audit quality can reduce the need for incentives. The trade-off between investments to improve audit capability and the corresponding reduction in incentive payouts is an area of ongoing research.

By discussing our approach with practitioners, we also gained important insights on the implementation of the information governance approach with escalation and incentives. For example, escalation must be done within the allowable zone dictated by regulatory requirements; escalation must provide an audit trail, including records of who requested it, when, what data was accessed, and what value was created (e.g., the type of transaction being performed) (Rissanen et al., 2004); and the firms need to understand employees' private benefit in order to properly design escalation options. One interesting advantage of an escalation-based system is the possibility of organizational learning. By observing employee behavior, firms can learn more about the dynamics of the business environment from employees.

References

Antle, R. and Eppen, G. D. "Capital Rationing and Organizational Slack in Capital Budgeting," *Management Science* (31:2), 1985, pp.163–174.

Arrow, K. J. "The Economics of Agency," in *Principals and Agents: The Structure of Business*, Pratt, J.E., Zeckhauser, R.J and Arrow, K.J. (Eds.) Harvard Business School Press, Boston, MA. 1985, pp. 37–53.

Aveksa. "Enterprise Roles-based Access Governance," *Technical Report*, White Paper, 2007.

Baiman, S. "Agency Research in Managerial Accounting: A Second Look," *Accounting Organizations and Society* (15:4), 1990, pp. 341–371.

Baker, N. R. and Freeland, J. R. "Structuring Information Flow to Enhance Innovation," *Management Science* (19:1) *Theory Series*, 1972, pp. 105–116.

Baron, D. P. and Besanko, D. "Regulation, Asymmetric Information, and Auditing," *The RAND Journal of Economics* (15:4), 1984, pp. 447–470.

Chen, P.-C.; Rohatgi, P., and Keser, C. "Fuzzy MLS: An Experiment on Quantified Risk-Adaptive Access Control," in Proceedings of *DIMACS Workshop on Information Security Economics*, 2007.

Dye, R. A. "Optimal Monitoring Policies in Agencies," *The RAND Journal of Economics* (17:3), 1986, pp. 339–350.

Ferreira, A., Cruz-Correia, R., Antunes, L., Farinha, P., Oliveira-Palhares, E., Chadwick, D., and Costa-Pereira, A. "How to Break Access Control in a Controlled Manner," in *Proceedings of the 19th IEEE Symposium on Computer-Based Medical Systems (CBMS'06)*, 2006, pp. 847–854.

Ferraiolo, D.F., Kuhn, D.R. and Chandramouli, R. *Role-based Access Control*, Ar tech House, Norwood, MA, 2007

Goetz, E. and Johnson, M. E. "Security through Information Risk Management." I3P Technical Report. Dartmouth College. http://mba.tuck.dartmouth.edu/digital/Programs/CorporateEvents/CISO2007/Overview.pdf.

Harris, M., Kriebel, C., and Raviv, A. "Asymmetric Information, Incentives and Intrafirm Resource Allocation," *Management Science* (28:6), 1986, pp. 604–620.

Harris, M. and Raviv, A. "Optimal Incentive Contracts with Imperfect Information," *Journal of Economic Theory* (20), 1979, pp. 231–259.

Harris, M. and Raviv, A. "The Capital Budgeting Process: Incentives and Information," *Journal of Finance* (51:4), 1996, pp. 1139–1174.

Holmstrom, B. "Moral Hazard and Observability," *Bell Journal of Economics* (10:1), 1979, pp. 74-91.

Johnson, M. E. and Goetz, E. "Embedding Information Security Risk Management into the Extended Enterprise," *IEEE Security and Privacy*, 5(3), 2007, pp. 16–24.

Jolly, D. "Fraud Costs French Bank $7.1 Billion," *New York Times,* 2008.

Kannan, K. and Telang, R. "Market for Software Vulnerabilities? Think Again," *Management Science* (51:5), 2005, pp. 726–740.

Kim, S. K. and Suh, Y. S. "Conditional Monitoring Policy Under Moral Hazard," *Management Science* (38:8), 1992, pp. 1106–1120.

Krishnan, V. and Zhu, W. "Designing a Family of Development Intensive Products," *Management Science* (52:6), 2006, pp. 813–825.

Lee, H. L., So, K. C., and Tang, C. S. "The Value of Information Sharing in a Two-level Supply Chain," *Management Science* (46:5), 2000, pp. 626–643.

Motta, M. "Endogenous Quality Choice: Price vs. Quantity Competition," *Journal of Industry Economics* (41:2), 1993, pp. 113–131.

Povey, D. "Optimistic Security: a New Access Control Paradigm," in *Proceedings of the 1999 Workshop on New Security Paradigms*, ACM Press, 2000, pp. 40–45.

Rathnam, S., Mahajan, V., and Whinston, A. B. "Facilitating Coordination in Customer Support Teams: A Framework and Its Implications for the Design of Information Technology," *Management Science* (41:12), 1995, pp. 1900–1922.

Richardson, R. "The 12th Annual Computer Crime and Security Survey," Computer Security Institute, 2007.

Rissanen, E., Firozabadi, S. B., and Sergot, M. "Towards a Mechanism for Discretionary Overriding of Access Control," in *Proceedings of the 12th International Workshop on Security Protocols*, Cambridge, 2004.

Sinclair, S., Smith, S.W., Trudeau, S., Johnson, M.E., and Portera, A. "Information Risk in Financial Institutions: Field Studyand Research Roadmap," in *Proceedings for the 3rd International Workshop on Enterprise Applications and Services in the Finance Industry* (FinanceCom 2007), 2007, Montreal, Canada.

Shavell, S. "Risk Sharing and Incentives in the Principal and Agent Relationship," *Bell Journal of Economics* (10:1), pp. 55–73.

Townsend, R. M. "Optimal Contracts and Competitive Markets with Costly State Verification," *Journal of Economy Theory* (21:2), 1979, pp. 265–293

Tsai, W. "Knowledge Transfer in Intraorganizational Networks: Effects of Network Position and Absorptive Capacity on Business Unit Innovation and Performance," *The Academy of Management Journal* (44:5), 2001, pp. 996–1004.

US Department of Defense. "Department of Defense Trusted Computer System Evaluation Criteria," DoD 5200.28-STD, Washington, D.C., US Department of Defense, 1985.

US Department of Defense. "National Computer Security Center, Glossary of Computer Security Terms," NCSC-TG-004-88, Ft. Meade, Md, National Computer Security Center, 1988.

von Hippel, E. "Sticky Information and the Locus of Problem Solving: Implications for Innovation," *Management Science* (40:4), 1994, pp. 429–439.

Zhao, X and Johnson, M.E, "Access Governance: Flexibility and Control through Escalation and Incentives," Center for Digital Strategies working paper, Tuck School of Business, Dartmouth College, 2008.

[illegible] independent [illegible]
[illegible]
[illegible]
[illegible] and [illegible], pp. 756–760.
[illegible] pp. 119–130.
[illegible] 2006 [illegible]
[illegible] Supply [illegible] Information Sharing [illegible]
[illegible] 2007.
[illegible] 2004.
[illegible] Information [illegible]
[illegible] and [illegible] Incentives for Information Sharing [illegible]

Reinterpreting the Disclosure Debate for Web Infections

Oliver Day [1], Brandon Palmen [1] and Rachel Greenstadt [2]

[1] StopBadware Project, Berkman Center for Internet and Society, Harvard University

[2] Center for Research in Computation and Society, Harvard University

Abstract Internet end users increasingly face threats of compromise by visiting seemingly innocuous websites that are themselves compromised by malicious actors. These compromised machines are then incorporated into bot networks that perpetuate further attacks on the Internet. Google attempts to protect users of its search products from these hidden threats by publicly disclosing these infections in interstitial warning pages behind the results. This chapter seeks to explore the effects of this policy on the economic ecosystem of webmasters, web hosts, and attackers by analyzing the experiences and data of the StopBadware project. The StopBadware project manages the appeals process whereby websites whose infections have been disclosed by Google get fixed and unquarantined. Our results show that, in the absence of disclosure and quarantine, certain classes of webmasters and hosting providers are not incentivized to secure their platforms and websites and that the malware industry is sophisticated and adapts to this reality. A delayed disclosure policy may be appropriate for traditional software products. However, in the web infection space, silence during this period leads to further infection since the attack is already in progress. We relate specific examples where disclosure has had beneficial effects, and further support this conclusion by comparing infection rates in the U.S. where Google has high penetration to China where its market penetration rate is much lower.

1 Introduction

Debate has raged for over a decade to determine the most responsible and productive way to disclose software vulnerabilities, so that software vendors, vulnerability researchers, and the public all benefit from the exchange of knowledge without facilitating the software vulnerability exploitation. While it sometimes makes sense for software vulnerabilities to be hidden for a short period of time if those vulnerabilities have not already been identified by malfeasants, the same cannot be

M.E. Johnson (ed.), *Managing Information Risk and the Economics of Security*,
DOI: 10.1007/978-0-387-09762-6_9, © Springer Science + Business Media, LLC 2009

said for websites which distribute malware, because the vulnerabilities in these websites have already been exploited, and because allowing these infections to remain hidden would harm Internet users while abetting attackers.

Compromised websites often infect visitor's computers automatically by exploiting vulnerabilities in Internet Explorer, Firefox, and other web browsers which allow the infected pages to execute malicious code and download additional malware components without the visitor's knowledge or consent. The HTML elements which attackers place on websites to make them infectious, such as hidden iframes and javascript references to third-party malware hosts, can be placed on compromised websites with such ease and automation that a growing number of unsophisticated attackers now participate in malware affiliate networks, which pay these attackers commissions for infecting legitimate websites with their malicious code (Finjan 2007).

Because Internet users who visit compromised websites often have no idea that their computers have been infected with malware, the operators of these websites have little incentive to disclose to their visitors that they may have been infected; doing so could damage the websites' brand or reputation, and failing to do so is unlikely to bear any negative consequence for the website owner. Thus, voluntary disclosure of website infections allows webmasters to conceal the risk that their websites pose to Internet users, and to inappropriately externalize the costs of poor website security. This has the potential to create a lemons market (Akerlof 1970), where webmasters and web hosting providers who invest in securing their websites against attack are driven out by others who do not invest in security, and who place the burden of resulting website infections on Internet users.

Mandatory disclosure of website infections forces webmasters to accept responsibility for the safety and security of their web properties, and removes the perverse incentives which lead webmasters to systematically underinvest in website security. Google and StopBadware's public disclosures of infected websites have caused webmasters and web hosting providers to pay greater attention to web security. They exemplify a mandatory disclosure regime which we believe should be uniformly enforced, either by public policy or by additional private web gatekeepers like search engines and Internet service providers.

Google attempts to protect users of its search products from these hidden threats with the "safe browsing" (Provos et al. 2007) program. This program identifies websites that are infected with malicious code through the use of instrumented browsers which reside in virtual machines. These machines create a score based on new network connections, processes spawned, and other criteria which are considered abnormal for machines that are only rendering a webpage. Those urls which are deemed bad are shielded from Google users by inserting interstitial warning pages behind links to these websites in returned search results. In addition to providing more information about these warning pages and malware threats in general, StopBadware (StopBadware 2008) provides education and technical resources to website owners who wish to clean and secure their websites and have Google's warning flags removed from their website's search results.

This chapter describes our experiences implementing and supporting the mandatory disclosure system developed by Google and StopBadware. In addition to describing the trends we have observed in malware infection technologies, we explore the characteristics of webmasters and web hosting providers that we consider most prone to attack, and compile statistics from our clearinghouse of infected websites, identifying particular web hosting providers that host an unusually large number of infections. We conclude the chapter with a discussion of the impact that unusual limitations on public disclosure may have had on the proliferation of infected websites in China, and we present our opinion that the mandatory disclosure paradigm which we have prototyped should be expanded to protect more Internet users, and to ensure that all Internet stakeholders make web security a priority.

2 Attack Trends

When the StopBadware project was founded, the Internet malware landscape was considerably simpler than it is today. We framed our software guidelines to define a class of software which causes unacceptable user harm, and focused on identifying borderline applications rather than on the uncontroversial malware that antivirus and security vendors seek to address. At that time, most of the software that violated our guidelines was packaged with popular consumer applications or tucked away in the so-called 'dark corners' of the Internet: websites promoting software and media piracy, pornography, drugs, and gambling. In order to have her PC compromised, an Internet user was first induced, by deception or ignorance, to manually download and run the malicious software. In that environment, the task of identifying, unmasking, and incentivizing the reform of distributors was more easily accomplished for many reasons. In particular, malware distribution was almost invariably an intentional act, either by software developers who packaged the exploits with their consumer applications, or by shadowy web hosts who deliberately added exploit links to their web pages. This made it fairly simple to encourage the reform or abandonment of particular applications and websites by inviting public scrutiny of the offenders and by contributing to public education about the hazards of downloading untrusted software. Unfortunately, the success that security watchdogs like StopBadware have had in improving public caution against traditional malware distribution channels has had the ancillary effect of encouraging malware creators to develop new methods of exploiting Internet users. Three important conditions of the malware environment have made it particularly difficult for web consumers to avoid malware threats and for StopBadware to combat them.

First, the malware community has embraced 'long-tail' network economics, which postulates that considerable value can be derived from exploiting a large number of small, niche markets. In the malware context, the expected value of stolen financial information, passwords, and other personal data that can be collected by attacking a large number of poorly secured niche websites exceeds the value of attacking a single, large website that is well protected. To this end, malware distribution networks often no longer attempt to create demand for false or dubious websites (against which the public is now fairly well warned), and instead invisibly hijack traffic from thousands of legitimate websites by exploiting security vulnerabilities or misconfigurations in those sites and then adding a small amount of malicious code to those sites which does not otherwise affect the website's functionality. Since exploits can now be downloaded and executed automatically upon visiting a compromised page, visitors to these normally safe websites are often unaware that they have become vulnerable to identity theft, or that their computers have been conscripted into the ranks of a botnet. When StopBadware's collaboration with Google to blacklist URLs that victimize the Internet users began in August, 2006, most of the sites that were added to our clearinghouse belonged directly to those parties who profit from the distribution of malware. Today, a large number of these domains belong to third-party hacking victims whose only responsibility for malware distribution is the mismanagement of their websites' security, and who often believe that StopBadware has mistakenly and carelessly advised web users to avoid visiting their personal blog or small business website.

The disconnect between webmaster perceptions of security and reality frames a second notable development in the malware environment: the emergence of a vulnerable class of web content providers we call 'consumer webmasters'. These are individuals who have benefited from the simplification of web publishing techniques without having gained a technical understanding of how to keep their websites secure. In addition to neglecting to use strong passwords and correct file permission settings, consumer webmasters tend to deploy off-the-shelf web scripts like blogging platforms and photo galleries which, especially when they are not updated with security patches in a timely manner, significantly increase the number of vulnerabilities composing a site's attackable 'surface area'. Mid-tier shared web hosting services also contribute to the problem. These high-volume, low-margin web hosts often pack thousands of clients onto each physical server, such that the exploitation of a single software vulnerability or poorly protected user account can result in thousands of compromised web sites. In order to cater to the widest variety of clients without incurring the costs of server customization, these web hosts often enable dozens of redundant or seldom-used features by default, the vulnerabilities of each of which can compound the vulnerability of the server as a whole. Finally, the threat that inexperienced consumer webmasters and insecure web hosts pose to Internet users is exacerbated by the fact that even when Google and StopBadware positively determine that a website has been compromised, the consumer webmaster of that site often has an insufficient understanding of the problem to identify and remove the malicious code and secure the site against future attacks.

The frequency with which StopBadware encounters webmasters and web hosts who are more concerned about losing traffic or customers than they are about making their websites safe for the public is alarming, and informs the third challenge which we now face in our campaign against the spread of malware: the ability of web content providers to conceal and externalize the costs of malware infection under voluntary disclosure policy, which does not require that webmasters disclose their infections to the public. Website owners who do not inform the public that their websites have been compromised possess asymmetric or insider information which systematically results in harm to Internet consumers. The user protections enabled by Google's interstitial warning pages and StopBadware's website review clearinghouse help to spread responsibility for Internet security among more Internet stakeholders, but are insufficient in scope to address the source of this incentive problem. Vulnerable Internet users who visit compromised webpages directly, or through links from other pages, rather than through Google's search results, are not protected from infection, and even Google's safe-browsing program lacks the capacity to identify all new malware threats before many Internet users are infected. While the impact of Google's warnings often prompts webmasters to clean the infections from their websites, it often takes some time for the problems to be fixed, during which many Internet users who access the infected websites directly are exploited. StopBadware hopes to form partnerships with additional web gatekeepers like search engines and potentially Internet service providers to make our threat disclosures more comprehensive, but these measures treat the symptoms of an incentive problem. If webmasters held web hosts responsible for the security of their servers, and if Internet users held webmasters responsible for the safety of their webpages, all Internet stakeholders would find it in their interests to protect themselves against malware infection.

2.1 Drive-By Downloads

In our experience, automatic or 'drive-by' downloads from trusted websites have become the most common form of malware distribution on the Internet today. In the past, Internet users could avoid malware infection simply by choosing not to download and run unknown applications, browser toolbars, or plug-ins — and a great deal of effort was spent teaching people to avoid these downloads. Although this education did reduce the effectiveness of traditional, deceptive but consent-driven malware distribution channels, it turned a blind eye to the automatic object downloads embedded in HTML webpages, like images, iframes, and JavaScript. When malware distributors learned to use these embedded web objects to exploit browser vulnerabilities (such as MDAC, Shell.Object, and ANI), it became unnecessary to induce web users to download and install exploits - Internet users could be infected simply by rendering the code of a compromised webpage in a vulnerable browser.

The 'hidden iframe' attack is one characteristic form of drive-by download that malware distributors utilize to deliver exploit payloads to unsuspecting Internet users. StopBadware first encountered this type of attack in December, 2006, when it received a review request from the owner of a website called SantaLinks, which Google had flagged as potentially harmful. When we tested the site, we were initially perplexed by Google's malware determination, since we did not discover any visible links to malicious downloads on the site; however, a closer inspection of the site's HTML code revealed a hidden iframe at the bottom of the page which automatically exploited a known Internet Explorer vulnerability to install malware. The website owner removed the offending iframe code in time for the holidays, but attackers soon reinfected the website because the initial site vulnerability was not repaired. Reinfections are common for websites whose infections are caused by the exploitation of software vulnerabilities which remain on the server, even after the symptoms of an initial infection, such as foreign iframes, have been removed. The iframe attack that SantaLinks suffered was relatively simple, but it illustrates several key developments in the way malware is distributed. Most importantly, SantaLinks was an extremely innocent appearing website whose credibility Internet users had no reason to doubt. Previously, malware distributors expended great effort concealing the nature of their exploits as desirable downloads, and typically preyed upon appetites for pornography and illicit software which overcame Internet users' defenses against the known risks of such downloads. Now, no such efforts need to be made, except to ensure that the iframe or javascript that loads an exploit is not discovered by the user or the webmaster. Placed in the midst of a long document, a simple tag of the form:

```
<iframe src="third_party_url" height=0></iframe>
```

can easily avoid the detection of an inexperienced webmaster, but can launch a visitor's web browser through a chain of JavaScript tests and additional iframes which ultimately results in the automatic download and execution of the precise exploit that will compromise that particular visitor's computer. If a concerned user or webmaster does investigate the source of a mysterious iframe, he often finds that the resulting JavaScript code has been obfuscated, and is unintelligible to casual human readers as well as to many text signature-based anti-virus scanners.

Example: The following script for inserting a malicious iframe:

```
<SCRIPT>window.status='Done';document.write('<iframe
name=0b617b46901 src=\'http://77.221.133.188/.if/go.html?'
+Math.round(Math.random()*55640)+'5\' width=214 height=260
style=\'display: none\'></iframe>')</SCRIPT>
```

...might appear on an infected website in this obfuscated form:

```
<script>function v47befeddcf5b2(v47befeddcf9ba){ var v47befe
ddcfdac=16;return(parseInt(v47befeddcf9ba,v47befeddcfdac));}
function v47befeddd09a0(v47befeddd1198){ var v47befeddd1d9
5=2;var v47befeddd15ac='';for(v47befeddd1991=0;v47befeddd19
```

```
91<v47befeddd1198.length;v47befeddd1991+=v47befeddd1d95)v47b
efeddd15ac+=(String.fromCharCode(v47befeddcf5b2(v47befeddd11
98.substr(v47befeddd1991, v47befeddd1d95))));}return v47befe
ddd15ac;}document.write(v47befeddd09a0('3C5343524950543E7769
6E646F772E7374617475733D27446F6E65273B646F63756D656E742E7772
69746528273C696672616D65206E616D653D306236313762343639303120
7372633D5C27687474703A2F2F37372E3232312E3133332E3138382F2E69
662F676F2E68746D6C3F272B4D6174682E726F756E64284D6174682E7261
6E646F6D28292A353536343029B27355C272077696474683D323134206B
65696768743D3236302737474796C653D5C27646973706C61793A206E6F6E6
55C273E3C2F696672616D653E27293C2F5343524950543E'));</script>
```

Adding to the sophistication of this exploit-chain approach, many of the links in this chain can be hosted in different domains, on different servers, and in different countries, making it very difficult to disable or even map the complete malware network, since a single URL change at any level of the distribution infrastructure can introduce new exploits or replace a server that has been blocked or disabled by Internet service providers or law enforcement officials.

2.2 *Weaponized Exploit Packs*

Because the hidden iframes and obfuscated javascript discussed previously are invisible to web users, attackers no longer need to customize the placement and appearance of exploits to blend into each page that those attackers compromise; thus, the process of adding these tags can be automated. Using new toolsets, an attacker who has accessed a vulnerable server can add the same hidden iframe or obfuscated javascript to every web page on that server with trivial effort. If this server belongs to a shared web host, hundreds or thousands of different websites with vastly different audiences will all be simultaneously converted into malware distribution channels. Because of the ease with which these commoditized attacks can be performed, the expertise required of attackers who hope to profit from malware distribution has diminished—any person who possesses a basic understanding of web code is capable of launching a scripted attack. To further enhance the labor productivity of these freelance attackers, malware distributors now market weaponized exploit solutions like 'Icepack,' and 'Mpack', which package complicated hacking procedures with push-button simplicity to black market entrepreneurs who desire a share of the malware bounty (OMurchu 2007). These software packages were initially sold for as much as $1000, but they are now freely distributed on hacking forums, and allow almost anyone to deploy a private malware distribution network. The producers of these 'weaponized' exploit kits even sell technical support and software updates containing new exploits and evasive techniques like IP-filtering and geo-targeting, which allow attackers to minimize exposure to security firms and maximize the value of each infection.

Although obtaining and deploying these weaponized exploit packs is relatively simple and inexpensive, there remains a certain amount of risk associated with running a malware server. Black market entrepreneurs who are willing to assume this risk are known to develop affiliate networks around their exploit platforms, thereby employing many other attackers to place the entrepreneur's malicious iframes on vulnerable websites. The affiliate network tracks the number of infections generated by each affiliate, and returns a small fee which is usually dependent on the country where the infected computer resides (Finjan 2007). The similarity borne by these malware affiliate networks to legitimate publisher advertising networks is not coincidental - the success of each depends primarily on the number of webpages enlisted to display the syndicated content, rather than on the efficacy of that content. In fact, most of the 'commercial' exploit packs that exist target software vulnerabilities that have already been patched by vendors; however, if even 5% of the visitors to a compromised web page have failed to apply those security patches, and if links to the exploit server are sufficiently widespread, the aggregate number of resulting infections will be large. The similarity of advertising network and malware network economics has encouraged other black market entrepreneurs to bypass hacking altogether by simply using javascript or iframe-based advertising networks as malware vectors, or by developing their own dubious advertising networks which are then redistributed by syndicating ad networks like Clicksor.

3 Market Failure: Consumer Webmasters and Mid-Tier Web Hosts

With these new tools of exploitation and profit, a growing community of freelance attackers scours the web for server vulnerabilities which will allow attackers to add malicious code to innocent websites. Although the occasional discovery of vulnerabilities in a major website or web service can be exceptionally profitable, freelance attackers are much more likely to earn steady incomes by compromising a large number of small, poorly protected websites than by expending great effort attempting to penetrate the defenses of a few large sites. This increased demand for vulnerable websites to attack has prompted some hackers to compile lists of such sites, which they sell in bulk to the attackers. The simplest way to compile such voluminous lists is to identify vulnerabilities in off-the-shelf software products like database applications, webhost control panels, and blogging platforms, and then determine which websites have those vulnerable software products enabled and unpatched. This can often be accomplished just by searching for particular identifying text-strings in commercial search engines.

The efficiency of targeting websites which have inadequate defenses and standardized software that is out-of-date has led to the systematic exploitation of consumer webmasters. Consumer webmasters tend to be individuals who have no formal IT training, and who have learned to minimally use web server technologies for specific purposes such as publishing a blog, promoting a small business, or providing a topical discussion forum. Consumer webmasters face technological problems as they arise, rather than attempting to identify potential problems and prevent them in advance, and commonly ignore skill-demanding best practices in favor of expedient, functional solutions. Some consumer webmasters possess the skills required to install and tweak software platforms like WordPress or phpBB, but fear upgrading these platforms as security updates are released, lest the upgrades break the existing system and require repairs which demand greater technological sophistication than the webmaster possesses. Others hire third parties to customize open-source content management systems or e-commerce applications for their small businesses, and then neglect to maintain the websites in any way, imagining that because they have not altered the sites since their creation, the sites remain pristine and secure. In short, consumer webmasters want their websites to 'just work', and invest little effort in developing the fundamental understanding of Internet technology that would inform decisions to deliberately address website security risks before they are exploited. Although an understanding of Internet security is certainly not a prerequisite for operating a website, forcing webmasters to accept responsibility for the safety of their web properties ensures that webmasters are incented to demand better security from their web hosting providers.

The websites operated by consumer webmasters rarely require much processing and network bandwidth, so these site owners are unwilling to pay the extra costs associated with obtaining and supporting dedicated web hosting. Instead they purchase basic shared web hosting packages that firms market by competitively increasing the number of features available on each plan while reducing their prices to nearly the marginal cost of administrating a single additional user account. In many ways, this competitive pressure on web hosts is a positive development, since it allows many more web users to operate websites affordably. Unfortunately, our experience has been that consumer webmasters tend to choose between these mid-tier hosting providers on the basis of comparative feature propositions marketed by the web hosts, rather than by determining which web hosts offer the best combination of features and security. Because competition between mid-tier web hosts is intense, and the fixed cost of adding additional features to bargain hosting plans is low compared to the marginal revenue to be gained by expanding the host's client base, many of these web hosts now bundle multiple database applications, several popular scripting languages, and dozens of 'one-click-install' web applications with every plan that they sell. This feature bloat constitutes a significant threat to the security of servers operated by mid-tier web hosts not only because the vulnerabilities of each feature compound the vulnerability of the server as a whole, but also because many of these mid-tier web hosts are unprepared to uniformly deploy the hundreds of security patches that the vendors of these products release each year. Each time a web host attempts to update features, it risks breaking one or more of the many software dependencies inherent to its complicated systems. Since server stability is a far more visible feature of hosting quality to consumer webmasters than server security, mid-tier web hosts often refrain from updating their older systems even when they apply security patches to brand new servers. Finally, some mid-tier web hosts make themselves particularly vulnerable to attack by deploying off-the-shelf server control-panel software like cPanel or Plesk, whose standardized vulnerabilities can be exploited to commoditize the attack of multiple web hosts, thousands of servers, and potentially millions of websites (Geer et al. 2003).

Because a large number of vulnerabilities can exist in a single website and server, when a website does become compromised it is often difficult for exploited Internet users to assign blame for the security lapse that permitted the attack, and to determine which parties, if any, were negligent. Ideally, website attackers would be discovered and punished by law enforcement, but the structure of malware distribution networks is such that it is extremely difficult to identify and prosecute these criminals. Web hosting providers typically argue that website security is the responsibility of website owners, and that they are not responsible for the safety or security of their clients' websites. But when an attack on a single client's website has the potential to compromise additional websites and servers, the web host should play an active role in enforcing the security even of client websites, in the same way that a landlord might require certain safety practices of his tenants. Web hosts are loathe to perform this monitoring, because doing so would result in added costs, a slippery-slope toward content censorship, or legal liability; and because there is little way for the public to know just how secure or insecure any particular web host's services are, the web hosting market exhibits traits of a 'lemons' market (Akerlof 1970), where secure web hosts are driven out at the cost-margins by impune, insecure web hosts. Website owners bear similarly little liability to Internet users for the safety of their websites, and therefore have little incentive either to secure their websites or to disclose attacks when they occur. The ability of web hosts and website owners to externalize the costs of lax web security to Internet users by failing to disclose the potential for harm constitutes a market failure that must be addressed to ensure that all Internet stakeholders take effective precautions against malware infection.

4 Vulnerability Disclosure

The debate surrounding the proper way to disclose software security vulnerabilities is intense and unresolved. This problem has been studied extensively by the economics and information security community (Anderson 2005; Arora et al. 2004; Arora, Telang, & Xu 2004; Camp & Wolfram 2004; Cavusoglu, Cavusoglu, & Zhang 2006; Choi, Ferstman, & Gandal 2007; Granick 2005; Rescorla 2005; Schechter 2002; Swire 2005).

Software vendors insist with some force that when a software vulnerability is discovered, the vendor of that software should be notified sufficiently in advance of public disclosure to allow the vendor to produce and deploy a patch. In theory, this would prevent malfeasants from becoming aware of vulnerabilities until it is too late to exploit them; but in practice, attackers may discover the vulnerabilities independently and may then exploit them even more effectively because they are not publicly acknowledged (Granick 2005). Unfortunately, software vendors almost always prefer to hide the vulnerabilities in their products, and are willing to pay considerable bounties to independent vulnerability discoverers in exchange for non-disclosure by the discoverers (Schechter 2002). Since there is no general consensus on which policy is socially optimal (or rather, the optimal solution depends on the case), voluntary or delayed disclosure has become the norm for software vendors and independent security analysts alike. Because the public is left unaware of the vulnerabilities, it is unable to defend against the exploitation of those vulnerabilities; and perhaps more importantly, it fails to sufficiently pressure vendors to focus on security, detect vulnerabilities, and patch them expediently (Camp & Wolfram 2004). However, the context in which the problem has been studied is that of application software running on end hosts, not web infections.

Like software vendors, website owners commonly object to Google's immediate public warnings about their websites when it is determined that they host or distribute malware, believing that they should be entitled to a grace period during which they can clean and secure their websites before they suffer the financial or reputational consequences of public disclosure[35]. These webmasters value the reputation of their brands more than they value the safety of their visitors. Their websites are not merely vulnerable, they are already compromised; they are actively harming internet users, and they need to be quarantined immediately. Arora, Telang, and Xu summarized the effects of late disclosure in traditional software products as reducing the time window that customers are exposed to attack, but decreasing the vendor's willingness to deliver a quick patch (Arora et al. 2004). To use this logic for web infections is disingenuous; in this case, late disclosure increases the amount of time that customers are exposed to attacks, decreases the vendor's willingness to deliver patches, and limits the ability of customers to discover that they have been compromised. Keeping these infections secret even for a short period of time would abet attackers, whereas publicly disclosing the infections ensures that internet users are informed of the risks of visiting the infected websites. By publicly disclosing and, to the extent that websites depend on Google for traffic, quarantining websites that distribute malware, StopBadware and Google force website owners to address the security issues that they would otherwise force their visitors to bear without consent. Although this can be frustrating for website owners who are themselves victims of attack, we believe that it is their responsibility to ensure that their web properties do not threaten public

[35] Google does attempt to contact webmasters when their sites are initially added to Google's blacklist, but there is no reliable system to ensure that webmasters receive these communications.

safety. Still, many website infections are caused not entirely by the negligence of website owners themselves, but also by the lax security standards of their web hosts. Just as novice or apathetic webmasters externalize the costs of poor website security to internet users, impune web hosts externalize the costs of poor server security to consumer webmasters, who have few means of recourse.

5 Methods for Identifying Most-Infected Web Hosts

StopBadware's list of infected websites is currently derived from a single data source: Google. Google's Security Team sends us a list of URLs that Google has determined to host malware, which we tag in our clearinghouse with the information we develop through our own testing and through interaction with webmasters and the public. Google's method of constructing this list of infected URLs is described by Provos et al. (Provos et al. 2007). Because StopBadware's list of infected websites is dependent on Google's malicious website collection and detection methods, it is possible that some systematic bias exists in our data, reflecting the limitations of the scope and depth of Google's index, or the particular types of infection detected by Google. For example, if Google only tests websites using Internet Explorer, it will fail to detect infections that exclusively exploit other web browsers. We believe that Google's data is representative of the Internet as a whole, but it is probably not comprehensive. Because many website infections are caused by links to third-party servers, the availability of these referenced servers can affect the infectiousness of the compromised webpages. Other infections are cleared by website owners or advertising networks after Google has reported the sites to us but before StopBadware has independently tested those sites. Either of these factors can create inconsistency between Google's list of infected websites and StopBadware's testing and reporting process, since a site that infects users at one moment might appear to be clean in the next. In order to maximize the accuracy of our data by limiting our study to websites which we know firsthand to be infected, we constrained our study to the list of websites whose infections StopBadware had confirmed. StopBadware does not attempt to confirm infections on websites whose owners have not requested reviews from us, so the list of confirmed infections used in this study reflects the subset of website owners who requested StopBadware's assistance, and therefore excludes those websites which are likely owned by malfeasants directly, and those whose owners chose to deal with the infections without our assistance. The IP addresses for these confirmed, infectious websites were resolved using a DNS server controlled by StopBadware. Although it is common for malware distribution servers to change IP addresses rapidly in order to avoid detection and blacklisting, we believe that the IP addresses of the compromised personal and consumer websites that predominate our sample are unlikely to change frequently. In the future, we plan to resolve IP addresses for all URLs supplied to us by Google or other data partners at the time we receive those URLs, not just those which we have confirmed to be infected. Once this list of IP addresses was compiled, we used a free 'who-is' lookup server provided by Team Cymru in Chicago to group the IPs by Autonomous System Number (ASN), registered AS name, registration date, country of registration, and registrar. This information was then linked in our database to the original website URLs and IP addresses, allowing us to determine which ASNs hosted the largest number of infections. ASN grouping is not perfect, since some IP addresses do not map to any existing ASN, and some ASNs are subleased, which can make certain web hosts appear more secure than they really are. Furthermore, some ASNs are relatively small, while others are Class B blocks, which can contain tens of thousands of IP addresses, each of which could host thousands of URLs. To add granularity to our investigation, URLs were also grouped by IP address, which revealed a few cases in which nearly all of an ASN's infections were hosted on a single host IP.

6 Web Host Infection Results

Although StopBadware does not conduct comprehensive vulnerability scans of web hosts or particular servers, we use the information contained in our website clearinghouse to identify web hosts that host an unusually large number of compromised websites, an indicator that those hosts are either structurally insecure or undedicated to clearing infections after they occur. We publish this information to inform webmasters about the hidden risks of contracting hosting services with these web hosts, and to encourage the public to pressure the web hosts to reform their security practices. Our first public report on highly infected web hosts was issued in May '07, and highlighted the security risk posed by one hosting company in particular: IPowerWeb (StopBadware 2007). At that time, IPowerWeb hosted over 10,800 infected websites, which composed more than 20% of all websites in our sample, and nearly four times the number hosted by the second most infected host. As it happened, IPowerWeb was undergoing a merger at the time StopBadware released its report, which resulted in enormous public and private pressure for the company to take security more seriously. As of January '08, only 129 of the infected websites in our clearinghouse were hosted by IPowerWeb - a commendable improvement. Even so, the total number of infected websites reported to us by Google increased over 400% during the period between March '07 and December '07, and another web host has developed an unusually large number of infections. The Planet, which is controlled by the private equity firm GI Partners, now hosts roughly 8,300 infectious websites as shown in Figure 1. No matter which party is responsible for the initial security lapses that caused these infections, if The Planet ceased to abdicate responsibility for the security of its servers and forced its clients to clean and secure their websites, it could have a substantial positive impact in the fight against the spread of malware.

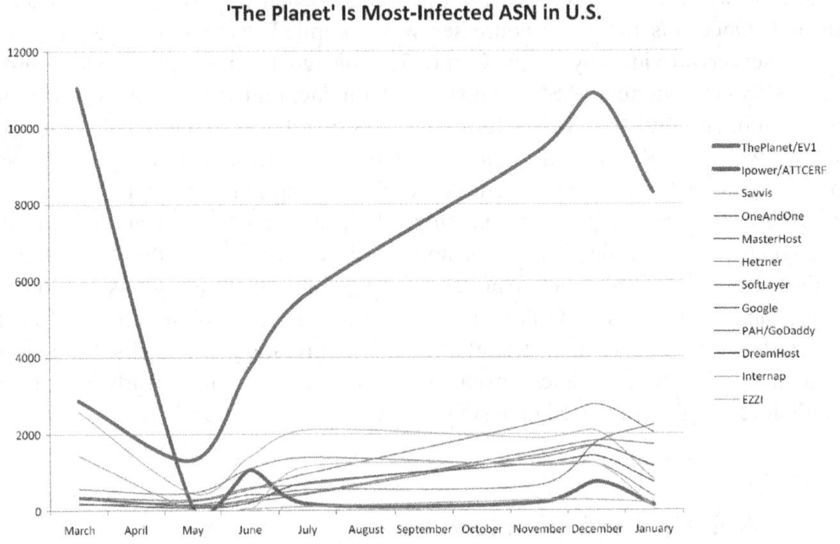

Figure 1. 'The Planet' Is Most-Infected ASN in US

6.1 *The Panda in the Room*

Although The Planet hosts far more infected websites than any other host in the United States or Europe, even this threat is overshadowed by the volume of infectious websites which are hosted in China. China's single most infected ASN (#4134) hosted nearly 83,600 infectious websites in December '07, as seen in Figure 2, which constituted approximately 30% of our entire website sample. The top 5 Chinese ASNs host over 50% of the world's infectious websites, while the top five ASNs in the rest of the world account for a mere 7.6% of this total. Although the Chinese population is large, internet penetration in China does not exceed that of the rest of the world, and even if Chinese websites are concentrated on fewer ASNs in general, the total number of infections in China far exceeds the total in the rest of the world. We can only speculate why China has an abnormally high rate of infections. Although the value of financial information stolen from Chinese internet users may be low compared to financial information stolen from Americans, the ease with which some Chinese websites can be attacked and many Chinese internet users infected creates a comparative advantage for the production of Chinese bot-networks, which can be used to mount distributed denial-of-service attacks or to send enormous quantities of spam worldwide. Furthermore, many Chinese internet users possess virtual assets in online community and game accounts, which are commonly stolen, aggregated, and exchanged on online auction sites for real currency and value.

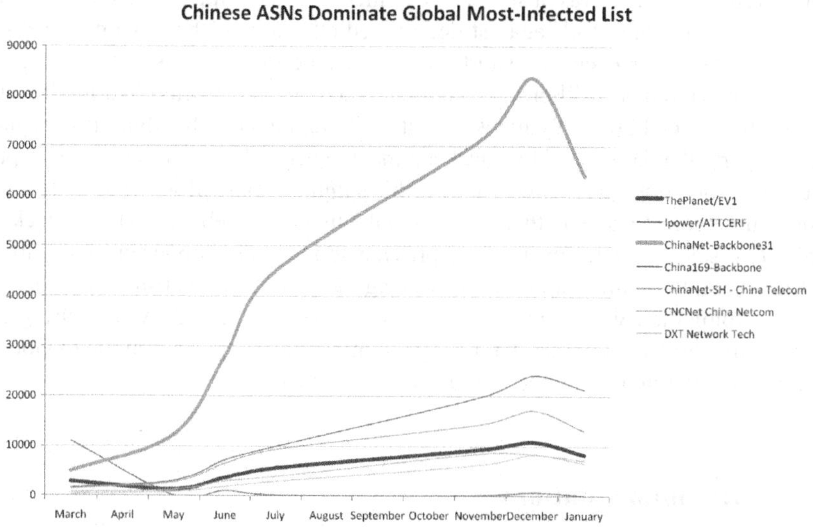

Figure 2. Chinese ASNs Dominate Global Most-Infected List

We propose that the single most important factor which leads Chinese websites to become infected at a higher rate than websites in the rest of the world is the relative lack of public disclosure and quarantine. Although Google does provide interstitial warnings in its Chinese search results as it does elsewhere, Google controls only about 24% of the Chinese search market. Baidu, China's leading search engine, holds a 61% share of the Chinese search market, and currently offers no clear warnings or protections against harmful websites in its search results. Because Chinese internet users generally do not know which websites host malware and have no clear recourse mechanism to punish or publicly shame insecure web hosts, many Chinese web hosts and website owners do not make the security and safety of their websites a priority.

The Chinese disclosure environment can be viewed as a worst-case scenario for what can happen when web content providers are not accountable to web consumers for the safety of their internet properties. This observation informs the importance of our quest to disclose website infections to the public, to pressure web hosts to take an active role in ensuring the security and safety of their servers, and to educate and support consumer webmasters and internet users who seek information and resources to protect themselves from attack and exploitation on the web. It will be interesting to observe timed attacks on Chinese websites during the 2008 Summer Olympic Games in Beijing. The official website of the 2008 Olympic Games (beijing2008.cn) is hosted on the China Netcom network, which currently hosts over 8,000 infected websites. As the Olympic Games approach and progress, many Olympics-oriented web properties which are hosted on Chinese networks will become highly valuable temporal attack targets. Like the Superbowl

2007 website, which was also attacked, the 2008 Olympics website has little experience defending itself against determined attackers. If the Olympics website is compromised for even one short, peak-traffic period, perhaps surrounding the opening ceremonies, millions of computers could be infected worldwide. Of course, the official 2008 Olympics website will not be the only Olympics-oriented web property that is targeted by attackers; many other websites owned by Olympics enthusiasts and opportunists will appear this summer, some of which may be even more vulnerable to attack than the official Olympics website. Baidu's lack of malware disclosure mechanisms may provide an interesting opportunity to further test the theories of this chapter, by observing the patterns of website infection and visitor exploitation which occur in relation to the games, and by measuring the comparative protective effect that Google's interstitial warnings provide to Google Search users within the limited scope and timeframe of the games.

7 Recommendations

The current voluntary disclosure paradigm for software vulnerabilities is broken. It allows vendors to systematically underinvest in software security while externalizing the costs of resulting software vulnerabilities to end users without those users' informed consent. In the Internet context, voluntary disclosure leads web hosting providers and website owners to take inadequate measures to secure their services against attackers, since they are unlikely to be held responsible for damages to Internet users in the event that their websites become infected. Even when website owners are aware that their websites have been compromised and are actively harming Internet users, many of these website owners deliberately attempt to conceal the attacks, because they value the reputation of their brands more than they value the welfare of their visitors. Similarly, web hosts fail to disclose their security failures because their reputations are guarded from public scrutiny by the intermediating brands of their clients; and thus, the market for web hosting services is also a 'lemons' market.

Google and StopBadware's mandatory disclosure of web infections begins to solve this market failure by informing consumers of risks that website owners and software vendors would otherwise attempt to hide. Other potential remedies, such as civil suits by exploited Internet users against negligent webmasters, could also be effective in shifting the burden of responsibility for web security from consumers to web content providers[36]. One example of mandatory disclosure policy that could be expanded to require webmasters to disclose infections to their

[36] Some have cited the increased investment in fraud-prevention technology resulting from placing the burden of liability for ATM fraud on banks, rather than on account holders, as an example of how civil liability could be used to promote greater investment in Internet security (Anderson 2001).

visitors is California Senate Bill 1386, which demands that companies disclose incidents which have resulted in the exposure of sensitive customer information. Unfortunately, these legal remedies would be difficult to apply and enforce consistently across the varying legal landscapes of the many countries where malware infections occur. For example, it would be unreasonable to expect American product liability laws to have a substantial impact on Internet security in China. Mandatory disclosure of infected websites, whether publicly or privately enforced, can be sufficient protection and remedy for Internet consumers, provided that the disclosures actually succeed in informing all visitors to those websites of their risk of infection. Our warnings play an important role in protecting and informing consumers of the risks of visiting particular websites, but our defensive efforts will not be sufficient to stem the malware tide without the aid of other web gatekeepers, ranging from search engines to web hosting providers. Furthermore, our public warnings about infected websites succeed only in correcting the misallocation of the economic burdens of malware, and do not directly address the underlying security issues which allow these infections to occur. Ultimately, we hope that the pressure on webmasters that our warnings create will encourage them to learn about Internet security, and to demand better security from their hosting providers, so that infections are prevented and neither Internet users nor consumer webmasters become victims of attack. Similarly, web hosts and Internet service providers should be held responsible for the safety of properties hosted on their networks. The positive change enacted at iPowerWeb following StopBadware's report on infected web hosts confirms our belief that mandatory disclosure policy can be effective in encouraging web hosts to invest in good security practices. We therefore propose that in general, when particular websites are determined to host or distribute malware, web service providers should be required to clear the infections or to quarantine those websites. This will extend the protections currently enjoyed by users of Google Search to the rest of the Internet public.

The 2008 Olympic Games in Beijing will provide an interesting opportunity for the global public to pressure China to address its disproportionate malware infection problem. If China fails to contain and clear these infections in time, many 'virtual visitors' to the games around the world will likely fall prey to identity theft and other forms of Internet crime as a result of visiting compromised Olympics-oriented websites. China is already expected to make compromises in certain areas of its Internet policy, such as permitting specific IP addresses assigned to Internet cafes, hotels, and conference centers in the vicinity of the games to access web content that is ordinarily blocked by the 'Great Firewall of China', in order to present itself well to the visiting international community this summer (Fallows 2008). Thus, it seems possible that Chinese authorities might be more responsive than usual to complaints about China's malware problem, if enough people are made aware of the issue. We hope that the exposure produced by this chapter will help inform the public about the perverse incentives that are created when website infections are concealed instead of cleared, and that it will encourage more web gatekeepers, in China and elsewhere, to begin to address these problems with greater responsibility and openness.

8 Conclusion

Website owners and web hosting providers externalize the costs of lax web security by concealing website infections from the public, which harms Internet users. Google's interstitial warning pages force disclosure of website infections, and cause significant reductions of traffic to these infected websites during the period that the warnings are active. This causes website owners to accept responsibility for the safety of their services, and prevents many Internet users from becoming infected and exploited online.

The consequences of inadequate website infection disclosure are seen in Chinas high malware infection rate, where Google's limited market share implies that fewer Internet users are warned against infected websites. To correct this lack of disclosure in China, we encourage Baidu, China's leading search engine, to adopt a private mandatory infection disclosure regime similar to Google's; thereby expanding protection for Internet users and ensuring that expectations and responsibilities for website security are consistent around the world.

Acknowledgments

This work has been supported in part by the Berkman Center for Internet and Society and The Center for Research and Computation and Society (CRCS).

We would also like to thank Team Cymru for providing IP to ASN translation service, Google for the use of their data on malicious websites, and John Palfrey, Jonathan Zittrain, Maxim Weinstein, and the rest of the StopBadware team for help and support.

References

Akerlof, G. A. "The Market for 'Lemons': Quality Uncertainty and the Market Mechanism," *The Quarterly Journal of Economics* (84:3), 1970, pp. 488–500.

Anderson, R. "Why Information Security is Hard—An Economic Perspective," in *17th Annual Computer Security Applications Conference (ACSAC)*, 2001.

Anderson, R. "Open and Closed Systems are Equivalent (That Is, in an Ideal World)," in *Perspectives on Free and Open Source Software,* The MIT Press, 2005, pp. 127-142.

Arora, A., Krishnan, R., Nandkumar, A., Telang, R., and Yang, Y. "Impact of Vulnerability Disclosure and Patch Availability: An Empirical Analysis," in *Workshop on Economics and Information Security*, 2004.

Arora, A., Telang, R., and Xu, H. "Optimal Policy for Software Vulnerability Disclosure," in *Workshop on Economics and Information Security*, 2004.

Camp, L. J., and Wolfram, C. D. "Pricing Security: Vulnerabilities as Externalities." *Economics of Information Security* (12), 2004.

Cavusoglu, H., Cavusoglu, H., and Zhang, J. "Economics of Security Patch Management," in *Workshop on Economics and Information Security*, 2006.

Choi, J.-P., Ferstman, C., and Gandal, N. "Network Security: Vulnerabilities and Disclosure Policy," in *Workshop on Economics and Information Security*, 2007.

Fallows, J. "The Connection Has Been Reset," *The Atlantic Monthly*. http://www.theatlantic.com/doc/200803/chinese-firewall, 2008.

Finjan. 2007. "Finjan Web Security Trends Report q2-2007." http://www.finjan.com.

Geer, D., Bace, R., Gutmann, P., Metzger, P., Pfleeger, C. P., Quarterman, J. S., and Schneier, B. "Cyberinsecurity: The Cost of Monopology." *Computer and Communications Industry Association (CCIA)*, 2003.

Granick, J. S. "The Price of Restricting Vulnerability Publications," *International Journal of Communications Law and Policy* (9), 2005.

OMurchu, L. "Honor among Thieves?" http://www.symantec.com/enterprise/security_resp onse/weblog/%2007/11/honour_among_thieves.html. Symantec, 2007.

Provos, N., McNamee, D., Mavrommatis, P., Wang, K., and Modadugu, N. "The Ghost in the Browser Analysis of Web-based Malware," in *Proceedings of the first conference on First Workshop on Hot Topics in Understanding Botnets (HotBots'07),* 4–4. USENIX Association, 2007.

Rescorla, E. "Is Finding Security Holes a Good Idea?" *IEEE Security and Privacy* (3:1), 2005, pp. 14–19.

Schechter, S. E. "How to Buy Better Testing: Using Competition to Get the Most Security and Robustness for Your Dollar," in *Infrastructure Security Conference*, 2002.

StopBadware. http://www.stopbadware.org. Berkman Center for Internet and Society, 2008.

StopBadware. "Stopbadware.org Identifies Companies Hosting Large Numbers of Websites that Can Infect Internet Users with Badware." http://www.stopbadware.org/home/pr 050307, 2007.

Swire, P.P. "Security Market: Incentives for Disclosure of Vulnerabilities," in *Proceedings of the 12th ACM Conference on Computer and Communications Security (CCS '05)*, 2005, pp. 405–405.

The Impact of Incentives on Notice and Take-down

Tyler Moore and Richard Clayton

Computer Laboratory, University of Cambridge, UK

Abstract We consider a number of notice and take-down regimes for Internet content. These differ in the incentives for removal, the legal framework for compelling action, and the speed at which material is removed. By measuring how quickly various types of content are removed, we determine that the requester's incentives outweigh all other factors, from the penalties available, to the methods used to obstruct take-down.

1 Introduction

Almost all schemes for the removal of undesirable content from the Internet are described as being a 'notice and take-down' (NTD) regime, although their actual details vary considerably. In this chapter we show that the effectiveness of removal depends rather more on the incentives for this to happen, than on narrow issues such as the legal basis or the type of material involved.

It is impractical for Internet Service Providers (ISPs) to police the entirety of the content that their users place upon the Internet, so it is generally seen as unjust for ISPs to bear strict liability, viz: that they become legally liable for the mere presence of unlawful content. However, the ISPs are in an unrivalled position to suppress content held on their systems by removing access to resources – webspace, connectivity, file access permissions, etc. – from their customers. Hence many content removal regimes make ISPs liable for content once they have been informed of its existence, viz: once they have been put on 'notice'. If they fail to 'take-down' the material then sanctions against them may then proceed.

The ISP is often the only entity that can identify customers in the real world, and so they must necessarily become involved before the true originator can be held accountable for the presence of unlawful content. This gives rise to various complexities because the ISP may be bound by data protection legislation or by common law notions of confidentiality, from disclosing the information haphazardly. Equally, ISPs are reluctant to get drawn into acting as the plaintiffs' agent against their own customers – and at the very least demand recompense for their efforts,

M.E. Johnson (ed.), *Managing Information Risk and the Economics of Security*,
DOI: 10.1007/978-0-387-09762-6_10,

along with immunities when errors are made. Nevertheless, some benefits do accrue from including the ISP in the process. They may be more familiar with the process than their customers, allowing them to reject flawed requests and assist in dealing with vexatious claims. The ISP's experience, along with their assessment of the standing of their customer, will enable them to assess the merits of the case, and perhaps advise their customer that the claim should be ignored. An ISP does not have any incentive to annoy a major commercial customer by suspending their website merely because of a dubious claim of copyright in a photograph it displays.

In fact, when we examine NTD regimes, we find that incentives are at the heart of the effectiveness of every process, outweighing the nature of the material or the legal framework for removal. Where complainants are highly motivated, and hence persistent, content is promptly removed. Where the incentives are weak, or third parties become involved with far less of an incentive to act, then removal is slow or almost nonexistent.

In this chapter we examine a number of notice and take-down regimes, presenting data on the speed of removal. We start by considering defamation in Section 2, which has an implicit NTD regime. In Section 3 we look at copyright which has, particularly in the United States, a very formalised NTD mechanism. In Section 4 we consider the removal of child sexual abuse images and show how slow this removal can be in practice. In Section 5 we contrast this with the removal of many different categories of 'phishing' websites, where we are able to present extensive data that illustrates many practical difficulties that arise depending upon how the criminals have chosen to create their fake websites. In Section 6 we consider a range of other criminal websites and show that their removal is extremely slow in comparison with phishing websites, and we offer some insights into why this should be so. In Section 7 we consider the issues surrounding the removal of malware from websites and from enduser machines, and discuss the incentives, such as they are, for ISPs to act to force their users to clean up their machines – and in particular to stop them from inadvertently sending out email 'spam'. Finally, in Section 8 we draw the various threads together to compare and contrast the various NTD regimes.

2 Defamation

Until very recently, access to mass media was limited by professionals (printers, newspaper editors, etc.) acting as gatekeepers, so that people could rarely express defamatory opinions to large audiences. Consequently, actions for defamation (sometimes technically distinguished by terms such as slander or libel) were also rare, and would typically involve a handwritten note (*Wilde v. Marquis of Queensbury 1895*), a letter (*Huff v. Huff 1915*), or a message on a golf club noticeboard (*Byrne v. Dean 1937*).[37] The defamation itself was usually obvious, and these cases were decided upon the interpretation of the law, or the unmasking of perjury by one of the protagonists.

Conversely, where books or mainstream journalism are involved, the gatekeeper has already formed an opinion that the material should be published, and may have edited the content to reduce the risk of action. These court cases typically revolve around 'justification' (whether the claim was in fact true) such as in *Irving v. Lipstadt 2000*, whether the court has jurisdiction (*Kroch v. Rossell 1937*), or the extent of the actual defamation (*Whistler v. Ruskin 1878*).

The Internet, and the ease of posting articles to Usenet (*Godfrey v. Demon Internet 1998*) or to web sites (*Totalise v. Motley Fool 2001*), has fundamentally changed the landscape to one in which there are no gatekeepers, but individuals are capable of rapidly propagating their words to a wide audience. This makes defamation more common – although since it is a civil matter, state aid for plaintiffs is seldom available, meaning that only the well-heeled, or those with the most open-and-shut cases, ever take action.

In the United Kingdom the law was revised by the Defamation Act 1996, when the Internet was already widely being used, albeit with 'user-generated content' still in its infancy. The Act enshrined the existing common law principle of 'innocent dissemination', and made it clear that distributors of defamatory material had a statutory immunity until they became aware of the nature of the material. In the context of Internet content this means that ISPs are not liable for a defamatory statement until they are put on notice of the existence of the material, and court actions will not succeed if they promptly take-down the material.

In 1999, in a pre-trial hearing of *Godfrey v. Demon Internet*, Morland J. set out the extent of the statutory (and common law) immunity in a lengthy judgment that struck out part of Demon Internet's defence (Morland 1999). The case was then settled out of court. This immediately led to a step-change in the number of notices being served upon Demon Internet – as people became aware of serving notices as a simple and effective method of removing defamatory material (Clayton 2000).

In the USA, defamation has some subtle differences from UK law. In particular if the statement relates to a public figure then it is necessary to prove 'actual malice'. More relevant to the present discussion, American ISPs also have a qualitatively different defence in that s230 of the Communications Decency Act 1996 gives an immunity where information is merely being transmitted and was originated by a third party. The leading case is *Zeran v. AOL* from 1997, which made it crystal clear that, in the US, serving a notice does not put an ISP under any obligation to take-down defamatory content.

Very few people can afford to pursue defamation cases to court, and those who do so are often very well-known. This leads to 'forum shopping', where cases are

---

37 In this chapter we cite UK cases; similar developments occurred in the US, Australia and other jurisdictions.

pursued in the British or Australian courts rather than in the United States. Conversely, where a court action is unlikely, the practical effect of the different US and UK regimes is that when defamatory content is published on a UK web site it will be fairly promptly removed by the ISP. When it is republished on a US site, it then remains available for a considerable time.[38]

3 Copyright Violations

Rights holders have long complained about copyright violation by Internet users. As individuals have been able to access more and more bandwidth, the focus of attention has moved from photographs, to songs, to feature films. Although most 'sharing' now takes place on peer-to-peer networks, the original mechanisms were the use of websites or Usenet articles. To deal with the dominance of client/server architectures of the time, the US passed Title II of the Digital Millennium Copyright Act 1998 (DMCA).

The DMCA gives an immunity (a 'safe harbor') to ISPs operating web or Usenet servers if they follow certain rules. They must provide a contact address, and if served with a valid notice alleging copyright infringement, they acquire 'actual knowledge' and must 'expeditiously' remove the material. However, if they are served with a 'counter notification' (a 'put-back' request) by their customer, then they must restore the material 10 to 14 days later unless the matter has gone to court. The put-back notice has to identify the customer, who must submit to the court's jurisdiction, viz: they must firmly identify themselves as standing behind their claim that the take-down notice was mistaken.

Similar take-down provisions exist in the 2000 European Union 'Directive on Electronic Commerce', which gives a similar immunity to ISPs using very similar language – 'actual knowledge', 'expeditiously' etc. However, the Directive does not set out a put-back provision.

There have been many claims that the EU regime creates incentives for ISPs to remove items first without even bothering to ask questions afterwards. Two experiments have been performed to demonstrate this. In 2003, an Oxford research group posted material onto UK and US websites (Ahlert 2004). The material was an extract of John Stuart Mill's 1869 'On Liberty', discussing freedom of speech. The experimenters then wrote anonymously to the two hosting ISPs, falsely claiming that the material was still in copyright. The UK ISP removed the

[38] It would be possible to give numerous instances of sites that have migrated to the US, however we have not provided any examples of this alternative type of 'forum shopping' because the authors are currently residing in the UK. In this jurisdiction there is some case law about providing pointers to defamatory material: in *Hird v. Wood 1894*, the court held that the defendant had defamed the plaintiff by merely standing on a road and mutely pointing out a path which, if followed, allowed one to view a notice on which a defamatory statement had been written, even though the authorship of that statement was never proved.

material, whereas the US ISP insisted upon the provision of the legally necessary 'on pain of perjury' declaration on the DMCA notice – which the researchers were not prepared to make, so the material remained available. The researchers concluded that there was a substantial difference between the US and UK in how easily websites are removed, although one suspects that if they had perjured themselves, the difference would have disappeared.

In 2004 a similar experiment was performed by the Netherlands-based 'Multatuli Project' (Nas 2004). They placed some out-of-copyright material from a famous 1871 tract onto webspace provided by ten different Dutch ISPs. Their results were mixed, with some ISPs losing their first complaint and only acting on a follow-up message. By the end of the experiment, seven of the ten ISPs had removed the material, taking between 3 hours and 3 days to do so. However, in neither investigation did the customer protest the removal decision and suggest that the ISP taking the complaint at face value was incorrect. Hence the experiments do not necessarily represent the true situation, but merely show that ISPs are generally keen to avoid liability, do not establish the accuracy of complaints, and may need to be asked more than once before they act.

4 Child Sexual Abuse Images

Child sexual abuse images are often perceived as the most widely condemned form of Internet content, but this universality is relatively recent and remains inconsistent. For example, Japan did not pass its 'Child Prostitution and Child Pornography Prevention Law' until 1999.

Harmonisation of the laws in this area was one of the aims of the 2001 Convention on Cybercrime, but this has several optional aspects: the age limit should be 18, but can be as low as 16; simple possession need not be made a crime; and computer-generated material, no matter how realistic, may be tolerated. The last of these issues is a point of departure between the UK and the US. In the UK, child sexual abuse images generated on a computer are illegal if they are realistic enough to appear to be a photograph (viz: they are a 'pseudo-photograph'), whereas the US Supreme Court held in *Ashcroft v. Free Speech Coalition 2002* that since no real children were involved in creating this type of material, it was unconstitutional to ban it.

Notwithstanding these minor variations, the bulk of child sexual abuse images are illegal to distribute in all relevant jurisdictions, and hence it should be expected that any such material is promptly removed.

The Internet Watch Foundation (IWF) was founded in the UK in 1996 to operate a 'hotline' for reports of child sexual abuse images from the public. It employs trained staff to check these reports and pass them on to the UK police if illegal material is found. If the sites are in the UK then the police will act upon them directly, whereas if they are hosted elsewhere in the world then a report will be passed to the authorities in that country. Within the UK, the IWF will also pass the report directly to the ISP and, in the case of illegal images circulating on Usenet, will pass a report to all UK ISPs so that they can remove the article from their servers. The IWF is a member of INHOPE,[39] and it will send a report to another INHOPE member if the material appears to be hosted in their country.

The IWF regularly publish statistics on where illegal images are hosted, but until recently they have not measured how long it takes to get them removed, and their figures still remain patchy. Anecdotally their view is that sites are generally removed in weeks rather than months, although they have much higher expectations for sites in the UK – where removal is expected within hours, or a couple of days at most. Removal became so rapid that at one stage the IWF were reporting sites to the police first, so that evidence of what was on the site could be collected, and only two days later would they report the site to the relevant UK ISP.

The IWF have published a smattering of data on site longevity, which – since only fractions of a percent of all sites are now hosted in the UK – will in practice measure the speed of take-down of internationally hosted content. In mid-2006 they checked which sites were available at the start and end of a six week period and found that 287 (circa 20%) of sites had survived, including one dating from 1999 which had been the subject of 20 separate reports to the authorities (IWF 2006a). In 2007 (IWF 2007) they reported that 94 sites had been active for a year or more, 33 for two years and 32 for longer, and in late 2006 (IWF 2006b) that of the commercial sites they tracked (about half of the total), 62% were removed in a month, and 2% lasted more than a year.

To supplement the published reports, the IWF kindly provided us with sanitised data on the websites they track. They use an automated system which performs daily checks on whether the offending content remains available. Whenever the system detects removal, operators manually inspect the page to ensure it has been removed. The logs given to us include a pseudonym for the suspected URL, the date reported, the date removed and the date of reappearance (if observed).

We computed the lifetimes for websites reported during the calendar year 2007, which in some cases were already known to the IWF, but were mainly new. The total number of domains was 2585, although of course the number of individual pages with child sexual abuse images was much higher. We excluded 8 domains which had more than 100 individual reports, which we believe to be well-known 'free' web-hosting sites.

The lifetime of each website was calculated by comparing the date of first report to the date of first removal. Consequently, we do not consider how long it takes to remove any subsequent reappearance of images on the same website.[40]

---

[39] The International Association of Internet Hotlines: http://www.inhope.org

[40] The data provided by the IWF presents numerous difficulties whenever images reappear on the same website. Using the sanitised data they made available, it is impossible to distinguish between similar and distinct removals on the same website.

The results are given in Table 1. Of the 2585 website domains reported to be hosting child sexual abuse images in 2007, nearly all (2531) of the websites removed images at least once on or before April 3, 2008. It took an average of 562 hours – over three weeks – to take down images hosted on these websites. The median lifetime is 264 hours, or 11 days. Fifty-four websites reported in 2007 (2.1% of the total) have never had images removed. The average lifetime for these sites is 338 days (and growing). Combined together, the mean lifetime of all websites found to be hosting child sexual abuse images in 2007 is 719 hours (30 days).

Table 1. Lifetimes for Websites Hosting Child Sexual Abuse Images

-	Sites	Lifetime (hours)	
		mean	median
Removed websites	2531	562	264
Unremoved websites	54	≥8027	≥9216
Total	2585	719	288

While we have not measured the time to remove images when they reappear on websites, we have determined that within 24 weeks, images reappeared on 1070 sites, 41% of the total. Sometimes offenders reload new images onto free webspace, while at other times insecure websites are simply recompromised (we describe techniques for publishing illicit content below).

5 Phishing

Phishing is the term used when criminals entice people into visiting websites that impersonate the real thing, duping them into revealing passwords and other credentials, which will later be used for fraud. Many types of companies are attacked in this way, from domain registrars, through auction sites and multi-user games to online merchants, but the vast majority of attacks are against financial institutions: banks, credit unions, credit card companies, online share brokers and so on.

In previous work we have identified wide variations in take-down time for different financial institutions and different types of attacker (Moore and Clayton 2007). We have subsequently determined that some of the variation can be ascribed to the company charged with removing the sites being unaware of its existence, viz: that no notice was issued, so no take-down occurred (Moore 2008).

In this chapter we examine phishing attacks against a particular e-commerce company that conducts business using two very well-known brands, both of which are in the top 600 most visited websites in the world. We consider the data for attacks that were first reported during the month of January 2008. The lifetime figures we give are from the earliest point at which we know the site existed, to the last time that our monitoring system[41] indicates that it was hosting a fake page. Where we can do no better, we use the timestamp from when we receive the URL, but almost all of our feeds, including the one from the brand owner we are considering, provide a timestamp from when they entered the URL into their internal systems – which we assume to be within a few minutes of when they start to verify the nature of the site and set their take-down processes into motion.

To avoid being traced, phishing attackers will not host the fake websites on their own personal machines. Some attackers use free webspace, where anyone can register and upload pages, but it is more common to encounter sites that are hosted on compromised machines; perhaps a residential machine, but often a server in a data centre. The hijacked machine will have come under the attacker's control either through a security vulnerability (typically unpatched applications within a semi-abandoned 'blog' or messageboard), or because the user is running some malware, delivered by email or downloaded during a visit to a malicious website.

It is possible to distinguish these cases by examining the URL and by checking the IP address of the website. We now consider the various different types of hosting for phishing websites, and how NTD works in each case. The website lifetimes for the different phishing attack methods discussed in this section are listed in Table 2.

Table 2. Phishing Website Lifetimes by Attack Type

-	Sites	Lifetime (hours)	
		Mean	median
Free web-hosting			
all	395	47.6	0
brand owner aware	240	4.3	0
brand owner missed	155	114.7	29
Compromised machines			
all	193	49.2	0
brand owner aware	105	3.5	0
brand owner missed	155	103.8	10
Rock-phish domains	821	70.3	33
Fast-flux domains	314	96.1	25.5

[41] For a detailed account of our 'feeds' of URLs of phishing websites and our monitoring system, we refer the interested reader to (Moore 2008; Moore and Clayton 2007; Moore and Clayton 2008). In the current context, the key point is that because we receive data from a number of disparate sources, we believe that our database of URLs is one of the most comprehensive available, and the overwhelming majority of phishing websites will come to our attention.

5.1 Free Web-hosting

A typical URL for a website that has been set up at a free web-hosting provider is http://www.bankname.freehostsite.com/login, where the bankname is chosen to match or closely resemble the domain name of the financial institution being attacked. We compiled a list of known free web-hosting domains, and used this to determine which websites we were monitoring were hosted on free space. We also checked the IP addresses of the websites against the IP address ranges used by the free providers.

To get the phishing website removed, all that is necessary is to contact the webspace provider and draw their attention to the fraudulent site. They will then remove it and cancel the hosting account. In earlier work we commented on the wide disparity in take-down times between different providers, and upon a 'clued-up' effect, whereby when webspace providers were first exploited they would not know how to deal with the situation, but after awhile they would acquire 'clue' and settle down to a steady-state removal time (Moore and Clayton 2007).

Some attackers favour hosting attacks on free webspace. In January 2008, for the two brands we are considering, we learned of 395 phishing websites that were hosted on free webspace. The majority of these websites were removed before we could visit them, giving a median lifetime of 0 hours. However, there are a number of very long-lived websites, which dragged the mean lifetime up to 47.6 hours.

To understand why the mean is so much larger than the median, it is necessary to examine which websites were known about by the brand owner. Only 240 of the 395 free-hosting phishing websites impersonating the brands turned up in the company's own feed of phishing website URLs. This subset of websites was removed very quickly – 4.3 hours on average, with a 0 hour median. By contrast, the 155 websites that we learned about from other sources, but the company remained ignorant of, had an average lifetime of 114.7 hours with a median of 29 hours.

5.2 Compromised Machines

For compromised machines, attackers may have restricted permissions, and are limited on where files can be placed. They add their own web pages within an existing structure, leading to URLs for their websites that have the typical form http://www.example.com/user/www.bankname.com/ where, once again, the bankname is present to lend specious legitimacy should the user check which site they are visiting, yet fail to appreciate the way in which URLs are really structured.

The attacker may occasionally find that the existing DNS configuration permits URLs of the form www.bankname.com.example.com, but if this is not possible, and if the example part of the hostname makes it unlikely that the URL will be convincing, then the URL may use just the IP address of the compromised machine, perhaps encoded into hexadecimal to obscure its nature. Alternatively, to further allay suspicion, the fraudsters will sometimes go to the effort of registering their own domain name, which they will then point at either free webspace (as just discussed), which can often be configured to allow this to work, or to a compromised machine where they have sufficient control of the web server configuration so that it will respond to page requests. The domain names are usually chosen to be a variation on bankname.com such as bankname-usa.com, or they will use the bank's name as a subdomain of some plausible, but superficially innocuous domain, such as bankname.xtrasecuresite.com. A halfway house to an actual domain name is the use of systems that provide domain names for dynamic IP address users, which results in the usage of domains such as bankname.dyndns.org.

In order to get a website removed from a compromised machine it is generally necessary to get in touch with the system administrator who looks after it. In some cases that information can be gleaned from public records or from the rest of the website. In other cases it is necessary to work through the ISP to get a message delivered. Less commonly, where a domain name has been registered especially for the phishing attack, it is necessary to approach the appropriate domain name registrar and ask them to suspend the name.

We examined the attacks on the two brands by phishing websites that were hosted on compromised machines in January 2008 and found 193 websites[42] with an average lifetime of 49.2 hours and a 0 hour median, which is very similar to the lifetimes we measured for free web-hosting sites.

The similarities between compromised machines and free web hosts continue once we break down the lifetimes according to whether the brand owner was aware of the website. The 105 phishing websites hosted on compromised machines known to the company are removed within 3.5 hours on average (0 hour median). The 88 websites missed by the company remain for 103 hours on average, with a median of 10 hours.

Thus, for ordinary phishing websites, the main differentiator appears to be whether the organisation responsible for the take-down is aware of the site's existence. Free web-hosting companies and the administrators of compromised machines both appear to comply promptly with the take-down requests they received. However, the website administrators do need to be notified of the problem – phishing websites that brand owner did not know about, and so did not issue any notices for, remain up for considerably longer.

[42] While our method for identifying compromised websites from the structure of phishing URLs has confirmed 193 websites, there are additional websites that we have not yet verified. Hence, the 193 websites should be viewed as a sample of a significantly larger population of compromised websites.

5.3 *Rock-phish and Fast-flux Attacks*

The 'rock-phish' gang operate in a completely different manner from the ordinary phishing attacks just described. This group of criminals perpetrates phishing attacks on a massive scale (McMillan 2006). The gang purchases a number of domains with meaningless names such as lof80.info. Their spoof emails contain a long URL of the form http://www.bank.com.id123.lof80.info/vr. Although the URL contains a unique identifier (to evade spam filters), all variants are resolved to a single IP address using 'wildcard DNS'. The IP address is of a machine that acts as a proxy, relaying web traffic to and from a hidden 'mothership' machine. If the proxy is removed, the DNS is adjusted to use another proxy, and so the only practical way to remove the website is to get the appropriate registrar to remove the domain name from the DNS.

A related form of attack is dubbed 'fast-flux'. The mechanism is similar to the one employed by the rock-phish gang, except that the domain name is resolved to many IP addresses in parallel (typically 5 or 10) and the IP addresses used are rapidly changed (sometimes every 20 minutes). For these attacks the only practical approach is to have the domain name suspended. We have identified several disjoint fast-flux networks. Interested readers can find more details of fast-flux in (Honeynet Project 2007), which gives many details about one of the networks that we also encountered, and about its use in phishing attacks in (Moore and Clayton 2007). Unlike rock-phish attacks, fast-flux networks are made available for hire as a type of 'bulletproof' hosting. Hence, they are used for other types of attack in addition to phishing. We discuss the use of fast-flux domains for hosting online pharmacies in Section 6.3.

Besides using an innovative architecture, the rock-phish gang also attack multiple banks in parallel, with the URL path distinguishing between them. Since these bank 'microsites' generally appear and disappear together, we monitor the rock-sites generically, tracking whether the domain name remains active. For convenience, we track fast-flux sites in a similar manner, although they may attack only a single bank.

The rock-phish and fast-flux attack methods are not universally understood by the registrars who are asked to suspend domains. Splitting up the components of the attack (domains, compromised machines and hosting servers) obfuscates the phishing behaviour. Hence, each individual decision maker cannot easily recognise the nature of the attack – the domain registrar does not see an obviously impersonated domain name (e.g., barclaysbankk.com) and the ISP system administrator does not find HTML for a bank site in a hidden subdirectory on a hijacked machine. Recent activities have highlighted the confusion domain name registrars are experiencing in addressing the threat from rock-phish attacks. Email-blacklist operator Spamhaus engaged in a public row with the Austrian domain registrar nic.at over the registrar's initial refusal to remove rock-phish domains (Spamhaus 2007).

The two brands we have studied so far have only been very briefly targeted by rock-phish and fast-flux attacks, so we instead examine all attacks of this type, irrespective of brand. The lifetime of the 821 rock-phish domains we monitored in January 2008 reflects the added difficulty faced during take-down procedures. The domains lasted 70.3 hours on average (median 33 hours), despite the additional attention rock-phish domains attract by impersonating many banks simultaneously. The lifetimes for the 314 fast-flux domains were similar, lasting 96.1 hours on average with a 25.5 hour median.

5.4 Common Features of Phishing Website Removal

As has been seen, phishing websites are generally removed fairly promptly. This might be viewed as quite remarkable given the multiple jurisdictions involved. The site may be in a different country than the bank, and the take-down company making the request may be in a third location. Furthermore, it is most unusual for the police or the courts to be involved in the procedure. There is no legislation anywhere prescribing the elements that need to be present on the notice – or indeed specifying what the penalties might be for ignoring the notice. In practice the vast majority of system administrators have an understanding of what phishing is, they recognise the site as being part of a criminal enterprise, and they remove it. This was not always so – we have been told that when phishing was first starting in 2003 it was often more effective to point out the intellectual property infringements apparent on the website: the unauthorised use of logos, the similarity of design and text, and even in some cases, the unauthorised use of a particular rights-encumbered font.

Although the phishing sites are usually taken down it is, unfortunately, quite common for similar sites to reappear quickly. This occurs because the free web-hosting site does not have mechanisms to check for identical content being uploaded by a 'different' person; because the system administrator for a compromised machine does not patch the security hole that led to the compromise; or because the registrar does not tighten up their procedures to prevent the purchase of domain names using the same *modus operandi* as the instance just suspended. Looking at comprehensive phishing data from October 2007 to March 2008, we found that approximately 22% of all compromised machines were recompromised within 24 weeks. A more detailed analysis of phishing website recompromise and its causes can be found in (Moore and Clayton 2008). The recompromise rate for phishing is noticeably smaller than the 41% rate found for websites hosting child sexual abuse images. However, the comparison is somewhat inexact, since we cannot exclude all of the instances of free web-hosting from the analysis of child sexual abuse images due to our sanitised data source.

6 Fraudulent Websites

As the preceding discussion of the take-down of phishing websites shows, institutions being impersonated often have a very strong incentive to remove offending content. Consequently, miscreants have designed a number of scams that escape such scrutiny by creating websites for entirely fake institutions. While many types of fraudulent websites exist, we discuss three classes in this section: fake escrow agents, mule-recruitment websites and online pharmacies.

6.1 Fake Escrow Agents

One lucrative type of fraud is to set up fake escrow agents. Escrow agents serve as trusted intermediaries to facilitate large financial transactions between untrusted parties. For instance, someone buying a car on eBay might not want to pay the seller until she has received the car; likewise the seller might not want to ship the car until she has been paid. An escrow agent takes the money and the goods and completes the transaction once both parties have acted. In an escrow scam, a rogue seller offers an expensive item at a reasonable price. Once a buyer has been found, the seller suggests that they use an escrow agent of her choosing and points the buyer to the web page of the fake agent. The buyer sends her money to the fake escrow agent, only to later realise a fraud has occurred.

Fake escrow websites have been used extensively for the past few years. Because no organisation is being impersonated, no company tries to remove the websites. Only motivated volunteers, primarily acting through Artists Against 419 (AA419),[43] attempt to take down the websites. Initially, removing fake escrow websites took a very long time. Eventually, escrow website lifetimes diminished as volunteers developed efficient take-down procedures and established trust with ISPs. Meanwhile, the creators of the fake escrow agents have continued to turn the handle, creating 'new' companies with websites that borrow generously from prior incarnations. Hence, the battle between the fake escrow agents and volunteers has reached somewhat of a steady state.

We examined 696 fake escrow websites appearing between October and December 2007. On average, these websites remained for 222 hours, or over 9 days. The median lifetime was 24.5 hours, approximately one day. The volunteers are definitely making an impact, but given their limited resources they are certainly not as successful as the banks removing phishing websites.

Note that our analysis of lifetimes only includes escrow websites known to AA419, which is the only group we are aware of that are actively removing the

---

[43] http://www.aa419.org

websites.[44] It is undoubtedly the case that additional fake escrow websites exist. Most fake escrow pages include curious phrases such as:

> "Thanks to our innovative view of courier transport and to our commitment to provide a competitive service, we soon were ahead in the sector, leaving all the traditional Trans companies behind."

While the names of the companies are changed frequently along with the URLs, the website content often remains the same. Using targeted web searches for 81 peculiar phrases repeatedly used on the escrow pages, we identified many more websites than those listed by AA419. Each web search found 9.8 domains on average, while approximately 2.4 of these domains were picked up by AA419.

In all likelihood, these additional websites remain for much longer than those identified by the volunteers. So the fairest comparison between escrow and phishing websites is between the lifetimes of sites known to both removing parties. The average removal time of 4 hours (0 hour median) for the websites the brand owner knows about compares very favourably to the lifetimes of 222 hours (24.5 hour median) of escrow sites that are known to the volunteers.

6.2 *Mule-recruitment Websites*

One of the biggest challenges for phishing attackers is to 'launder' the proceeds obtained from victims. One method is to recruit 'money mules', who receive transfers of money from compromised phishing victim accounts, take a cut, and then forward the rest to third parties using non-revocable transactions, typically Western Union transfers. When the fraudulent transfers are detected, they are often reversed, and so it is often the case that the mule ends up out of pocket, rather than the original phishing victim.

Prospective mules are mainly recruited by sending spam email. Often the spam includes only an email address for correspondence. Other times there are links to a website of the purported company which is 'hiring' for jobs such as 'transaction processors', or 'sales executives'. Sometimes the mule-recruitment websites impersonate a legitimate business, but the company may be entirely fictitious. The existence of the website must be assumed to be important in engendering trust by the mule – who may even receive signed 'contracts of employment'. The apparent legitimacy makes the mules far more likely to ignore warnings given by Western Union against sending money to 'strangers'.

---

[44] Occasionally the legitimate escrow service **escrow.com** goes after fake sites that infringe upon their brand. Of course, additional volunteer groups may be operating, but we are unaware of any.

Table 3 Lifetimes of Mule-Recruitment Websites

Company Name	Real?	Period	Sites	Lifetime (hours)	
				mean	median
Lux Capital	✓	Mar–Apr 2007	11	721	1050
Aegis Capital	✓	Apr–May 2007	11	292	311
Sydney Car Centre	✗	Jun–Aug 2007	14	171	170
Harvey Investment	✓	Sep–Oct 2007	5	239	171
Cronos Investment	✗	Oct–Nov 2007	12	214	200
Waller Truck	✓	Nov–Feb 2008	14	237	3
Overall			67	308	188

We tracked several sets of mule-recruitment websites during the course of 2007/8. These sites were clearly linked by the style of spam email sent and the way in which a new set of sites commenced when an old set tailed off. Table 3 summarises the mule-recruiting companies, the number of different domain names that were used and for how long the websites remained available.

Where the websites impersonated existing companies, we found that the usual response has been that a warning notice is placed onto the company's legitimate website, as in Figure 1. This appears to be intended to discourage correspondence, rather than to actively combat the money laundering. However, in one case the impersonated company does seem to have been more proactive. On the 7th and 8th of October 2007, the Draper Investment Company was impersonated under 7 different domain names. They were simultaneously removed around noon on the 9th of October (maximum lifetime 62 hours, mean 40 hours, median 39 hours). On the 17th of October, the fictitious Cronos Investment Company made an entrance – the website design was identical to that of Draper Investment, except for the name. These sites clearly didn't engender the same reaction because they lasted considerably longer.

Even though the money laundering advertised by these sites directly harms banks attacked by phishing, none of the banks or take-down companies actively pursue the mule-recruitment websites. Although individual companies occasionally take action, we believe that in general only volunteer groups such as AA419 attempt to remove these sites. Even the volunteers treat these sites as less of a priority because the mules are seen as being complicit in phishing crimes. The lifetimes certainly reflect the lack of priority. The mule-recruitment websites we tracked had a lifetime of 308 hours (188 hours median). This is noticeably longer than for phishing, where the banks are actively seeking removal. It is also considerably longer than for escrow websites, which may again reflect the priorities of the volunteers.

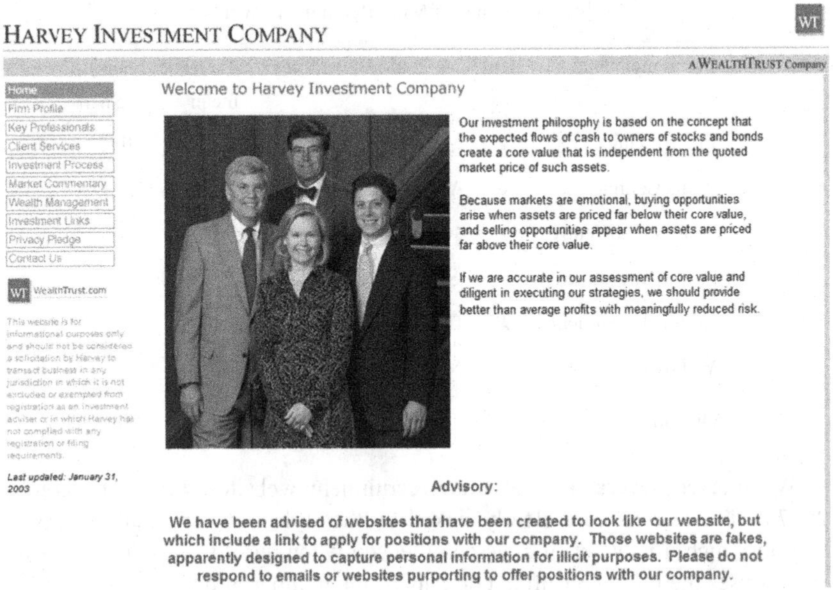

Figure 1. Warning Message on the Real Harvey Investment Web Page

For one set of phishing websites, impersonating Waller Truck, we also made a collection of 256 incoming spam emails received by one of the authors between 27 Nov 2007 and 20 Feb 2008, which promoted 44 different URLs. By assuming that the sites were live at the moment each email was sent, we were able to calculate an alternative view of the lifetimes. The 33 URLs, for which more than one email was received, had a mean lifetime of 265 hours (median 124 hours).

We also applied 'capture-recapture' analysis to this data: AA419 and PhishTank[45], between them, knew of 18 sites, of which 14 were in the emails received. Hence we estimate the total population to be 57.[46] We were also able to do a similar analysis for the Cronos websites. In this case we did not have the timestamps for the URLs, but the other sources knew of 12 sites, 10 of which overlapped with the email collection of 31 sites. In this case the overall population is estimated to be 37. Venn diagrams indicating the overlap are given in Figure 2.

---

[45] http://www.phishtank.com

[46] We use the standard formula for capture-recapture: $\frac{|sample_1| \times |sample_2|}{|overlap|}$ Our data does not satisfy all of assumptions necessary for this formula to hold – notably the population is dynamic, with sites appearing and disappearing. (Weaver and Collins 2007) computed the overlap between two phishing feeds and applied capture-recapture analysis to estimate the number of overall phishing attacks. They discuss how the capture-recapture assumptions can be accommodated for phishing. We leave deriving a more accurate estimate to future work.

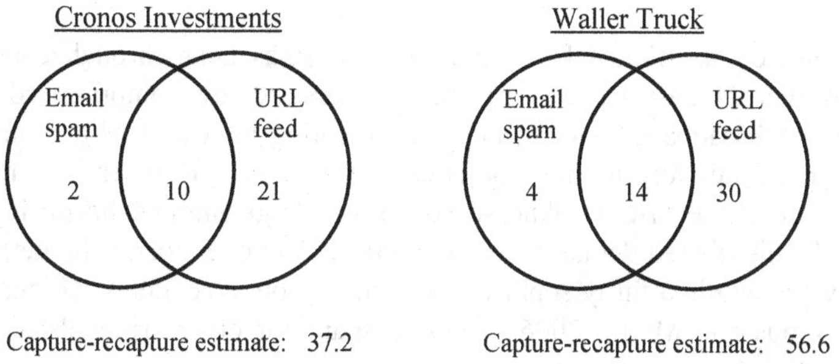

Figure 2. Venn Diagram Comparing Coverage of Mule-Recruitment Websites from an Email Spam Source and the URL Feeds

The similarity of results from the email analysis and from the website lifetime measurements, and the relatively small number of sites that are likely to have been missed, means that even though relatively small numbers of sites have been tracked, the estimates of lifetimes seem reasonably robust.

6.3 Online Pharmacies Hosted on Fast-flux Networks

In Section 5.3 we described a particular category of phishing attacks called 'fast-flux'. Some online criminals have constructed a fast-flux network and made it available for hire. Clients include any group wishing to host material that is the target of NTD procedures. We have already presented lifetime figures for phishing websites hosted on fast-flux networks. We also examined 82 domains used by an online pharmacy from October to December 2007. The lifetimes of these domains is much longer than for the fast-flux domains used for phishing websites. The pharmacy domains remain for an average of 1370.7 hours, or over 8 weeks. The median lifetime is slightly longer at 1404.5 hours.

From these figures, it appears that almost no one is attempting to remove the online pharmacies, even though they are illegal and advertised through spam email. There is a large disparity between how long pharmacy websites remain available and the lifetimes of fast-flux phishing websites. This demonstrates that the longevity of the domains depends less on the hosting method used, and more on whether anyone is motivated to remove the offending content.

7 Spam, Malware and Viruses

The sending of unsolicited bulk email ('spam') has gone through considerable evolution over the past decade. The main senders are now compromised end user machines on broadband links, which are operating as a part of a 'botnet'. The 'zombie' machines forming the botnet can be commanded to send spam, to scan other systems for security weaknesses, or to send large amounts of traffic as a part of a DDoS (distributed denial of service) attack. The operators of botnets hire out their services within a fairly sophisticated 'underground economy' (Franklin et al. 2007; Thomas and Martin 2006), sending spam for other criminals to promote their activities.

Until relatively recently, recruitment of machines into these botnets was done by the sending of email viruses – code that executed when the user was tricked into opening email attachments. The virus would then replicate itself by emailing everyone in the user's address book, while contacting a botnet controller for further instructions. A later refinement was to avoid the replication – which attracted attention – and only send out new copies of the code when the botnet was too small. The main infection vector at present appears to be placing malware onto websites in such a way as to infect visitors who have not applied security patches to their systems, or who can merely be inveigled into executing code supplied by the website.

Various volunteer organisations track these disparate activities. For example, Spamhaus[47] collates lists of IP addresses that are known to send spam email; Team Cymru[48] tracks various botnets by their characteristic scanning activities; and researchers such as (Enright 2007) and (Dagon et al. 2006) have developed ways of tracking particular botnets. In a slightly different realm, the StopBadware project[49] tracks websites that are infected with malware.

Some of these activities generate reports to the ISP whose customer's machine has been compromised. Additionally, many major ISPs (such as AOL[50] and MSN[51]) operate 'feedback loops', to let other ISPs know about incoming spam email to their servers. Finally of course, individual recipients of spam emails, or DDoS attacks, may generate reports of their own.

These reports are, in essence, notices of bad activity, and the expectation is that the ISP will pass the report on to their customer and the wickedness will be 'taken down'. The incentives for this take-down are weak, boiling down to implicit threats to block further traffic, or to name-and-shame ISPs that fail to act effectively.

---

[47] http://www.spamhaus.org

[48] http://www.team-cymru.org

[49] http://www.stopbadware.org

[50] AOL Feedback Loop Information: http://postmaster.aol.com/fbl/

[51] Microsoft Smart Network Data Services: https://postmaster.live.com/snds/

Some of the dynamics of blocking were discussed by (Serjantov and Clayton 2005), but there has been little other academic study.

The lack of incentives has been commented upon by legislators such as the UK House of Lords Science and Technology Committee, who recommended (House of Lords 2007) that after a short period the ISP should become legally liable for ongoing bad traffic (#3.69). However they found it hard to square the incentives with a wish to see ISPs being more proactive in monitoring (#3.68), and in any event, the UK Government totally rejected the proposal (United Kingdom Government 2007). Incentives to increase ISP participation in cleaning up compromised end user machines also feature strongly in the recommendations made by (Anderson et al. 2008) in their report to the European Network and Information Security Agency (ENISA).

It would be instructive to measure the take-down times for this category of material because there are weak incentives on ISPs to act, but at the same time, there are strong incentives by complainants to see action taken. However, there are no published figures for the lifetimes of spam-sending (or DDoS-participating) machines. A key reason for this is that many of the end user machines involved use dynamic IP addresses. Consequently, lifetimes may be artificially lowered (and the number of sources greatly exaggerated) by the problem machines regularly changing to new IP addresses – altering the only marker by which they can be distinguished.

8 Comparing Take-down Effectiveness

We have just described many of the different categories of web content subject to NTD requests. For several categories we have obtained data on the associated websites' lifetimes. While the circumstances and assumptions for each category often vary, we can still draw useful comparisons. Table 4 summarises the lifetime data we have presented.

It is apparent that the presence of incentives to remove offending material has the greatest impact on website lifetimes. By far, phishing websites are removed fastest. Banks are highly motivated to remove any impersonating website because their continued appearance increases losses due to fraud and erodes customers' trust in online banking. Solid legal frameworks do not seem to matter as much. Courts almost never get involved in issuing orders to remove phishing websites. By contrast, other clearly illegal activities such as online pharmacies do not appear to be removed at all.

However, the banks' incentives are not perfectly aligned. Most banks remain narrowly focused on actively removing only those websites that directly attack their brand. Another key component of the phishing supply chain, mule-recruitment

Table 4. Website Lifetimes by Type of Offending Content

-	Period	Sites	Lifetime (hours)	
			mean	median
Child sexual abuse images	Jan–Dec 2007	2585	719	288
Phishing				
Free web-hosting (two brands)	Jan 2008	240		0
Compromised machines (two brands)	Jan 2008	105		0
Rock-phish domains (all brands)	Jan 2008	821		33
Fast-flux domains (all brands)	Jan 2008	314		25.5
Fraudulent websites				
Escrow agents	Oct–Dec 2007	696	222.2	24.5
Mule-recruitment websites	Mar 07–Feb 08	67	308.2	188
Fast-flux pharmacies	Oct–Dec 2007	82	1370.7	1404.5

websites, is completely ignored and left to volunteers. Removing mule-recruitment websites is a collective-action problem: many banks are harmed by these websites, yet none takes action because they cannot be sure whether removing them will help themselves or their competitors. This lack of cooperation is somewhat surprising, given that there are numerous organisations within the financial sector whose remit includes tackling collective threats (e.g., the Financial Services Technology Consortium (FSTC), the Financial Services ISAC in the US, APACS in the UK, and the Anti-Phishing Working Group (APWG)).[52]

Duped consumers are harmed most by fake escrow agents, yet they are in no position to remove the websites. Auction houses such as eBay do have a weak incentive to remove escrow websites, in that their continued existence undermines trust in online commerce. Volunteers are likely motivated by a sense of justice, but the figures demonstrate such an incentive is not entirely sufficient. Even the two experiments with spurious copyright infringement removal requests show what matters most is the perseverance of the requesters.

The technology chosen by the attacker does affect the speed of take-down, but the impact is much smaller than the incentive to remove. While the use of free web-hosting and compromised machines for hosting phishing websites exhibited similar lifetimes, the evasive techniques employed by the rock-phish gang and in fast-flux attacks leads to substantially longer lifetimes. However, online pharmacies using fast-flux techniques remain 14 times longer than phishing websites using the same approach. This provides further evidence that the defender's motivation for removal matters far more than the attacker's implementation strategy.

[52] Financial Services Technology Consortium: http://www.fstc.org; Financial Services Information Sharing and Analysis Center: http://www.fsisac.com; Association for Payment Clearing Services: http://www.apacs.org.uk; Anti-Phishing Working Group: http://www.antiphishing.org.

8.1 Lifetimes of Child Sexual Abuse Image Websites

The long lifetimes of websites hosting child sexual abuse images is particularly striking. In spite of a robust legal framework and a global consensus on the content's repulsion, these websites are removed much slower than any other type of content being actively taken down for which we have gathered data. An average lifetime of 719 hours is over 150 times slower than phishing websites hosted on free web-hosting and compromised machines. Since we are not privy to the hosting method used by child sexual abuse image websites, we do not know whether sophisticated techniques, such as those employed by the rock-phish gang, are used. Even here, the take-down time is around 10 times slower than for phishing. Take-down is more than twice as slow than for mule-recruitment websites, which are ignored by banks and only removed by volunteers. Only online pharmacies using fast-flux mechanisms are removed more slowly, and we have found no evidence that anyone is attempting to remove these websites at all!

The latest IWF Annual Report (IWF 2008) presents the website lifetimes using analysis that is similar to ours – they show 71% of websites removed within 50 days, and only 16 lasting all year. Data from earlier reports is much harder to directly compare. We therefore ran some additional tests to provide a more direct comparison to the previous IWF approach of checking which sites were still alive at the beginning and end of two particular four and six week periods. Note that this is not the same as counting the number of websites that are removed within six weeks. Using the IWF's approach, all websites alive on a starting date (whether they first appeared the day previously or three years before) are rechecked at the end of the period. This type of test tends to emphasise long-lived websites.

We conducted a similar test for phishing websites alive at midnight on October 1, 2007, counting the proportion of websites still alive four and six weeks later. The complete results are given in Table 5. Overall, a smaller proportion of phishing websites than child sexual abuse image websites are long-lived. 10.4% of all phishing websites were alive six weeks later, compared to 20% for websites hosting child sexual abuse images. 12.5% of all phishing websites were alive four weeks later, which is notably smaller than the 38% of commercial websites hosting child sexual abuse images.

Table 5. Proportion of Websites Still Alive After 6 and 4 Weeks Respectively

-	Sites > 6 weeks	Sites > 4 weeks	Sites
Child sexual abuse images	20.0%	38.0%	1400
Rock-phish domains	0.0%	0.0%	33
Fast-flux phishing	10.5%	15.7%	38
Ordinary phishing	24.0%	24.0%	25
All phishing combined	10.4%	12.5%	96

Examining the proportion of long-lived phishing sites broken down by type is instructive. Fast-flux and ordinary phishing sites suffered a few long-lived websites. By contrast, all rock-phish domains were removed within four weeks. This could be because rock-phish domains draw the attention of several banks, making it far less likely that they all let the domain slip through the cracks. Fast-flux and ordinary phishing attacks typically impersonate a single bank, making the occasional oversight possible.

However, it must be noted that exceptionally long-lived phishing websites are much less of a concern to the banks than long-lived child sexual abuse image websites are to groups such as the IWF. Phishing websites require spam advertisements to attract victims. If spam is no longer being sent on behalf of months-old websites, then little harm is being done. Long-lived websites hosting illicit pictures cause continued offence until their removal. Hence, the relatively poor performance in removing websites that host child sexual abuse images is especially troubling.

Applying the IWF's methods of analysis, child sexual abuse image websites fare worse than other types of offending content. But it remains difficult to construct a complete picture using these methods alone. Comparing the average website lifetime, as we have done in Table 4, unequivocally demonstrates that there is scope for hastening the removal of child sexual abuse images from the Internet.

An examination of the incentives can again shed light on why these websites are not removed more quickly. In the UK, the IWF works directly with the ISPs to remove offending websites. Websites hosted in the UK are claimed to be removed within 48 hours, which is believed to explain why only 0.2% of such websites are now hosted there (IWF 2006a). When the websites are hosted in other countries, the IWF notifies the appropriate law enforcement agency and perhaps a local INHOPE hotline, but then takes no further action.

Only 29 countries have hotlines that are members of INHOPE, and their policies vary on what to do with incoming reports. For example, the United States hotline 'CyberTipline' operated by the National Center for Missing and Exploited Children (NCMEC) states that they issue take-down notices to ISPs "when appropriate".[53] However, the IWF tells us that they only issue notices to members, which suggests that the incentive here is to use the notices as part of a 'carrot and stick' approach to growing their community.

Similarly, law enforcement responses also vary. Typically, reports are passed to a central agency operating at a national level. It is then up to this agency to pass the necessary information to the appropriate local jurisdiction, who then deal with passing information on to the responsible ISP. At any stage delays can be introduced, with further slowdowns triggered by evidence collection and assessment. The police are institutionally motivated to seek out the criminals, which is not always consistent with getting the material removed in the most timely manner.[54]

---

[53] http://www.ncmec.org/en_US/documents/CyberTiplineFactSheet.pdf

[54] In this chapter we have not considered whether 'take-down' of child sexual abuse images is the optimal strategy. It could be argued that the correct approach is to locate the people behind

Furthermore, law enforcement budgets are always very tight, and organisations may choose not to devote the necessary resources to process the reports quickly because they are not as highly motivated as INHOPE members.

Almost all the other types of material we have considered are dealt with on an international basis. While language can be a barrier to prompt action, borders are essentially immaterial to those seeking to have content taken down. However, because the police are made central to the process of dealing with child sexual abuse images, we can see a clear emphasis on jurisdiction since the police do not operate across national (or sometimes state or county) borders. The IWF told us that they would be "treading on other people's toes" if they contacted ISPs outside the UK, and that they "are not permitted or authorised to issue notices to take down content to anyone outside the UK". The defamed, the rights holders, the banks, the take-down companies and the various groups of volunteers just do not think this way.

9 Conclusion

In this chapter we have examined a range of notice and take-down regimes. We have developed insights by comparing differing outcomes where underlying commonalities exist. The banks have adopted a narrow focus on phishing while overlooking mule-recruitment. The evasive techniques of fast-flux networks appear unimportant, given that seemingly permanent online pharmacies and short-lived phishing websites use the same scheme.

The Internet is multi-national. Almost everyone who wants content removed issues requests to ISPs or website owners throughout the world, believing – not always correctly – that the material must be just as illegal 'there' as 'here'. Unexpectedly, in the one case where the material is undoubtedly illegal everywhere, the removal of child sexual abuse image websites is dealt with in a rather different manner. The responsibility for removing material has been divided up on a national basis, and this appears to lead directly to very long website lifetimes.

In sum, the evidence we have presented highlights the limited impact of legal frameworks, content types and attack methods on take-down speed. Instead, take-down effectiveness depends on how the responsibility for issuing requests is

---

the websites and that removing websites merely leads to a 'whack-a-mole' game that rapidly removes individual websites without decreasing the availability of the material. The attention that has recently been paid to site lifetimes in the IWF annual reports indicates that removal is now seen by them to be important. However (Callanan 2007) found that only 11% of all websites are reported to ISPs by member hotlines. They wish "not to interfere with any ongoing law enforcement investigation" and say that "depending on national legislation, the ISP sometimes prefers not to be informed about potentially illegal content." We do not understand this comment, unless it refers to the necessity, in some jurisdictions, for the ISP to make a report to the authorities.

distributed, and the incentives on the organisations involved to devote appropriate resources to pursue the removal of unwanted content from the Internet.

Acknowledgments

We would like to thank the companies and voluntary groups who provide us with data about phishing website URLs. We are also extremely grateful to the IWF for their assistance in providing detailed statistics about website longevity. Tyler Moore is supported by the UK Marshall Aid Commemoration Commission and by US National Science Foundation grant DGE-0636782.

References

Ahlert, C., Marsden, C., and Yung, C. "How 'Liberty' Disappeared from Cyberspace: The Mystery Shopper Tests Internet Content Self-regulation," 2004, http://pcmlp.socleg.ox.ac.uk/text/liberty.pdf

Anderson, R., Böhme, R., Clayton, R., and Moore, T. "Security Economics and the Internal Market," ENISA, January 2008, http://www.enisa.europa.eu/doc/pdf/report_sec_econ_&_int_mark_20080131.pdf

Callanan, C., and Frydas, N.P. "2007 Global Internet Trend Report," INHOPE, September 2007, https://www.inhope.org/en/system/files/inhope_global_internet_trend_report_v1.0.pdf

Clayton, R. "Judge and Jury? How 'Notice & Take Down' Gives ISPs an Unwanted Role in Applying the Law to the Internet," July 2000, http://www.cl.cam.ac.uk/~rnc1/Judge_and_Jury.pdf

Dagon, D., Zou, C.C., and Lee, W. "Modelling Botnet Propagation Using Time Zones," in *13th Annual Network and Distributed System Security Symposium (NDSS),* San Diego, California, February 2006, pp. 235–249.

Enright, B. "Exposing Stormworm," October 2007, http://noh.ucsd.edu/~bmenright/exposing_storm.ppt

Franklin, J., Paxson, V., Perrig, A., and Savage, S. "An Inquiry into the Nature and Causes of the Wealth of Internet Miscreants," in *14th ACM Conference on Computer and Communications Security (CCS'07)*, Alexandria, Virginia, October 2007, pp. 375–388.

Honeynet Project and Research Alliance. "Know Your Enemy: Fast-flux Service Networks, an Ever Changing Enemy," July 2007, http://www.honeynet.org/papers/ff/fast-flux.pdf

House of Lords Science and Technology Committee. *Personal Internet Security, 5th Report of Session 2006–07*, The Stationery Office, London, August 2007.

Internet Watch Foundation. 2006 Half-yearly Report, IWF, July 2006, http://www.iwf.org.uk/documents/20060803_2006_bi-annual_report_v7_final4.pdf

Internet Watch Foundation. "IWF Reveals 10 Year Statistics on Child Abuse Images Online," Press Release, IWF, October 2006. http://www.iwf.org.uk/media/news.archive-2006.179.htm

Internet Watch Foundation. "IWF Reports Increased Severity of Online Child Abuse Content," Press Release, IWF, April 2007, http://www.iwf.org.uk/media/news.archive-2007.196.htm

Internet Watch Foundation. "2007 Annual and Charity Report," IWF, April 2008. http://www.iwf.org.uk/documents/20080417_iwf_annual_report_2007_(web).pdf

McMillan, R. "'Rock Phish' Blamed for Surge in Phishing," *InfoWorld* (12 December), 2006, http://www.infoworld.com/article/06/12/12/HNrockphish_1.html

Moore, T. "Cooperative Attack and Defense in Distributed Networks," Tech Report UCAM-CL-TR-718, Computer Laboratory, University of Cambridge, June 2008.

Moore, T., and Clayton, R. "Examining the Impact of Website Take-down on Phishing," in *Anti-Phishing Working Group eCrime Researcher's Summit (APWG eCrime)*, Pittsburgh, Pennsylvania, October 2007, pp. 1–13.

Moore, T., and Clayton, R. "Evaluating the Wisdom of Crowds in Assessing Phishing Websites," in *12th International Financial Cryptography and Data Security Conference (FC 2008)*, Tsudik, G. (Ed.), LNCS 5143, Springer-Verlag, Berlin, Germany, 2008, pp. 16–30.

Moore, T., and Clayton, R. "Evil Searching: Compromise and Recompromise of Internet Hosts for Phishing", *in submission*, June 2008.

Morland J. "Laurence Godfrey v. Demon Internet Limited. Case No: 1998-G-No 30," March 1999. http://www.hmcourts-service.gov.uk/judgmentsfiles/j932/godfrey2.htm

Nas, S. "The Multatuli Project: ISP Notice & Take Down," in *SANE*, October 2004. http://www.bof.nl/docs/researchpaperSANE.pdf

Serjantov, A., and Clayton, R. "Modelling Incentives for Email Blocking Strategies," in *4th Workshop on the Economics of Information Security (WEIS)*, Cambridge, Massachusetts, June 2005.

Spamhaus. "Report on the Criminal 'Rock Phish' Domains Registered at nic.at," Press Release, Spamhaus, June 2007. http://www.spamhaus.org/organization/statement.lasso?ref=7

Thomas, R., and Martin, J. "The Underground Economy: Priceless," *USENIX ;login* (31:6), December 2006, pp. 7–16.

United Kingdom Government. "The Government Reply to the Fifth Report from the House of Lords Science and Technology Committee Session 2006–07 HL Paper 165 Personal Internet Security," Cm7234, The Stationery Office, London, October 2007.

Weaver, R., and Collins, M. "Fishing for Phishes: Applying Capture-recapture to Phishing," in *Anti-Phishing Working Group eCrime Researcher's Summit (APWG eCrime)*, Pittsburgh, Pennsylvania, October 2007, pp. 14–25.

Studying Malicious Websites and the Underground Economy on the Chinese Web

Jianwei Zhuge[1], Thorsten Holz[2], Chengyu Song[1], Jinpeng Guo[1], Xinhui Han[1], and Wei Zou[1]

[1]Peking University, Institute of Computer Science and Technology, Beijing, China

[2]University of Mannheim, Laboratory for Dependable Distributed Systems, Mannheim, Germany

Abstract The World Wide Web gains more and more popularity within China with more than 1.31 million websites on the Chinese Web in June 2007. Driven by the economic profits, cyber criminals are on the rise and use the Web to exploit innocent users. In fact, a real underground black market with thousands of participants has developed, which brings together malicious users who trade exploits, malware, virtual assets, stolen credentials, and more. In this chapter, we provide a detailed overview of this underground black market and present a model to describe the market. We substantiate our model with the help of measurement results within the Chinese Web. First, we show that the amount of virtual assets traded on this underground market is huge. Second, our research proves that a significant amount of websites within China's part of the Web contain some kind of malicious content: our measurements reveal that about 1.49% of the examined sites contain malicious content that tries to attack the visitor's browser.

1 Introduction

The World Wide Web (WWW) becomes more and more important each day within China. A large number of Chinese Internet users enjoy the convenience and flexibility the Web brings them, from searching for information, online entertainment to e-business, and e-finance (CNNIC 2007). According to the latest Alexa Global top 500 websites list (Alexa 2008) (32 Chinese websites are in the list), there are four different types of successful and well-known sites within the Chinese Web: the first type of websites are search engines, including Baidu, Google.cn, Yahoo! China, Tencent's SoSo, and Suhu's Sogou. Among them, Baidu and Google are the most popular ones. The second category contains portals and navigation sites. Among the seven sites belonging to this category, Tencent's QQ,

M.E. Johnson (ed.), *Managing Information Risk and the Economics of Security*,
DOI: 10.1007/978-0-387-09762-6_11,

Sina, NetEase 163, Sohu, and TOM are listed in the top ten Chinese websites. The third type of sites is related to e-business: the Taobao C2C (*customer-to-customer*) online business platform and the Alibaba B2B (*business-to-business*) platform – both operated by the Alibaba group – are well-known within the Chinese Web. The last type of sites contains sites in the area of online entertainment and virtual personal space, including YouTube-like sites such as 56.com, toodou, ku6, several myspace-like sites such as poco, bokee, and others.

But there is also the other side of the coin: targeting the virtual assets owned by the normal Chinese Internet users, malicious attackers discover the Web as a new venue for making money by exploiting innocent users. A common theme is to inject malicious code into a bought or compromised website. The injected code exploits an unpatched client-side vulnerability: each time a user with a vulnerable version of a browser or related application visits this site, his machine is compromised and some kind of malware is automatically installed. This kind of attack is also called *drive-by-download attack* (Wang et al. 2006). The malware is quite often some kind of Trojan Horse that searches for valuable information on the victim's machine and then sends the information back to the attacker, who in turn can sell this virtual good to other attackers or innocent users.

In this chapter, we study this phenomenon on the Chinese Web in more detail. We propose a model to describe the underground economy which drives the malicious websites phenomenon and the individual actors within this ecosystem. The model describes the underground economy that we have studied within the Chinese Web, and thus some aspects of it are specific to China. However, our model can also be used to describe the market for malicious tools and stolen goods for other parts of the Web or the Web as a whole. Our measurements show that there are thousands of participants within this market and there are strong relations between the underground black market and the public virtual assets trading. Furthermore, we also measure the extent of malicious websites within China's part of the Web with the help of client honeypots. During our measurement of about 145,000 of the most commonly visited websites on the Chinese Web, we found that 2,149, i.e., 1.49% of them, contained some kind of malicious content. We also performed redirection link analysis which can disclose the relationship between malicious websites and the hosts of web-based exploits, as well as the top active exploiters.

This chapter is outlined as follows: In Section 2, we provide an overview of related work in the area of malicious websites and the underground black market. We introduce a model to describe the underground economy and the different actors within this ecosystem, together with a case study, in Section 3. In Section 4, we show different mechanisms used by attackers to create malicious websites which we found by studying a large amount of actual attacks on the Chinese Web. The results of a measurement study on the underground black market and malicious websites within the Chinese Web are presented in Section 5. Finally, we conclude the chapter in Section 6.

2 Related Work

The work most closely related to ours is a study on the underground black market by Franklin et al. (Franklin et al. 2007). The authors study a large number of underground IRC channels and keep track of advertisements for virtual goods. Based on the collected information, they examine the size of the underground black market, the number of virtual goods traded, and similar characteristics. Our work is orthogonal to the work by Franklin et al.: We study the aspects of the underground market visible as part of the World Wide Web. We examine the relationship between the individual actors within the market and also study the size of the actual market via different metrics. Furthermore, we also propose a model for the underground economy and substantiate our model with the help of real-world data collected on the Chinese Web. Other studies orthogonal to ours focus on different aspects of the underground economy (Cymru 2006; Thomas and Martin 2006).

One of the first research efforts to analyze malicious websites were published by Wang et al. (2006) and Moshchuk et al. (2006). The key idea in both projects is to automatically browse the Web and analyze all content in order to detect sites that try to infect an unprotected user. Both projects show that such an effort is viable and they could detect malicious sites in an automated way. We extend the original idea by combining ideas from both projects in order to achieve a more scalable solution that still has the capability of detecting unknown exploits. The most detailed overview of the threat posed by malicious websites is given by Provos et al. (Provos et al. 2007; Provos et al. 2008). Using Google's cache of crawled websites, they analyzed the extent of this threat and could give, for the first time, numbers showing the maliciousness of a significant part of the Web. We focus on the Chinese Web and show that this part of the Web also hosts a significant amount of malicious content. In addition, we also analyze parts of the Web that are not easily reachable by Google, e.g., the virtual goods offered at the Taobao online business platform or the advertisements posted at the Baidu Post Bar. The Honeynet Project has released several papers which deal with the phenomenon of malicious websites. One of the papers deals with attacks against web applications (Honeynet Web Application 2007), while the other focuses on client-side honeypots (Honeynet Web Servers 2007). We extend the original idea of client honeypots by combining two techniques that allow us to significantly speed-up the analysis platform.

3 Underground Economy Model

3.1 *Modeling the Individual Actors*

In this section, we introduce a model to describe the interaction between different actors within the underground black market. We explain the economic aspects of the phenomenon and for each actor, we illustrate their role, what kind of information/goods they trade, and what the common price for such goods/services is. This model is adapted to the Chinese Internet, since the social aspects within China enable a unique ecosystem. However, our model can also be extended to describe the blackhat underground economy in other countries and is not specific to China per se.

3.1.1 Virus Writers

Virus Writers are malicious Internet users driven by economic profits. They have a certain degree of technical background of computer networks and programming skills, e.g., they are able to find vulnerabilities in software (so called *0-day* vulnerabilities) themselves, or they use recently public disclosed vulnerabilities and the corresponding exploits. Furthermore, these actors have the technical skills to develop their own exploits or malware based on the original vulnerability reports and available exploit codes. Then they sell their tools and malware for profit, and provide evasion service to their customers.

To find potential customers, they post advertisements on the underground black market. The markets are typically online discussion boards, so called *bulletin board systems*, within the World Wide Web that are used for discussions. Furthermore, the boards provide a platform for sellers and buyers of this kind of resources. In addition, experienced Virus Writers often release some limited version of their tools or malware for free, in order to raise their status and reputation within the community.

We searched within the underground black market and found the following prices for typical "services" within this market: the market price of a Trojan is between tens to thousands Renminbi (RMB), and a package of powerful Trojan generator and evasion service can be up to several ten thousands RMB. 10 RMB is as of February 2008 equivalent to $1.40 US dollar. This means that such software has a certain value and Virus Writers have the incentive to invest time and knowledge into this area.

3.1.2 Website Masters/Crackers

The second actors within the underground market are *Website Masters* and *Website Crackers*. The administrators of certain personal websites attract visitors with the help of free goodies, e.g., free movies, music, software, or tools. These websites often betray their visitors: they sell the traffic (i.e., *website visits*) of their websites to *Envelopes Stealers* (see next section) by hosting the web-based Trojans. This means that innocent website visitors are redirected via these malicious websites to other sites that then attack the victims. If the attack is successful, a piece of malware is installed on the victim's machine.

Website Crackers can also compromise well-known – but unsafe – websites by exploiting vulnerabilities that exist on these sites. Via the command line access on the compromised machines, they then redirect the traffic for this website to another malicious machine, i.e., they then sell the traffic of their victim's website. Our research revealed a market price of about 40 – 60 RMB per ten thousand IP visits.

3.1.3 Envelopes Stealers

"*Envelopes*" is a jargon word used in the underground market which means the stolen pair of account and password, i.e., the credentials for a given site. We will use this term throughout the chapter. *Envelopes Stealers* have very limited technical knowledge and commonly buy ready-to-use Trojans or even malware generators from Virus Writers, and website traffic from Website Masters/Crackers. All they need to do is to create a web-based Trojan network from which they can harvest envelopes: they combine a web-based Trojan (which exploits vulnerabilities in the browsers, underlying components, or related applications) with a conventional Trojan for stealing certain envelopes and link the generated Trojan to the bought websites.

They then sell the harvested envelopes to *Virtual Asset Stealers*, which we introduce in the next section. We found that the market price of an envelope varies from some Jiao to tens of RMB. They also sell access to the compromised machines, which are called *flesh chicken* (because "chicken" has the same pronunciation as "machine" in Chinese), in the underground market. The market price of a "flesh chicken" is between 0.1 – 10 RMB, thus it is rather cheap for an attacker to control a compromised machine.

3.1.4 Virtual Asset Stealers

Virtual Asset Stealers do not have any technical knowledge about hacking and programming, but they have a rather good understanding of the underground market itself. Typically, they know which online games are currently popular and which virtual asset (for example, equipment in games) can be sold for a good price. They buy envelopes from the Envelopes Stealers, and log-in to the online games or QQ accounts to steal valuable virtual assets like game equipments or QQ coins. Besides these monetary goods, these actors also steal other valuable, virtual goods including "beautiful" QQ accounts, i.e., accounts with a short name, or a name that can be easily remembered.

After getting access to the virtual assets, they commonly sell them to others. Besides a prospering market for QQ accounts, we also found evidence that they sell other virtual assets like powerful equipments for various online games. The market price varies for each virtual good, e.g., game equipment is typically sold for 10 – 10K RMB/equipment, whereas 1 QQ coin commonly costs 0.2 – 0.3 RMB. It is interesting to observe that the official exchange rate by the vendor Tencent is 1 RMB for 1 QQ coin. During the "Super Voice Girls" competition, an annual national singing contest, the black market price rose to 0.3 – 0.5 RMB since enthusiastic fans were seeking QQ coins to vote for their favorite contestants.

3.1.5 Virtual Asset Sellers

Another party within the whole underground are the *Virtual Asset Sellers*, which can also be (but not need to be) Virtual Asset Stealers. They contribute to the circulation section of the industry chain by setting up virtual shops on the World Wide Web. These shops can be commonly found at Taobao, Tencent's PaiPai, and eBay, the three biggest online business platforms within China.

Our research shows that the Virtual Asset Sellers usually buy the virtual assets from the underground market on bulletin board systems with a very low price. They then sell them to *Players* on the public marketplaces, making profit due to the price difference between buying and selling. For example, they typically buy QQ coins on bulletin boards and then sell the coins for 0.5 – 0.8 RMB on Taobao, making a certain profit with each transaction.

3.1.6 Players

The sixth actor within our economic model are the *Players*, who are enthusiastic online games players (or QQ users), often spending large amounts of money on virtual assets. The Players are commonly male teenagers who dispense their parents' money for fun on the World Wide Web and in online games. They are the foundation of the whole underground market since they stimulate demand for all virtual goods and drive the market.

3.2 Market Interaction

In Figure 1, we provide an overview of the interaction of the individual actors within the underground market. The business between the six different actors within the ecosystem takes place in different locations. For example, businesses between Envelopes Stealers, Virus Writers, and Website Masters/Crackers takes place in the underground black market on different kinds of bulletin board systems. These systems also provide a marketplace for Envelopes Stealers and Virtual Asset Stealers as well. On the other hand, the circulation of virtual assets is open on the World Wide Web. This is due to the fact that they need benign players to find them easily and there are very weak controls on the circulation of stolen virtual assets in China.

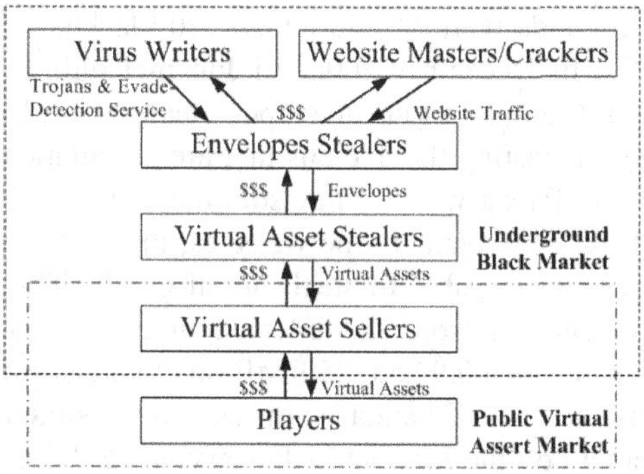

Figure 1. Interaction of the Individual Actors within the Underground Market on the Chinese Web

As noted previously, the underground market commonly uses bulletin board systems to connect the individual actors. One of the most prominent places for such markets within China is the Baidu Post Bar, the largest bulletin board community in China. Advertisements can be commonly found on several pertinent post bars at the site *post.baidu.com*. This system has a keyword-based structure, and there are no other entries to the post bar: if you do not know the keyword to search for, you will not find any malicious entries. The actors within the black market have their own, unique jargon, and thus it is hard for an outsider to find information about this threat.

The actual trading of virtual assets happens on public marketplaces like Taobao. These very common online business platforms within the WWW are used by the cyber criminals to advertise and sell their goods. After a trade was successful and a Player has bought a virtual good, the money is sent commonly via Alipay, the leading Chinese online payment service similar to PayPal. The goods, i.e., the virtual assets, are exchanged through different online mechanisms. They can for example be sent via e-mail or transferred with the help of other services within the Internet.

3.3 Case Study: PandaWorm

The most well-known security incident on the Chinese World Wide Web during the year 2007, which also follows the economy model we introduced above, was committed by a Chinese blackhat team. The most important actor is Li Jun, a Virus Writer. He implemented the *Panda worm* (also known as *Worm.Nimaya.w* or "panda burning joss stick") based on his experience from implementing several other kinds of malware, for example *QQTailEKS* and *QQpass*, two popular pieces of malware. He sold Panda worm to more than 120 blackhats for a price between 500 and 1000 RMB. In December 2006, Li Jun met online with Wang Lei (a Website Master) and Zhang Sun (an Envelopes Stealer). Jun Li and Lei Wang set up several websites for hosting the Trojans that are automatically downloaded by users infected with the Panda worm. They sold the website traffic to Zhang Sun, who linked his web-based Trojans to the websites, thus the victims were infected with several Trojans that are able to steal virtual goods. The attackers stole the envelopes for online games from the infected machines. Zhang Sun sold the envelopes for a price between 0.9 and 2.5 RMB on the underground market.

The attackers lost control of Panda worm and this resulted in an infection of thousands of computers on the Internet in January and February 2007. The losses due to this incident are estimated to be up to 100 million RMB. This huge amount of damage raised the attention of several anti-virus vendors and the police: in February 2007, the criminals were arrested and put into jail. Before they were arrested, all of them made a certain profit: Li Jun made an estimated profit of about 150,000 RMB, Wang Lei 80,000, and Zhang Sun 12,000. In September 2007, Li Jun was sentenced to four years in prison, Wang Lei two and a half years, and Zhang Sun two years. Compared to other countries, the imprisonment for crime on the World Wide Web is high in China. For example, the author of Agobot, a bot that caused high damage, was sentenced by a German court for only 12 months on probation.

4 Mechanisms Behind Malicious Websites on the Chinese Web

4.1 Overall Technical Flow

The overall technical flow of the malicious websites phenomenon is shown in Figure 2. The Virus Writers take care of implementing web-based and conventional Trojans, and use evasion methods to create covert Trojans, and then they sell the malware and evasion service. Website Masters/Crackers betray their customers or crack unsafe websites, and sell the visitor's traffic. Envelope Stealers construct a web-based Trojan network by hosting the bought web-based and conventional Trojans on compromised computers, and redirect the website visitors to their web-based Trojans. When the web-based Trojan network is ready, the victims who visit the malicious websites will be redirected to and exploited by the web-based Trojans, and infected with further conventional Trojans. These Trojans then steal envelopes and virtual assets from the victim's machine.

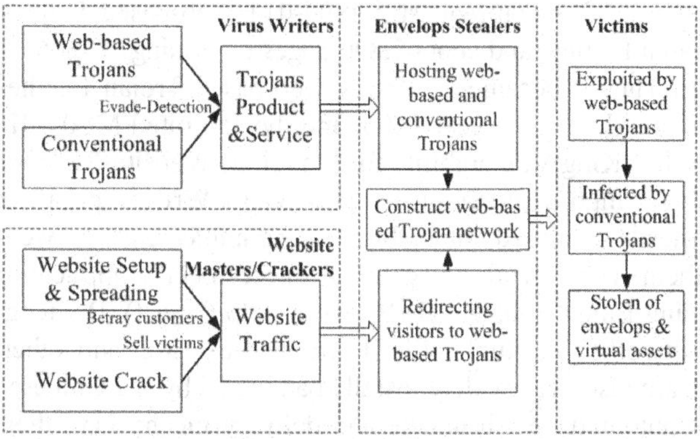

Figure 2. Overview of the Overall Technical Flow for the Malicious Websites Phenomenon

In the following subsections, we discuss in detail the mechanisms used by the Chinese attacker community in the different steps of this technical flow. We focus on the web-based and conventional Trojans, vulnerabilities used for web-based Trojans, and strategies for redirecting visitors to web-based Trojans.

4.2 *Web-based and Conventional Trojans*

There are two different types of Trojans involved in the technical flow of malicious website, i.e., Web-based Trojans and conventional Trojans. Web-based Trojans are used for exploiting the vulnerabilities in the web browser or third-party extensions and injecting the conventional Trojans. The purpose of conventional Trojans is to remotely control the victim's machine and steal envelopes from them.

4.2.1 Web-based Trojans and Generators

Web-based Trojans are a kind of client-side attack, and typically exploit certain system- or application-level vulnerabilities to obtain complete control of the client system once the vulnerable client visits the malicious site. Web-based Trojans are typically implemented in scripting languages including JavaScript and PHP. Virus Writers commonly implement *generators* which can generate web-based Trojans automatically and which can be used by other actors in the market without any programming skills.

In the following, we provide a brief example of a web-based Trojan. A well-known and widely used web-based Trojan family on the Chinese Web is the *MS06-014 Trojan*. The source code of the malware is quite easy to understand and it can be downloaded for free from the Internet, e.g., there are about 3,670 result pages by issuing the search request "MS06-014 Web-based Trojans" (in Chinese) to Baidu Search Engine, and about 2,800 pages by issuing "MS06-014 Generators" (in Chinese). Thus it became a primary web-based Trojan for the attacker community in China during the year 2006, and the exploited MS06-014 vulnerability was entitled the "King Vulnerability for Malicious Websites" accordingly.

To achieve a high exploitation rate, the Virus Writers are always seeking for zero day or newly disclosed vulnerabilities, and implement new web-based Trojans exploiting them. They are also targeting Chinese-specific applications and components including Baidu Soba BHO (Browser Help Object), Baofeng media player, PPStream network TV, Xunlei file download software, and others. Since these applications are also very widely installed and used by the Chinese Internet users, and lack an automatic patch update and delivery mechanism, they have become one of the most important targets of the web-based Trojans.

4.2.2 Conventional Trojans

Conventional Trojans are also essential tools which contribute to the remote control of the infected "flesh chickens", and the harvesting of stolen envelopes. The history of the conventional Trojans is quite long in the Chinese attacker community. The Virus Writers are constantly developing more powerful Trojans and they struggle against anti-virus vendors and their software.

The most famous and widely used full-functional Trojan after *Binghe* is the *Hack.Huigezi* tool, which was developed and maintained by a blackhat group called *Huigezi Lab*. Although Huigezi was advertised as a network management software, it contains many powerful functions that are beyond the demands of a network administrator, including remote control of a large amount of client computers to build botnets, downloading and uploading files, keystroke recording, remote desktop monitoring, setting up proxy servers, and hiding of itself by API hooking and process injection. Due to its powerful capacities and customized service provided by Huigezi Lab, Huigezi has been widely used by the Chinese blackhat community, also in the area of malicious websites. It was listed as a top ten malware for three years from 2004 to 2006 in a row by almost all of the Chinese anti-virus vendors.

There is also a large amount of dedicated stealer Trojans available on the Chinese Web or the underground market. Most of them are QQ stealers and online game stealers driven by the virtual asset market requirements. We could easily find free downloads or advertisements of up to ten different QQ stealer families and stealer Trojans for almost all of the popular online games on the Chinese Web. Other types of Trojans, such as dedicated web-based bots for click fraud, stealers for online banking and stock trading credentials, are also seen on the Chinese public Web and the underground market.

4.3 Vulnerabilities Used for Web-based Trojans in China

Table 1 provides an overview of the number of published system- and application-level vulnerabilities used for web-based Trojans in China for the years 2003 until 2007. This table shows two major trends. First, malicious websites are more and more popular, and the number of disclosed and exploited vulnerabilities is increasing. Second, the attackers are moving to the vulnerabilities of common applications instead of system-level vulnerabilities.

Table 1. Number of System- and Application-level Vulnerabilities Related to the Malicious Websites Phenomenon for Several Years

Year	System Vulnerabilities	Application Vulnerabilities	Total
2003	1	0	1
2004	6	0	6
2005	5	0	5
2006	9	2	11
2007 (January – August)	8	7	15

In Table 2, we provide a more detailed overview of the vulnerabilities for the year 2007. We list the date of the public disclosure, the availability of a patch, and the availability of an exploit for this particular vulnerability. The table shows that the time between public disclosure and availability of a patch or exploit is often rather short: for a normal user, the *time to patch*, i.e., the time between the announcement of a vulnerability and the active exploitation in the wild, is rather short and it is hard to keep up with the latest information. Especially in the area of the Web, this is an increasing problem since patching third-party applications or browser add-ons / ActiveX controls is still a manual and error-prone process.

We also examined the relationship between vulnerabilities and their usage on the Chinese Web. The two left columns of Table 2 list for all vulnerabilities the date when an exploit was seen on a malicious website within the Chinese Web and when an exploit for this vulnerability was advertised on the underground black market. For all vulnerabilities we found information about the corresponding exploit available on the Chinese Web, and also most of the exploits were advertised on the underground market. This means that the attackers are very active and they also react fast to new vulnerabilities.

Table 2. Time between Public Disclosure, Patch Availability, and Exploit Availability for Selected Vulnerabilities on the Chinese Web in the Year 2007
The table also includes information when the first exploit was found on websites and when advertisements for exploits were found on the black market. N/A means that we did not find freely accessible information for patches or exploits.

Vulnerability ID	Disclosure	Patch	Exploit	Exploit on Websites	Advertisements
MS07-004	09.01.2007	09.01.2007	16.01.2007	26.01.2007	22.01.2007
MS07-009	24.10.2006	13.02.2007	26.03.2007	28.03.2007	N/A
MS07-017	28.03.2007	03.04.2007	08.04.2007	30.03.2007	10.04.2007
MS07-020	10.04.2007	10.04.2007	N/A	15.09.2007	24.07.2007
MS07-027	08.05.2007	08.05.2007	10.05.2007	30.03.2007	10.04.2007
MS07-033	14.03.2007	12.06.2007	14.03.2007	07.07.2007	13.06.2007
MS07-035	12.06.2007	12.06.2007	N/A	11.07.2007	08.07.2007
MS07-045	15.08.2007	14.08.2007	N/A	02.09.2007	02.09.2007
CVE-2007-3148	06.06.2007	N/A	06.06.2007	08.06.2007	N/A
CVE-2007-4105	02.08.2007	02.08.2007	03.10.2007	18.08.2007	23.09.2007
CVE-2007-4748	19.08.2007	N/A	31.08.2007	19.08.2007	08.09.2007
CVE-2007-4816	07.09.2007	20.09.2007	N/A	06.09.2007	08.09.2007
CVE-2007-5017	19.09.2007	N/A	19.09.2007	26.09.2007	N/A
CVE-2007-3296	30.05.2007	01.06.2007	N/A	25.06.2007	28.06.2007
CVE-2007-5064	30.08.2007	N/A	19.09.2007	30.08.2007	14.09.2007

4.4 *Strategies for Redirecting Visitors to Web-based Trojans*

To redirect the visitors of the trojanized websites to the actual web-based Trojan, attackers are typically using one of the following three categories of strategies.

4.4.1 Embedded HTML Tags

The first category uses embedded HTML tags such as *iframe*, *frame*, and others, to embed the web-based Trojan into the source code of the website. In order to achieve better covertness and flexibility, the attackers often introduce some intermediary stepping stones and dispatchers to build complex and obfuscated Trojan networks, by recursively using embedded tags and obfuscating the destination location.

The most used tag in the wild for redirection is *iframe*: the purpose of this HTML element is to create an inline frame that contains and displays another document. When the including page is opened, the included document is displayed in the inline frame. The attackers take advantage of this characteristic to include the web-based Trojan directly or recursively, but always set the iframe to be invisible. This can be easily achieved by setting the height or width of the iframe to zero or a very small value.

The frame tag can also be used to include web-based Trojans, but it is a little bothering to define a frameset and include the URL to the web-based Trojan in an invisible frame, so it is rarely used by attackers in the wild. Other strategies belonging to this category include using the *body onload* event to load web-based Trojan, and injecting links to web-based Trojans into CSS and various other tags.

4.4.2 Malicious Scripts

The second and also popular category uses the script tag to include web-based Trojan scripting or redirector scripting, which are often XSS (Cross-Site Scripting) vulnerabilities. The redirector scripting typically uses *document.write* to generate an *iframe* tag which includes the web-based Trojan or further stepping stones, or rarely seen *windows.open* function to obviously pop-up a new HTML window to perform exploitation.

4.4.3 Embedded Objects

The third category of strategies for including a web-based Trojan is based on the embedded object tag for activating third-party applications (e.g., Flash or Baofeng media player) or Browser Helper Objects (BHOs) to display the embedded object. When vulnerabilities in these applications and BHOs are found, attackers then use this strategy to inject the carefully constructed objects to the vulnerable applications, which exploit them in order to remotely execute code on the victim's machine.

A classical example belonging to this category is a technique widely used by Chinese attackers during the last year to include web-based Trojans. This technique is based on an exploit of a vulnerability within Internet Explorer (MS06-021): the attackers can generate a malicious Flash file by injecting the URL to web-based Trojans into a normal, benign SWF Flash file, and then they can include this specially prepared Flash file in a website which they control or other well-known websites which provide the Flash uploading and browsing service. When the malicious Flash file is displayed by a vulnerable version of Internet Explorer, the visiting computers are then attacked and redirected to execute the web-based Trojans. The machine of the visitor is then compromised.

5 Measurements and Results

To understand the situation posed by the malicious websites phenomenon and the prevalence of the underground economy on the Chinese Web, we performed a comprehensive measurement study in October 2007. Our measurement setup covers the observation and analysis on the underground black market, the analysis on the public marketplace for the virtual assets trading, and a detailed and in-depth evaluation of the threats raised by malicious websites to the normal Chinese Internet users.

5.1 Measurements on the Underground Black Market

Unlike the US or European blackhat communities, Chinese blackhats are typically not familiar with IRC (*Internet Relay Chat*). They typically use bulletin board systems on the Web or IM software like QQ to communicate with each other. Orthogonal to a study on the underground black market located within IRC networks (Franklin et al. 2007), we measure the Chinese-specific underground black market on the Web. We focus on the most important part located at *post.baidu.com*, the largest bulletin board community in China. We crawled the portal and stored all posts and replies posted on certain post bars which are all dedicated for the underground black market on this particular website. The post bars we examined include *Traffic bar*, *Trojans bar*, *Web-based Trojans bar*, *Wangma bar* (acronyms of Web-based Trojans in Chinese), *Box bar*, *Huigezi bar*, *Trojanized websites bar*, and *Envelopes bar*.

Each post and reply in the bar contains a title, information about the poster, post time, and the actual content. If the poster is not registered, the poster field is filled with the Class C IP range from where the poster connects to the server. Although it is possible that one person connects to the server from different IP ranges, we can still use this information to represent the poster since this situation happens only rarely due to the lack of IP addresses in China. For each of the IP addresses, we queried the geographical location of the poster using *ChunZhen*, a well-known IP2Location library within the Chinese Internet community.

Our measurements show that 23,606 distinct posters were involved in the underground market between January 2006 and September 2007. In total, they posted 90,679 posts or replies during this period of time. As shown in Figure 3 and 4, the numbers of posts published on these post bars per month are increasing over time, as well as the numbers of posters. At the peak point in August 2007, almost 3,500 posters published nearly 14,000 posts on the underground market, which shows that the underground black market is quite active in China. We also provide an overview of the province distribution of the underground market participants in Table 3, based on the location query results of the posters. This data is obtained with the help of a Geo-IP database.

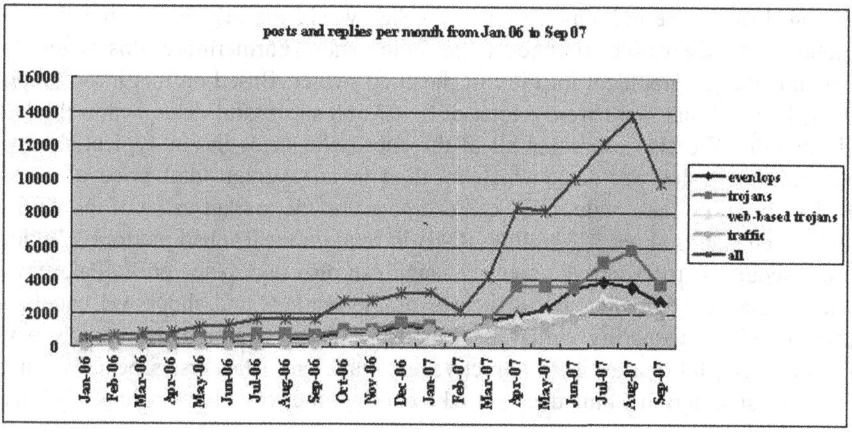

Figure 3. Posts and Replies per Month from January 2006 to September 2007

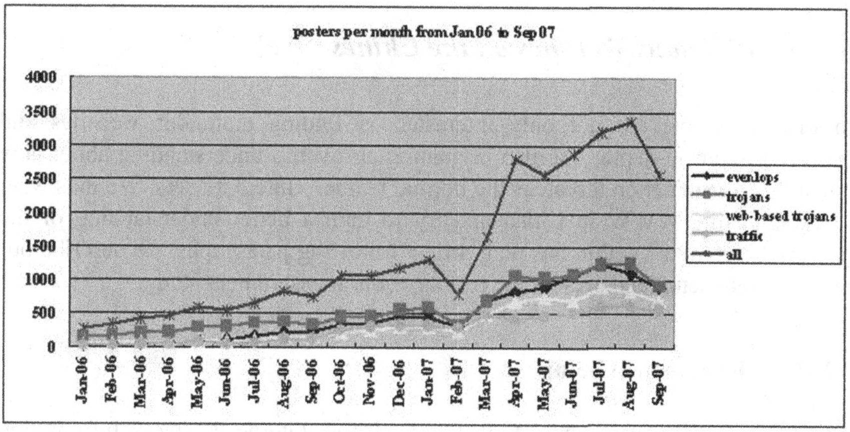

Figure 4. Posters per Month from January 2006 to September 2007

5.2 *Measurements on the Public Virtual Assets Marketplace*

We also studied the public assets marketplace visible via the Taobao online business platform. We found 42,561 online shops in total, and 34,450 of them had bargained deals successfully. Furthermore, our measurements show that there are a total of 1,220,181 virtual goods in all of these shops available, which means that each shop has on average 28 goods.

To estimate the market value of the whole virtual asset exchange market on the Taobao platform, we crawled the credit history pages of all the shops. From these pages it is possible to retrieve more information about the overall trading activity during different periods, including in the last week, the last month, the last six months, and the whole lifetime of the online shop. Furthermore, this page also contains the geographical location of the shop owner. Based on this information, we calculated that there were a total of 8,907,568 successful deals within the last six months. We also examined all of the successful deals in one typical shop to estimate the value per deal, which resulted in an average total price of 12.56 RMB. Based on these values, we can estimate that the market value of the virtual asset exchange is about 223 million RMB in total on the Taobao platform. Taking into account that the virtual asset exchange can also take place on PaiPai, eBay, and thousands of smaller, but dedicated online markets and shops, we conclude that there is a prospering virtual asset industry. These numbers also explain why the underground market is so attractive for malicious attackers, especially since the legal situation in China does not take cyber crime related to stealing of virtual assets into account.

5.3 Malicious Websites on the Chinese Web

In this work, we are not only interested in finding malicious websites and analyzing them in-depth, but also in gaining an overall understanding about how much this phenomenon threatens the normal Chinese Internet users. We thus want to examine the WWW in China and try to gain a better understanding of the malicious "corners" within the Web. In the following paragraphs, we describe our measurement setup and present the results of our measurement study.

5.3.1 Measurement Setup

According to the status report published by China Internet Network Information Center (CNNIC), there are a total of 1.31 million websites on the Chinese WWW in June 2007 (CNNIC 2007). Since checking the whole content of the Chinese Web is infeasible due to the size of the Web, we need to find a way to efficiently inspect a representative part of it. We thus need a good *sampling strategy* in order to find the parts of the Web that are most commonly accessed by normal Internet users. According to the same report by CNNIC, about 75% percent of the Internet users within China use search engines to find their information and target websites on the WWW. To sample the Chinese WWW effectively and focus on the major threats to the majority of Chinese Internet users, we thus use search engines to find the starting points of our experiments. We used two input sources to obtain the most commonly used keywords by Chinese Internet users to find their information: first, we used the Baidu top search keywords list provided at *http://top.baidu.com*. Second, we included the Google Chinese ReBang ("Top hot search keywords") provided at *http://www.google.cn/rebang/home*. Using the combined list of both inputs, we then categorized the searched websites into the following twelve categories: *portal/navigation*, *movie/TV*, *game*, *news/information*, *sport/entertainment*, *free download*, *e-business*, *industry information*, *chat/virtual society*, *e-finance*, *warez*, and *user content*. By issuing the most commonly used keywords for the specific content area to the Baidu and Google search engines, we obtained about 145,000 domain names. This set of sites represents our sampling set. Furthermore, we built a blacklist category containing the recently reported malicious websites by the Chinese Internet community during a one-week period before our measurements. We inspected all these websites to examine whether they are malicious or not. We also categorized the websites to learn whether there are some specific areas on the Chinese WWW that are more risky than others.

To actually inspect these websites, we developed a client honeypot that is capable of efficiently examining whether or not a given website is malicious. In contrast to previous work in this area, we split the task in two steps: in the first step, we examine websites with a *high-interaction honeypot*. A honeypot is a system which is intended to be probed, accessed, or compromised (Provos and Holz 2007). In this context high-interaction means that we use a real system for performing the analysis: The basic idea is to execute a web browser within a *honeypot* environment, automatically "surf" websites, and closely observe all activities on the honeypot. If we open a web page within the honeypot and this website exploits a vulnerability in our browser, we can detect this malicious behavior and issue an alert. In a second step, we use a *low-interaction honeypot*: instead of using a real system, we use a web crawler to automatically download and analyze larger amounts of data. As a starting point for these crawls, we use malicious websites identified in the first step. This two-tier architecture helps us to scale the system and analyze content in more depth. More technical details about the setup are available in the extended version of this chapter.

5.3.2 Malicious Websites

Based on the measurement setup we introduced in the former subsection, we identified a total of 2,149 malicious websites from 144,587 distinct hosts which represent the most commonly visited websites by normal Chinese Internet users. Table 3 provides an overview of the measurement results for the twelve different categories, the blacklist, and the total sites. We found that the categories including free download, sport/entertainment, movie/TV and chat/virtual society are more risky than others, which is consistent with our anticipation. The results also reveal that all categories contain a significant amount of malicious content: this is an important discovery as it means any Chinese Internet user accessing the web is at risk, regardless of the type of content they browse. Given the fact that all these sites were found using a search engine, this proves that the threat is significant.

Table 3. Measurement Results for Malicious Websites on the Chinese Web

Category	Keywords	Inspected	Malicious	%
Free Download	22	20,547	394	1.92
Sport / Entertainment	31	27,649	520	1.88
Movie / TV	25	23,472	423	1.84
Chat / Virtual Society	6	8,115	140	1.73
Game	23	20,105	269	1.34
News / Information	29	36,700	459	1.25
Warez	14	13,237	164	1.24
Portal / Navigation	6	8,829	106	1.20
Industry Info	17	20,518	246	1.20
e-Finance	15	19,138	139	0.73
e-Business	6	9,799	64	0.65
User Content	6	7,402	33	0.45
Total with overlaps	200	215,511	2,965	1.38
Distinct Total	200	144,587	2,149	1.49
Blacklist	N/A	796	28	3.52

The measurement results for the different categories reveal that different parts of the Web have a different degree of maliciousness: we found that user content is only malicious in 0.45% of the sites, while free download sites have a significant higher chance of hosting malicious content.

5.3.3 Link Analysis

Based on the collected data, we can also generate interrelations between different malicious websites. This allows us to connect different attacks and we can learn more about relations between the involved domains. We have generated several graphs revealing the link relations between the involved domains, redirectors, and the hosts of the web-based Trojans discovered during our measurement. In Figure 5, we show an example of such a graph, in which we see that different domains are connected via malicious content included as an embedded link.

Trojanized websites are drawn as ellipses, the redirector websites are drawn as parallelograms, and the exploit-hosting websites are drawn as boxes.

Similar to the node ranking strategy adopted by HoneyMonkey (Wang et al. 2006), we also assign the incoming and outgoing ranks to all of the hosts in the overall graph. We focus on the top-level domain names and not the low-level redirection links. Our strategy can reflect the popularity of the exploiters more precisely than the graphs generated by HoneyMonkey. Ordered by the incoming

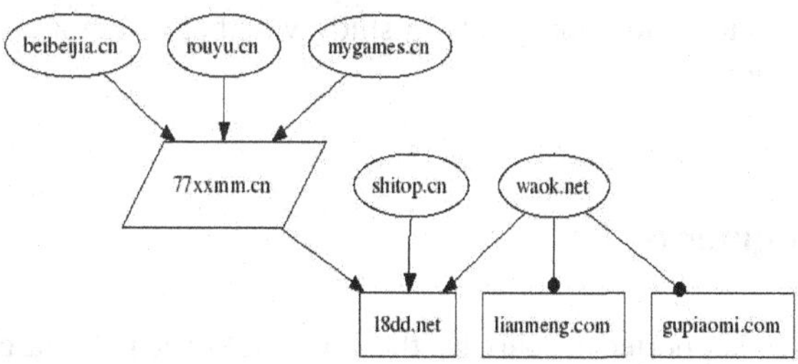

Figure 5. Example of Link Analysis of Malicious Websites

ranks, we were able to list the top malicious sites, together with the number of directly linked malicious websites or redirectors. Shutting down these domains would effectively lower the total amount of malicious websites on the Chinese Web since these domains are one of the root causes.

We also analyzed the top exploiter in more depth, and found out that 490 malicious websites (22.8% of total) located at 206 different top domains redirected their traffic to this particular attacker. The links were either direct or via 26 redirectors. The attacker used heavily obfuscated hosted dispatcher scripts and web-based Trojans to evade detection. In total, we found 21 different executables being used in this attack, and the majority of them are identified as online game stealers.

An interesting observation we can find from the link analysis is that the attackers register large amounts of *.cn* domains and use them for their attacks. This is specific to the Chinese Web since starting in March 2007, the register fee for .cn domains is only 1 RMB for the first year to encourage the development of the Chinese Web. Attackers abuse this in order to have many domains which redirect innocent Internet users to malicious websites. To even enhance the effectiveness of this strategy, the attackers generate many second-level domain names on these cheap domains. The domain names themselves seem to be generated in a random fashion and follow no obvious pattern.

6 Conclusions

In this chapter, we studied several aspects of malicious activities within the World Wide Web. First, we introduced a model of the underground black market which describes the interaction of the different actors within the market. This model is based on empirical data collected within China. Based on this model, we presented the first empirical measurements of malicious websites within the Chinese part of the World Wide Web. We studied the activities of attackers, how they trade the virtual goods (e.g., exploits or envelopes), and where they are located. Furthermore, we also examined malicious content within the Chinese Web. We combine high- and low-interaction honeypots to study whether or not a given site contains malicious content.

Acknowledgments

This work was supported in part by the 863 High-Tech Research and Development Program of China under Grant No. 2006AA01Z445. Jianwei Zhuge was supported by IBM Ph.D. Fellowship Plan. The views and conclusions contained here are those of the authors and should not be interpreted as representing the official policies or endorsements of the C.N. Government or any of its agencies.

References

Alexa, The Web Information Company. Global Top 500 Sites, May 2008. http://alexa.com/site/ds/top_sites?ts_mode=global.

China Internet Network Information Center (CNNIC). 20th Statistical Reports on the Internet Development in China, July 2007. http://cnnic.cn/download/2007/20thCNNICreport-en.pdf.

Franklin, J., Paxson, V., Perrig, A., and Savage, S. "An Inquiry into the Nature and Causes of the Wealth of Internet Miscreants," in *Proceedings of ACM Conference on Computer and Communications Security*, 2007.

Moshchuk, A., Bragin, T., Gribble, S.D., and Levy, H.M. "A Crawler-based Study of Spyware in the Web," in *Proceedings of 13th Network and Distributed System Security Symposium* (*NDSS'06*), 2006.

Provos, N. and Holz, T. *Virtual Honeypots: From Botnet Tracking to Intrusion Detection*, Addison-Wesley, July 2007.

Provos, N., Mavrommatis, P., Rajab, M. A., and Monrose, F. "All Your iFrames Point to Us," in *Proceedings of 17th USENIX Security Symposium*, 2008.

Provos, N., McNamee, D., Mavrommatis, P., Wang, K., and Modadugu, N. "The Ghost in the Browser: Analysis of Web-based Malware," in *Proceedings of HotBots 2007*, 2007.

Team Cymru. "Cybercrime: An Epidemic," *ACM Queue* (4:9), 2006, pp. 24–35.

The Honeynet Project. Know Your Enemy: Malicious Web Servers, August 2007. http://www.honeynet.org/papers/mws/.

The Honeynet Project. Know Your Enemy: Web Application Threats, February 2007. http://www.honeynet.org/papers/webapp/.

Thomas, R., and Martin, J. "The Underground Economy: Priceless," *USENIX;login:* (31:6), 2006, pp. 7–16.

Wang, Y.-M., Beck, D., Jiang, X., Roussev, R., Verbowski, C., Chen, S., and King, S. T. "Automated Web Patrol with Strider HoneyMonkeys: Finding Web Sites That Exploit Browser Vulnerabilities," in *Proceedings of 13th Network and Distributed System Security Symposium* (*NDSS'06*), 2006.

Botnet Economics: Uncertainty Matters

Zhen Li[1], Qi Liao[2] and Aaron Striegel[2]

[1]Department of Economics and Management, Albion College,

[2]Department of Computer Science and Engineering, University of Notre Dame

Abstract Botnets have become an increasing security concern in today's Internet. Thus far the mitigation to botnet attacks is a never ending arms race focusing on technical approaches. In this chapter, we model botnet-related cybercrimes as a result of profit-maximizing decision-making from the perspectives of both botnet masters and renters/attackers. From this economic model, we can understand the effective rental size and the optimal botnet size that can maximize the profits of botnet masters and attackers. We propose the idea of using virtual bots (honeypots running on virtual machines) to create uncertainty in the level of botnet attacks. The uncertainty introduced by virtual bots has a deep impact on the profit gains on the botnet market. With decreasing profitability, botnet-related attacks such as DDoS are reduced if not eliminated from the root cause, i.e. economic incentives.

1 Introduction

A hot topic nowadays in the Internet security community is botnets - referring to collections of compromised computers, or bots, controlled by botnet masters. It is widely accepted that botnets impose one of the most serious threats to the Internet since they are predominantly used for illegal activities. For example, Rajab et al. find that a major contributor of unwanted Internet traffic – 27% of all malicious connection attempts – can be directly attributed to botnet-related spreading activity (Rajab et al. 2006).

The attackers or hackers on the Internet were generally thought to be less financially driven in the past, i.e. motivated by self-fulfilment, fun, and proof of skills. Recently however, cybercriminals have been moving toward business models that involve building, exploiting and maintaining botnets. These cybercriminals collect, use, rent and trade botnets to make economic gains. Botnets can be exploited for various purposes, the most dominant uses including distributed denial-of-service attacks (DDoS), SMTP mail relays for spam (Spambot), ad click fraud, the theft of application serial numbers, login IDs, and financial information such as credit card

M.E. Johnson (ed.), *Managing Information Risk and the Economics of Security*,
DOI: 10.1007/978-0-387-09762-6_12,

numbers and bank accounts, etc. Almost all these tasks can be used to make money or have the potential to make money.

Researchers and Internet Service Providers (ISPs) have largely explored sophisticated technical only solutions with limited success. Recent trends note that the problems themselves are only growing, not abating. Existing technical approaches aim at either to prevent infected machines from reaching the target, or to redirect the visit of infected computers to a different site (Mahajan et al. 2002; Yau et al. 2005). Such defenses tend to be passive and inefficient mainly because current Internet architecture makes it extremely hard if not possible to differentiate a "pretend-to-be-legitimate" request from a "true legitimate" visit. Especially as botnets evolve quickly to become a significant part of the Internet, they are also increasingly hidden. New directions of thinking and effective alternatives are imminently required to deal with the problems at the root cause.

Today's botnet masters and attackers are seeking money, driven by profits, and motivated more by a desire to gain financially than to create havoc. Taking away the financial incentives that lead them to join malicious Internet activities in the first place is hence a promising new line of thinking in fighting the battle against botnet attacks. This study explores the worth and benefits by learning from economics, and applys economic theories in the analysis of botnet-based attacks and activities.

Rational people think at the margin, one of the essential economic principles, suggests that when making economic decisions, people compare costs and benefits, and will only do things if the benefit of doing it exceeds the costs. The *cost-benefit analysis* would guarantee the maximum profit to an economic agent. Applying the principle to for-pay attacks or other illegal activities, both botnet masters and attackers (who rent bots from previous) are by nature economic agents who participate in the botnet market, seeking economic returns. Similar to other rational behaviors like consumers or firms, botnet masters/attackers make economic decisions in order to reach the highest level of satisfaction, i.e., profit-driven botnet masters and attackers make their decisions regarding the optimal size of botnets, the effective size of bot rental, etc. to reap the maximum level of profit. Based upon the above, the contribution of this study is the systematic modeling of the botnet operation and utilization as a result of *profit-maximizing decision-making* from the perspectives of both botnet masters and attackers. The economic model developed in this study can help in understanding the interaction between botnet masters, attackers, and defenders, the effective rental size and the optimal botnet size, cost and benefit, and many other aspects.

Another key contribution of this chapter is to propose an interesting economic solution to the botnet problem. By introducing *virtual bots* (honeypots running on virtual machines that are to be compromised by the botnet masters), we create *uncertainties* and *interference* in the botnet market. As shown in this chapter, these uncertainties have a tremendous impact on the effective botnet size and therefore the profitability of botnet operators and attackers. Botnet masters and attackers, being profit-driven rational economic agents, make decisions to seek the maximized profit, whose level depends on factors such as costs of operating botnets, payoff received for successfully disabling victim web sites, market rental price of botnets, etc. Given rational profit-driven botnet masters and attackers, both the size of rental and the size of botnets determined on a honeypot-free Internet black market are economically efficient. At any point in time, the capacity of the server limits the number of compromised machines supported, further limiting the number of bots rented and used to attack victims (Rajab et al. 2007). Therefore, having virtual bots in botnets reduces the probability of launching a successful attack and thus reduces the profitability of botnet market. The profit margin of the market is reduced not only through lowering revenue levels of market participants, but also through increasing costs of operating botnets. With falling profit margins, botnets and the associated attacks will eventually decrease, if not outright disappear.

The remainder of the chapter is organized as follows. Section 2 discusses technical background on botnet style DDoS attacks and defense mechanism, our threat model and the related work. Section 3 develops the assumptions, the variables, and profit levels of botnet masters and attackers in the benchmark model where virtual bots are not around. The profit maximization problem is formalized for both botnet masters and attackers. The fact of modeling botnet masters' and attackers' decision-making as a profit maximization problem allows us to find the optimal sizes of botnets, honeypots, and rentals used for attacks. Section 4 extends the benchmark model to accommodate the existence of honeypots. We first assume the probability for a rental machine to be virtual is fixed, and then relax the assumption to analyze a more informative case in which the probability of fake bots is unknown to botnet masters and attackers. It also describes how this method can be used to understand and undermine botnet attacks from the root cause, i.e. economic incentives. The impacts on botnet masters, attackers, and defenders introduced by this uncertainty are analyzed in detail. Section 5 discusses technical deployment feasibility and a few challenges. We walk through examples with concrete numeric values coupled with graphical illustration. Finally, we conclude and propose future work in Section 6.

2 Background and Related Work

In a botnet-style distributed denial of service (DDoS) attack, the attacker chooses a subset of botnets to either flood or consume end servers' resources. Since those requests are not spoofed, they all appear *legitimate*, but are much more intense than normal use and cause the system to become busy, rendering the site unavailable to other legitimate users. Regardless of the type of DDoS attack, bandwidth depletion or resource depletion schemes, the goal of a DDoS attack is to impair the target's functioning, effectively shutting down the victim by forcing it to spend resources handling the attacker's traffic. An example of the botnet DDoS attack is illustrated in Figure 1.

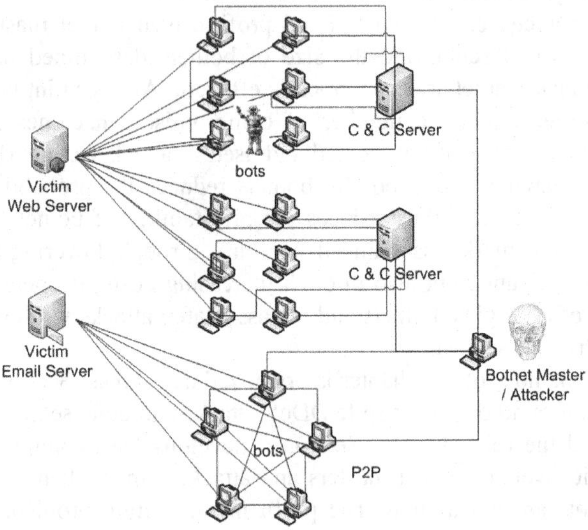

Figure 1. A Scenario of Botnet Attacks Launched by Robot Computers (bots) Controlled by the Botnet Master and Attacker

Defending against botnet DDoS attacks is an extremely challenging problem. Traditionally, defenses against those attacks have focused only on technical solutions. Approaches include rate limiting/filtering the offense hosts (Mahajan et al. 2002; Yau et al. 2005), tracing back (Park and Lee 2001; Savage et al. 2000; Snoeren et al. 2001), or host-based anomaly filtering (Jin et al. 2003, Jin and Yeung 2004; Xu and Lee 2003). These methods require either accurately identifying the source as "bad" or "good", constant updating signatures, or support from network architecture. This results in a never ending arms race between attackers and defenders, which is an undesirable position for a content provider.

We note that as researchers become more aware of the economic nature of Internet security problems, recent research has been seeking help from economic principles. To stem the flow of stolen credit cards and identity thefts, Franklin and Perrig propose two technical approaches to reduce the number of successful market transactions, aiming at undercutting the cybercriminals' verification or reputation system (Franklin and Perrig 2007). The approach by Xu and Lee uses game theory to model the attackers and defenders (Xu and Lee 2003). Although their approach is by nature a technical DDoS defense, it is interesting to notice that they use a game-theoretical framework to analyze the performance of their proposed defense system and to guide the design and performance turning of the system.

The closest study to ours is Ford and Gordon (Ford and Gordon 2006), which targets malicious code generated revenue streams. We both aim at designing botnet-disabling mechanisms from an economic perspective that are in the direct control of defenders. Nevertheless, there are noticeable differences between the two studies. In contrary to the focus on online advertising fraud, our model covers more general botnet attacks with a threat model focusing more on botnet DDoS attacks. Our contribution is that we model botnet masters' and attackers' decision-making as solving a profit maximization problem. Notably, we also incorporate the *diurnal pattern* and live population when modeling the botnet behavior. Depending on the optimal strategies botnet masters and attackers adopt, we illustrate in detail how honeypots can be deployed to change economic motivations of illegal Internet practitioners. In this sense, we are in line with these researchers by claiming that botnet-related crimes will dramatically decrease if botnet masters give up on it – that is, when maintaining botnets becomes more troublesome than worthwhile.

We also propose a fresh new method of using virtual bots to introduce the *uncertainties* to the optimizing problem through analysis of those virtual bots' impact on the botnet market. Although the idea of honeypots is not new (Bacher et al. 2005), honeypots have primarily been used for data collecting to understand the botnet or mapping the infected machines to track the control channel rather than undermining botnets by removing the financial incentives of running and employing the botnet. By extending the functioning of honeypots in the direction of interfering with the money-driven Internet malicious activities, the value of honeypots is fundamentally improved, especially when taking into account the potential effectiveness of our proposed method.

3 The Benchmark Model

In this section, we consider a benchmark model in which virtual machines are not present to interfere with the botnet. We present the assumptions of the model, the variables and constant parameters, and the profit levels of both botnet masters and attackers as a result of their profit maximization decision-making.

3.1 *Profit-driven Cybercriminals*

Internet-based crimes have been shifting from reputation economy to cash economy. Today, a large fraction of Internet-based crimes is profit-driven and can be modeled roughly as rational behavior. The Internet underground market creates a large fortune. The exponential growth of botnet with millions of infected computers bought and traded on an underground market has evolved into billion-dollar "shadow industry" (ScienceDaily 2007). Being such a lucrative business, Internet illegal activities have been popular and hard to kill. Any effective approach aiming at eliminating such activities must remove the financial incentives out of them. Economic theories would help.

Botnet economics is by nature similar to other economics, whereby rational individuals driven by profits make economic decisions to maximize their well-being. Applying the cost-benefit principle from economics to Internet crimes, a botnet master will keep botnets if the benefit of doing so is larger than the costs. Similarly, attackers will be better off if they commit an action whose benefits are larger than costs.

Evidence has been found that compromised machines are actually rented on underground markets (Franklin and Perrig 2007). It is realistic to model Internet market as the trading place where bots are rent to attackers for launching DDoS attacks. We choose to model botnet-based DDoS attacks first because of their straightforwardness. Moreover, (botnet-related) DDoS is still the primary concern for network security operations (Arbor Network 2006). In the rest of the section, we build a theoretical model to illustrate how the two parties – botnet masters and attackers – make economic decisions in order to reap maximum profit.

3.2 Assumptions

The key assumption is the rationality of botnet masters and attackers. For any market, there must be a long-run equilibrium in which all market forces have been balanced. Suppose the Internet black market is in long-run equilibrium. We note the following assumptive parameters.

1. n^e is the minimum number of machines required to achieve a task (e.g. disable a website) [55]. We assume that technical capability determines the size of n^e, which both botnet masters and attackers take as given. We refer to n^e as the effective number of rentals (and as we will see later, since it costs money to rent botnets, in the steady state, attackers' profit-maximizing size of rental is equal to n^e).
2. An attacker is only paid if the attack successfully disables the target site. The payment received by the attacker is denoted as M.
3. The rental price per bot (denoted as P) is determined on Internet black markets, which both botnet masters and attackers take as given.
4. Botnet masters who manage bots use Command and Control (C&C) channel[56] to communicate with zombie computers in botnets. A typical C&C channel can host q machines simultaneously, which is also the live population on the C&C

[55] Alternatively, we can view n^e as the minimum number of accesses required to disable a website, and further define the number of accesses per machine to figure out the size of rental. We do not see it necessary to go into such details and believe our conclusions are not affected.

[56] Although we are considering Internet Relay Chat (IRC), which is the dominant C&C channel in today's botnet, the parameter for botnet maintenance costs can be defined accordingly based on the underlying technique adopted to control bots, whether through IRC or other decentralized systems such as P2P.

channel at any point in time.[57] The unit cost of maintaining a C&C channel is given at m.

5. A real bot machine operates on average t hours per day and d days per week due to the owner's diurnal patterns and physical constraints. Of all the live population, botnet masters randomly select bots to lease out.

In summary, the exogenous/given variables are the effective size of rentals (n^e), the number of machines a C&C channel can support at a point in time (q), the average cost of maintaining a C&C channel (m), the unit rental price of compromised machines (P), the payment for a successful attack (M), and how often a real machine operates (t and d).

3.3 Model Without Virtual Machines

In the benchmark model, we set up the profit maximization problems for a representative botnet master and a representative attacker where virtual machines are not present to interfere with the botnet. Profit is the difference between revenue and costs, and both can be monetary and psychological. Since it is hard to measure or quantify psychological benefits and costs, we focus only on the monetary aspect of the analysis.

The profit maximization problems for a representative botnet master and a representative attacker are as follows, respectively.

For the attacker:

$$\begin{aligned} &\max_{n}(Profit) = M - P \times n \\ &\text{s. t.} \qquad n \geq n^{e} \end{aligned} \tag{1}$$

where the subject condition requires that the attacker must rent at least the effective number of machines to launch a successful attack.

For the botnet master:

$$\begin{aligned} &\max_{k,N}(Profit) = P \times n - m \times k - a(N) \\ &\text{s. t.} \qquad k \geq \frac{n}{q} \\ &\qquad\qquad N \geq \frac{n}{(t/24) \times (d/7)} \end{aligned} \tag{2}$$

where N is the size of a typical botnet, which is simply the number of machines in a botnet. N is called the footprint of the botnet. $a(N)$ is the penalty function for the

---

57 Similar to the determination of n^e, how many bots, q, a C&C channel can host is determined by technological progresses and limited by the capacity of the channel. Given technology, q is fixed.

botnet master, measuring the economic losses suffered from being detected and arrested. Since the chance of being identified and arrested is higher as the size of the botnet increases, the penalty function is increasing in the size of the botnet ($a'(N)>0$). The second restriction for the botnet master implies that the active members in the botnet ($N \times (t/24) \times (d/7)$) must be no smaller than the live population (n) because the botnet master can only rent out active machines. The first restriction for the botnet master suggests that the total number of C&C channels must be enough to support the n machines being leased.

The control variable for the attacker is the size of the rental (n). The control variables for the botnet master are the number of C&C channels (k) and the size of the botnet (N) to maintain.

Given the consideration of both the attacker and the botnet master, the order of the decision making and the first-best model solutions are the following.

1. The attacker rents n machines to launch a successful attack; After the victim is taken down, the attacker receives M payment. Since it costs money to rent machines, at given M, the attacker's profit is maximized at $n = n^e$. In other words, in the steady state, the equilibrium number of rental is equal to the effective size of rental.
2. After observing the number of machines the attacker is willing to rent, the botnet master chooses the size of the botnet to maintain that will satisfy the rental needs of the attacker. Without uncertainty, since a typical machine runs t hours a day and d days a week, the steady-state size of the botnet is $N = n^e / \{(t/24) \times (d/7)\}$. Meanwhile, the botnet master needs to maintain enough C&C channels to host the n^e rental machines. Given the total revenue $P \times n^e$, maximizing profit is equivalent to minimizing costs, which is further equivalent to maintaining the minimum number of C&C channels $k = n^e/q$.

From above, when the botnet master and the attacker do not have to worry about virtual machines, efficient market results are achieved by realizing the effective level of rental, number of C&C channels, and size of the botnet. Without uncertainty, the botnet master's and the attacker's benchmark profits are deterministic. Let π_b be the profit earned by the botnet master and π_a be the profit for the attacker; their profit levels can be represented as follows, respectively.

$$\pi_b = P \times n^e - m \times \frac{n^e}{q} - a\left(\frac{n^e}{(t/24) \times (d/7)}\right) \tag{3}$$

$$\pi_a = M - P \times n^e \tag{4}$$

Examining the expressions of steady-state profits for the botnet master and the attacker, it can be seen that for the existence of the business, both profits must be non-negative. Combining the botnet master (seller of the botnet) and the attacker (buyer of the botnet), the market is profitable as long as both sides of the market are profitable,

$$M \geq P \times n^e \geq m \times \frac{n^e}{q} + a\left(\frac{n^e}{(t/24)\times(d/7)}\right) \tag{5}$$

Adding (3) and (4), the size of the gains on the market is

$$\pi_a + \pi_b = M - m \times \frac{n^e}{q} - a\left(\frac{n^e}{(t/24)\times(d/7)}\right) \tag{6}$$

On current Internet black markets, the chance for a botnet master to be arrested is small. The widespread (and increasing) illegal botnet practices suggest that the profitability of the business may be quite significant, and hence participating in the market is attractive and rewarding.

One thing we do not take into account is the idle time of botnets – the time periods when botnets are not leased. The attacks do not happen all the time. The botnet master cannot rent the botnet as often as he/she would like. When the botnet is at idle, it receives no revenue and occurs only costs. The calculation of profits in the benchmark model is per successful attack. We can accommodate the concern of idle time straightforwardly by specifying the profit as the profit reaped in a period of time. The setup and solutions of the model are unchanged.

4 Optimization Model With Virtual Machines

In the benchmark model, botnet masters and attackers earn profits and thus will remain in the market. To push them away from the market, we ought to reduce their profit level and make the business less attractive. Economic theory suggests that uncertainty is costly. When market situation becomes less clear for some reason, market participants would be reluctant to do the business and ask for higher compensation for the increased risks resulting from ambiguity. The idea provides a new approach to interfering with the Internet underground market – to make it less efficient and less deterministic. We propose that creating honeypots for botnet masters to compromise will do the job.

In this section, we extend the benchmark model to allow the existence of honeypots in botnet. We first assume that the probability for a rental machine to be virtual is fixed, and later relax the assumption to analyze a more realistic and informative case in which market participants have no idea about the number of honeypots having been created.

4.1 Fixed Probability for a Rental Bot Being Virtual

The introduction of virtual machines creates uncertainty to the botnet in large. Virtual bots will not attack the victim as ordered. If still $n = n^e$ machines were rented, a number of inactive machines would make the attack unsuccessful. The actual size of rental (n) can no longer be equal to the effective size of rental (n^e). With some of n being virtual machines, renting n^e is not enough, implying that the new equilibrium size of rental must be larger than n^e.

We model the profit maximization problems for the botnet master and the attacker to show what happens with the introduction of virtual machines. For the time being, we assume that the probability for a rental machine to be virtual is fixed.

Let p_v denote the probability for a rental machine to be virtual, and p_v is fixed. The profit maximization problem for a typical attacker now looks as follows.

$$\max_n(Profit) = M - P \times n \qquad \text{s.t.} \quad n \times (1 - p_v) \geq n^e \tag{7}$$

For the botnet master, the profit maximization problem is the same as in the benchmark model since his/her decision-making is based upon the size of rental chosen by the attacker.

Solving the problems results in two conclusions:

1. To launch a successful attack, the attacker now has to rent $n = n^e/(1 - p_v)$ machines, larger than in the benchmark model.
2. To accommodate the $n = n^e/(1 - p_v)$ machines leased, the botnet master has to maintain $k = n^e/\{(1 - p_v) \times q\}$ C&C channels. In the meantime, the new equilibrium size of botnet increases to

$$N = \frac{n^e}{(1 - p_v) \times (t/24) \times (d/7)} \tag{8}$$

If everything else remains unchanged, the profit for both the botnet master and the attacker are different from the benchmark model. For the botnet master, the profit may either go up or go down. On one hand, the botnet master's revenue increases due to more machines rented; on the other hand, the botnet master has to acquire more C&C channels to support the increased rental and also suffers a higher chance of being arrested. The botnet master's profit margin is now:

$$\pi_b^{v1} = P \times \frac{n^e}{1 - p_v} - m \times \frac{n^e}{(1 - p_v) \times q} - a\left(\frac{n^e}{(1 - p_v) \times (t/24) \times (d/7)}\right) \tag{9}$$

where π_b^{v1} represents the profit margin for the botnet master when the probability for a rental machine to be virtual is fixed at p_v.

The attacker's profit must decline. With the same payment for successfully taking down the victim, the attacker incurs larger costs of renting machines. The new profit level for the attacker is therefore

$$\pi_a^{v1} = M - P \times \frac{n^e}{1 - p_v} \tag{10}$$

where π_a^{vl} stands for the profit margin for the attacker when the probability for a rental machine to be virtual is fixed at p_V.

Adding (9) and (10), the size of the total gains on the market shrinks to

$$\pi_a^{vl} + \pi_b^{vl} = M - m \times \frac{n^e}{(1-p_v)\times q} - a\left(\frac{n^e}{(1-p_v)\times(t/24)\times(d/7)}\right) \tag{11}$$

Obviously, the existence of virtual machines lowers the incentives for attackers to rent machines. For the botnet master, the profit level depends on the rental price of machines P. The profit level decreases as the rental price P falls. If relaxing the assumption of a given rental price (that is, if P is allowed to adjust to market situations), the attacker's decreased demand for botnets will push down the rental price of machines (that is, P will fall). Market price P is further decreasing in p_V, thus a higher p_V will lower the botnet master's profit through two channels: lowered revenue due to lower price and higher costs of maintaining more C&C channels (Figure 2). Alternatively, Figure 3 illustrates the botnet rental market where botnet masters are price-takers.

In the following analysis, we will hold market price as given. Price changes are not essential to our analysis because the rental price received by the botnet master is just the price paid by the attacker. Price fluctuations cause income redistribution between botnet masters and attackers rather than affecting the combined benefits of the market.

The analysis in this subsection shows how the introduction of virtual machines may alter economic benefits to interested parties. By creating virtual bots to disturb botnets, we've seen the possibility of reducing profitability of participating in Internet black markets, and hence reducing the incidence of black market activities. By reducing the potential profit levels of both botnet masters and attackers, creating virtual machines has a large potential to reduce unfavorable Internet practices.

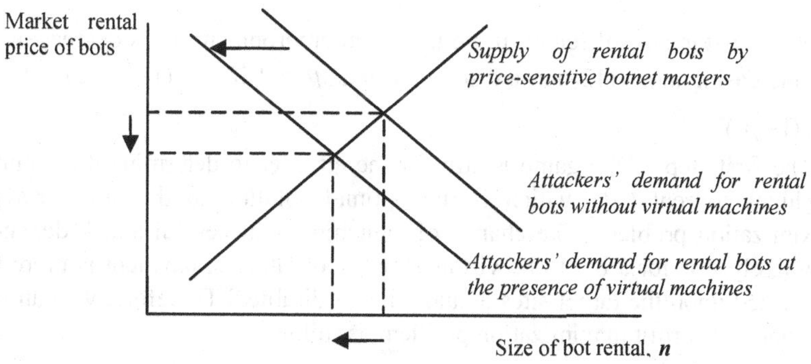

Figure 2. In the Underground Market for Botnets Where Botnet Masters Are Price-sensitive, a Supply and Demand Model Suggests the Decreased Price and Bot Rental After Introducing Virtual Machines

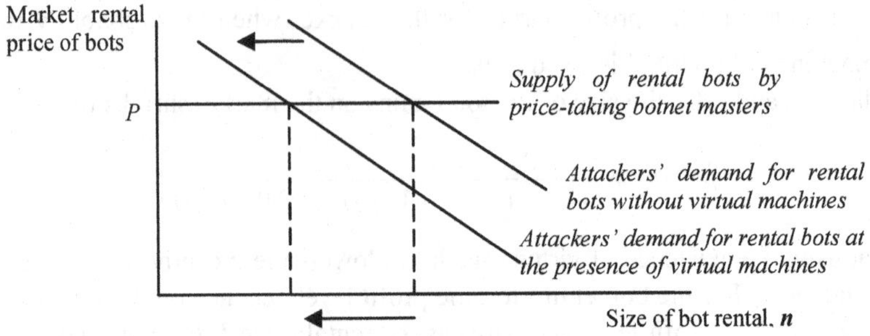

Figure 3. In the Botnet Market Where Botnet Masters are Price-takers, a Decreased Bot Rental is Suggested at the Presence of Virtual Bots

4.2 *Uncertainty for a Rental Bot Being Virtual*

In the previous subsection we demonstrate that creating honeypots reduces the attractiveness of participating in the black market for botnets. In this section we relax the assumption of a fixed p_V and introduce *uncertainty* to the market. In other words, this time p_V becomes unknown to black market participants (botnet masters, attackers, etc.). The following analysis shows that an uncertain proportion of virtual machines will make the situation even more harsh for botnet masters and attackers.

To that end, the model needs to be modified. We continue denoting the probability for a rental bot to be virtual as p_V, but it is unknown to the market this time. We denote the probability for a botnet-style attack to be successful as p_S, which depends on p_V and the total number of machines rented,

$$p_s = f(p_v, n^u) \tag{12}$$

where n^u is the size of rental in the uncertain environment. p_S is decreasing in p_V and increasing in n^u. (12) has a discrete format: $p_S = 1$ if $n^u \times (1 - p_v) \geq n^e$; $p_S = 0$ if $n^u \times (1 - p_v) < n^e$.

The first step of the game is still for the attacker to determine the number of machines to rent (n^u), which is the optimal solution to the attacker's profit maximization problem. The chance of launching a successful attack depends on how likely it is for a bot to be virtual. For DDoS attacks, payment is more likely predicated upon the target sites actually being disabled. Therefore, we can model the attacker's profit maximization problem as follows.

$$\max_{n^u}(Profit) = E - P \times n^u = M \times p_s - P \times n^u = M \times f(p_v, n^u) - P \times n^u \tag{13}$$

$$\text{s. t.} \quad n^u \times (1 - p_v) \geq n^e$$

where we replace the probability of launching a successful attack p_S with its determinants p_V and n^u. E stands for the *expected* revenue of the attacker. To make the attack successful, the attacker has to rent at least $n^u = n^e/(1-p_v)$ machines. As $p_V \to 1$, $n^u \to \infty$.

Taking the first order derivative of the objective function with respect to n^u, we get the first order condition for the maximizing problem, $M \times f'(p_v, n^u) - P = 0$, or $f'(p_v, n^u) = P/M$, which implies that by observing market price of renting machines and the payment to be received after launching a successful attack, the attacker rents n^u such that the first order condition holds true.

If p_V were known to the attacker, the minimum size of rental would be $n^e/(1-p_v)$. The unknown probability p_V makes it impossible for the attacker to pin down the size of rental: renting too many, unnecessary costs incur; renting too few, the attack fails.The attacker receives no payment and only pays rental costs. Thus, there is a trade-off between rental costs and the odds of a successful attack.

The solutions to the botnet master's profit maximization problem still take the format: $k = n^u/q$ and $N = n^u/\{(t/24)\times(d/7)\}$. The uncertainty of n^u due to the unknown p_V leads to the uncertainty of k and N, and both are increasing in n^u.

The machines that the botnet master can rent to the attacker must be live machines. When the botnet master needs to choose n^u machines from the botnet, he/she has to choose live machines. A real machine may have idle time as well as live time, while a virtual machine can run 24/7. The chance for a virtual machine to be chosen is likely to be higher than that of a real machine. If the botnet master selects machines randomly from the live population, the chance for a virtual machine to be picked c_V and the chance for a real machine to be picked c_r have the following relationship: $c_v = (24/t)\times(7/d)\times c_r \geq c_r$.

Without virtual machines, the attacker rents $n = n^e$ machines and the botnet master keeps the size of the botnet at $N = n^e/(1-p_v)$. The chance for a real machine to be picked is $c_r = (t/24)\times(d/7)$. With the existence of virtual machines, the number of virtual machines in the botnet (V), the uncertain botnet size (N^u) and the uncertain size of rental (n^u) have the following relationship.

$$V + (t/24)\times(d/7)\times(N^u - V) = n^u \tag{14}$$

From (14) we can derive the probability for a machine in the n^u rental machines to be virtual,

$$p_v = \frac{V}{n^u} = \frac{V}{V + (t/24)\times(d/7)\times(N^u - V)} \tag{15}$$

The profit margins for the botnet master and the attacker are calculated as

$$\pi_a^{v2} = M \times f(p_v, n^u) - P \times n^u \tag{16}$$

$$\pi_b^{v2} = P \times n^u - m \times \frac{n^u}{q} - a\left(\frac{n^u}{(t/24)\times(d/7)}\right) \quad (17)$$

Adding (16) and (17), the size of the gains on the whole market is now

$$\pi^u = M \times f(p_v, n^u) - m \times \frac{n^u}{q} - a\left(\frac{n^u}{(t/24)\times(d/7)}\right) \quad (18)$$

Since $f(p_V, n^u) \leq 1$, $n^u > n$, and $a(\cdot)$ is increasing in n^u, the market profitability shrinks, meaning that the total benefit available for the two parties is smaller. Indeed, both parties are only left with a smaller profit margin than in the previous two cases.

It is important to go over the motivation and preferences of each interest party, and see the effects of an uncertain p_V.

- **The attacker.**
  The attacker decides the minimum/effective size of rental that guarantees a successful attack n^u, which is determined according to $f'(p_v, n^u) = P/M$. Given market prices of rental and attack, n^u is increasing in p_V. The attacker's profit is decreasing in p_V.

- **The botnet master.**
  By observing the number of machines the attacker is willing to rent, the botnet master decides the minimum/effective number of C&C channels and the size of the botnet to maintain that at least n^u machines are alive, ensuring there are always enough machines for renting. An uncertain p_V increases the botnet master's operation costs and may eventually reduce his/her profit if the market rental price of "low-quality" botnet drops and he/she further suffers reputational losses and an increased chance of being arrested. Note for both the attacker and the botnet master, undesirable costs incur.

- **The defenders[58].**
  The strategy is simply to create virtual slices/images on their computers to interfere with the botnet market. Both the botnet master's and the attacker's costs are directly and positively related to the probability for a bot to be virtual among the n^u rental machines. That is, p_V is the essential factor that is, if not fully, at least partially controlled by the defenders. Higher p_V will effectively reduce the profits earned by both the botnet master and the attacker. If p_V is high enough, renting botnets to launch attacks or other illegal activities may no longer be profitable.

[58] Defenders refer to whoever has the incentive to run/maintain honeypots such as researchers and government agencies. While these organizations by law have desire to fight against cybercriminals, private parties may also be motivated to create honeypots if they are financially compensated. For example, a honeypot server may collect data on the botnet to sell to customers for development of infrastructure protection techniques.

Even if some profits remain, the reduced profit margin will certainly make the business not as attractive as before[59].

Although we have modeled the profit maximization decision-making for the attacker and the botnet master separately, the model conclusions will be the same if the two parties are combined to model the optimal results on the whole market. Therefore, if botnets are not rent to attackers but are used by botnet masters themselves to launch attacks, the model predictions work equally well.

5 Further Discussion and Case Study

First, a few countervirtual measurements that might be adopted by the botnet master are discussed in this section, for example, what if the botnet master selects machines according to lifetime of being a botnet member rather than selecting machines randomly (or, what if the botnet master adopts a "first-in-first-out" strategy). What about insurance; would that help? Second, we walk through examples as case study coupled with graphical analysis of the model. Last, some technical deployment feasibility is discussed.

5.1 Countervirtual Strategies

First, let us look at "first-in-first-out" strategy. First-in-first-out means that the botnet master selects machines according to the length of being compromised. "Older" member bots are more likely to be chosen. This strategy may seem more advantageous than random selection at first sight, but it will not nullify our method. The first-in-first-out strategy simply imposes more challenges for researchers to develop approaches for preventing a virtual machine from being detected by the botnet master. Meanwhile, since virtual machines are not subject to the life cycle of a real machine, they tend to have longer lifetimes, which can even increase the probability for a virtual machine to be selected.

If the botnet market becomes aware of the problems created by virtual machines, the botnet master may consider offering warranty or insurance to attackers and promises to replace inactive machines. This seems like a good idea but it would be very difficult for the botnet master to implement it because:

1. All the warranty depends on the capability for the attacker/botnet master to find out which machine is inactive, which takes time;

---

[59] Furthermore, the increased likelihood for an attack to fail also increases the psychological costs of launching such an attack, which makes the practice even less interesting.

2. Even if the previous is possible, having virtual machines distributed widely among botnets, and the fact that a virtual machine is more likely to be picked, further complicate the situation;
3. Some type of attacks (such as DDoS) may be time-restricting. Once the first wave of attack fails, the target site may have been aware of the attack and initiated counterattacking.

To counter the uncertainty created by unknown p_v, the attacker may rent $n^u = n/(1-p_v^g)$ machines at an estimated level of $p_v = p_v^g$. If $n^u = n/(1-p_v^g)$ turns out to be insufficient, the attacker then increases the intensity of attacks per (real) machine (upon detecting virtual machines). There are again two major difficulties with this countervirtual strategy. The first is about the timing, i.e. how likely and quickly is it for the attacker and the botnet master to detect virtual machines? The second issue is the increased chance of being blocked if each real bot has to send more access requests. That is, it will be harder for the attacker to mimic a human visitor. In other words, the heavier each machine attacks, the more likely it will be detected and filtered. Therefore, it is concluded that the strategy of creating virtual machines to blur Internet black markets is robust to the above various possible counterstrategies that cybercriminals may adopt.

Indeed the most obvious and challenging countervirtual strategy the botnet master may explore is to improve the detection of fake bots. For example, the botnet master may monitor whether bots participate in the attack or respond to other malicious commands as instructed. Section 5.3 discusses issues related to such countermeasure in more details.

5.2 Examples and Illustration

We now look at a case study with numerical examples and graphical illustration. From above, the essential component of our strategy is the uncertainty of p_v, or the ambiguous number of virtual machines that have been created (V). An interesting question is how large should V be to completely wipe off the profits reaped from participating in the market. Since modeling botmasters and attackers, respectively, is equivalent to modeling the entire market, we focus on analyzing how the total size of the market profit is affected by changing the number of virtual machines, and figuring out the cutoff value of it.

Substituting (8) into (15), we express the number of virtual machines V as a function of the probability for a rental machine to be virtual p_v.

$$V = \frac{n^e \times p_v}{(1-p_v)\{1-p_v \times [1-(t/24)\times(d/7)]\}} \tag{19}$$

The uncertainty of p_V makes it impossible to solve for the botnet size N^u and the size of market profit π^u. We assign some values to the parameters and show how the two variables (N^u and π^u) change with p_V.

For simplicity, suppose $n^u \geq n^e/(1-p_v)$ is satisfied, hence $f(p_V, n^u) = 1$. We also drop the penalty function from the market profit function[60]. The market profit (18) is simplified as

$$\pi^u = M - m \times \frac{n^e}{(1-p_v) \times q} \tag{20}$$

Given the parameters (M, m, n^e and q), we can solve for the cutoff p_V that reduces the market profit to break even (and if p_V exceeds the cutoff value, the market profit becomes negative). The formula of the cutoff p_V is

$$p_{v,cutoff} = 1 - \frac{m \times n^e}{M \times q} \tag{21}$$

Based upon the relationship between p_V and V as shown in (19), we can derive the critical number of virtual machines required.

For example, if the parameters take the following values: $M = 1{,}000$, $m = 40$, $n^e = 1{,}000$, and $q = 50$[61], The corresponding cutoff value is $p_{V,cutoff} = 0.2$.

Suppose the average hours during which a real machine is alive is $t = 8$. The average days for a real machine to be at work is $d = 5$. To reach $p_{V,cutoff}$, the number of virtual machines that the researcher needs to create is $V_{cutoff} = 295$. The size of the botnet is accordingly $N = 5{,}250$.

The numerical example suggests that given the parameters, the market profit will be lowered down to zero if the chance for a rental bot to be virtual is 0.2. For a technically-determined effective size of rental $n^e = 1{,}000$, 295 virtual machines are required. Without virtual machines, the botnet master only needs to maintain the botnet size at $N = n^e / \{(t/24) \times (d/7)\} = 4{,}200$. The interference by virtual machines enlarges the botnet size by the rate of $1/(1 - p_V)$. At the cutoff $p_V = 0.2$, the botnet size is enlarged by 1.25 times.

Note the previous numerical example is based upon the assigned parameter values. If they change, the cutoff probability and the number of virtual machines also change. m and n^e affect p_V negatively, and M and q affect p_V positively. From the perspective of researchers, a negative impact on p_V is favorable since a lower p_V requires fewer virtual machines to be in place. Increasing cost of maintaining

---

60 In reality, the chance for a botnet master to be detected and arrested is small. Dropping the penalty component of the costs does not damage the model conclusions. Effects of non-zero legal punishment and how legal enforcement can be combined with honeypots to fight botnets, especially when botnets are used to launch attacks with linearly increasing payoffs such as spams, are studied in a related work.

61 The actual values of the parameters can be estimated from empirical studies. The numbers assigned here are for illustrative purposes.

channels (higher m)[62] and a larger number of machines required to disable the target site (larger n^e) raise the operation burden of the botnet master. By contrast, the more payoff for disabling the victim (larger M) and the more machines a C&C channel can support (larger q) enhance the motivation for attacks and reduce the operation costs for the botnet master.

We now illustrate graphically how the key variables are related, using the same parameter values specified.

First of all, the market profit margin depends on the probability for a rental machine to be virtual p_v. It is interesting to know how this profit margin changes with p_v. Figure 4 illustrates the mathematical relationship

$$\pi^u = 1{,}000 - 40 \times \frac{1{,}000}{(1-p_v)\times 50}$$

Secondly, the number of virtual machines (V) varies with the probability for a rental bot to be virtual (p_v). The relationship between V and p_v is

$$V = \frac{1{,}000 \times p_v}{(1-p_v)\times\{1-p_v\times[1-(8/24)\times(5/7)]\}}$$

Recalling the relationship between p_v and the botnet size N^u, we get the following formula linking the two at the given parameter values:

$$N^u = \frac{1{,}000}{(1-p_v)\times(8/24)\times(5/7)} = \frac{4{,}200}{1-p_v}$$

The graphical illustration of how V and N^u are related to p_v is given in Figure 5.

The above numerical and graphical illustration shows that uncertainty matters given the cutoff probability of fake rental bots $p_{v,cutoff}$. The availability of virtual machines largely reduces economic payoffs for participating in the Internet black market, which reduces the attractiveness of the practice. Making p_v a random number will make the situation even more challenging for botnet masters and attackers.

More likely, the rough ranges of the parameter values are common knowledge. Botnet masters and attackers could also figure out the cutoff value of p_v. By increasing the size of the botnet, they may be able to convert a loss into a profit. To counterreact, researchers may have to increase the number of virtual machines, which may further force the botnet masters to expand botnets. Consequently, having p_v fixed may result in an unpleasant situation similar to arms race.

Our proposed strategy becomes much more effective by making p_v uncertain. Without researchers' and defenders' commitment to creating just the "right" number

[62] Botnet masters may seek for innovation in response to the increased use of honeypots. For example, they may develop cheaper means of C&C (i.e., lower m). According to (20) and (21), profit may increase and the cutoff p_v has to be larger. Cheaper means of C&C is unfavorable innovation concerning fighting attacks. Nevertheless, it does not affect the nature of model conclusions.

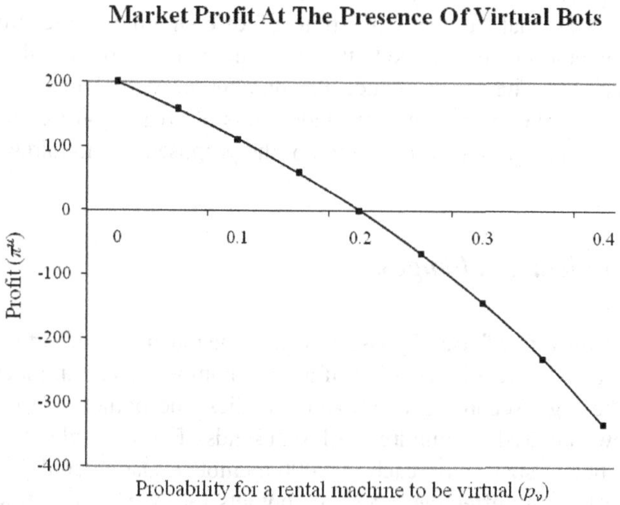

Figure 4. Botnet Market Profit Decreases with Increasing Chance of Fake Rental Bots

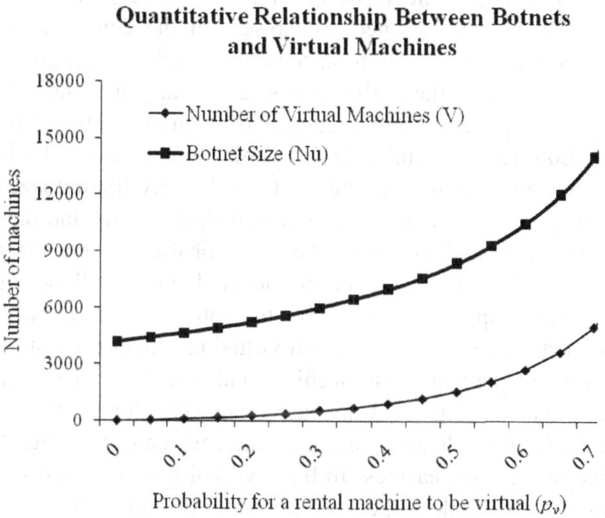

Figure 5. Optimal Botnet Size and Rental Size Increase as the Chance for a Rental Bot to be Virtual Increases

of virtual machines to reach $p_{v,cutoff}$, it is difficult, if ever possible, for the illegal practitioners to guess the actual number of virtual machines. Therefore, there is no way to make optimal decisions. Since the attacker receives no money if the attack fails, one safe bet may be just to rent as many as possible. The botnet master has to expand the size of botnets as well. The increased costs for both parties reduce the profit margins. If the costs increase by too much, all the profit margins may be disappearing. Note that, at the same time of discouraging botnet masters and attackers from entering the market, the uncertainty helps reduce the operation costs of defenders. They may reduce the number of virtual machines without being aware of it. The uncertainty (or randomness of creating virtual machines in some sense) facilitates the implementation of the proposed methodology.

5.3 Technical Challenges

We further discuss a few feasibility issues such as the magnitude of virtual machines and counterdetection techniques. First of all, the number of virtual machines does not have to be big. According to previous studies, the botnet size ranges from roughly a few hundred to hundreds of thousands. For example, Dagon et al. establish that botnet sizes may reach 350,000 members (Dagon et al. 2006). Rajab et al. indicate that the effective sizes[63] of botnets rarely exceed a few thousand bots (Rajab et al. 2006). A recent study by Rajab et al. revisits the question of botnet size and draws the distinction between footprint (the overall size of the infected population at any point in the lifetime of a botnet) and live population (the number of live bots simultaneously present in the command and control channel). They show that while the footprints of the botnets can grow to several tens of thousands of bots, their effective sizes usually are limited to a few thousand at any given point in their lifetime. For example, botnet footprint sizes can exceed 100,000 infections, and their live populations are normally in the range of a few thousand bots (Rajab et al. 2007). The relatively limited size of botnets suggests that it may not be easy to enlarge botnets dramatically and rapidly due to some practical or technological barriers. If the probability for a machine to be virtual in the rental botnet is at a decent level, botnets will be significantly affected. For example, suppose $p_V = 0.1$; then the botnet size has to be 11 percent[64] larger compared with the situation in which virtual machines are not around. The attacker has to rent 11 percent more machines and suffers an 11 percent increase in costs. There is also an 11 percent increase in the costs for the botnet master to maintain more C&C channels and more machines, which can by significant. The contrast between the relative easiness to build virtual machines and the difficulty in enlarging botnets implies the opportunities for our plan to work.

---

[63] The effective size of a botnet is the number of bots connected to the IRC channel at a specific time. While the effective size has less impact on long-term activities such as executing commands posted as channel topics, it significantly affects the number of minions available to execute timely commands such as DDoS attacks.

[64] The size of the botnet is 1.11 (=1/(1 – 0.1)) times the size in the benchmark case. The increase in size is 11 percent.

The functioning of honeypots is pivoting on camouflaging fake bots. Indeed, botnets are not equally complicated. They diversify in terms of technological complexity. Botnets can be roughly categorized into three groups, depending on the botnet master's technological proficiency:

- Case I. Low: It should not be a big problem for defenders to make virtual machines to join a botnet.
- Case II. Medium: Botnet masters only check compromised machines at the entry of a bot. If a virtual machine passes this entry test, it will not be evaluated again.
- Case III. Advanced: The most challenging situation is when a sophisticated botnet master sends commands to test machines not only at the entry, but also from time to time. In this case, some anti-detecting technique or strategy is required. For example, allowing virtual machines to fulfill some trivial tasks would make virtual machines trustworthy to the botnet master. To follow this "I-fool-you, catch-me-if-you-can" strategy, it is crucial to find ways for virtual machines to judge which orders are innocuous to follow. What technical tools/progresses are necessary to disguise honeypots from being detected is also a promising further research topic.

The dynamic features of botnets also facilitate our method. According to Karasaridis et al. (Karasaridis et al. 2007), the botnets are very dynamic in nature. Based on long-term monitoring of validated malicious botnets, they estimate that the average bot stays about two to three days on the same botnet controller, switching controller addresses and domains very frequently. A duration of a couple of days makes it harder and less productive to conduct test orders frequently. More likely, botnet masters may only command a newly compromised machine to do a simple task at entry. Botnet masters also steal each others' machines. Honeypots may function equally well if being lost from one botnet to another. Furthermore, newer bots can automatically scan their environment and propagate themselves using vulnerabilities and weak passwords. Generally, the more vulnerabilities a bot can scan and propagate through, the more valuable it becomes to a botnet controller community. Therefore, a virtual machine-created pseudo-bot can propagate by including more virtual machines into a botnet, and enhance the higher weights and the "importance" of the virtual machines to botnet masters.

The botnet controller community features a constant and continuous struggle over who has the most botnets, and the largest amount of "high-quality" infected machines, like university and corporate machines. It may be economically reasonable for a botnet master to create larger botnets. For example, advertising a larger botnet may send a positive signal to potential buyers on Internet underground markets indicating the botnet master is experienced and ought to have a good reputation. Operating a larger botnet may also facilitate certain tasks that botnets are for. For example, a larger botnet may be more effective to disable a target by overwhelming it, or more spam emails can be sent in a short period of time by having more machines do the job. Since botnet masters have to keep recruiting new machines, even though they are fully aware of the existence of honeypots, the virtual bots' entry to botnets can never be shut down.

Meanwhile, the size of a botnet is subject to an upper bound, sometime specified by the width of the C&C channel. Therefore, there is a tradeoff between hacking more machines and increasing C&C channels. The more machines hacked, the larger the size of the botnet, and more buffer can be obtained, but more machines require more C&C channels, which increases operating costs of the botnet and the chance of being detected. The existence of honeypots makes maintaining a botnet more costly and risky since the botnet master may have to increase the size of the botnet to compensate for the uncertain inactive honeypots. One thing to note, instead of increasing the size of the botnet, the botnet master may rather reduce the size of the botnet, and only keep those "safe" and active machines. It is certainly a strategy botnet masters may use, the risk of that is a continuously declining botnet due to the life cycle of a comprised machine. Figuring out the optimal size of botnet given the complicated scenario then becomes mission impossible.

6 Conclusion and Future Work

Profit-driven botnet attacks impose serious threats to the modern Internet. Given that money is perhaps the single determining force driving the growth in botnet attacks, we propose an interesting economic approach to take away the financial incentives. By introducing the uncertainty level, we make the optimal botnet size infeasible for the botnet operators. As the chance of uncertainty increases, both botnet masters' and attackers' profits can fall dramatically.

The proposed scheme is advantageous versus existing schemes in that it strikes at the root motivation for the botnets themselves, i.e., the profit motivation. Regardless of the type of command and control structure, the sophistication of compromising new hosts, or the creation of new avenues to market botnet services, we believe this chapter nicely demonstrates how the application of economic principles can offer significant benefit to combatting botnets.

The chapter is the stepping stone of a series of analyses. In a related work, we include non-zero legal punishment into the profit maximization problem and discuss how the coordination of legal engagement and honeypots works to reduce financial incentives of non-DDoS botnet-related cybercrimes whose payoffs are linearly increasing in the use of botnet. Moreover, with varying qualities of botnets and diversified reputation of botnet masters, Internet botnet markets may be more monopolistic competitive or price discriminated. The assumptions of price-taking market participants and a single rental price of bots may be relaxed to study price discrimination, and such modification of the problem setup may result in some interesting results. Legalizing Internet black markets is another attractive and challenging idea. Besides economic factors, technical, social, ethical and legal considerations all play certain roles. A wealth of research can be carried out along this line of thinking.

References

Bacher, P., Holz, T., Kotter, M., and Wicherski, G. "Know Your Enemy: Tracking Botnets," The *Honeynet Project & Research Alliance*, March 2005.

"Computer Scientist Fights Threat of Botnets," *ScienceDaily*, Nov. 10 2007. Available at http://www.sciencedaily.com/releases/2007/11/071108141303.htm

Dagon, D., Zou, C., and Lee, W."Modeling Botnet Propagation Using Time Zones," in *Proceedings of the 13th Annual Network and Distributed System Security Symposium (NDSS'06)*, Febuarary. 2006.

Ford, R., and Gordon, S. "Cent, Five cent, Ten cent, Dollar: Hitting Botnets Where It Really Hurts," in *New Security Paradigms Workshop*, 2006, pp. 3–10.

Franklin, J., and Perrig, A. "An Inquiry into the Nature and Causes of the Wealth of Internet Miscreants," in *Proceedings of the 14th ACM conference on Computer and Communications Security*, SESSION: Internet Security, Alexandria, Virginia, 2007, pp. 375–388.

Jin, C., Wang, H., and Shin, K. "Hop-Count Filtering: An Effective Defense Against Spoofed DoS Traffic," in *Proceedings of the 10th ACM Conference on Computer and Communications Security*, 2003, pp. 30–41.

Jin, S. and Yeung, D. "A Covariance Analysis Model for DDoS Attack Detection," in *Proceeding of the IEEE International Conference on Communications (ICC)*, vol. 4, June 2004, pp. 1882–1886.

Karasaridis, A., Rexroad, B., and Hoeflin, D. "Wide-scale Botnet Detection and Charaterization," in *USENIX Workshop on Hot Topics in Understanding Botnets (HotBots'07)*, 2007.

Mahajan, R., Bellovin, S., Floyd, S., Ioannidis, J., Paxon, V., and Shenker, S. "Controlling High Bandwidth Aggregates in the Network," *ACM SIGCOMM Computer Communication Review* (32:3), July 2002, pp. 62–73.

Park, K., and Lee, H. "On the Effectiveness of Probabilistic Packet Marking for IP Traceback under Denial of Service Attack," in *Proceedings of INFOCOM 2001*, 2001, pp. 338–347.

Rajab, M. A., Zarfoss, J., Monrose, F. and Terzis, A. "A Multifaceted Approach to Understanding the Botnet Phenomenon," in *6th ACM SIGCOMM conference on Internet Measurment*, SESSION: Security and Privacy, 2006, pp. 41–52.

Rajab, M. A., Zarfoss, J., Monrose, F., and Terzis, A. "My Botnet is Bigger Than Yours (Maybe, Better Than Yours): Why Size Estimates Remain Challenging," in *Proceedings of the first conference on First Workshop on Hot Topics in Understanding Botnets*, Cambridge, MA, 2007, pp. 5.

Savage, S., Wetherall, D., Karlin, A. P., and Anderson, T. "Practical Network Support for (IP) Traceback," in *Proceedings of SIGCOMM*, 2000, pp. 295–306.

Snoeren, A., Partridge, C., Sanchez, L., Jones, C., Tchakountio, F., Kent, S. and Strayer, W. "Hash-Based IP Traceback," in *Proceedings of SIGCOMM*, 2001, pp. 3–14.

"Worldwide Infrastructure Security Report vol.ii (2006)," *ARBOR NETWORK*. Available at http://www.arbornetworks.com/report

Xu, J., and Lee, W. "Sustaining Availability of Web Services under Distributed Denial of Service Attacks," *Transactions on Computers* (52:2), Feburary 2003, pp. 195–208.

Yau, D.K.Y., Lui, J.C.S., Liang, F., and Yam, Y."Defending against Distributed Denial-of-Service Attacks with Max-min Fair Server-centric Router Throttles," *IEEE/ACM Transactions on Networking* (13:1), 2005, pp. 29–42.

[illegible] Available at [illegible] worms.

Cyber Insurance as an Incentive for Internet Security

Jean Bolot[1] and Marc Lelarge[2]

[1]SPRINT, California, USA
[2]INRIA-ENS, Paris, France

Abstract Managing security risks in the Internet has, so far, mostly involved methods to reduce the risks and the severity of the damages. Those methods (such as firewalls, intrusion detection and prevention, etc) reduce but do not eliminate risk, and the question remains on how to handle the residual risk. In this chapter, we consider the problem of whether buying insurance to protect the Internet and its users from security risks makes sense, and if so, identifying specific benefits of insurance and designing appropriate insurance policies.

Using insurance in the Internet raises several questions because entities in the Internet face correlated risks, which means that insurance claims will likely be correlated, making those entities less attractive to insurance companies. Furthermore, risks are interdependent, meaning that the decision by an entity to invest in security and self-protect affects the risk faced by others. We analyze the impact of these externalities on the security investments of the users using simple models that combine recent ideas from risk theory and network modeling.

Our key result is that using insurance would increase the security in the Internet. Specifically, we show that the adoption of security investments follows a threshold or tipping point dynamics, and that insurance is a powerful incentive mechanism which pushes entities over the threshold into a desirable state where they invest in self-protection.

Given its many benefits, we argue that insurance should become an important component of risk management in the Internet, and discuss its impact on Internet mechanisms and architecture.

1 Introduction

The Internet has become a strategic infrastructure in modern life and as such, it has become critical to the various entities (operators, enterprises, individuals,...) which deliver or use Internet services to protect that infrastructure against risks.

M.E. Johnson (ed.), *Managing Information Risk and the Economics of Security*, DOI: 10.1007/978-0-387-09762-6_13,

The four typical options available in the face of risks are to: 1) avoid the risk, 2) retain the risk, 3) self-protect and mitigate the risk, and 4) transfer the risk. Option 1 involves preventing any action that could involve risk, and it is clearly not realistic for the Internet. Option 2 involves accepting the loss when it occurs. Option 3 involves investing in methods to reduce the impact of the risk and the severity of the damages. Option 4 involves transferring the risk to another willing party through contract or hedging.

Most entities in the Internet have so far chosen, or are only aware of the possibility of, a mix of options 2 and 3. As a result, these entities have been busy investing in people and devices to identify threats and develop and deploy countermeasures. In practice, this has led to the development and deployment of a vast array of systems to detect threats and anomalies (both malicious, such as intrusions, denial-of-service attacks, port scanners, worms, viruses, etc., and non-intentional, such as overloads from flash crowds) and to protect the network infrastructure and its users from the negative impact of those anomalies, along with efforts in the area of security education in an attempt to minimize the risks related to the human factor (Cheswick et al. 2003).In parallel, most of the research on Internet security has similarly focused on issues related to option 3, with an emphasis on algorithms and solutions for threat or anomaly detection, identification, and mitigation.

However, **self-protecting against risk or mitigating risk does not eliminate risk**. There are several reasons for this. First, there do not always exist foolproof ways to detect and identify even well-defined threats; for example, even state of the art detectors of port scanners and other known anomalies suffer from non-zero rates of false positives and false negatives (Jung et al. 2004). Furthermore, the originators of threats, and the threats they produce, evolve on their own and in response to detection and mitigation solutions being deployed, which makes it harder to detect and mitigate evolving threat signatures and characteristics (Vojnovic et al. 2005). Other types of damages caused by non-intentional users, such as denial of service as a result of flash crowds, can be predicted and alleviated to some extent but not eliminated altogether. Finally, eliminating risks would require the use of formal methods to design provably secure systems, and formal methods capture with difficulty the presence of those messy humans—even non-malicious humans—in the loop (Odlyzko 2003).

In the end, despite all the research, time, effort, and investment spent in Internet security, there remains a residual risk: the Internet infrastructure and its users are still very much at risk, with accounted damages already reaching considerable amounts of money and possible damage even more daunting (e.g. (Gordon et al. 2005), (Weaver et al. 2004)) for a discussion on worm damage and conference web site for an opinion on damage cost estimation.) **The question then is how to handle this residual risk.**

One way to handle residual risk which has not yet been considered in much detail is to use the fourth option mentioned above, namely transfer the risk to another willing entity through contract or hedging. A widely used way to do this is through insurance, which is one type of risk transfer using contracts. In practice, the risk is transferred to an insurance company in return for a fee, which is the insurance premium. Insurance allows individuals or organizations to smooth payouts for uncertain events (variable costs of the damages associated with security risks) into predictable periodic costs. **Using insurance to handle security risks in the Internet raises several questions: does this option make sense for the Internet, and under which circumstances? Does it provide benefits, and if so, to whom, and to what extent?** Our goal in this chapter is to consider those questions.

In this chapter, we take the economic approach which considers that a limit to insurability cannot be defined only on the characteristics of the risk distribution, but should take into account the economic environment. We consider a sequence of increasingly complex, but simple models, to examine the impact of insurance in the Internet.

Our first model is the classical, expected utility model with a single entity or user. We use it to present known results from the literature, and in particular to examine the interplay between self-protection and insurance. The main relevant result is that the insurance premium should be negatively related to the amount invested by the user in security (self-protection). This parallels the real life situation where homeowners who invest in a burglar alarm and new locks expect their house theft premium to decrease following their investment.

The single user model is not appropriate for our purpose because the entities in the Internet face risks that are correlated, meaning that the risk faced by an entity increases with the risk faced by the entity's neighbors (e.g. I am likely to be attacked by a virus if my neighbors have just been attacked by that virus). Furthermore, entities face risks that are interdependent, meaning that those risks depend on the behavior of other entities in the network (such as their decisions to invest in security). Thus, the reward for a user investing in security depends on the general level of security in the network, leading to the feedback loop situation shown below:

$$\begin{array}{ccc} \text{self-protection} & \rightarrow & \text{state of the network} \\ \uparrow & & \downarrow \\ \text{strategy of the user} & \leftarrow & \text{pricing of the premium} \end{array}$$

We analyze the impact of these externalities on the security investments of the users with and without insurance being available. We focus on risks such as those caused by propagating worms or viruses, where damages can be caused either directly by a user, or indirectly via the user's neighbors. Users can decide whether or not to invest some amount c in security solutions to protect themselves against risk, which eliminates direct (but not indirect) damages. In the 2-user case, (Kunreuther et al. 2003) proved that, in the absence of insurance, there exists a Nash equilibrium in a "good" state (where both users self-protect) if the security investment cost c is low enough. These results were recently extended by the authors to a network setting in (Lelarge et al. 2008a) and (Lelarge et al. 2008b).

We first build upon this result to add insurance to the *2*-user case. We then consider the general case of a *n*-user network for which damages spread among the users that decide whether or not to invest in security for self-protection. We compare both situations when insurance is available and when it is not. We show that **if the premium discriminates against users that do not invest in security, then insurance is a strong incentive to invest in security.** We also show how **insurance can be a mechanism to facilitate the deployment of security investments by taking advantage of network effects such as threshold or tipping point dynamics.**

The models we use in the chapter are simple, and our results will not by themselves establish insurance markets for the Internet and its users. Still, the models and results are significant because they provide a convenient way to formulate the problem of deploying insurance in the Internet, they provide a methodology to evaluate the impact of insurance and design appropriate insurance policies, and they bring out the significant benefits of insurance. Given those benefits, we believe that insurance ought to be considered as an important component of Internet security, as a mechanism to increase the adoptability of security measures Internet-wide, and as a mechanism that could have significant impact on Internet architecture and policies.

The rest of the chapter is organized as follows. In Section 2, we describe related work. In Section 3, we introduce the classical expected utility model for a single user and present the standard results about risk premium and the interplay between self-protection and insurance. In Section 4, we describe the 2-user model, present the known results for self-protection in the absence of insurance, then build on this model to include insurance and prove our main results in the 2-user case. In Section 5, we extend those results to the case of a general network of *n* users. In Section 6, we discuss the impact of insurance and risk transfer on Internet mechanisms and architecture. Section 7 concludes the chapter. We refer to (Bolot et al. 2008) for an extended version of this work.

2 Related Work

Risk management in the Internet has typically involved approaches that retain the risk (i.e. accept the loss when it occurs) and self-protect against the risk. As a result, a vast amount of research has been published in the area of protection against risk in the Internet, ranging from risk or threat detection, identification, mitigation, to ways to survive or recover from damages. In parallel, researchers in the insurance community published a vast body of results in the area of insurance against risk (e.g. Gollier 2004).

Comparatively little has been carried out or published at the intersection of insurance and the Internet. We can divide relevant contributions into three areas: Internet economics (without insurance), cyberinsurance or insurance of computer risks in general (without much focus on network effects), and insurance of correlated or interdependent risks.

Research on Internet economics aims at increasing our understanding of the Internet as an economic system and at developing policies and mechanisms to achieve desirable economic goals (much the same way early research on the Internet aimed at developing policies and mechanisms - such as the IP protocol- to achieve desirable design goals such as those described in (Clark 1988), or more recent research aims at developing clean-slate policies and mechanisms to achieve the desired goals of the future Internet). The importance of the economic aspects of the Internet was recognized very early on. In 1974, Kleinrock mentioned that "[H]ow does one introduce an equitable charging and accounting scheme in such a mixed network system. In fact, the general question of accounting, privacy, security and resource control and allocation are really unsolved questions which require a sophisticated set of tools" (Kleinrock 1974). More recently, (Clark et al. 2002) mention economic drivers as key drivers to revisit old design principles and suggest new ones. Research in Internet economics has examined several issues, such as the economics of digital networks (refer to (Varian et al. 2004) for pointers to recent work in the area, and e.g. (Gong 2002) for the analysis of a point problem, specifically the impact of layering), pricing models and incentive mechanisms for resource allocation that align the interests of possibly selfish users with the interests of the network architect (Davis et al. 2004, MacKie-Mason et al. 1995, Shenker et al. 1996), and the economics of security (refer to (Anderson et al. 2006) for a recent survey and references, also (Camp et al. 2000) and the proceedings of the Workshop on economics of information security).

Using cyberinsurance as a way to handle the residual risk after computer security investments have been made was proposed more than 10 years ago in the computer science literature (Lai et al. 1994), but popularized only recently by (Schneier 2001, 2002). The problem of residual risk and cyber insurance has been analyzed by (Gordon et al. 2003). (Kesan et al. 2005a, 2005b) make the economic case for insurance, arguing that insurance results in higher security investments (and therefore increases the global level of safety), that it encourages standards for best practices to be at the socially optimum level, that it solves a market failure (namely the absence of risk transfer opportunity), and they see the emerging market for cyberinsurance as a validation of the case they make in the paper.

The market for cyberinsurance started in the late 90s with insurance policies offered by security software companies partnering with insurance companies as packages (software + insurance). The insurance provided a way to highlight the (supposedly high) quality of the security software being sold, and to deliver a "total" risk management solution (risk reduction + residual risk transfer), rather than the customary risk reduction-only solution (combined with risk retaining); for example, solutions offered by Cigna (Cigna's Secure System Insurance) or Counterpane/Lloyd's of London. More recently, insurance companies started offering stand-alone products (e.g. AIG's NetAdvantage). (Majuca et al. 2005) provides a recent and comprehensive description of the history and the current state of computer insurance.

A challenging problem for Internet insurance companies is caused by correlations between risks, which makes it difficult to spread the risk across customers - a sizeable fraction of worm and virus attacks, for example, tend to propagate rapidly throughout the Internet and inflict correlated damages to customers worldwide (Saniford et al. 2004, Zou et al. 2002). Furthermore, entities in the Internet face interdependent risks, i.e. risks that depend on the behavior of other entities in the network (e.g. whether or not they invested in security solutions to handle their risk), and thus the reward for a user investing in security depends on the general level of security in the network. Correlated and interdependent risks have only very recently started being addressed in the literature. (Böhme 2005) considers insurance with correlations in the extreme case of a monoculture (a system of uniform agents) with correlated Bernoulli risks and argues that the strong correlation of claims in that case may indeed hinder the development of a cyberinsurance industry. Subsequent work in (Böhme et al. 2006) argues that correlations are actually two-tiered and supports the argument with honeypot data. One tier represents the correlations across risks within an entity such as a corporation, and the other tier represents the correlations of risks across independent entities. Correlations in the different tiers impact the insurance process in different ways: the tier-1 correlations will then influence an entity to seek insurance, whereas the tier-2 correlations influence the price of the premium set by the insurance company. (Ogut et al. 2005) show that interdependent risks reduce the incentives of firms to invest in security and to buy insurance coverage. Our simple model (without premium discrimination) will recovery of this result (see Section 4.3). We will show how premium discrimination can overcome this difficulty.

(Kunreuther et al. 2003) consider the situation of agents faced with interdependent risks and propose a parametric game-theoretic model for such a situation. In the model, agents decide whether or not to invest in security, and they face a risk of damage which depends on the state of other agents. They show the existence of two Nash equilibria (all agents invest or none invest), and suggest that taxation or insurance would be ways to provide incentives for agents to invest (and therefore reach the "good" Nash equilibrium), but they do not analyze the interplay between insurance and security investments. The model in (Kunreuther et al. 2003) is extended by (Hofmann, 2006) to include compulsory insurance offered by a monopolistic insurer. The results show that a compulsory monopoly may lead to a higher social level of security investment if the insurer engages in premium discrimination, and that the level of investment is higher in a compulsory insurance monopoly market than in competitive insurance markets. Our work also builds on the model of (Kunreuther et al. 2003), and considers a single insurance market. However, our work differs from (Kunreuther et al. 2003) and (Hofmann, 2006) because it models all three desirable characteristics of an Internet-like network, namely correlated risks, interdependent agents, and a general model of a network with a flexible and controllable topology, and it derives general results about the state of the network and the behavior of the agents, with and without insurance being available.

Next, we describe the classical expected utility model for a single agent and present the standard results about premium computation and the interplay between self-protection and insurance.

3 Insurance and Self-protection: Basic Concepts

3.1 Classical Models for Insurance

The classical expected utility model is named thus because it considers agents that attempt to maximize some kind of expected utility function $u[.]$. In this chapter, we assume that agents are rational and that they are risk averse, i.e. their utility function is concave (see Proposition 2.1 in (Gollier 2004)). Risk averse agents dislike mean-preserving spreads in the distribution of their final wealth.

We denote by w_0 the initial wealth of the agent. The risk premium π is the maximum amount of money that one is ready to pay to escape a pure risk X, where a pure risk X is a centered random variable: $\mathbb{E}\,[X] = 0$. The risk premium corresponds to an amount of money paid (thereby decreasing the wealth of the agent from w_0 to $w_0 - \pi$) which covers the risk; hence, π is given by the following equation: $u[w_0 - \pi] = \mathbb{E}\,[u[w_0 + X]]$.

The risk premium plays a fundamental role in the economics of risk, and we refer to Gollier (2004) for a detailed account. We will focus in the rest of this section on the interplay between insurance and self-protection investments. To simplify our analysis, we consider simple one-period probabilistic models for the risk, in which all decisions and outcomes occur in a simultaneous instant; we do not consider dynamic aspects such as first mover advantage or the time value of money.

Each agent faces a potential loss ℓ, which we take in this chapter to be a fixed (non-random) value. We denote by p the probability of loss or damage. There are two possible final states for the agent: a good state, in which the final wealth of the agent is equal to its initial wealth w0, and a bad state in which the final wealth is $w_0 - \ell$. If the probability of loss is $p > 0$, the risk is clearly not a pure risk. The amount of money m the agent is ready to invest to escape the risk is given by the equation:

$$pu[w_0 - \ell] + (1 - p)u[w_0] = u[w_0 - m]. \tag{1}$$

As shown by (Mossin 1968), we clearly have $m > p\ell$. We can actually relate m to the risk premium defined above. Note that the left-hand side of Equation (1) can be written as $\mathbb{E}[u[w_0 - p\ell - X]]$ with X defined by $\mathbb{P}(X = \ell(1-p)) = p$ and $\mathbb{P}(X = -p\ell) = 1-p$. Hence we have $\mathbb{E}\,[u[w_0 - p\ell - X]] = u[w_0 - p\ell - \pi[p]]$, where $\pi[p]$ denotes the risk premium when the loss probability equals p. Therefore: $m = p\ell + \pi[p]$. The term $p\ell$ corresponds to what is referred to as the fair premium, i.e. the premium which exactly matches the expected. On the left-hand side of the equation, m corresponds to the maximum acceptable premium for full coverage: if an insurer makes a proposition for full coverage at a cost of $\wp$, then the agent will accept the contract if $\wp \leq m$.

3.2 A Model for Self-protection

Investments in security involve either self-protection (to reduce the probability of a loss) and/or self-insurance (to reduce the size of a loss). For example, intrusion detection and prevention systems are mechanisms of self-protection. Denial-of-service mitigation systems, traffic engineering solutions, overprovisioning, and public relations companies are mechanisms of self-insurance (overprovisioning to reduce the impact of overloads or attacks, PR firms to reduce the impact of security attack on a company stock price with crafty messages to investors). It is somewhat artificial to distinguish mechanisms that reduce the probability of a loss from mechanisms that reduce the size of the loss, since many mechanisms do both. Nevertheless, we focus on self-protection mechanisms only and consider a very simple model for self-protection. We refer to the work of (Gordon et al. 2002) for a more elaborate model.

We first look at the problem of optimal self-protection without insurance. We denote by c the cost of self-protection and by $p[c]$ the corresponding probability of loss. We expect larger investments in self-protection to translate into a lower likelihood of loss, and therefore we reasonably assume that p is a non-increasing function of c. The optimal amount of self-protection is given by the value c^* which maximizes

$$p[c]u[w_0 - \ell - c] + (1 - p[c])u[w_0 - c]. \tag{2}$$

Note that if ℓ increases, then c^* has to increase too because the gain caused by self-protection is increased. Consider the simple case where the loss probability is either one of two values, namely $p[c] = p^+$ if $c < c_t$ or $p[c] = p^-$ if $c > c_t$, with $p^+ > p^-$. The optimization problem (2) above becomes easy to solve: indeed, the optimal expenditure is either 0 or c_t.

In the rest of the chapter, we assume that the choice of an agent regarding self-protection is a binary choice: either the agent does not invest, or it invests ct, which will be denoted c for simplicity. In our case, if the agent does not invest, the expected utility is $p^+u[w_0 - \ell] + (1 - p^+)u[w_0]$; if the agent invests, the expected utility is $p^-u[w_0-\ell-c]+(1-p^-)u[w_0-c]$. Using the derivation in the subsection above, we see that these quantities are equal to $u[w_0-p^+\ell-\pi[p^+]]$ and $u[w_0-c-p^-\ell-\pi[p^-]]$, respectively. Therefore, the optimal strategy is for the agent to invest in self-protection only if the cost for self-protection is less than the threshold

$$c < (p^+ - p^-)\ell + \pi[p^+] - \pi[p^-] =: c^{sp}{}_1 . \tag{3}$$

Recall that $p\ell + \pi[p]$ corresponds to the amount of money the agent is willing to pay to escape a loss of probability p. Hence we can interpret Equation (3) as follows: $c^{sp}{}_1 + p^-\ell + \pi[p^-] = p^+\ell + \pi[p^+]$. The left-hand term corresponds to the scenario where the agent invests $c^{sp}{}_1$ in self-protection (and hence lower the probability of loss to p^-) and then pays $p^- \ell + \pi[p^-]$ to escape the risk. The right-hand term is exactly the amount he would pay to escape the original risk of a loss of probability p^+. Clearly the first scenario is preferred when $c < c^{sp}{}_1$, which corresponds exactly to Equation (3).

3.3 *Interplay between Insurance and Self-protection*

We now analyze the impact that the availability of insurance has on the level of investment in self-protection chosen by the agent.

Consider first the case when Equation (3) is satisfied, namely it is best for the agent to invest in self-protection. We assume that the agent can choose between insurance with full coverage and self-protection. Clearly if the agent chooses full coverage, he will not spend money on self-protection since losses are covered and the utility becomes $u^{fc} = u[w_0 - \wp]$. In the case of optimal self-protection, the utility has been computed above: $u^{sp} = u[w_0 - c - p^- \ell - \pi[p^-]]$ since Equation (3) holds. Hence the optimal strategy for the agent is to use insurance if

$$c^{sp}{}_4 := \wp - p^- \ell - \pi[p^-] < c \tag{4}$$

Note that because of Equation (3), we must have

$$\wp < p^+ \ell + \pi[p^+]. \tag{5}$$

If Equation (3) does not hold, then it is best for the agent to not invest in self-protection, and the choice is between insurance and no self-protection. It is easy to see that if Equation (5) holds, then the premium is low enough and the optimal strategy is to pay for insurance.

The combination of insurance and self-protection raises the problem of what is referred to as moral hazard. Moral hazard occurs when agents or companies covered by insurance take fewer measures to prevent losses from happening, or maybe even cause the loss (and reap the insurance benefits from it). Indeed, if the premium does not depend on whether or not the agent invests in self-protection, then insurance becomes a negative incentive to self-protection. A known solution to the problem is to tie the premium to the amount of self-protection (and, in practice, for the insurer to audit self-protection practices and the level of care that the agent takes to prevent the loss) (Ehrlich et al. 1972). Note that this condition is necessary to avoid moral hazard: if the premium is not designed as above, then self-protection will be discouraged by insurance and we would observe either a large demand for insurance and a small demand for self-protection, or the converse.

A natural candidate for such a desirable premium proposed by (Ehrlich et al. 1972) is the fair premium: $\wp[\mathrm{S}] = p^- \ell$, and, $\wp[\mathrm{N}] = p^+ \ell$.

To agents who invest in self-protection, the insurer offers the premium $\wp[S]$ and to agents who do not invest in self-protection, he offers the premium $\wp[N]$.

Since $p^- \leq p^+$, with such a choice, the price of insurance is negatively related to the amount of self-protection. With this premium, it is proved in (Ehrlich et al. 1972) that insurance can coexist with an incentive to invest in self-protection in some cases (if the probability of loss is not very small).

We will show that, even if the fair premium is negatively related to the amount spent in self-protection, it is not always sufficient for insurance to be an incentive for self-protection when risks are interdependent. In order to raise the social level of self-protection, the insurer may engage in premium discrimination. In particular, he may design different contracts for different risk types, relying on the policyholders' categorization: he may offer a premium rebate for low risk agents, and/or he may impose a premium loading for high risk agents and let agents voluntarily decide whether or not to invest in self-protection. The sequence of the considered game between the insurer and its customers may then be seen as follows: at a first stage, the insurer offers appropriate contracts including a premium loading and/or rebate on fair premiums. At a second stage, the customers choose a contract and decide simultaneously whether or not to invest in prevention. To agents who do not invest in prevention, the insurer may offer a premium $\wp[N] + \gamma$, where $\gamma \geq 0$ denotes a premium penalty (loading). To agents who invest in prevention, the insurer may offer a premium $\wp[S] - \gamma$, where γ denotes a premium rebate.

Table 1. Utility with Insurance and Self-protection: Single User Case

(I,S)	$u[w_0 - c - p^- \ell + \gamma]$
(I,N)	$u[w_0 - p^+ \ell - \gamma]$
(NI,S)	$u[w_0 - c - p^- \ell - \pi[p^-]]$
(NI,N)	$u[w_0 - p^+ \ell - \pi[p^+]]$

The utility for all possible cases is summarized in Table 1. The first column denotes the choice made by an agent. It is denoted by the pair (U, V), where $U = I$ means that the agent pays for insurance and $U = NI$ otherwise, and $V = S$ means that the agent invests in self-protection and $V = N$ otherwise. Note that for any non-negative value of γ, the strategy (I, S) always dominates the strategy (NI, S). Now for (I, S) to dominate (I,N), we need $c < (p^+ - p^-)\ell + 2\gamma$. For (I, S) to dominate (NI,N), we need $c < (p^+ - p^-)\ell + \gamma + \pi[p^+]$.

4 Interdependent Security and Insurance: the 2-agent Case

Recall that interdependent risks are risks that depend on the behavior of other entities in the network (e.g. whether or not they invested in security solutions to handle their risk). In the presence of interdependent risks, the reward for a user investing in self-protection depends on the general level of security in the network.

4.1 Interdependent Risks for 2 Agents

(Kunreuther et al. 2003) was the first to introduce a model for interdependent security (IDS), specifically a model for two agents faced with interdependent risks, and it proposed a parametric game-theoretic model for such a situation. In the model, agents decide whether or not to invest in security, and they face a risk of damage which depends on the state of other agents. As in Section 3 above, the decision is a discrete choice: an agent either invests or does not invest in self-protection. We assume that loss can happen in two ways: it can either be caused directly by an agent (direct loss), or indirectly via the actions of other agents (indirect loss). We assume that the cost of investing in self-protection is c, and that a direct loss can be avoided with certainty when the agent has invested in self-protection.

Table 2. Probability of States

	S	*N*
S	*P[S,S]=0*	*P[S,N]=pq*
N	*P[S,S]=p*	*P[N,N]=p+(1-p)pq*

The cost of protection should not exceed the expected loss, hence $0 \leq c \leq p\ell$. Four possible states of final wealth of an agent result: without protection, the final wealth is w_0 in case of no loss and $w_0 - \ell$ in case of loss. If an agent invests in protection, its final wealth is $w_0 - c$ in case of no loss and $w_0 - c - \ell$ in case of loss. Consider now a network of 2 agents sharing one link. There are four possible states denoted by (i, j), where $i, j \in \{S,N\}$, i describes the decision of agent 1 and j the decision of agent 2, S means that the agent invests in self-protection, and N means that the agent does not invest in self-protection. We examine the symmetric case when the probability of a direct loss is p for both agents, where $0 < p < 1$. Knowing that one agent has a direct loss, the probability that a loss is caused indirectly by this agent to the other is q, where $0 \leq q \leq 1$. Hence q can be seen as a probability of contagion. To completely specify the model, we assume that direct losses and contagions are independent events. The matrix $P[i, j]$ describing the probability of loss for agent 1, in state (i, j), is given in Table 2.

Table 3. Expected Payoff Matrix for Agent 1

	Agent 2: *S*	Agent 2: *N*
Agent 1: *S*	$u[w_0 - c]$	$(1-pq)u[w_0 - c]+pqu[w_0 - c - \ell]$
Agent 1: *N*	$(1 - p)u[w_0] +$ $pu[w_0 - \ell]$	$pu[w_0 - \ell]+(1-p)(pqu[w_0 - \ell]$ $+(1-pq)u[w_0])$.

The simplest situation of interdependent risks, involving only two agents, can be analyzed using a game-theoretic framework. We now derive the payoff matrix of expected utilities for agents 1 and 2. If both agents invest in self-protection, the expected utility of each agent is $u[w_0 - c]$. If agent 1 invests in self-protection (S) but not agent 2 (N), then agent 1 is only exposed to the indirect risk pq from agent 2. Thus the expected utility for agent 1 is $(1-pq)u[w_0 - c] + pqu[w_0 - c - \ell]$, and the expected utility for agent 2 is $(1 - p)u[w_0] + pu[w_0 - \ell]$. If neither agent invests in self-protection, then both are exposed to the additional risk of contamination from the other. Therefore, the expected utilities for both agents are $pu[w_0 - \ell] + (1-p)(pqu[w_0 - \ell] + (1-pq)u[w_0])$. Table 3 summarizes these results and gives the expected utility of agent 1 for the different choices of the agents.

Assuming that both agents decide simultaneously whether or not to invest in self-protection, there is no possibility to cooperate. For investment in self-protection (S) to be a dominant strategy, we need $u[w_0 - c] \geq (1 - p)u[w_0] + pu[w_0 - \ell]$ and $(1 - pq)u[w_0 - c] + pqu[w_0 - c - \ell] \geq pu[w_0 - \ell] + (1 - p)(pqu[w_0 - \ell] + (1 - pq)u[w_0])$. With the notations introduced earlier, the inequalities above become: $c \leq p\ell + \pi[p] =: c_1$, and $c \leq p(1 - pq)\ell + \pi[p + (1 - p)pq] - \pi[pq] =: c_2$.

In most practical cases, one expects that $c_2 < c_1$, and the tighter second inequality reflects the possibility of damage caused by the other agent. Therefore, the Nash equilibrium for the game is in the state (S, S) if $c \leq c_2$ and (N,N) if $c > c_1$. If $c_2 < c \leq c_1$, then both equilibria are possible and the solution to the game is indeterminate. More precisely, the situation corresponds to a coordination game. Overall, we have the following:

- if $c < c_2$: the optimal strategy is to invest in self-protection;
- if $c_2 < c < c_1$: if the other users in the network do invest in self-protection, then the optimal strategy is to invest in self-protection;
- if $c_1 < c$: then the optimal strategy is to not invest in self-protection.

4.2 IDS and Mandatory Insurance

We now build on the model and the results above and introduce our more general model in which insurance is available to the agents (the ability to self-protect remaining available, of course). We assume that a full coverage insurance is mandatory. As noted in Section 3.3, if we want to avoid a moral hazard problem, the insurance premium has to be tied to the amount spent on self-protection. Note that the probability of loss for agent 1 depends on the choice made by agent 2, however it seems necessary (at least from a practical point of view) to link the premium applied to agent 1 to the behavior of agent 1 only. A possible choice (which is profit-making for the insurance) is to choose for each decision of the agent the fair 'worst case' premium as follows, $\wp[S] = pq\ell$, $\wp[N] = (p + (1 - p)pq)\ell$.

In this case the payoff for the agent is deterministic: if it chooses S, the payoff is $u[w_0 - c - pq\ell]$; if it chooses N, the payoff is $u[w_0 - (p + (1-p)pq)\ell]$. Hence the dominant strategy is to invest in self-protection only if $c < p(1 - pq)\ell =: c_3 < c_2$. As in the single-agent case, we see that even if the premium is related to the amount spent on self-protection, insurance is a negative incentive for protection. To correct this effect, we apply the same strategy as in the single-agent case, namely we engage in premium discrimination. Let γ denote the premium rebate for agents investing in security and the premium penalty for agents not investing. Clearly, in our situation, the new condition for S to be the dominant strategy becomes: $c < p(1 - pq)\ell + 2\gamma =: c_3[\gamma]$. In particular for $2\gamma = p^2 q\ell$, we have $c_3[\gamma] = c_1$ and then for any $c < c_1$, the strategy S is dominant (whereas coordination was required in absence of insurance). Note that we have assumed a symmetric penalty and rebate, but our result easily extends to the general case.

4.3 IDS and Full Coverage Insurance

We now consider the situation where the choice is left to the agent as to whether to invest in self-protection and/or in a full coverage insurance. We assume that the premiums are those given above (with penalty/rebate). We summarize the payoff for agent 1 in Table 4, depending on the investment of agent 2 and for the four possible choices of the agent (notations are the same as in Section 3.3). We denote $c_4[\gamma] := p(1 - pq)\ell + \pi[p + (1 - p)pq] + \gamma$. Let us examine the situation depending on the behavior of agent 2. If agent 2 invests in self-protection (denoted by S_2), then for $c < c_1$, agent 1 chooses to invest in self-protection also and not otherwise. Consider now the case when agent 2 does not invest in self-protection (denoted by N_2). Then if $c < \min(c_3[\gamma], c_4[\gamma]) := c[\gamma]$, the optimal strategy is (I, S). Note that we have $c_4[\gamma] \geq c_2$ for all values of γ and we proved above that we can choose γ such that $c_3[\gamma] \geq c_2$. Therefore it is possible to tune γ such that $c[\gamma] \geq c_2$.

We have (in decreasing order)

$$c_1 = p\ell + \pi[p],$$
$$c[\gamma] = p(1 - pq)\ell + \gamma + \min(\pi[p + (1 - p)pq], \gamma),$$
$$c_2 = p(1 - pq)\ell + \pi[p + (1 - p)pq] - \pi[pq],$$
$$c_3 = p(1 - pq)\ell.$$

Note in particular that when insurance with discrimination is available, (S, S) becomes a Nash equilibrium for $c < c[\gamma]$ with $c[\gamma] > c_2$ for well-chosen values of γ. In such a case, insurance is an incentive to self-protection. However, if insurance is available at a fair premium, without discrimination, (i.e. $\gamma = 0$), then we see that $c[0] = c_3 < c_2$ and insurance is no longer an incentive to self-protection.

The main features present in the single-agent are also present in the 2-agent case. However a new feature comes into play because of the interdependent risks, namely the existence of a new threshold c_2 which takes into account the externality modeled by the possible contagion via the other agent. We see that the externalities due to the interdependent risks tend to lower the incentive for investing in self-protection (as shown in (Ogut et al. 2005, Lelarge et al. 2008)). However, we also see that the effect of the insurance (with discrimination) is unaffected by these interdependent risks. As a result the relative efficiency of insurance is higher in the presence of externalities.

Next, we extend the results of this section to the general case of a network of n users.

5 Interdependent Security and Insurance on a Network

Many phenomena in the Internet can be modeled using epidemic spreads through a network, e.g. the propagation of worms, of email viruses, of alerts and patches, of routing updates, etc. (e.g. see (Vojnovic et al. 2005; Zou et al. 2002) for models of worm propagation). As a result, there is now a vast body of literature on epidemic spreads over a network topology from an initial set of infected nodes to susceptible nodes (see for example (Ganesh et al. 2005)). The 2-agent model introduced in the previous section, although very basic, fits in that framework: the probability for an agent to be infected initially is p and the probability of contagion is q. It is then natural to consider the following extension: agents are represented by vertices of a graph $G = (V,E)$, and

- if an edge $(i, j) \in E$ then contagion is possible between agents i and j with probability q; otherwise the probability of contagion is zero;
- if agent i invests in protection, no direct loss can occur; otherwise direct loss occurs with probability p;
- the contagion process of agent i is independent of the process of agent j and independent of the direct loss process (characterized by p).

As in the previous section, we are considering a one-period model. The quantity of interest here is the value of the damages due to the epidemics. We assume that the damage caused by the epidemics is ℓ for all agents that have been infected. The topology of the underlying graph G is arbitrary. Note that G might not correspond to a physical network. For example, when modeling the spread of email viruses, we might choose a graph which reflects the social network of the email users. When modeling insurance against BGP router failures, we might choose a complete graph; indeed, BGP routers belonging to the top level ASes of the Internet form a completely connected graph, and internal BGP routers are often organized in a set of completely connected route reflectors - thus, the behavior of routers failing and recovering is, in a first approximation, modeled as the spread of an epidemic on a complete graph (Coffman et al. 2002).

In the rest of this section, we consider two important classes of topologies: the complete graph and the star-shaped graph. The study of star-shaped networks is of interest for several reasons. First, star-shaped networks exhibit a new tipping point phenomenon not observed in fully connected networks. Also, the spreading behavior of a large class of power law graphs, of particular interest given their relevance to Internet topology graphs (Doyle et al. 2005), is determined by the spreading behavior of stars embedded within them.

5.1 The Complete Graph Network

We assume here that G is a complete graph with n vertices, namely a graph with an edge between each pair of nodes. By symmetry, it is possible to define P_k^S, the probability that an agent investing in security experiences a loss when k users (among the $n - 1$ remaining ones) also invest in security. Similarly, we define P_k^N to denote the probability that a user not investing in security experiences a loss when k other users invest in security. Then we define:

$$c_k^n = P_k^N \ell + \pi\left[P_k^N\right] - P_k^S \ell - \pi\left[P_k^S\right]. \tag{6}$$

We have of course $P_k^N \geq P_k^S$, and we assume that the utility function u (which defines the function π) is such that $c_{k+1}^n \geq c_k^n$ for all $0 \leq k \leq n - 1$. Note that in the single user case, $n = 1$, we have $c_0^1 = c_1^{sp}$ defined in Equation (3). In the 2-user case, we have $c_1^2 = c_1$ and $c_0^2 = c_2$ defined in Section 4.1.

Results of Section 4 extend in a straightforward manner to the n-users case as follows:

- if $c < c_0^n$: the optimal strategy is to invest in self-protection;
- if $c_{k-1}^n < c < c_k^n$: if at least k users in the network do invest in self-protection, the optimal strategy is to invest in self-protection;
- if $c_{n-1}^n < c$: the optimal strategy is to not invest in self-protection.
- It is natural to define the following function: $k^n[c] = \inf\{k, c_k^n > c\}$.
- $k^n[c]$ is an important threshold value, because of the following:
- if the number of initial users investing in self-protection is less than $k^n[c]$, then all users will choose not to invest in self-protection;
- if the number of initial users investing in self-protection is greater than $k^n[c]$, then all users will choose to invest in self-protection.

Concerning the effect of an insurance, we only consider the case where the insurance company engages in premium discrimination. It is then easy to extend the results above with the function $c^n[\gamma]$ such that if $c <$ $c^n[\gamma]$, then the optimal strategy is to invest in self-protection regardless of the behavior of the other users. Furthermore, $c^n[\gamma]$ is a non-decreasing function of γ that tends to infinity as γ tends to infinity. In summary, we have the following simple situation: in presence of insurance, the optimal strategy for all users is to invest in self-protection as soon as the cost of self-protection is low enough, $c <$ $c^n[\gamma]$.

The situation is simple, but artificially so, because we are considering a purely symmetric case. Let us now consider the more general case of heterogeneous users, when the cost of self-protection is different for different users (but the effect of self-protection is not changed). Intuitively, users with low cost will tend to invest in prevention while those with high cost will not. We now derive the threshold $\hat{c}$ for which users with cost less than $\hat{c}$ invest in self-protection whereas others do not. We denote by $F^n[c]$ the fraction of users with self-protection cost lower than *c*. Let s_j denote the different possible values for the cost of self-protection. The function F^n is piecewise constant and increases at each s_j by the fraction of nodes having a cost of s_j.

Consider now the following dynamic process where all the users of the network are initially in state (*N*), i.e. they have not invested in self-protection. First consider the users with minimal cost, say s_0. If $s_0 < c_0^n$, then $nF^n[s_0]$ users switch and invest in self-protection. If $s_0 > c_0^n$, all users stay in state (*N*) and the process terminates. Next, consider the users still in state (*N*) with minimal cost s_1. If $s_1 < c^n_{nF^n[s_0]}$, then all those users will switch and invest in self-protection. Note that the condition above can be written as $k^n[s_1] < nF^n[s_0]$. Iterating the procedure, we see that the threshold is characterized by the following equation

$$\hat{c} = \min\left\{ s_{j-1}, F^n[s_{j-1}] < \frac{k^n[s_j]}{n} \right\}. \tag{7}$$

In order to analyze the impact of insurance on the dynamics of the process above, we approximate the *n* users by a continuum of heterogeneous users. Showing that this mean-field approximation is appropriate for large values of *n* is outside the scope of this chapter and requires a scaling of the probabilities *p* and *q* as *n* tends to infinity. However we present the following heuristic argument. We denote by *F*[*c*] the distribution function of the users and by *k*[*c*] the limit of $k^n[c]/n$, both of which are now continuous. Then Equation (7) reduces to

$$\hat{c} = \min\{c > c[\gamma], F[c] < k[c]\}.$$

When adding assurance, the same argument as above holds, but this time we can start with an initial condition where all users with cost less than $c[\gamma]$ invest in self-protection. Hence the final equilibrium will be given by

$$\hat{c}[\gamma] = \min\{c > c[\gamma], F[c] < k[c]\}.$$

Note that for any value of $\gamma \geq 0$, we have $\hat{c}[\gamma] \geq c[\gamma]$ which shows that more users choose to invest in self-protection in presence of insurance. Furthermore, if

$$F[c] = k[c] \tag{8}$$

has only one solution, then $\hat{c}[\gamma] = \max\{c[\gamma], \hat{c}\}$.

The results above show that insurance increases the adoptability of self-protection investments for all users in the network. We finish this section by showing that the increase in adoptability can be quite dramatic, nonlinearly so as a function of γ.

Assume now that the population is divided into classes of users with roughly the same cost for self-protection, and consider the case when users corresponding to the class with the smallest cost invest in self-protection. If the size of that population (of users in the class with the smallest cost) is small, it might not be sufficient to stimulate the second class to invest in self-protection too. Then the dynamics of the 'contagion process' for self-protection described earlier is stopped and only a small fraction of the total population has invested in security in the end. It turns out that insurance can be of significant help to boost the contagion process, as we explain next. Note that the function F is approximately a step function and Equation (8) might have more than one solution. The scenario described above corresponds to the case when the system is stuck at the low value $\hat{c}$. We see that if we tune the parameter γ in order for $c[\gamma]$ to reach the second fixed point, then the system will naturally increase its level of self-protection up to the next fixed point $\hat{c}[\gamma] >> c[\gamma] > \hat{c}$. In other words, insurance gives exactly the right incentive to a small portion of the population that would not have invested without insurance, so that the switch to self-protection of that fraction of the population induces a larger fraction of the population to invest also. In summary, insurance provides incentives for a small fraction of the population to invest in self-protection, which in turn induces the rest of the population to invest in self-protection as well, leading to the desirable state where all users in the network are self-protected. Furthermore, the parameter γ provides a way to multiply the benefits of insurance, by lowering the initial fraction of the self-protected population needed to reach the desirable state.

5.2 *The Star-shaped Network*

Consider a star-shaped network, with $n+1$ nodes, where the only edges are $(0, i)$, with $i = 1, \dots, n$. The same analysis as in previous section applies but we have to deal separately with the root and the leaves. First consider the root. The probability of a loss when exactly k leaves invest in self-protection is given (depending on the state (S) or (N) of the root) by $P_k^N = p + (1-p)(1-(1-pq)^{n-k})$, and $P_k^S = 1-(1-pq)^{n-k}$. Then, one can do the same analysis as in the previous section and compute the function $k^n[c]$ that would give the threshold for the number of leaves required to invest in self-protection in order for the root to also invest. Note that as n tends to infinity, the probability of loss tends to one as soon as the number of leaves not investing in self-protection tends to infinity. In this case, the agent at the root is sure to be contaminated by a leaf regardless of its choice regarding investment in self-protection. As a result, it will not invest in self-protection.

We next consider the leaves. An important remark is that for a leaf to be infected the root must also be infected. First assume that the root is in state (N).

The probabilities of loss when there are k other leaves investing in self-protection are: $\tilde{P}_k^N = p + (1-p)qP_k^N[n]$, and $\tilde{P}_k^S = qP_k^N[n]$, where $P_k^N[n]$, is the quantity computed above but for a network of size n. Now assume that the root is in state (S), the corresponding probabilities are given by (with the same notations) $\overline{P}_k^N = p + (1-p)qP_k^S[n]$, and $\overline{P}_k^S = qP_{k-1}^S[n]$. It is easy to see that $\overline{P}_k^N - \overline{P}_k^S \le \tilde{P}_k^N - \tilde{P}_k^S$, and as a result, we have

$$\overline{c}_k^{n+1} \le \tilde{c}_k^{n+1}, \tag{9}$$

where the parameters $\overline{c}_k^{n+1}$ and $\tilde{c}_k^{n+1}$ are defined as in Equation (6) with the appropriate probabilities. The incentive for a leaf to invest in self-protection is higher when the root is already invested in self-protection. We observe a tipping point phenomenon. More generally, we expect that nodes with low connectivity (i.e. low degree) will imitate the node with the highest connectivity they are connected to. The heuristic argument (which is captured in our model by (9)) is that the node with the largest connectivity an agent is connected to will be the main source of contagion (in term of probability). Hence, if that node invests in self-protection, it substantially decreases the probability of contagion of the agent and, as in the 2-agent case, that action increases the reward of investing in self-protection. In such a context, insurance could act as an incentive for highly connected agents to invest in self-protection and then trigger a cascade of adoption of self-protection. A precise analysis of this phenomena is left for future research.

6 Discussion

The results presented in this chapter show that insurance provides significant benefits to a network of users facing correlated, interdependent risks. Essentially, insurance is a powerful mechanism to promote network-wide changes and lead all users of the network to the desirable state where they all invest in self-protection.

The benefits of insurance are such that we believe that the development of insurance products and markets, and the large scale deployment of insurance in the Internet is likely, if not inevitable.

However, we have found that mentioning “Internet insurance” rapidly attracts comments about the uniqueness of the Internet environment, and in particular questions around the estimation of damages. The assumption is that estimating damages in the Internet is so difficult and fraught with peril that insurance is not inevitable at all, but rather destined to remain a niche or an oddity. We first note that reliably estimating damages is indeed an important task because it controls the profit (or the ruin) of the insurer and the incentives for agents to invest in self-protection. Also, it is true that quantifying risks for a good or an optimal premium value is difficult because the assets to be protected are intangible (such as a company stock price), because damages might be visible only long after a threat or an attack was identified (e.g. “easter egg” with timed virus or exploit in a downloaded piece of software), because risk changes can occur quickly (zero day attacks), and because evaluating the insurability (and the level of protection) of new and existing customers is likely to be a complex and time-intensive task. However, the insurance industry has been dealing with those problems for decades or centuries in other areas of life - if warships can be insured in time of war (as indeed they can), it is difficult to argue convincingly that Internet risks and damages absolutely cannot be insurable.

Questions about damage estimation might also be the wrong questions. A better question might be how to help insurers do a better job, i.e. how the current Internet might be used to help insurers do a better job of estimating damages, and how to evolve the Internet or create a new design that will make that job even easier. One way suggested by the discussion above on estimating damages would be to develop metrics and techniques for that purpose. Another related way is to develop metrics for the security related issues of interest. Some interesting propositions have been made in that sense, for example the "cost to break" metric described in (Schechter 2002), but we believe this is an important area ripe for further research (see also (Aspnes et al. 2002)). Note that metrics of interest are not limited to "core security" metrics such as cost to break, but need to be developed for all relevant activities facing threats and risks; for example, metrics quantifying risks and damages to insure against BGP router failures (mentioned in Section 5).

The deployment of insurance raises architectural issues. In particular, insurance relies heavily on authenticated, audited, or certified assessments of various kinds to avoid fraud and other issues such as the moral hazard examined earlier in the chapter. This argues, along with security metrics, for effective and efficient ways to measure and report those metrics. It might also require better traceability of events. But it will certainly impact other mechanisms and protocols in other, subtle ways. Consider for example a peering point between operators, some of which are insured, others of which are not. It is very reasonable to imagine that, in such a situation, policies would be developed to route traffic from insured peers (or neighbors in general) differently than traffic from uninsured peers - a latter-day QoS routing (where QoS means Quality of Security, of course).

Overall, we believe that Internet insurance, in addition to providing the benefits shown in the chapter, offers a fertile area of reflection and research. It is a timely area, as well, given the recent activities around clean-slate Internet design. We propose to add to the slate a broader definition of risk management, which includes the transfer of risk in addition to only the mitigation of risk, and to explore the benefits and consequences of that broader definition.

7 Conclusion

One of our main contributions in this chapter is to develop and solve simple models that explain why economically rational entities would prefer a relatively insecure system to a more secure one, to show that the adoption of security investments follows a threshold or tipping point dynamics, and that insurance is a powerful incentive mechanism to "push the mass of users over the threshold". Our second main contribution is to ask the question: if economics plays an essential role in the deployment of security technologies, then why deny ourselves the use of economics tools? Our purpose here is not to shift the problem of network security to the marketplace but to give a new perspective on Internet security. Finally, we argue that network algorithms and network architecture might be designed or reevaluated according to their ability to help implement desirable economic policies (such as the deployment of insurance) and help achieve desirable economic goals.

References

Anderson, R., and Moore, T., "The Economics of Information Security: A Survey and Open Questions," *Science* (314), October 2006, pp. 610-613.

Aspnes, J., Feigenbaum, J., Mitzenmacher, M., and Parkes, D., "Towards Better Definitions and Measures of Internet Security," in *Proceedings of Workshop on Large-Scale-Network Security and Deployment Obstacles*, Landsdowne, VA, March 2003.

Barnes, D.A. "Deworming the Internet," *Texas Law Review* (83:1), 2004. Available at SSRN:http://ssrn.com/abstract=622364.

Bolot, J., and Lelarge, M. "A New Perspective on Internet Security using Insurance," *INFOCOM 08*.

Bolot, J. and Lelarge, M., "Cyber Insurance as an Incentive for Internet Security," in *Proceedings of Workshop on the Economics of Information Security (WEIS)*, 2008.

Böhme, R. "Cyber-insurance Revisited," in *Proceedings of Workshop on the Economics of Information Security (WEIS)*, 2005.

Böhme, R., and Kataria, G., "Models and Measures for Correlation in Cyber-insurance," in *Proceedings of Workshop on the Economics of Information Security (WEIS)*, 2006.

Camp, L.J., and Wolfram, C., "Pricing Security," in *Proceedings of CERT Information Survivability Workshop*, Boston, MA, pp. 24-26, Oct. 2000.

Chan, H., Dash, D., Perrig, A., and Zang, H., "Modeling Adoptability of Secure BGP Protocols," in *Proceedings of ACM Sigcomm* 06, Pisa, Italy, September 2006.

Cheswick, W.R., Bellovin, S., and Rubin, A., *Firewalls and Internet Security: Repelling the Wily Hacker*, 2nd Ed., Addison-Wesley, 2003.

Chen, P., Kataria, G., and Krishnan, R. "Software Diversity for Information Security," in *Proceedings of the Workshop on Economic of Information Security 2005*, Harvard, MA, June 2005.

Clark, D. "The Design Philosophy of the DARPA Internet Protocols," in *Proceedings of ACM Sigcomm 88*, Stanford, CA, Aug 1988.

Clark, D., Wroclawski, J., Sollins, K., and Braden, R., "Tussle in Cyberspace: Defining Tomorrow's Internet," in *Proceedings of ACM Sigcomm 02*, Pittsburgh, PA, Aug. 2002.

Coffman Jr., E.G., Ge, Z., Misra, V., and Towsley, D. "Network Resilience: Exploring Cascading Failures within BGP," in *Proceedings of 40th Annual Allerton Conference on Communications, Computing and Control*, October 2002.

Davie, G., Hardt, M., and Kelly, F., "Network Dimensioning, Service Costing, and Pricing in a Packet Switched Environment," *Telecommunications Policy* (28), 2004, pp. 391-412.

Doyle, J., Alderson, D., Li, L., Low, S., Roughan, M., Shalunov, S., Tanaka, R., and Willinger, W. "The 'Robust yet Fragile' Nature of the Internet," in *Proceedings of National Academy Sciences* (102-41), October 2005.

Ehrlich, I., and Becker, G.S., "Market Insurance, Self-insurance, and Self-protection," *The Journal of Political Economy* (80:4), 1972, pp. 623-648.

Ganesh, A., Massoulie, L., and Towsley, D. "The Effect of Network Topology on the Spread of Epidemics," in *Proceedings of IEEE Infocom 2005*, Miami, FL, March 2005.

Gollier, C., *The Economics of Risk and Time*, MIT Press, 2004.

Gong, J., and Srinagesh, P., "The Economics of Layered Networks," *Internet Economics*, MIT Press, Cambridge, MA, 1997.

Gordon, L., and Loeb, M., "The Economics of Information Security Investment," *ACM Transaction Information Systems Security* (5: 4), November 2002, pp. 438-457.

Gordon, L., and Loeb, M., *Managing Cybersecurity Resources*. McGraw-Hill, Sept. 2005.

Gordon, L., Loeb, M., and Sohail, T. "A Framework for Using Insurance for Cyber-risk Management," *Communication of ACM* (46:3), 2003, pp. 81-85.

Hofmann, A., "Internalizing Externalities of Loss Prevention through Insurance Monopoly," in *Proceedings of Annual Meeting of American Risk and Insurance Association*, Washington DC, Aug 2006.

Jung, J., Paxson, V., Berger, A., and Balakrishnan, H. "Fast Portscan Detection Using Sequential Hypothesis Testing," in *Proceedings of IEEE Symposium Security and Privacy*, 2004.

Kearns, M., and Ortiz, L.E., "Algorithms for Interdependent Security Games," in *Advances in Neural Information Processing Systems*, Thrun, S., Saul, L. K., and Schoikopf, B. (Eds.), MIT Press, Cambridge, 2004.

Kesan, J., Majuca, R., and Yurcik, W., "The Economic Case for Cyberinsurance," In *Securing Privacy in the Internet Age*, Chander, A. et al. (Eds.), Stanford University Press, 2005.

Kesan, J., Majuca, R., and Yurcik, W. "Cyberinsurance as a Market-based Solution to the Problem of Cybersecurity: a Case Study," in *Proceedings of Workshop on the Economics of Information Security 2005*, Harvard, MA, June 2005.

Kleinrock, L. "Research Areas in Computer Communications," *Computer Communication Review* (4:3), July 1974, pp. 1-4.

Kunreuther, H. and Heal, G., "Interdependent Security: the Case of Identical Agents," *Journal of Risk and Uncertainty* (26:2), 2003, pp. 231-249.

Lelarge, M., and Bolot, J. "Network Externalities and the Deployment of Security Features and Protocols in the Internet," in *Proceedings of the 2008 ACM SIGMETRICS International Conference*, pp. 37-48.

Lelarge, M., and Bolot, J. "A Local Mean Field Analysis of Security Investments in Networks", *ACM NetEcon 08*, available at: http://arxiv.org/abs/0803.3455

Lai, C., Medvinsky, G., and Neuman, G.C., "Endorsments, Licensing, and Insurance for Distributed Systems Services," in *Proceedings of 2nd ACM Conference Computer and Communication Security (CCS)*, Fairfax, VA, November 1994.

MacKie-Mason, J., and Varian, H. "Pricing the Internet," in Kahin, B. and Keller, J. (Eds.), *Public Access to the Internet*, MIT Press, 1995.

Majuca, R.P., Yurcik, W., and Kesan, J.P. "The Evolution of Cyberinsurance," available at: arxiv:cs/060120

Mossin, J., "Aspects of Rational Insurance Purchasing," *Journal of Political Economy* (76), 1968, pp. 553-568.

Odlyzko, A. "Economics, Psychology, and Sociology of Security," in *Proceedings of Financial Cryptography 2003*, Wright, R.N. (Ed.), LNCS #2742, Springer, April 2003.

Ogut, H., Menon, N., and Raghunathan, S., "Cyber Insurance and IT Security Investment: Impact of Interdependent Risk," in *Proceedings of Workshop on the Economics of Information Security (WEIS)*, 2005.

Ozment, A., and Schechter, S., "Bootstrapping the Adoption of Internet Security Protocols," in *Proceedings of Workshop of the Economics on Information Security*, Cambridge, June 2006.

Saniford, S., Moore, D., Paxson, V., and Weaver, N. "The Top Speed of Flash Worms," in *Proceedings of ACM Workshop Rapid Malcode WORM'04*, Fairfax, VA, October 2004.

Schechter, S., "Quantitatively Differentiating System Security," in *Proceedings of Workshop on the Economics of Information Security (WEIS)*, Berkeley, CA, May 2002.

Schneier, B. "Insurance and the Computer Industry," *Communications of ACM* (44:3), March 2001, pp. 114-115.

Schneier, B. "Computer Security: It's the Economics, Stupid," in *Proceedings of Workshop on the Economics of Information Security (WEIS)*, Berkeley, CA, May 2002.

Shenker, S., Clark, D., Estrin, D., and Herzog, S., "Pricing in Computer Networks: Reshaping the Research Agenda," *ACM CCR* (26), April 1996, pp. 19-43.

Varian, H., Farrell, J., and Shapiro, C. *The Economics of Information Technology*. Cambridge University Press, Dec. 2004.

Vojnovic, M., and Ganesh, A., "On the Race of Worms, Alerts and Patches," in *Proceedings of ACM Workshop on Rapid Malcode WORM05*, Fairfax, VA, Nov. 2005.

Weaver, N., and Paxson, V., "A Worst-case Worm," in *Proceedings of 3rd Workshop on the Economics of Information Security*, Univ. Minnesota, May 2004. See web site for opinion by S. Saniford.

Zou, C.,Gong, W., and Towsley, D., "Code Red Worm Propagation Modeling and Analysis," in *Proceedings of 9th ACM Conference Computer Communication Security CCS'02*, Washington, DC, Nov 2002.

Conformity or Diversity: Social Implications of Transparency in Personal Data Processing

Rainer Böhme

Technische Universität Dresden, Germany

Abstract Consider the hypothetical situation of a society with virtually unconstrained storage and exchange of personal information, and shameless exploitation thereof for decision making, for example in contract negotiation. In this chapter we develop a stylised formal model to tackle the question if public knowledge about *how exactly* personal information is used in decision making changes aggregate behaviour. Simulation results suggest a slightly positive relationship between transparency and conformity, i.e., people tend to behave alike. This has implications on the common conjecture that collection and processing of personal information is tolerable as long as transparency is warranted.

1 Introduction

Individuals, in participating in social interaction, share information about themselves with others. The advent of information and communication technologies as tools and means for social interaction reduces the cost to collect, store, combine, and process such information. It is well-understood that accumulated personal information from past transactions can create information asymmetries in future transactions between the same agents (Acquisti and Varian 2004) and, if information is traded, even for transaction between agents who have never interacted before (Calzolari and Pavan 2005; Kim et al. 2005). Hence, data collection has attracted criticism from consumer and civil rights organisations, which reinforced a debate on privacy rights and informational self-determination. As a result, since the 1970s, most countries have passed legislation to deal with privacy concerns in state-to-individual and business-to-individual (consumer) interactions.

Since the 1980s, following the earlier vision of Baran (1965), computer scientists have increasingly researched into technical solutions to combat the privacy problems caused by technological progress. Technologies such as anonymous communication infrastructures, formalisation of privacy policies (e.g., P3P (Cranor 2003) or EPAL (Schunter and Powers 2003)), automatic enforcement (access control (Ferraiolo and Kuhn 1992)), as well as protocols for pseudonymous but accountable

M.E. Johnson (ed.), *Managing Information Risk and the Economics of Security*,
DOI: 10.1007/978-0-387-09762-6_14, © Springer Science + Business Media, LLC 2009

transactions are nowadays subsumed as *privacy-enhancing technologies* (PETs) (Goldberg et al. 1997; Camp and Osorio 2003; Adams 2006). Most PETs are designed to support data avoidance, which allows the construction of systems that are secure against relatively strong adversaries by relying on distributed architectures. The objective is to minimise the amount of trust required in individual transaction partners. Although some PETs can be designed very securely in theory, their principle of data avoidance/reduction is deemed impractical for many applications and the prospects for a wide adoption of PETs in the near future remain dim.

PETs are typically designed for 1 : 1 or 1 : *n* interactions in which each partner has full control over his or her devices and the signals they emit. We are not aware of practical solutions for privacy-preserving *n* : *m* interactions (although problem descriptions can be found in the literature, e.g., Borcea-Pfitzmann et al. (2007)) beyond very specific protocols for transactions with clearly defined semantics (for instance, cryptographic voting schemes or private multi-party auction protocols (Brandt 2003)).

1.1 From PETs to TETs

In the light of online social networking sites, sensor networks, ambient intelligence and behavioural biometrics, where *n:m* interactions and untrusted devices (sensors) are the rule rather than exception, it becomes evident that data avoidance most likely will not offer a solution to privacy threats in general social interactions. Data avoidance cannot be enforced at all by individuals alone, and only at unacceptably high costs by regulation (i.e., in the last consequence, only through restrictions on the ownership of freely programmable devices or sensors). Therefore, operable alternatives are sought.

Transparency-enhancing technologies[65] (TETs) are believed to be more viable options in these situations (Hildebrandt 2007; Bellotti and Sellen 1993). The idea is to inform people in detail how personal attributes (might) affect decisions concerning themselves. Consider an example where personal information is used for insurance redlining or credit scoring. If affected individuals cannot escape the data collection, then they should at least know how exactly a certain data disclosure, such as moving in a statistically more 'risky' area, will affect their future premium or credit conditions. One can argue that transparency limits excessive discrimination on the basis of personal information through three channels: First, on an individual level, pre-emptive transparency-enhancing technologies assist people in making decisions which do not affect their personal score adversely. Second, on a mechanism level, scoring procedures that are not strategy proof, or the effectiveness

[65] The notion of 'technology' is rather broad. For example, a sign informing pedestrians about video surveillance in public places can be seen as a (low-tech) TET.

of which depends on the scoring details to remain obscure, become less useful and would thus be avoided. Third, on a social level, if public scrutiny reveals that a particular scoring function is arbitrarily discriminating and as such incompatible with the society's values, the risk of public uproar and reputation damage might put social pressure on data controllers not to implement abusive practices in the first place. Note that all these outcomes depend on the optimistic assumption that the TET is honest about the true data processing habits, a requirement that is difficult to verify and enforce. So TETs, like PETs, are no panaceas that solve all privacy concerns of a modern society.

1.2 TETs and Individual Behaviour

The topic of this chapter is to study the effects of TETs on social behaviour, more precisely on its impact to diversity in behaviour. Diversity between individuals, i.e., the extent to which individuals live their own lifestyle, is considered as a valuable precondition in political and economic theory, where diversity is linked to concepts of pluralism and competition, respectively.

At first sight, two conflicting hypotheses on the relation between transparency and diversity can be formulated intuitively.

- **Transparency supports conformity** because, in the absence of information asymmetries and strategic interaction with others, the optimal path is obvious and becomes 'mainstream'.
- **Transparency supports diversity** because, without transparency, individuals are herded together by uncertainty and fear. The rationale under uncertainty is not to stand out of the mass because the mass would barely err (cf. Lundblad's (2004) notion of a *noise society*).

The objective of the remainder of this chapter is to develop a formal model with which the conflict between these two hypotheses can be resolved. While fully acknowledging the potential problems of formal models, we will propose (and put up for discussion) a multi-period game with heterogeneous preferences and analyse under which conditions this prior heterogeneity is best preserved in rational individuals' actions.

2 Model

Imagine a world where each individual stores all information about social interactions, possibly combines his or her database with others (in a market for information, so prices for database peering may be negotiated), and uses this information as decision support in future transactions. For simplicity, we rule out any ambiguity and assume that all information is authentic and individuals are perfectly identifiable.

2.1 Assumptions

The following list of assumptions defines our model. The rationales behind them are reported separately in Sect. 2.3 for the sake of clarity. A list of all symbols used in this chapter can be found in the appendix.

1. Individuals $I^{(1)},\ldots,I^{(n)}$ are endowed with heterogeneous private preferences $p^{(i)}$ and initial wealth $v^{(i)} = 1$.
2. The preference space is the circumference of a unit ring, with position drawn independently from a uniform distribution between 0 and 1, i.e., $p^{(i)} \in [0,1)$.
3. The system is updated in rounds. In each round *k*, all individuals emit a signal $s_k^{(i)} \in [0,1)$.
4. The cost of emitting a signal is a function of the signal, more precisely a weighted sum of two components $c_{\text{emit}}^{(i)} = \alpha\, c_{\text{pret}}^{(i)} + \beta\, c_{\text{disc}}^{(i)}$.
   - The *pretence* component increases with the distance from the individual private preference $p^{(i)}$, hence $c_{\text{pret}}^{(i)} = D(s_k^{(i)}, p^{(i)})$. We define function $D:[0,1)^2 \rightarrow [0,1]$ as four times the square of the (shortest) distance between two points on the ring.

$$D(x,y) = \begin{cases} 4(x-y)^2 & \text{for } |x-y| \leq \frac{1}{2} \\ 4(1-|x-y|)^2 & \text{otherwise} \end{cases} \tag{1}$$

     Note that *D* is symmetric and invariant to translation of its arguments on the unit ring: $D(x,y) = D(y,x)$ and $D(x,y) \equiv D(x+k \bmod 1,\, y+k \bmod 1)$.
   - The *discontinuity* component is proportional to the distance between the emitted signal in the current round $s_k^{(i)}$ and in the past round $s_{k-1}^{(i)}$, hence $c_{\text{disc}}^{(i)} = D(s_k^{(i)}, s_{k-1}^{(i)})$. $c_{\text{disc}}^{(i)} = 0$ in the first round of each individual.

   Parameters α and β control the discomfort of dynamic adjustment in relation to the discomfort of pretending different preferences.
5. There exists a global entity which punishes individuals depending on their emitted signals. The *penalty* is calculated as inverse distance between the signal *s* and a focal point *d*: $c_{\text{pen}}^{(i)} = \left(1 - D(s_k^{(i)}, d)^{\frac{1}{2}}\right)^2$.
6. The existence of TET is modelled as knowledge about the value of *d*. We will compare a scenario without TET, where individuals do not know *d*, with one in which all individuals know the exact position of *d* (through TET).
7. Total cost is deducted from wealth $v^{(i)}$ at the end of each round.

$$c_{\text{tot}}^{(i)} = c_{\text{emit}}^{(i)} + \gamma c_{\text{pen}}^{(i)} + \nu = \alpha\, c_{\text{pret}}^{(i)} + \beta\, c_{\text{disc}}^{(i)} + \gamma c_{\text{pen}}^{(i)} + \nu \tag{2}$$

8. Individuals default if their wealth $v^{(i)}$ turns negative. There is no possibility to transfer wealth between individuals, so no borrowing is allowed. Defaulted individuals are reinitialised in the next round ($v^{(i)} = 1$, new realisation of $p^{(i)}$), thereby losing their history of observations.
9. Individuals know the global parameters α, β, γ and ν as well as the set of emitted signals from the last round. Apart from that, there is no communication between individuals (in particular no sharing of knowledge about the possible position of focal point *d*).
10. Individuals act fully rational and maximise their own expected time to default. When indifferent between two alternatives which would lead to the same number of rounds before default, they prefer the option where $\left|v^{(i)}\right|$ is smaller after default.

2.2 Problem Statement

We use this model to study the relation between transparency and conformity with Monte-Carlo simulations. After initialisation, the model is updated over *N* rounds. At the end of each round, we compute two dependent variables:

1. A measure of *conformity* between individuals ψ_k, which is defined as the square sum of the (shortest) absolute distance between neighbouring signals $s_k^{(i)}$ on the preference ring, linearly scaled to the range from $\psi_{\min} = 0$ (perfect distribution; all signals are equidistant) to $\psi_{\max} = 100$ (full conformity; all signals equal). This metric, aggregated over all rounds, serves as the indicator variable to answer the research question.
2. The *mean time to default* of all individuals who have defaulted in this round. This metric can be interpreted as a covariate for a concept like (negative) 'social cost of information asymmetries'.

Both measures are calculated *per round* and then aggregated *over time*. This means that conformity should not be interpreted in an intertemporal fashion, like concepts such as stability over time. Note that the valuation of diversity (i.e., inverse conformity) as a desirable property, as outlined in Sect. 1.2, is exogenous to this model and not accounted (e.g., as negative social cost) in our metric for the mean time to default. We do not make an attempt to combine both metrics to a single scalar utility metric.

2.3 Rationales for the Assumptions

In the following we list the rationales that have led to our model formulation. The ones printed in bold are important for understanding our design decisions.

- As to assumption 2: We choose the circumference of a unit circle to avoid discontinuities at the margins of the preference space. This also ensures that a pair of locations is always equally distant from *d*. The distribution between these points, based on individual preferences, can be interpreted as diversity.
- As to assumption 3: Signals correspond to information disclosed in social interactions. Individuals have the possibility to hide their true preferences if they deem this advantageous in the long run. However this comes at a cost. For example, if someone prefers not to disclose his home address to an online retailer, he or she has to bear the transaction costs of going to a bricks-and-mortar store. Also refraining from engaging in a transaction for privacy concerns can be seen as incurred opportunity cost.
- As to assumption 4: A quadratic distance function is a technical assumption to ensure that unique minima exist (apart from some pathologic cases where two options are possible due to symmetry).
- As to assumption 4: The discontinuity component constrains dynamic adjustment and thus learning. If adjustment is too cheap, then some individuals will infer the centre of the penalty distribution from observations so that they gain 'transparency by experience' even in the condition without transparency. Contrary, if adjustment is expensive, then the expectations formed in the very first round of each individual are much more important for its survival. Aside from technical considerations, discontinuity costs can be interpreted as the social cost of changing one's image, or sunk costs associated with previous actions. The fact that discontinuity costs are quadratic in the distance between two signals implies that individuals prefer making small steps over a couple of rounds rather than a single big leap.
- As to assumption 5: The punishing entity models the disadvantage individuals might incur from disclosing particular personal information. Although in reality privacy risks are caused by other people, we have chosen this asymmetric setting (in fact, a player-versus-nature game) to keep the number of strategic interdependencies low. We do not believe that this is a major factor constraining the model's external validity.
- As to assumption 7: Cost $\nu > 0$ is a small technical offset charged in each round independent of the individual's preference and behaviour to ensure that all individuals have finite time to default. (Otherwise the model could converge in a deterministic state.)
- As to assumption 10: Assuming unbounded rationality is often criticised (rightly so). In assuming rational behaviour, our model abstracts from what we call *awareness* aspects, which deal with the problem that people do not understand or cannot interpret the information they have – in theory – at their disposal. We acknowledge that awareness is at least as important in practice as transparency, but both concepts must be differentiated and studied separately before drawing conclusions about their joint effect.

2.4 *Analytical Approach*

We will first discuss the optimal strategy for individuals in the simpler case of full information before we advance to cases where d is unknown.

Strategy of individuals in regime with TET Individuals $I^{(i)}$ enter the game with knowledge of d and adjust $s_k^{(i)} = s^{(i)}\ \forall k$ with respect to $p^{(i)}$ to maximise their expected lifetime, that is minimise $c_{\text{tot}}^{(i)} - \nu$.

$$c_{\text{tot}}^{(i)} - \nu = \alpha\, c_{\text{pret}}^{(i)} + \beta\, c_{\text{disc}}^{(i)} + \gamma c_{\text{pen}}^{(i)}\,. \tag{3}$$

$$= \alpha\, D(s^{(i)}, p^{(i)}) + \beta \cdot 0 + \gamma\left(1 - D(s^{(i)}, d)^{\frac{1}{2}}\right)^2. \tag{4}$$

Using the fact $\left|s^{(i)} - d\right| \le \frac{1}{2}$ (from symmetry) and regarding only cases where $d \le \frac{1}{2}$, $d \le p^{(i)} \le 1$ and thus $d \le s^{(i)} \le 1$,

$$c_{\text{tot}}^{(i)} - \nu = 4\alpha(s^{(i)} - p^{(i)})^2 + \gamma\left(1 - 2(s^{(i)} - d)\right)^2. \tag{5}$$

The first-order condition of the minimisation problem (for parameters $\alpha + \gamma > 0$) is

$$s^{(i)} = \frac{\alpha\, p^{(i)} + \gamma\,(d + \frac{1}{2})}{\alpha + \gamma}. \tag{6}$$

Using translation invariance of D, we obtain the formula for $d > p$:

$$s^{(i)} \equiv \frac{\alpha(1 - d + p^{(i)}) + \frac{\gamma}{2}}{\alpha + \gamma} + d \bmod 1 \tag{7}$$

Equations (6) and (7) define the strategy for all individuals in the scenario where TET is available and d is public (by definition). As the cost function is fully deterministic and does not depend on other individuals' behaviour, there is no need to adjust the position in rounds $k > 1$. As a result, the weight for discontinuity costs β does not appear in the optimal strategy in this case.

We will further derive a number of metrics as a function of the absolute distance $|x - d|,\ 0 \le x \le \frac{1}{2}$, which are needed below for the strategy in a regime without TET. The probability distribution function for 'young' individuals (age $k = 1$) directly follows from the uniform distribution assumption for realisations of $p^{(i)}$ in $[0,1)$ and Eq. (6) solved for $p^{(i)}$.

$$f_{s_1}(x) = \Pr\left(\left|s_1^{(i)} - d\right| < x\right) = \begin{cases} \dfrac{x(\alpha+\gamma) - \frac{\gamma}{2}}{\alpha} & \text{for} \quad \dfrac{\gamma}{2(\alpha+\gamma)} < x \le \dfrac{1}{2} \\ 0 & \text{otherwise} \end{cases} \tag{8}$$

As can be seen, $f_{s_1}(s^{(i)}) \equiv f_{s_1}(x + d \bmod 1)$ is a uniform distribution in the interval $\left[d + \frac{\gamma}{2(\alpha+\gamma)} \bmod 1, d - \frac{\gamma}{2(\alpha+\gamma)} \bmod 1\right]$ with density $\frac{\alpha+\gamma}{\gamma}$.

The expected time to default (measured in rounds) of young individuals with observed signals $s^{(i)}$ as a function of $x = \left|s^{(i)} - d\right|, x < \frac{1}{2}$ can be obtained directly from the cost function (assumption 7):

$$K(x) = \left\lfloor \left(c_{\text{tot}}^{(i)}\right)^{-1} \right\rfloor = \left\lfloor \left[\alpha D\left(x, \left|p^{(i)} - d\right|\right) + \gamma\left(1 - D(x,0)^{\frac{1}{2}}\right)^2 + \nu\right]^{-1} \right\rfloor \tag{9}$$

$$= \left\lfloor \left[4\alpha \left(x - \underbrace{\frac{1}{\alpha}\left(x(a+\gamma) - \frac{\gamma}{2}\right)}_{\text{Eq. 6 solved for } p^{(i)}} \right)^2 + \gamma(1-2x)^2 + \nu \right]^{-1} \right\rfloor \tag{10}$$

$$= \left\lfloor \frac{\alpha}{\gamma(\alpha+\gamma)(1-2x)^2 + \alpha\nu} \right\rfloor \tag{11}$$

Here we see that offset $\nu > 0$ is essential to avoid a zero denominator. Figure 1 (d) depicts the time to default as a function of $s^{(i)}$. In the repeated game, the distribution of all observable signals f_{s_k} (as opposed to f_{s_1} for young individuals only) is proportional to the time to default.

Strategy of individuals in regime without TET We use a heuristic strategy to model the behaviour of individuals if *d* is unknown.[66]

---

[66] Although we cannot prove that our strategy is optimal in the sense that it makes best use of all available information to narrow down the position of *d* as tightly as possible, we believe that our algorithm is a quite good approximation. This conjecture is supported by evaluation of numerical gradients in our simulation environment.

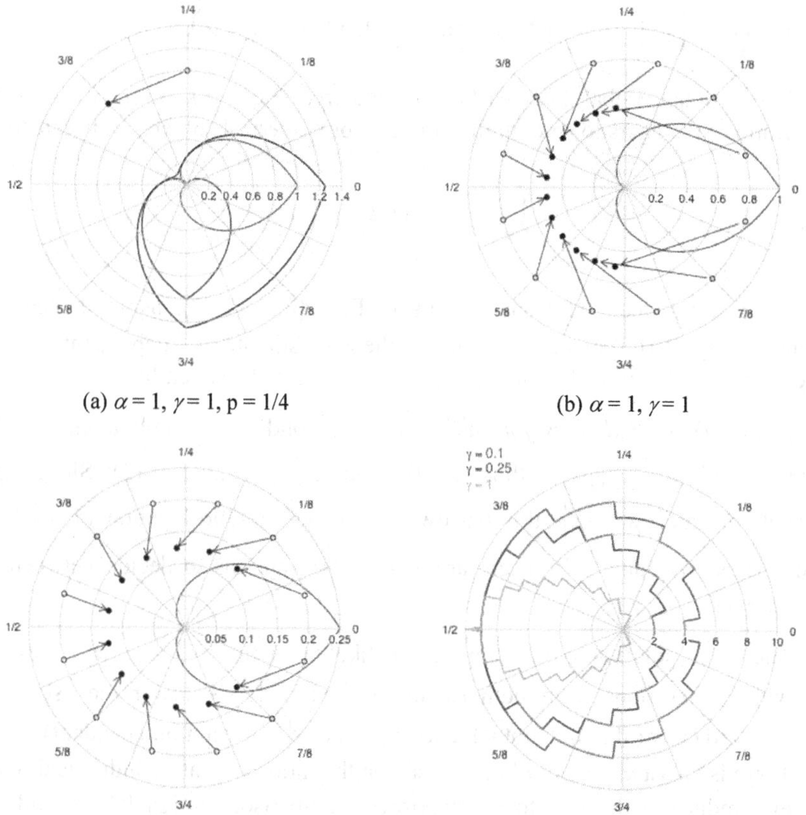

(a) $\alpha = 1$, $\gamma = 1$, p = 1/4

(b) $\alpha = 1$, $\gamma = 1$

(c) $\alpha = 1$, $\gamma = 1/4$

(d) $\alpha = 1$, $\nu = 1/10$

Figure 1. Preference and emitted signals under transparency. Radial plots of preference space. Symbols ○ for preferences p, ● for emitted signals s; connected lines are functions of s: red for penalty, blue for pretence cost, and black for total cost. (a): cost components and adjustment for example individual; (b) + (c): adjustment of heterogeneous individuals for varying γ (different radius for presentation clarity only); (d): time to default (in rounds) for young individuals as a function of emitted signal $s^{(i)}$ for varying γ. Focal point $d = 0$ in all plots.

Step 1 – Choice of $s_1^{(i)}$*:* After initialisation, an individual $I^{(i)}$ knows the rules of the game, the global parameters (α, β, γ, ν), its own preference $p^{(i)}$ and $m < n$ signals $s_o^{(j)}$ emitted by individuals in the previous round. Neither $p^{(j)}, v^{(j)}, (j \neq i)$, nor the age of other individuals are observable.

The best guess of d is a solution to the maximum-likelihood (ML) problem

$$\hat{d}_1^{(i)} = \arg\max_x \Pr\left(s^{(1)},\ldots,s^{(j)},\ldots,s^{(m)} \middle| d = x, \forall j \neq i\right) \tag{12}$$

$$= \arg\max_x \prod_j \Pr\left(s^{(j)} \middle| d = x\right) = \arg\min_x \sum_j - \log \Pr\left(s^{(j)} \middle| d = x\right).$$

The conditional probability can be obtained from Eq. (11), where we omit the truncation to integers to smooth the gradient for numerical solvers, and scale to

$$\int_{\frac{\gamma}{2(\alpha+\gamma)}}^{1-\frac{\gamma}{2(\alpha+\gamma)}} f_{s_k}(x)\, dx = 1. \tag{13}$$

Then, $s_1^{(i)}$ is calculated from $\hat{d}_1^{(i)}$ using Eqs. (6) and (7), as in the case of transparency. Performance indicators for the ML estimate of d dependent on γ and the number of individuals n are reported in Table 2 in the appendix.

Step 2 – Two candidates for $\hat{d}_2^{(i)}$: In the second round, individual $I^{(i)}$ has experienced cost $c_{\text{tot},1}^{(i)}$ and thus can find out $c_{\text{pen},1}^{(i)}$ using Eq. (2). Since $c_{\text{pen},1}^{(i)}$ reveals distance $\left|s_1^{(i)} - d\right|$, this narrows down the possible location of d to two candidates, $\hat{d}_{2+}^{(i)}$ and $\hat{d}_{2-}^{(i)}$. There are at least two options to decide between the candidates:

1. The *static* solution is to compare the likelihood for $\hat{d}_{2+}^{(i)}$ and $\hat{d}_{2-}^{(i)}$, possibly with observations from both rounds $s_o^{(j)}$ and $s_1^{(j)}$ to lower the estimation standard error (although not a lot, as $s_o^{(j)}$ and $s_1^{(j)}$ are not independent).
2. There is also a *dynamic* solution based on the rationale that no individual would ever reduce its distance to *d*. Therefore a comparison of signals $s_o^{(j)}$ and $s_1^{(j)}$ contains information about the dynamic adjustment of other individuals and therefore conveys information about the most likely location of *d*.

In practice, both solutions come to the same conclusions in the large majority of cases. We have not investigated ways to combine the information optimally or resolve conflicting results. Our experiments are based on a static update of $\hat{d}_2^{(i)}$. Signal $s_2^{(i)}$ is chosen using the step size rule described below (Eq. 17), with a target position calculated from the refined estimate $\hat{d}_2^{(i)}$.

Step 3 and later – Optimal adjustment to d: The focal point d can be obtained exactly from $c_{\text{pen},1}^{(i)}$, $c_{\text{pen},2}^{(i)}$, $s_1^{(i)}$ and $s_2^{(i)}$. Finding the optimal step sizes to approach the ideal position, $s_*^{(i)}$ conditional to *d*, is a discrete dynamic optimisation problem. However, we argue that for $0 < \beta \leq 5$, the problem is posed in such a way that a reasonably good solution can be found sequentially by minimising the cost *in the current round.*[67] So, again, we minimise $c_{\text{tot},k}^{(i)} - \nu$.

[67] This means that individuals are myopic or uncertain about the default threshold.

$$c^{(i)}_{\text{tot},k} - \nu = \alpha c^{(i)}_{\text{pret},k} + \beta c^{(i)}_{\text{disc},k} + \gamma c^{(i)}_{\text{pen},k} \tag{14}$$

$$= \alpha D(s^{(i)}_k, p^{(i)}) + \beta D(s^{(i)}_k, s^{(i)}_{k-1}) + \gamma\left(1 - D(s^{(i)}_k, d)^{\frac{1}{2}}\right)^2 \tag{15}$$

Restricting the analysis to cases where $d \leq \frac{1}{2}, d \leq p^{(i)} \leq 1$ and thus $d < s^{(i)}_k, s^{(i)}_{k-1} \leq 1$.

$$c^{(i)}_{\text{tot},k} - \nu = 4\alpha\left(s^{(i)}_k - p^{(i)}\right)^2 + 4\beta\left(s^{(i)}_k - s^{(i)}_{k-1}\right)^2 + \gamma\left(1 - 2\left(s^{(i)}_k - d\right)\right)^2 \tag{16}$$

This leads to the first-order condition (and symmetric equivalents)

$$s^{(i)}_k = \frac{\alpha p^{(i)} + \beta s^{(i)}_{k-1} + \gamma (d + \frac{1}{2})}{\alpha + \beta + \gamma}. \tag{17}$$

We have also implemented a numeric iterative solver for the dynamic minimisation problem and found that it leads to substantially better solutions only when β is large (see Figure 2) and initial estimates $\hat{d}^{(i)}_1$ poor. Either occurs rarely in our experiments.

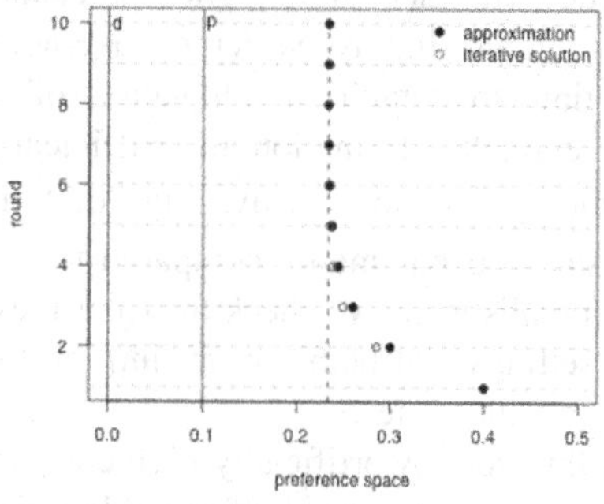

(a) $\beta = 1$

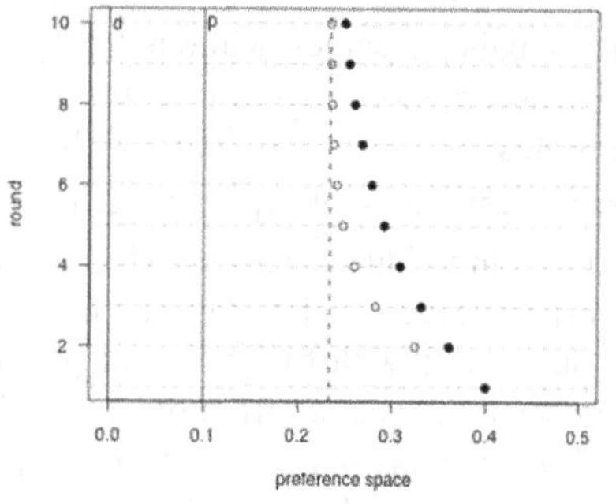

(b) $\beta = 5$

Figure 2. Difference in adjustment step sizes between myopic and intertemporal optimal solution. $d = 0$, $p = 1/10$, $\alpha = 1$, $\gamma = 1/2$. Signal $\hat{d} = 0.4$ is very unrealistic and only chosen to emphasise the difference. The total cost disadvantage of the approximation (until convergence) is 0.7% (left) and 4.7% (right).

3 Results

It is obvious that the diversity measure depends on parameters *(α, β, γ, ν)* as discontinuity costs clearly determine the individuals' ability to emit favourable signals. Therefore, we will compare the diversity of systems conditional to these parameters.

To structure the discussion of results, we fix parameters $\alpha = 1$, $\nu = 1/10$ and $n = 100$ for what we call *baseline results*. We compare the case of transparency (TET available) with no transparency for different severity of disadvantage due to unfavourable personal attributes: small (γ = 1/10), medium (γ = 1/2), and substantial (γ = 1) penalty. In the case of diversity, we further differentiate between low (β = 1/10), medium (β = 1) and high (β = 4) discontinuity costs.

Figure 3 shows two simulation snapshots for selected parameters with and without transparency (see figure caption for more details), and aggregate measures of conformity and time to default are reported in Table 1 for all relevant parameter combinations.

For the *baseline results*, it turns out that conformity ψ is always maximal in the case of transparency, although the relative difference to the simulations without transparency is rather small. We could confirm this tendency in many other parameter settings not reported here. We interpret this as a tentative support of our first hypothesis (transparency supports conformity), but the probably more interesting result is that the influence of transparency on diversity is so small. The much higher differences in ψ and mean time to default *between* different values for γ are not surprising, as γ directly influences the dispersion of the ideal distribution of individuals in the signal space (see Eq. 8). The mean time to default is approximately independent of transparency (in fact, at a higher precision, individuals in games without transparency default slightly earlier on average). This observation, as well as the constant time to default for all values of β, indicates that n = 100 individuals provide enough information for sufficiently precise estimates of $\hat{d}_1^{(i)}$. In other words, the information disadvantage of fully rational individuals without TET is rather small in our model compared to full transparency. Arguably, this can be seen as unrealistic, so we check the robustness of our results with two different parameter settings that both aim at limiting the 'information leakage' from older individuals to young ones.

The *early default* result set accomplishes this goal by artificially high constant costs ν. As a result, mean time to default drops to roughly one half of the baseline results. This ensures that the fraction of experienced (i.e., 'old' and thus better adjusted) individuals in the population decreases (see Figure 4 (a) in the appendix). Nevertheless, this does not alter our conclusion on conformity; quite the contrary: the relative conformity gain in the case of transparency even widens.

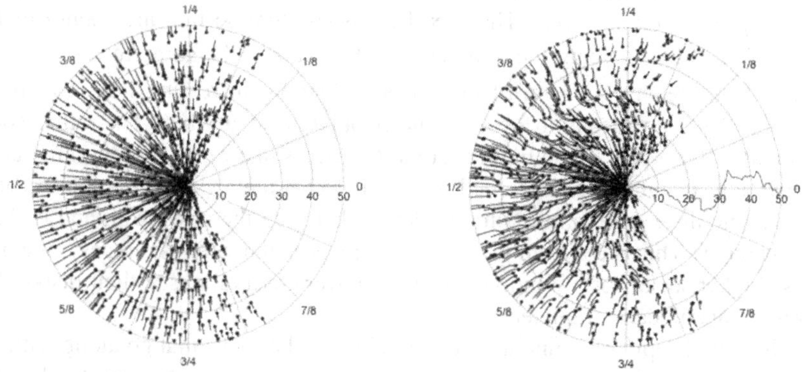

(a) transparency (b) no transparency, $\beta = 1$

Figure 3. Visualisation of a simulation snapshot of 50 subsequent rounds. The preference space is mapped to the polar axis and time increases with distance from the origin. Emitted signals from unique individuals are black connected lines. Each $s_1^{(i)}$ is annotated with symbol '*'. The red line shows the evolution of $\hat{d}_1$ over time. Parameters are $n = 100$, $d = 0$, $\alpha = 1$, $\gamma = 1/2$, $\nu = 1/10$.

Table 1. Simulation Results: Impact of Transparency-enhancing Technologies

	Conformity ψ				Mean time to default			
	Transparency	No transparency			Transparency	No transparency		
		$\beta = 1/10$	$\beta = 1$	$\beta = 4$		$\beta = 1/10$	$\beta = 1$	$\beta = 4$
Baseline results								
$n = 100$, $\nu = 1/10$								
$\gamma = 1$	27.5	27.3	26.3	26.2	5.6	5.6	5.6	5.6
$\gamma = 1/2$	12.8	11.6	12.2	12.4	6.3	6.3	6.3	6.3
$\gamma = 1/10$	2.0	1.5	2.0	1.9	8.4	8.4	8.4	8.4
Early default								
$n = 100$, $\nu = 1/4$								
$\gamma = 1$	26.1	24.5	24.5	23.7	3.1	3.1	3.1	3.1
$\gamma = 1/2$	12.4	11.7	11.5	10.0	3.4	3.4	3.4	3.4
$\gamma = 1/10$	1.9	1.4	1.2	1.4	4.0	3.9	3.9	3.9
Limited population sample								
$n = 10$, $\nu = 1/10$								
$\gamma = 1$	40.1	39.3	37.7	38.9	5.6	5.3	5.4	5.5
$\gamma = 1/2$	32.6	20.7	20.5	26.9	6.2	6.0	6.1	6.3
$\gamma = 1/10$	10.6	10.1	11.7	8.4	8.5	8.2	8.3	8.3

Aggregate metrics computed from 1000 iterations ($\alpha = 1$)

The findings on conformity remain broadly stable in the third result set tagged *limited population sample*.[68] The idea here is to increase the uncertainty of the estimate $\hat{d}_1^{(i)}$ by reducing the number of individuals in the game to $n = 10$. This can be interpreted as a kind of awareness constraint in reality, i.e., individuals typically have no means to observe the population as a whole but rather some randomly drawn peers. The higher estimation errors that cause discontinuity costs during adjustment can be observed in Fig. 4 (b) (in the appendix) and also cause measurable differences in the time to default between the cases with and without transparency. This is coherent with the interpretation that information asymmetries cause higher social costs if individuals have fewer observations at their disposal to approximate hidden parameters.

All in all, keeping in mind all the limitations and caveats that go along with the methodological approach, we conclude that our model suggests relatively little impact of transparency on diversity, although with a slight tendency towards a positive correlation between transparency and conformity. We did not find supporting evidence for the opposite hypothesis.

4 Discussion

We see this work as an attempt to conceive a formal model of individual behaviour in different regimes of public knowledge about the consequences of personal data exposure. It is far too early to draw relevant conclusions for the real world from such a small model, or to derive policy recommendations. Here it is important to recall that the model compares two 'second best' options, and favourable policies might include elements not captured in the models, say, a combination of transparency, restrictions on personal data processing and a ban of obvious discrimination by personal attributes (i.e., decreasing γ rather than communicating d). This is why we rather see our proposal as a framework to support structured reasoning about social aspects of privacy and transparency, as well as a subject for critique and improvement.

Our current list of ideas for model extensions which may be considered, one by one, in further refinements is given below. Where appropriate, we also comment qualitatively on the technical consequences for the model and possible interpretations.

- **Perception bias** In the current model, the maximum-likelihood estimate of d is efficient because the individual has access to a representative sample of the signals emitted in the population. This is unrealistic, as people observe their peers over connections in social networks, where nodes in close proximity tend to share similar preferences. The model could be augmented by an

[68] with one single exception for $\beta = 1$ and $\gamma = 1/10$

observability rule (technically, a filter on $s^{(j)}, j \neq i$) that reflects these restrictions.

- **Multi-modal preference distribution** In line with the previous point, preferences are most likely not distributed evenly between individuals, but rather in clusters. This is partly due to socialisation between peers, but since social adaptation is not captured in our model, an exogenous multi-modal (mixture) distribution for preferences could help to emulate this phenomenon. However, care must be taken to keep the number of parameters tractable, and whether individuals know them or not.
- **Higher-dimensional preference space** The low dimension of the preference space restricts individuals in the choice of trade-offs between their private preferences and their public 'image' (communicated through signals). Possible candidates for higher-dimensional preference spaces are surfaces of k-toruses, hyperspheres (both share the useful property that no discontinuities exists at margins) or, for a discrete case, a binary vector. Higher-dimensional preference spaces have the advantage that the penalty function can be a distance measure in a lower-dimensional projection. Knowledge about which dimensions are relevant (i.e., the coefficients of the projection matrix) could be a distinguishing feature between transparency and obscurity. This not only allows to adjust the degree of transparency more gradually, but might also be deemed as closer to reality where information asymmetries tend to exist on the *selection of attributes* used as discriminating features (e.g., high school degree for credit scoring), while the *direction* of influence is more obvious (e.g., better grades, on average, imply better jobs and thus lower credit risk). Higher-dimensional preference spaces also enable the reflection of dependencies between attributes.
- **Stochastic penalty** One problem in our model that might drive the results is the fact that individuals learn the position of the focal point so quickly from incurred cost (for large n, more than 90% of individuals know d in the second round, and with certainty in the third round). Although we try to compensate for this by keeping time to default short, and thus the proportion of uninformed individuals high, it would be desirable to find ways to cut the immediate feedback. One option is to make the penalty discrete and stochastic, so that individuals optimise over expected costs. This would clearly add noise to the observations and impede learning. However, stochastic penalty also complicates the model as lot, in particular since individuals would have to make trade-offs between expected value and volatility. So additional assumptions on risk aversion are needed.
- **Penalty dependent on other individuals' actions** Yet another direction are penalty functions that depend on the individuals' *behaviour relative to others* (e.g., the cost is born by the $q < n$ individuals closest to d). Such a penalty function could mirror the dynamics of social norms, which have empirically been found to affect individuals' cost to emit certain signals

(perceived abnormality implies higher cost (Huberman et al. 2005)). This seemingly simple change has tremendous implications, as the setting would become a non-zero sum game *between* individuals. So optimal strategies will need observations of others no longer just to compensate information asymmetries, but also to anticipate the (re-)actions of others. So making the penalty function dependent on others seems difficult and might not be a good idea unless the focus of study is strategic competition between individuals.

- **Endogenous penalty function** Related to the previous point, one could also consider making the penalty function dependent on the (aggregate) signals. This would reflect the property that the 'punishing entity' is part of the society and formed by it in more or less institutionalised ways, such as democratic decisions, populism in policy-making, or public uproar and revolution. Strictly speaking, endogenous penalty functions imply that the model turns into a game between individuals (see above). However, if n is large, one can make the common assumption that individuals are 'price-takers' to justify that strategic interactions are disregarded.
- **Behavioural features** Finally, the rationality assumption could be weakened by allowing for well-understood behavioural phenomena that are deemed relevant for perceptions (and following actions) in the area of privacy and transparency, for instance through hyperbolic discounting of uncertain costs in the future (Acquisti and Grossklags 2004).

We would like to stress that this list of options is not very specific to the research question studied in this chapter, but applies to more general aspects of modelling the distribution of personal information in a society. An overview of literature that addresses topics at the intersection between privacy and technology with a similar methodology, though in a more or less formal manner, is given in the next section.

5 Related Work

Social implications of permanent data traces have been studied by Friedman and Resnick (2001; 'social cost of cheap pseudonyms'), Blanchette and Johnson (2002; 'forgetfulness') and lately also by Mayer-Schönberger (2007). Odlyzko (2003) has added that costs of a lack of privacy can also materialise in supplier rents through better possibilities for price discrimination. A broader survey on the economics of privacy has been compiled by Hui and Png (2006).

Transparency as a remedy to personal information abuses has received little attention so far. TETs in conjunction with PETs can be seen as enabling tools for Jiang et al.'s (2002) *principle of minimum asymmetry*. This principle has been developed in the broader context of privacy issues in ambient intelligence. It is based on the assumption that information asymmetries between two parties, data owner and data controller, negatively impact the data owner in making informed decisions about disclosure of personal information to the data controller. This is so because the data owner is uncertain about negative externalities arising from the reuse of his or her personal information by third parties that collude with the data controller. These externalities correspond to our penalty function, and the logic that technology cures negative externalities indirectly (via reducing information asymmetries) is compatible with our model. The solutions proposed in this framework differ from our model in several ways. First, user-controllable data avoidance (i.e., PETs) are considered by Jiang et al. (2002) as complementary technologies, but do not appear in our model (data avoidance would mean to constantly hide the private preferences). Instead, we allow the individuals to alter their signal (personal attributes), though it comes at a cost. Finally, Jiang et al.'s (2002) framework includes the concept of prevention by deterrence: technology supports mechanisms to detect data abuse and a legal framework ensures that malicious data controllers are held accountable. This channel has no corresponding element in our model. Also Brin's (1998) – pointed and admittedly unrealistic – concept of a transparent society can be seen as a spiritual forerunner of our work, however without leaving individuals the choice to emit a different signal than their endowed preference (that is not private any longer).

One of the key ingredients of modelling privacy-related behaviour on the individual level is the assumption of heterogeneous attributes between individuals (our model does this by means of preferences). While this design decision is quite obvious – otherwise, if all individuals were identical, hiding attributes shared with all others is not very meaningful – researchers disagree in whether the attitude towards privacy should itself be modelled as heterogeneous (e.g., in Böhme and Koble 2007; Chellappa and Shivendu 2007) or not (for example Bouckaert and Degryse 2006). Clearly, empirical evidence suggests the existence of different stereotypes, such as privacy fundamentalists as well as pragmatists (Kumaraguru and Cranor 2005). However, adhering to the *lex parsimoniae* (parsimony principle), one may consider to omit this detail. Dodds (2007) approaches this important question with an evolutionary theory and proposes a model in which heterogeneous privacy concerns are more stable than homogeneity, although the exact transition paths depend on a number of (arbitrarily chosen) parameters. Note that privacy concerns are heterogeneous in our model as well. They follow implicitly from rational behaviour given heterogeneous preferences.

6 Summary and Outlook

Our research was motivated by the debate about appropriate tools and technologies to assist people in dealing with their personal information in a world where storage and processing of data becomes ever cheaper. We have argued that the data avoidance approach pursued by advocates of so-called privacy-enhancing technologies (PET) is impractical and unrealistic in many situations, so that transparency-enhancing technologies (TET) are seen as a promising alternative. This led us to the research question, how transparency on the consequences of disclosure of particular personal attributes affects aggregate behaviour, such as diversity and conformity. We have proposed a microeconomic model of rational agents adjusting their data disclosure under various constraints, and presented solutions for the optimal individual strategy in either case. Simulation results tentatively suggest that transparency in fact fosters conformity, although the effects we found are rather weak. Beyond this particular result, we see the main contribution of this chapter in the model proposal and the reflections on possible extensions. They may serve as a starting point for more complete (or more parsimonious) models, which one day may be augmented by a measurement part to be fit to empirical data.

Acknowledgments

We thank Thomas Gloe for stating the proposition “If TETs ever provide full transparency, then everybody will behave alike” in an informal conversation, which led us to the research question. The final model is a result of fruitful discussion with Mike Bergmann, Stefan Berthold, Matthias Kirchner, Stefan Köpsell, and Immanuel Scholz. As usual, the responsibility for errors and omissions remains our own.

This work was supported in part by the EU Network of Excellence “Future of Identity in the Information Society” (FIDIS, http://www.fidis.net) and a travel stipend by the Institute for Information Infrastructure Protection (I3P, http://www.thei3p.org). The views and conclusions contained herein are those of the authors and should not be interpreted as necessarily representing the official policies.

References

Adams, C. “A Classification for Privacy Techniques,” *University of Ottawa Law & Technology Journal* (3:1), 2006, pp. 5-52.

Acquisti, A., and Grossklags, J. “Privacy Attitudes and Privacy Behaviour: Losses, Gains, and Hyperbolic Discounting,” in *The Economics of Information Security*, Camp, L. J., and Levis, R. (Eds.), Kluwer, 2004, pp. 165-178.

Acquisti, A., Varian, H. R. “Conditioning Prices on Purchase History,” *Marketing Science*, (24:3), 2005, pp. 1-15.

Baran, P. “Communications, Computers and People,” Technical report, RAND Corporation, Santa Monica, CA, 1965.

Bouckaert, J., and Degryse, H. "Opt in Versus Opt Out: A Free-entry Analysis of Privacy Policies," in 5th *Workshop on the Economics of Information Security (WEIS)*, Cambridge, United Kingdom, June 2006.

Blanchette, J.-F., and Johnson, D. G. "Data Retention and the Panoptic Society: The Social Benefits of Forgetfulness," *Information Society* (18:1), 2002, pp. 33-45.

Böhme, R., and Koble, S. "On the Viability of Privacy-enhancing Technologies in a Self-regulated Business-to-Consumer Market: Will Privacy Remain a Luxury Good?", in 6th *Workshop on the Economics of Information Security (WEIS)*, Pittsburgh, PA, June 2007.

Borcea-Pfitzmann, K., Hansen, M., Liesebach, K., Pfitzmann, A., and Steinbrecher, S. "Managing One's Identities in Organisational and Social Settings," *Datenschutz und Datensicherheit [Data Protection and Data Security]* (31:9), 2007, pp. 671-675.

Brandt, F. "Fully Private Auctions in a Constant Number of Rounds," *in Proceedings of Financial Cryptography*, Wright, R. N. (Ed.), LNCS 2742, Springer-Verlag, Berlin, 2003, pp. 223-238. (Revised version available at http://www.tcs.ifi.lmu.de/~brandtf/papers/fc2003.pdf)

Brin, D., *The Transparent Society*, Perseus Books, Reading, MA, 1998.

Bellotti, V., and Sellen, A. "Design for Privacy in Ubiquitous Computing Environments," in *ECSCW'93: Proceedings of European Conference on Computer-Supported Cooperative Work*, Kluwer, 1993, pp. 77-92.

Camp, L. J., Osorio, C. "Privacy Enhancing Technologies for Internet Commerce," in *Trust in the Network Economy*, Petrovic, O., Ksela, M., Fallenböck, M., and Kittl, C. (Eds.), Springer-Verlag, Wien, 2003, pp. 317-329.

Calzolari, G., and Pavan, A. "On the Optimality of Privacy in Sequential Contracting," *Journal of Economic Theory* (30), 2005, pp. 168-204.

Cranor, L. F. "P3P: Making Privacy Policies More Useful," *IEEE Security & Privacy* (1:6), 2003, pp. 50-55.

Chellappa, R., and Shivendu, S. "An Economic Model of Privacy: A Property Rights Approach to Regulatory Choices for Online Personalization," *Journal of Management Information Systems* (24:3), 2007, pp. 193-225.

Dodds, S. "Hiding, Seeking, and the Evolution of Privacy Behaviour," in 6th *Workshop on the Economics of Information Security (WEIS)*, Pittsburgh, PA, June 2007.

Ferraiolo, D. F., and Kuhn, D. R. "Role Based Access Control", in *Proceedings of the 15th National Computer Security Conference*, 1992.

Friedman, E., and Resnick, P. "The Social Cost of Cheap Pseudonyms," *Journal of Economics and Management Strategy* (10:2), 2001, pp. 173-199.

Goldberg, I., Wagner, D., and Brewer, E. "Privacy-enhancing Technologies for the Internet," in *Proceedings of the 42nd IEEE Spring COMPCON*, 1997, pp. 103-109.

Huberman B. A., Adar, E., and Fine, L. R. "Valuating Privacy," *IEEE Security & Privacy* (3:5), 2005, pp. 22-25.

Hildebrandt, M. "Profiling into the Future: An Assessment of Profiling Technologies in the Context of Ambient Intelligence," *FIDIS In-house Journal*, 2007, online at http://journal.fidis.net/fileadmin/journal/issues/1-2007/Profiling_into_the_future.pdf.

Hui K.-L., and Png, I. "The Economics of Privacy," in *Handbooks in Information System and Economics*, Hedershott T. J. (Ed.), volume 1, Elsevier, 2006, pp. 471-493.

Jiang, X., Hong, J. I., and Landay, J. A. "Approximate Information Flows: Socially-based Modeling of Privacy in Ubiquitous Computing," in *UbiComp '02: Proceedings of Ubiquitous Computing*, LNCS 2498, Springer-Verlag, Berlin, 2002, pp. 176-193.

Kumaraguru, P., and Cranor, L. F. "Privacy Indexes: A Survey of Westin's Studies," Technical Report CMU-ISRI-5-138, Carnegie Mellon University, 2005.

Kim, E., Lee, B., and Zhu, K. "CRM and the Incentive to Share Customer Information," in *Workshop on Information Systems and Economics (WISE)*, UC Irvine, CA, 2005.

Lundblad, N. "Privacy in a Noise Society," in *WHOLES Workshop: A Multiple View of Individual Privacy in a Networked World*, Sigtuna, Sweden, 2004.

Mayer-Schönberger, V. "Useful void: The Art of Forgetting in the Age of Ubiquitous Computing," KSG Faculty Research Working Paper RWP07-022, 2007.

Odlyzko, A. "Privacy, Economics, and Price Discrimination on the Internet," in *The Economics of Information Security*, Camp, L. J., and Levis, R. (Eds.), Kluwer, 2004, pp. 187-211.

Schunter, M., and Powers, C. *The Enterprise Privacy Authorization Language (EPAL 1.1)*, 2003, online at http://www.zurich.ibm.com/security/enterprise-privacy/epal/ .

Appendix

List of Symbols

α	weight of pretence component in total cost
β	weight of discontinuity component in total cost
γ	weight of penalty component in total cost
ν	cost offset per round (technical constant to prevent convergence)
ψ	measure of conformity (variable of interest)
c_{disc}	discontinuity cost ($\propto$ distance to previous signals)
c_{pen}	penalty cost ($\propto$ neg. distance between signal s and focal point d)
c_{pret}	pretence cost ($\propto$ distance between preference p and signal s)
$c_{\text{tot}}^{(i)}$	total cost of i-th individual
d	location of focal point (max. penalty); transparency $\Rightarrow$ d is known
$\hat{d}_k^{(i)}$	estimate of d formed by the i-th individual in round k
D	distance function in preference/signal space
f_{s_1}	probability distribution of 'young' individuals' signals
f_{s_k}	probability distribution of all individuals' signals
i	index for individual
$I^{(i)}$	individual (agent in the model) with index i
j	alternative index for individual (used to iterate over others)
k	round index (as suffix)
K	expected time to default (function over signal/preference space)
m	number of observable signals from previous round
n	number of individuals in the model
$p^{(i)}$	private preference of i-th individual ($0 \leq p^{(i)} < 1$)
q	quantile among individuals ($0 \leq q \leq n$)
$s^{(i)}$	signal emitted by i-th individual ($0 \leq s^{(i)} < 1$)
$v^{(i)}$	wealth of i-th individual ($v^{(i)} < 1$)

Table 2. Performance of the ML Estimator for $\hat{d}$ (in % pts.)

	Mean absolute error (MAE)				
n	γ= 1/20	γ= 1/10	γ= 1/4	γ= 1/2	γ= 1
1	14.38	10.16	6.91	4.33	2.75
10	10.77	7.41	4.85	3.15	1.88
25	8.07	5.88	3.23	2.47	1.55
50	7.30	4.31	2.59	1.61	1.07
100	4.47	3.20	1.91	1.52	0.80
200	3.81	2.46	1.43	0.91	0.61

Metrics computed from 100 runs after 50 iterations (α= 1, ν =1/10)

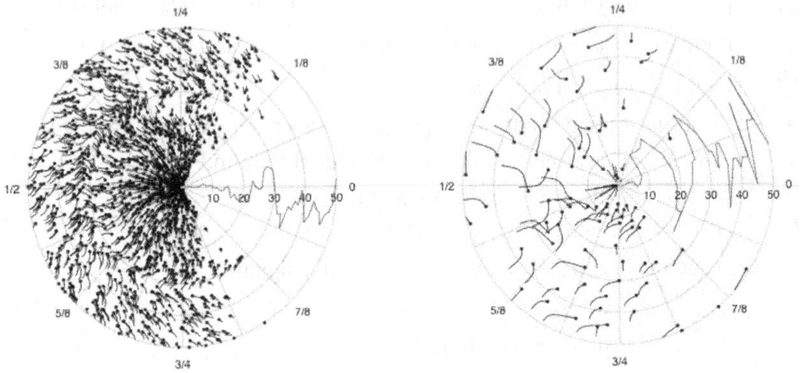

(a) no transparency, n = 100, ν= 1/4 (b) no transparency, n = 10, ν= 1/10

Figure 4. Supplemental simulation snapshots. d = 0, α = 1, β= 1, γ= 1/2. See caption of Fig. 3 for more details.

Is Distributed Trust More Trustworthy?

Kurt Nielsen

University of Copenhagen, Denmark

Abstract We provide a comparative economic analysis of a traditional trusted mediator, e.g. an auction or a consultancy house, and a mediator based on distributed cryptography (threshold trust). The two institutions are compared in a supergame that compares the immediate gain from corruption with future losses if corruption is detected. Corruption with threshold trust requires cooperation among $T+1$ out of N preassigned independent third parties, which results in relative higher detection rates. If all incidents of corruption are detected, traditional trust is the most trustworthy institution. This follows from the fundamental division problem that gain from corruption is divided among less than honest gain with threshold trust. On the other hand, if the threshold is $T = N-1$, threshold trust is the most trustworthy institution for any detection rate less than 1. In all intermediate situations, determining the most trustworthy institution depends on the institutional setup and payoffs. However, the required cooperation with threshold trust allows a public authority to enhance trust in various ways. Furthermore, conflicting interests may cause a TTP based on threshold trust to breakdown after detected corruption, and thereby make the punishment more harsh and threshold trust more trustworthy.

1 Introduction

We consider the institutional design of a Trusted Third Party (TTP) that is paid to confidentially coordinate private information according to a comprehensive protocol. One example could be a sealed bid auction, where the submitted bids are kept confidential and coordinated as prescribed in the auction rules.

In information economics the existence of a TTP is a basic assumption and a requirement for many economic mechanisms. One of the most well-known theoretical results in this field is *The Revelation Principle*, which says that for any mechanism there exists a weakly dominating mechanism where all participants reveal their type to a TTP that tells the participants what to do, see e.g. Gibbard (1973) or Myerson (1979). Economic theory has little to say about the ideal design

M.E. Johnson (ed.), *Managing Information Risk and the Economics of Security*,
DOI: 10.1007/978-0-387-09762-6_15, © Springer Science + Business Media, LLC 2009

of the required TTP and where it comes from. However, economic literature provides some insight to the nature of trust, see e.g. James Jr. (2002).

In practice the market provides many different TTPs that in one way or the other handle private information. Common for these is that the TTP is a single entity: a person or an institution. Almost by definition, the information revealed to the TTP is crucial and valuable to others or the TTP itself (e.g. when the commission depends on the turnover). To counteract corruption, the traditional TTP enhances its reputation, for example by enforcing strict procedures. Nevertheless, corruption happens, either independently by an individual or an institution or more organized among individuals or institutions.

In computer science the topic of designing TTP institutions has been a central challenge for many years. While traditional cryptography focuses on preserving privacy within a group of individuals with full access to the information, recent contributions show a fundamental break with the idea of placing all trust in a single entity at any time. The discipline of distributed cryptography provides a theoretical solution by the so-called *secure multiparty computation*, which allows a number of parties to jointly perform a computation on private inputs without releasing other information than agreed upon a priori. The seminal ideas go back to Shamir (1979) and the theory was founded in the 1980s, see e.g. Goldreich et al. (1988), Ben-Or et al. (1988) and Chaum et al. (1988), but only recently has the idea been refined and made applicable in practice, see e.g. Bogetoft et al. (2005), Bogetoft et al. (2008) and Malkhi et al. (2004)[69].

To provide an idea of how secure multiparty computation works, consider the following simplified problem of adding the two privately held numbers a and b. Let c be a secret key and the encrypted information submitted be c^a and c^b. Now multiplying the two numbers yield c^{a+b} and if you know c you know the result, though, unfortunately you also know the private inputs. To solve this problem, let c be the following solution to a linear function $f(0)=c$, and the $f(x_1)=y_1$ and $f(x_2)=y_2$ two random numbers on the function. Now, one of the points provides no information while both points provide all information about c. Although other operations like that of comparing two numbers require many more operations, the basic intuition is the same[70]; it is feasible without revealing any information other than what was agreed upon a priori.

This chapter compares two distinct trust institutions based on respectively, a single TTP (traditional trust) and an organized network of N TTPs using secure multiparty computation (threshold trust). The two institutions are compared in a game-theoretic model, where corruption is a tempting strategy. Unlike traditional

---

[69] The three papers represent the following two research projects: SIMAP (www.sikkerhed.alexandra.dk/uk/projects/simap/index.htm) and FAIRPLAY (www.cs.huji.ac.il/project/Fairplay/home.html).

[70] Comparing two numbers depends on the size of the numbers and requires a lot of communication between the involved TTPs. Comparing 2 32-bit integers in a NT-TTP where N=3 and T=1 takes approx. 1 second, see e.g. Bogetoft et al. (2006).

trust, no single TTP as a member of threshold trust can make corruption by misusing the private information. As in the example above, revealing the private information requires coordination. In general threshold trust is designed such that corruption is avoided as long as no coalition of T+1 colludes[71]. Although, the computational complexity depends on the choice of N and T, it is reasonable to consider N and T as fundamental design variables. This chapter aims at providing economic reasoning for this fundamental design issue. I will refer to the two different trust institutions as T-TTP (traditional TTP) and NT-TTP (threshold trust).

In the game-theoretic model, a TTP plays repeatedly against a market that demands a mediation job from the TTP. The TTP gets a high payoff from playing " corrupt" as opposed to playing " honest", but the market can punish the TTP by selecting another competing TTP. In an infinitely repeated game, a sufficient valuation of future punishment (weighted by a discount factor) makes it economically optimal to play honest as opposed to playing corrupt and getting a high payoff in the short run. The question is whether it requires a higher or a lower weight on future punishment to make corruption unattractive to NT-TTP as opposed to T-TTP. With NT-TTP, corruption can only happen if a predefined number of T+1 TTPs cooperate. By intuition such a system may seem superior to a T-TTP. However, if T+1 is less than N, payoff from playing honest is divided by more than payoff from playing corrupt. The analytical model illustrates these two counteracting effects.

The modeling has many similarities to models of cartels. Although the basic game typically has some of the same structures, the players in cartel games are competing firms and the demand side is represented by the underlying elastic demand function, see e.g. Motta (2004). Here we assume perfect competition where the market pays the competitive price or selects another TTP. In a cartel game, payoff from cooperation is the illegal collusion, and the tempting deviation is a unilateral deviation from the coordinated monopoly profit. In this model the cooperation strategy is the honest play, and the deviation the illegal corruption. Furthermore, the NT-TTP structure forces the deviation to be coordinated. How this coordination is taking place is not modeled, it is simply assumed that the most profitable number of T+1 TTPs form a collusive coalition[72]. From a welfare perspective, the deviation is a positive thing in a cartel game (since it may start a price war) and a negative thing in our model. On the other hand, the task of the authorities is to make collusion difficult in both cases. In traditional cartel games, the participating firms are looking for deviations from cooperation, and the punishment from deviation from the cartel's point of view, is to play the competitive

[71] Here the threshold T is the maximum number of TTPs that can not reveal the information; other parts of the literature operate with a threshold for the minimum number of TTPs that can reveal the information.

[72] It is assumed that the remaining N-T-1 participating TTPs have no more insight in the corruption than any other outside authority. This is supported by the technology.

equilibrium. In our setting the punishment for detected corruption comes directly from the exclusion from a large part of the market. In our model the information about corruption is modeled simply by an exogenous detection rate as opposed to the more advanced cartel models, where the market in one way or the other provides indications of deviation.For example, rotemberg and Saloner (1986) base the deviation on expected profit given demand fluctuations, while Porter (1983) introduces a certain trigger price that triggers the punishment period.

A related line of literature models the so-called leniency programs, where members of the cartel get reduced penalty for helping the authorities in cartel cases, see e.g. Motta and Polo (2003). These models involve exogenous probabilities about things like the chance of being reviewed by the authorities and the chance of being proved guilty in case of no co-operation with authorities. This model is more simple and operates with a single detection rate and that detection triggers punishment forever. In a leniency program, it may, e.g., be optimal to remain in the cartel although the firm is under review.

Another line of research considers the game-theoretical rational of sharing a secret using threshold trust. The primary setup is where the involved TTPs each have a higher value of the secret if no one else sees it. In a one-shot game (where all are supposed to submit their shares simultaneously) none of the parties have an incentive to distribute their share, see Halpern and Teague (2004). Several papers suggest mechanisms and setups that counteract this finding and make it rational to share the secret, see e.g. Halpern and Teague (2004) and Abraham et al. (2006). In addition, Recently Maleka et al. (2008) extend these ideas by modeling it as a repeated game, where lack of cooperation (not sending the share) is punished in future repetition of the game. In this chapter I differ from this line of research by considering a different setup, where the involved TTPs are paid to supply a service and hereby to participate with their individual shares[73].

The outline of the chapter is as follows. Section 2 describes the characteristics of threshold trust. Section 3 provides the game-theoretic modeling and an immediate comparison of the two trust institutions. More comparative results and policy recommendations are provided and discussed in Section 4, and Section 5 concludes.

2 Threshold Trust

The purpose of a TTP is to confidentially handle private information according to a prescribed protocol. In this chapter failure to do so is considered corruption. Corruption that does not involve the TTP, e.g. bidding rings, is not considered.

---

[73] It is assumed that defecting within the corrupt coalition may be sufficiently avoided or punished by the remaining members of the coalition. Meaning that the situation where a single member of the corrupt coalition tries to gain the others' shares without supplying his own is not considered.

Corruption may either be performed internally by the TTP or in coordination with an outside party that gains from the corruption. A simple example is a second price sealed bid auction where the price may be manipulated by an extra bid just below the highest bid. This is clearly valuable to the seller. Also, if the TTP's salary depends on the selling price, corruption may be directly beneficial for the TTP as well.

With NT-TTP, the choice of *N* and *T* are fundamental design variables that in different ways counteract corruption. To illustrate the differences between the two trust institutions, consider the following three general security concerns (Pfleeger and Pfleeger 2003):

Integrity: Prevent manipulation of the protocol.
Confidentiality: Prevent revelation of information outside the protocol.
Availability: Prevent the protocol from being blocked.

Corruption can be categorized as a violation of one or more of these three concerns. Clearly, all three concerns may be directly violated by a T-TTP. This is opposed to NT-TTP, where violation of each of the three concerns requires a different number of the *N* TTPs to cooperate[74]. Table 1 illustrates the required coordination in order to violate the three concerns in case of *N*=5 and varying threshold (*T*).

Table 1. Required Coordination to Violate the Three Security Concerns with NT-TTP

NT setup	Integrity	Confidentiality	Availability
(5,1)	5	2	4
(5,2)	5	3	3
(5,3)	5	4	2
(5,4)	5	5	1

Manipulating the protocol will involve all *N* TTPs. Therefore, integrity is independent of the chosen threshold, unlike confidentiality and availability that is inversely dependent on the threshold. Compromising confidentiality may be done independently by *T*+1 TTP without any traceable signals outside the coalition. On the other hand, *N-T* TTPs can prevent the protocol from being executed. This creates a fundamental trade-off between confidentiality and availability.

In this chapter it is assumed that the gain from a successful corrupt act is the same for a T-TTP and a coalition of *T*+1 out of *N* in case of NT-TTP. Hereby, we basically assume that breaking the confidentiality is both necessary and sufficient to get the high payoff from playing corrupt.

The neglected higher integrity with NT-TTP may be supported by the following statements: 1) that knowledge about the private inputs is sufficient to

[74] Corruption by software engineers is not considered in this chapter.

perform a corruption, like in the case of the second price auction and 2) that breaking the confidentiality is less detectable than manipulating the protocol, since the protocol is public and the public result has to correspond with each participant's submitted information.

Availability seems of less importance in terms of corruption, although it may be of value to prevent the protocol from being performed. As illustrated in Table 1, the higher the threshold the more coalitions may prevent availability. Especially with the maximum threshold of N-1 where each individual TTP may veto the protocol. Apart from intended blocking, unintended dropout may be a significant problem if N is large or if timely precision is important, e.g. in most online services. Also, if just one of the keys is lost, the collected information is useless. On the other hand, setting T=N-1 and letting each of the participants constitute a TTP makes up a perfect trust institution in terms of confidentiality.

Apart from the three security concerns, the complexity of secure multiparty computation is significant and depends on N and T. In general the computation time increases as N, T and the relation T/N increases. Altogether, there is no a priori dominating choice of N and T.

In the analysis we will assume that the N members are identical and independent and discuss the numeric choice of N and T. Though in reality, one might have prior expectations about likely coalitions among the N members and use this to select the threshold. In general one may consider the likely gain from corruption by any T+1 coalitions and select T according to this, like defining stable coalitions in a cooperative game. As an example, consider a sealed bid double auction between one seller and one buyer, where the mediator's job is to compute the trading price, e.g. the average of the two submitted bids. Consider a NT-TTP with N=3 and T=1 where the TTPs are the seller, the buyer and a consultancy house. Since likely corruption may happen in a coalition between either the buyer or the seller and the consultancy house, the required coordination with T-TTP is the same. On the other hand, if the NT-TTP consisted of three independent consultancy houses, any corruption would require fundamentally more coordination.

3 The Game-Theoretic Modeling

This section presents the applied game-theoretic models and some immediate comparative results. As mentioned above, for a successful coalition to maximize the gain from corruption, it is assumed that it consists of exactly T+1 TTPs. Hereby we consider the most profitable type of corruption. Stability of the corrupt coalition is discussed in section 4.

It turns out that the preferred trust institution is determined by two counteracting effects:

1. Unlike T-TTP, the gain from corruption is divided among less than the gain from playing honest with NT-TTP[75]
2. Unlike T-TTP, corruption requires cooperation among more independent TTPs with NT-TTP

The modeling is first presented in a simple basic model that only involves the division effect, and then extended to a model that captures both effects.

3.1 The Basic Model

It is assumed that the two trust institutions face the same competitive prices for a given mediation job. One may think of the job of handling the private bids in a second price sealed bid auction. **The TTP**'s opponent is customers (represented by **The Market**), who perceive **The TTP** as being reliable or unreliable. If **The TTP** is perceived unreliable, a large part of the customers drop the TTP, and the TTP gets a low payoff (V^l). If **The TTP** is perceived reliable, playing "honest" generates a medium payoff (V^m) while playing "corrupt" generates a high payoff (V^h). **The Market** has an advantage of using the same TTP but a disadvantage of facing corruption. The payoffs have the same properties as in the well-known game of the prisoners' dilemma. Below, the game is presented as a 2×2 matrix game between **The TTP** and **The Market.**

Table 2. The Basic Game.

		The Market	
		Reliable	*Unreliable*
The TTP	*Honest*	(V^m, V^h)	(V^l, V^m)
	Corrupt	(V^h, V^l)	(V^l, V^m)

The game has a weakly dominating Nash equilibrium in pure strategies, where **The TTP** plays corrupt, and *The market* considers **The TTP** to be unreliable and chooses another TTP. Although both players would have been better off by playing respectively "honest" and "reliable", it is not a best response. However, if the two players repeatedly meet and play the same game, supporting the cooperative strategy (honest, reliable) may be possible.

We assume that the players play this game in every period and that there is always a positive probability for another period - meaning that we consider an

---

[75] Unless T=N-1, where both gains from corruption as well as honest play are divided among N TTPs.

infinite number of periods. Also, we will consider the so-called *Grim trigger strategy*, which in this setup means that **The Market** plays "reliable" as long as **The TTP** plays "honest". If **The TTP** plays "corrupt" **The Market** will play " unreliable" in the next period and forever hereafter. It is well known, that with a sufficiently high discount factor, future punishment may ensure that the cooperative strategy (honest, reliable) is a Subgame Perfect Nash Equilibrium, see e.g. the seminal paper by Friedman (1971) for an introduction to this so-called supergame. The intuition is simple; a higher discount factor puts higher weights on future punishments which at some point make it economically optimal to play "honest".

In this chapter, the focus is on comparing two trust institutions facing the same supergame. Therefore, the simplified assumption that deviation from cooperation (honest, reliable) is punished by playing the Nash equilibrium (corrupt, unreliable) for infinity is less important. Alternatively, one may e.g. implement a return to the cooperative equilibrium after a given number of punishment periods, see e.g. Abreu (1986) for inspiration. This may reflect a situation where trust is reestablished after a period of corruption.

We are now ready to define discount factors that support cooperation. The expression below provides the smallest discount factor that makes "honest" the T-TTP's best response.

$$\begin{aligned} &V^{\text{honest}} > V^{\text{corrupt}} \Leftrightarrow \\ &V^m \cdot \frac{1}{1-\delta} > V^h + V^l \cdot \frac{\delta}{1-\delta} \Leftrightarrow \\ &\frac{V^h - V^m}{V^h - V^l} < \delta \end{aligned} \tag{1}$$

A similar expression is derived in the case of NT-TTP. As mentioned, the gain from playing "honest" is divided among N and the gain from playing "corrupt" is divided only among T+1. Clearly, any coalition with more than T+1 may also play corrupt, however the most profitable coalition consists of exactly T+1. The expression below represents the situation for one of the T+1 members of the corrupt coalition. If the T+1 plays "corrupt", the remaining N-T-1 TTPs are unaware of any corruption before the subsequent period. When corruption is detected, the assumption is that the NT-TTP institution continues with a smaller part of the market which is collectively shared among all N TTPs. Setting $V^l = 0$ is a simple way to model the case where the NT-TTP institution breaks down when corruption is detected - this is discussed further in section 4. Like before, the expression below provides the smallest discount factor that makes "honest" the best response for any member of the corrupt coalition[76].

[76] The result is independent of a proportional increase in the payoff i.e. independent of the market share.

$$
\begin{aligned}
&V^{\text{honest}} > V^{\text{corrupt}} \Leftrightarrow \\
&\frac{V^m}{N}\cdot\frac{1}{1-\delta} > \frac{V^h}{T+1} + \frac{V^l}{N}\cdot\frac{\delta}{1-\delta} \Leftrightarrow \\
&\frac{\frac{N}{T+1}V^h - V^m}{\frac{N}{T+1}V^h - V^l} < \delta
\end{aligned}
\tag{2}
$$

Note that the difference between the two situations is $N/(T+1)$, which is larger than or equal to 1. Therefore, all successful coalitions among at least T+1 and no more than N-1 require a higher discount factor to support "honesty" as opposed to T-TTP. This means that it is easier to support honesty with T-TTP in the sense that the required valuation of future punishments is less for T-TTP than for NT-TTP. This is illustrated in Figure 1 where payoffs are fixed at $V^l = 3$, $V^h = 10$ and , $V^m = 3 + w, w \in [0;7]$ and 4 different choices of N and T are pictured ((5,1), means $N = 5$ and $T = 1$).

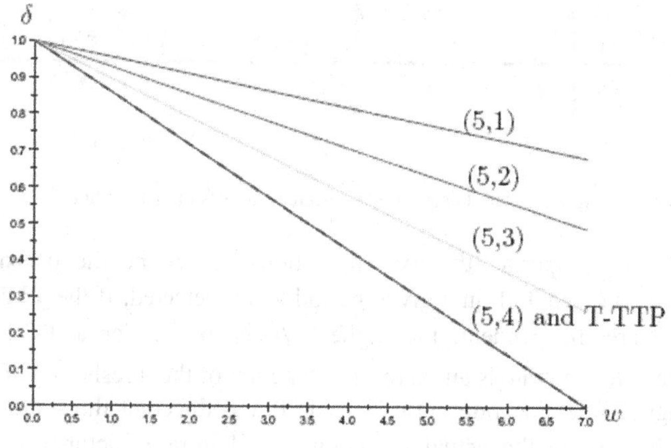

Figure 1. T-TTP is a Relatively More Trustworthy Institution If All Corruption is Detected

3.2 *The Extended Model*

In the analysis above, all corruption is detected with certainty and punished in the following period and forever hereafter. In the following we will assume that less than all incidences of corruption is detected. Though, if corruption is detected the TTP is punished in the following period and forever hereafter as before.

It is assumed that the payoffs are expected payoffs, supported by overlapping intervals, such that the realized payoffs do not leave **The Market** player with any certain signals about corruption. Corruption may be detected by the market participants or some third party supervising the market. The detection of corruption is assumed to be the same for all TTPs in every period, no matter if they operate individually as T-TTP or as a member of NT-TTP. Also, the detection rates for the individual TTPs are assumed to be independent.

Now, let β be the probability that corruption by a given trust institution (T-TTP or NT-TTP) in a given period is *not* detected. If $\beta = 0$ corruption is always detected as in the model above. For $\beta > 0$, the TTP can either be detected and receive V^l forever hereafter or move undetected to the next period. If no corruption is detected, the game is repeated, and the TTP plays "corrupt" again and receives V^h, which may or may not be detected and punished from the subsequent period. Figure 2 illustrates the different paths a TTP can take and the associated expected and discounted payoffs.

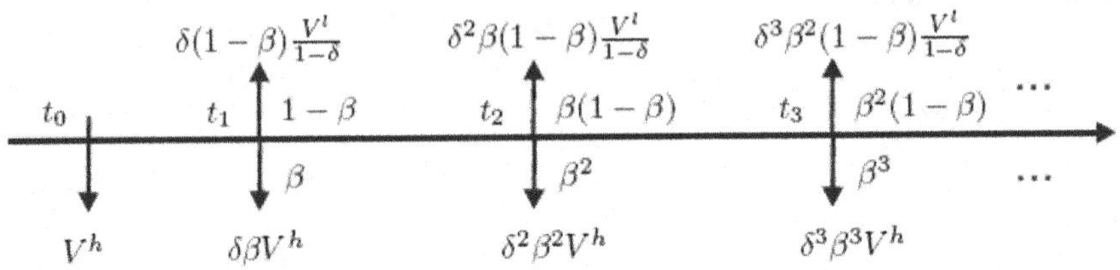

Figure 2. The Discounted Expected Payoffs on a Timeline

In terms of comparing the two institutions, let α be the probability that corruption by a given TTP in a given period is *not* detected. If the TTPs involved in NT-TTP are independent, the highest β is α^{T+1}. For a T-TTP $\beta = \alpha$. Clearly, the detection rate is an increasing function of the threshold *T*. Though, the relative higher detection rate between T-TTP and different threshold values for NT-TTP depends on the actual detection rate. Figure 3 pictures $\alpha - \alpha^{T+1}$ for different values of α and *T*. Hereby, the relative gain from the coordination effect is illustrated. For high and low values of α, the relative coordination effect is small. Also, the maximum relative coordination value increases with *T*. In the following, we study how this coordination effect counteracts the division effect, illustrated in the section 3.1.

Now, weighting the different paths a T-TTP can take (see Figure 2), the inequality that makes a "honest" the economically best response is given as:

$$\underbrace{\frac{V^m}{1-\delta}}_{\text{honest}} > \underbrace{V^h + \frac{\delta\alpha V^h}{1-\delta\alpha}}_{\text{not detected}} + \underbrace{\frac{\delta}{1-\delta\alpha}\frac{(1-\alpha)V^l}{1-\delta}}_{\text{detected}} \tag{3}$$

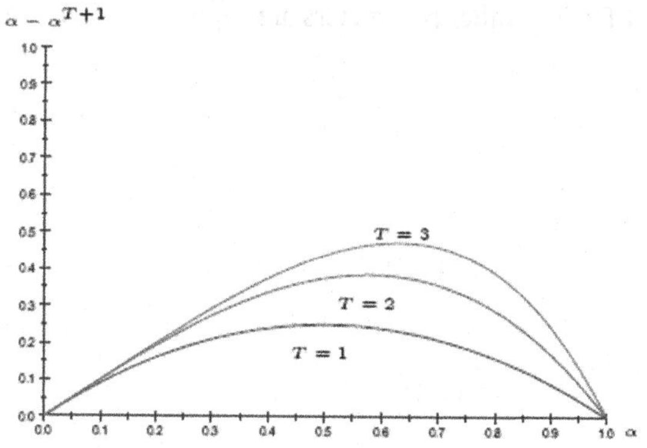

Figure 3. The Relative Coordination Effect

As above, solving for δ provides a lower bound on the discount factor in order to support "honest":

$$\begin{aligned}
&\frac{V^m}{1-\delta} > V^h + \frac{\delta\alpha V^h}{1-\delta\alpha} + \frac{\delta}{1-\delta\alpha}\frac{(1-\alpha)V^l}{1-\delta} \Leftrightarrow \\
&(1-\delta\alpha)V^m > (1-\delta)V^h + \delta(1-\alpha)V^l \Leftrightarrow \\
&0 > -\delta(V^h - V^l - \alpha V^m + \alpha V^l) + V^h - V^m \Leftrightarrow \\
&\delta > \frac{V^h - V^m}{V^h - V^l - \alpha V^m + \alpha V^l}
\end{aligned} \tag{4}$$

Likewise, the discount factors that makes "honest" the best response for any member of the corrupt coalition is given as:

$$\begin{aligned}
&\frac{1}{N}\frac{V^m}{1-\delta} > \frac{1}{T+1}V^h + \frac{1}{T+1}\frac{\delta\alpha^{T+1}V^h}{1-\delta\alpha^{T+1}} + \frac{1}{N}\frac{\delta}{1-\delta\alpha^{T+1}}\frac{(1-\alpha^{T+1})V^l}{1-\delta} \Leftrightarrow \\
&(1-\delta\alpha^{T+1})V^m > (1-\delta)\frac{N}{T+1}V^h + \delta(1-\alpha^{T+1})V^l \Leftrightarrow \\
&0 > -\delta(\frac{N}{T+1}V^h - V^l - \alpha^{T+1}V^m + \alpha^{T+1}V^l) + \frac{N}{T+1}V^h - V^m \Leftrightarrow \\
&\delta > \frac{\frac{N}{T+1}V^h - V^m}{\frac{N}{T+1}V^h - V^l - \alpha^{T+1}V^m + \alpha^{T+1}V^l}
\end{aligned} \tag{5}$$

A comparison of the two institutions while playing the same supergame is given in Figure 4. The result provides the lower bound on the discount factor δ in order to support the TTP to play "honest" as a function of α for respectively

T-TTP and NT-TTP. The other parameters are set to: $N = 5$, $T = 2$, $V^l = 3$, $V^m = 4$ and $V^h = 10$.

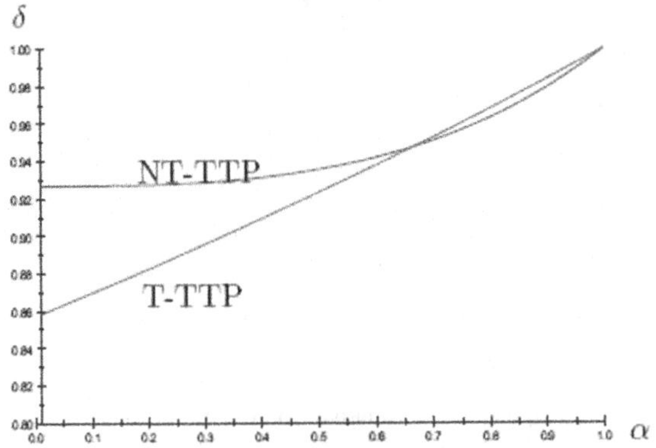

Figure 4. Comparing T-TTP and Threshold Trust with $N = 5$ and $T = 2$

The figure illustrates the counteraction between the division and the coordination effect. If all corruption is detected, the division effect makes it easier to support honesty with T-TTP. On the other hand, if no corruption is detected, there is no economic reasoning for any TTP to play "honest". The interesting point is where the curves cross - where the division effect is suppressed by the coordination effect and makes NT-TTP a relatively more trustworthy institution.

In the following we present some comparative results that follow the same logic as in Figure 4. We explore where the two curves cross with respect to the different application specific parameters. First we consider the choice of N and T and then the payoff matrix.

3.3 *The Choice of N and T*

To explore the effect of increasing the threshold, N is fixed at 7 and the threshold T is varied. In Figure 5, T-TTP is the thick dashed curve and the intersecting curves represent the 6 different NT-TTP setups. With (7,0) each of the individual TTPs may play "corrupt" and get the high payoff, while payoff from playing "honest" should be divided among all 7 TTPs. Hereby the division effect dominates and T-TTP will always be a relatively more trustworthy institution. As T increases, α for which NT-TTP is preferred increases rapidly. For T=5, NT-TTP is a dominating choice with the chosen payoffs: $V^l = 3, V^m = 4$ and $V^h = 10$. For $T = 6$ NT-TTP will always be a relatively more trustworthy institution. To see this, note that when $T = 6$ the division effect disappears and the coordination effect makes NT-TTP more trustworthy.

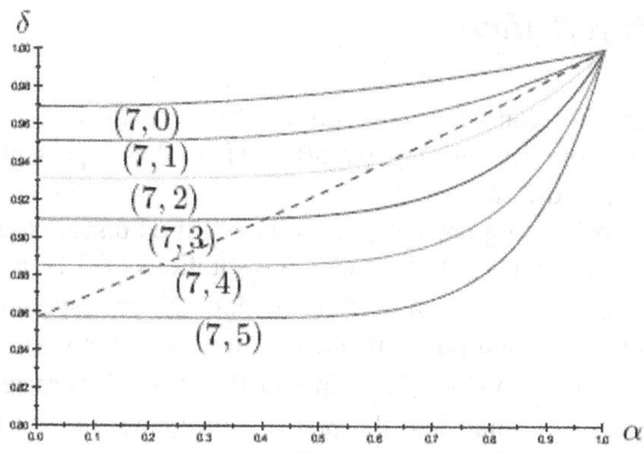

Figure 5. The Effect of T

Since majority trust has a computational advantage it may be relevant to consider the effect of majority trust with an increasing N. To explore this, majority trust based on (3,1), (5,2), (7,3), (9,4) and (11,5) are compared to T-TTP. Figure 6 provides the required discount factor as a function of α for each of the different setups. T-TTP is the thick dashed curve, and the intersecting curves represent the 5 different NT-TTP setups. Figure 6 shows that N has a small positive but diminishing effects in favor of NT-TTP. Also the figure shows that the order of the curves representing the different NT-TTP setups changes for smaller α. However, applying the same payoff matrix in the two institutional setups, an increasing N will always make NT-TTP a relatively more trustworthy institution. The intuition is that the division effect is approximately the same as N increases, while the coordination effect increases as T increases. Like before, the chosen payoffs are: $V^l = 3$, $V^m = 4$ and $V^h = 10$.

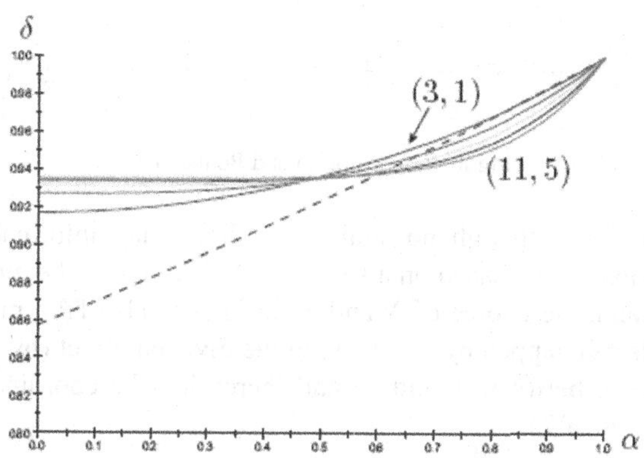

Figure 6: The Effect of N

3.4 The Payoff Matrix

Here we explore the relative trustworthiness between the two trust institutions when facing the same but varying payoffs. NT-TTP is represented as majority trust based on N=5 and T=2.

As mentioned before, Figure 7 provides the required discount factor as a function of α for T-TTP and NT-TTP. The two institutions (T-TTP and NT-TTP) are compared in three different situations (A, B and C), corresponding to different payoffs from corruption and punishment. In situation A, the gain from corruption is high and the punishment low (9:1). In situation C, V^m is raised such that the gain from corruption is small and the punishment higher (1:9). Situation B is in between. As the figure illustrates, the different corruption/punishment scenarios have a significant effect on the relative trustworthiness of the two institutions. As the gain from corruption decreases and the punishment increases, the T-TTP becomes relatively more trustworthy. The intuition is that with NT-TTP the high gain from cooperation is collectively shared among all N TTPs, while the small extra gain from corruption is only shared among the $T+1$ TTPs. Therefore, NT-TTP requires a higher weight on the future since punishment is relatively less.

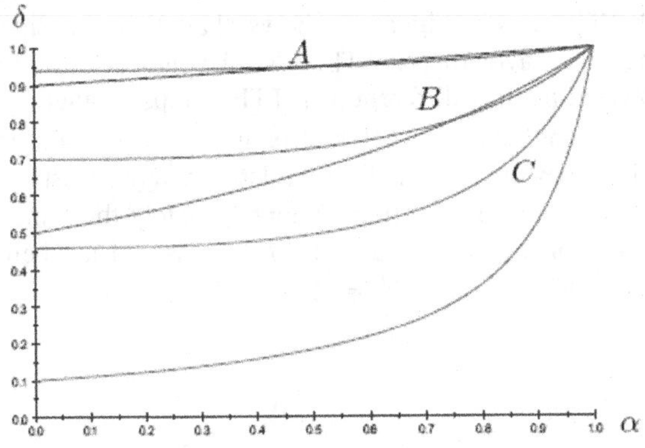

Figure 7. Corruption and Punishment

To conclude, even though no single TTP holds any information in case of NT-TTP, traditional trust based on a single TTP (T-TTP) can be more trustworthy. On the other hand, the choice of N and T can make NT-TTP a more trustworthy institution. This can happen by diminishing the division effect (by diminishing the relative difference between N and T) and increasing the coordination effect (by increasing the size of T).

4 Discussion and Policy Recommendation

From the previous section we have seen that neither of the two trust institutions is a dominating choice per se. In this section we discuss differences between the two trust institutions as well as initiatives that may counteract corruption and make NT-TTP a relatively more trustworthy institution.

4.1 NT-TTP Has a Different Cost Structure

It is sometimes suggested that a NT-TTP is a less costly way to establish trust. The basic argument is that no sensitive information is available to the individual TTP. This is opposed to a traditional TTP, where strict procedures prevent any leakage of information. On the other hand, the NT-TTP involves more TTPs. In terms of the game-theoretic modeling above, it is clear that the TTP institution that makes the most profit is the most trustworthy. The intuition is simply that the more profitable TTP has more to lose from playing "corrupt".

4.2 Breakdown of The NT-TTP

In the analytical model it is assumed that NT-TTP continues in a smaller market after corruption is detected - a cost that is collectively covered. However, corruption may cause the NT-TTP to break down with one or more TTPs leaving. Nevertheless, this may cause the NT-TTP institution to be more trustworthy for several reasons.

In the case that the remaining group of N-T-1 TTPs leave the NT-TTP after detected corruption, they may experience a temporary loss of reputation or business opportunities. This risk of being associated with a corrupt NT-TTP may affect the behavior of the TTPs in two opposite directions. In the initial phase of establishing the NT-TTP, the risk of sullying a good name may bias the selecting in a positive direction. On the other hand, if the TTPs expect the others to form a corrupt coalition, they might as well try to join it to get a part of the high payoff. However, if the later effect causes the corrupt coalition to include more than T+1 TTPs, the division effect makes corruption less attractive. Therefore, in both cases the NT-TTP becomes relatively more trustworthy.

A more direct effect comes from the fact that if a NT-TTP breaks down it can not continue in a smaller market, as opposed to a T-TTP. This makes the punishment more harsh to the NT-TTP and therefore corruption less tempting. Figure 8 illustrates the situation where $V^l = 0$ for the NT-TTP[77] and 0,1,2 and 3 for the T-TTP. The other parameters are chosen to be: $N = 3$, $T = 1$, $V^m = 4$ and $V^h = 10$. As the figure illustrates, a relatively more harsh punishment makes NT-TTP a relatively more trustworthy institution.

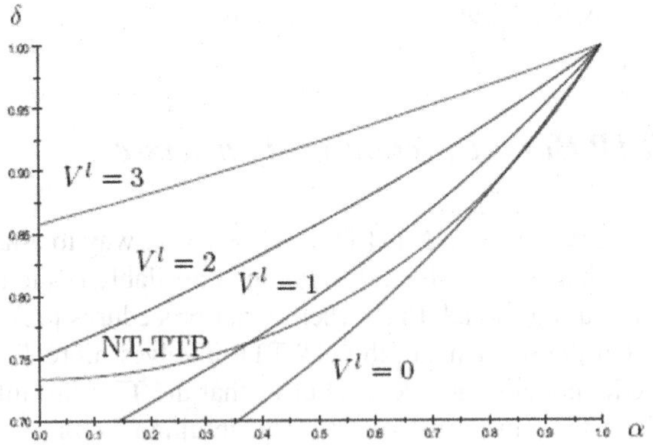

Figure 8. If NT-TTP Breaks Down It Becomes Relatively More Trustworthy

4.3 *Counteract Stable Coalitions*

If the information about corruption is disseminated outside the successful coalition, the risk of being detected increases, or the coalition may be forced to expand the coalition or bribe outside parties. Therefore, it seems reasonable to assume that, if possible, the coalition will consist of the same $T+1$ TTPs in every period in order to avoid disseminating information outside the coalition. Though, if one or more of the N TTPs are replaced in each round, playing corrupt in every period may involve new coalitions. Hereby a successful group of $T+1$ colluding TTPs in a given period should either choose to 1) bribe outside TTPs that hold superior information about likely corruption, 2) accept a higher detection rate or 3) only play corrupt when the same TTPs meet. Either way, the NT-TTP institution becomes relatively more trustworthy since the expected gain from corruption is lower one way or the other.

To give an example, consider the following simple extension where 4 TTPs are initially assigned and where the NT-TTP consists of N=3 and T=1. Now, in every new period, one of the 3 TTPs is replaced with the 4th TTP. Hereby, any given

[77] If the punishment V^l is negative, a comparison between T-TTP and NT-TTP may provide the NT-TTP with a weird advantage, since the "negative" punishment is less harsh because it is shared among all N members.

successful coalition of 2 TTPs will only meet every second period. Assuming that a successful coalition of 2 TTPs decide to play corrupt only when they meet, the situation may be modeled simply by lowering the payoff from playing "corrupt" with 50 % in the present model. However, the cost is that 4 instead of 3 TTPs have to share the same gain from playing "honest" as well as the payoff in the punishment period. Figure 9 illustrates 4 different situations. T-TTP and NT-TTP ^{A} represent the benchmark with the usual payoffs: $V^l = 3$, $V^m = 4$ and $V^h = 10$. 50 % less gain from corruption reduces V^h to 7, and dividing the honest gain and punishment with 4 instead of 3 reduces V^l and V^h to $2\frac{1}{4}$ and 3 respectively, this is represented by NT-TTP ^{B}. Although the figure shows significant improvement from introducing a fourth TTP, it is not unambiguously because V^l and V^m are relatively lower. However, if the fourth TTP is subsidized or represents a public authority, the effect is unambiguously in favor of NT-TTP. This is illustrated in Figure 9 by NT-TTP ^{C}, where the payoffs are $V^l = 3$, $V^m = 4$ and $V^h = 7$.

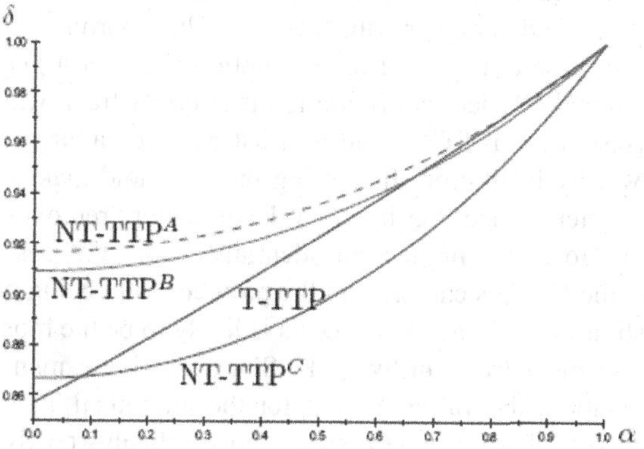

Figure 9. Replacing One TTP in Each Period, $N = 3$ and $T = 1$

4.4 *NT-TTP and Leniency Programs*

By assumption, if corruption is detected, the punishment is V^l in every future period. In reality there might be an additional penalty if the corruption can be proven in court. To the extent that corruption can be proven in court, an additional leniency program may counteract corruption with NT-TTP. With a leniency program a member of a corrupt coalition gets a reduced penalty for helping the authorities in court, see e.g. Motta and Polo (2003). Therefore, with a positive probability of being convicted in court (and detected in the first place), each of the colluding TTPs may be tempted to cooperate with the authorities for economic reasons. Although, the real effect of a leniency program may be limited, it will cause the detection rate to increase for each member of a NT-TTP.

5 Conclusion

Traditional trust is compared to threshold trust in a repeated game where corruption is a tempting deviation. If corruption is detected, a part of the market chooses another TTP, and the TTP is punished by a low payoff forever.

NT-TTP has a fundamental division problem where the gain from corruption is divided among less than are honest gains. Therefore, if all corruption is detected, corruption is a relatively more tempting deviation with NT-TTP, which makes T-TTP a more trustworthy institution.

On the other hand, if not all incidents of corruption are detected, the trustworthiness depends on the actual configuration of the NT-TTP. Since corruption with NT-TTP requires cooperation among at least two independent TTPs, the chance of being detected is higher with NT-TTP. This coordination effect counteracts the uneven division of payoffs from corruption and honest play.

One computational efficient configuration is majority trust, where any majority can use and misuse the NT-TTP. Majority trust based on a large number of TTPs is a more trustworthy institution. Increasing the threshold makes the NT-TTP an unambiguously better choice. Setting T=N-1 completely removes the problem of uneven division. However, higher confidentiality is at the cost of availability, since any one of the N TTPs can prevent the protocol from being performed.

The TTP institution with the lowest costs is likely to be the most profitable, and therefore also the most trustworthy TTP. Since no single member of NT-TTP holds any information, the variable costs for the individual TTPs is likely to be low. This is unlike a T-TTP, where strict and (probably) costly procedures are required for being reliable. This likely difference in cost structures is in favor of NT-TTP.

As a public authority, the structure of NT-TTP allows for efficient intervention. Introducing a fourth (subsidized) TTP that systematically replaces the TTPs in a simple majority trust based on 3 TTPs, makes the NT-TTP institution relatively more trustworthy. On the other hand, the classical leniency programs may have limited effect due to the problem of proving corruption in court.

The modeling neglects the cooperative game within the NT-TTP. The division of the gains may cause instability among the N TTPs while playing the cooperative strategy and the punishment period, and among the T+1 TTPs, while playing the deviation strategy. As an example, if the NT-TTP breaks down due to instabilities among the N TTPs after corruption is detected, the punishment period may be relatively more harsh to NT-TTP, which makes it relatively more trustworthy. However, incorporating the cooperative requirements in the present non-cooperative game is one of the more challenging extensions.

Another future challenge is to conduct laboratory or field experiments to uncover how the two trust institutions are perceived. The trust institution that is perceived to be the most trustworthy may attract a larger part of the market and hereby become even more trustworthy as a result of corruption being less tempting.

Acknowledgments

I would like to thank Ivan B. Damgaard, Jakob I. Pagter, Jens-Martin Bramsen and Philipp Festerling for their helpful comments. This work is sponsored by the Danish Strategic Research Council as part of the research project SIMAP: www.sikkerhed.alexandra.dk/uk/projects/simap.

References

Abraham, I., Dolev, D., Gonen, R., and Halpern, J. "Distributed Computing Meets Game Theory: Robust Mechanisms for Rational Secret Sharing and Multiparty Computation," in *Proceedings of the twenty-fifth annual 18 ACM symposium on Principles of distributed computing*, ACM Press, New York, NY, USA, 2006, pp. 53–62.

Abreu, D. "Extremal Equilibria of Oligopolistic Supergames," *Journal of Economic Theory* (39), 1986, pp. 191–225.

Ben-Or, M., Goldwasser, S. and Wigderson, A. "Completeness Theorems for Non-cryptographic Fault-tolerant Distributed Computation," in *Proceedings of ACM Symposium on Theory of Computing*, Chicago, Illinois, USA, 1988, pp. 1–10.

Bogetoft, P., Christensen, D. L., Damgaard, I., Geisler, M., Jakobsen, T., Krøigaard, M., Nielsen, J. D., Nielsen, J. B., Nielsen, K., Pagter, J., Schwartzbach, M. and Toft, T. "Multiparty Computation Goes Live," *Cryptology ePrint Archive*, Report 2008/068. http://eprint.iacr.org/. 2008.

Bogetoft, P., Damgaard, I., Jacobsen, T., Nielsen, K., Pagter, J. and Toft, T. "Secure Computing, Economy, and Trust - a Generic Solution for Secure Auctions with Real-World Applications," Report RS-05-18, Basic Research in Computer Science. 2005.

Bogetoft, P., Damgaard, I., Jacobsen, T., Nielsen, K., Pagter, J. and Toft, T. "A Practical Implementation of Secure Auctions Based on Multiparty Integer Computation," in *Proceedings of Financial Cryptography*, Lecture Notes in Computer Science, vol. 4107, Springer Verlag, 2006, pp. 142–147.

Chaum, D., Cr′epeau, C. and Damgaard, I. B. "Multi-party Unconditionally Secure Protocols," in *Proceedings of ACM Symposium on Theory of Computing*, Chicago, Illinois, USA, 1988, pp. 11–19.

Friedman, J. W. "A Non-cooperative Equilibrium for Supergames," *Review of Economic Studies* (38), 1971, pp. 1–12.

Gibbard, A.: 1973, "Manipulation of Voting Schemes: A General Result," *Econometrica* (41), 1973, pp. 587–601.

Goldreich, O., Micali, S., and Wigderson, A. "How to Play Any Mental Game or a Completeness Theorem for Protocols with Honest Majority", in *Proceedings of ACM Symposium on Theory of Computing*, New York, NY, USA, 1987, pp. 218–229.

Halpern, J., and Teague, V. "Rational Secret Sharing and Multiparty Computation: Extended Abstract", in *Proceedings of ACM Symposium on Theory of computing,* New York, NY, USA, 2004, pp. 623–632.

James Jr., H. S. "The Trust Paradox: A Survey of Economic Inquiries into the Nature of Trust and Trustworthiness," *Journal of Economic Behavior & Organization* (47), 2002, pp. 291–307.

Maleka, S., Shareef, A., and Rangan, C. P. "Rational Secret Sharing with Repeated Games," forthcoming at *Proceeding from The 4th Information Security Practice and Experience Conference*, 2008.

Malkhi, D., Nisan, N., Pinkas, B., and Sella, Y. "Fairplay - a Secure Twoparty Computation System", Presented at *Usenix Security Symposium*, San Diego, CA, USA, 2004.

Motta, M. *Competition Policy*, Cambridge University Press. 2004.

Motta, M., and Polo, M. "Leniency Programs and Cartel Prosecution," *International Journal of Industrial Organization* (21), 2003, pp. 347–379.

Myerson, R. B. "Incentives Compatibility and the Bargaining Problem," *Econometrica* (47), 1979, pp. 61–73.

Pfleeger, C. P. and Pfleeger, S. L. *Security in Computing*, 3rd edn., Prentice Hall, 2003.

Porter, R. H. "Optimal Cartel Trigger Price Strategies," *Journal of Economic Theory* (29), 1983, pp. 313–338.

Rotemberg, J. J., and Saloner, G. "A Supergame Theoretic Model of Business Cycles and Price Wars During Booms," *American Economic Review* (76), 1986, pp. 390–407.

Shamir, A. "How to Share a Secret", in *Proceedings of Communication of the ACM* (22:11), 1979, pp. 612–613.

Index